SPORTS CARS

SPORTS CARS
AUTOCAR

256 GBL

Third edition published 1997 by
Bay View Books Ltd
The Red House, 25-26 Bridgeland Street
Bideford, Devon EX39 2PZ

ISBN 1 870979 88 5

Printed in China

Publisher's Note
The forerunner of this book was a pair of magazine-format
publications compiled by Peter Garnier in the mid-1970s.
They covered the four-cylinder cars and the sixes, and they
were brought together in the first edition of *MG Sports
Cars* in 1979. The book was expanded and updated in
1989, and this 1997 edition is further expanded to
accommodate the MG RV8 and the MGF.

CONTENTS

Britain's Enduring Sports Car Marque
Described through the pages of

AUTOCAR

Thousands of words have been written by hundreds of authors in attempts to define the sports car. Apart from one or two unsporting vehicles forced by insensitive management to wear the octagonal badge, one of the simplest ways to explain 'sports car' was to point at any two-seater MG, for few MGs were anything other than sports cars first and foremost. The marque will always be associated with sports cars despite the fact that through most of the 1980s the badge was used on high-performance saloons.

MG sports cars occupied a unique position in motoring; they were not always the fastest, the most technically advanced or the most glamorous of cars, even if some outstanding racing and record-breaking feats were achieved with MGs before Second World War. Yet out of a somewhat prosaic beginning came a series of cars which were the ultimate ambition of many a young man pining for something more dashing than the family car which was so often his four-wheeled destiny. For half a century there was nearly always an MG cheap enough for him to achieve his ambition and even to give him a taste of competitive motoring.

William Morris began his remarkable career repairing and then building bicycles and (later) motor bikes. Disused stables in Longwall Street, Oxford, provided his workshops. By 1911, he had turned his attention to motor cars, selling various makes from the same premises, rebuilt and called The Morris Garage. Further expansion and new premises made the title plural – The Morris Garages – and the first Morris was actually assembled there.

Morris became engrossed in production of his new Oxford car, undertaken at an old school in Cowley, and he put The Morris Garages under a manager. In 1922 the manager was Cecil Kimber, an energetic man, who set about designing special bodywork for Morris chassis.

The name MG first appeared in 1923, when Kimber drove a re-bodied Morris Cowley, prepared by The Morris Garages, on the Land's End

The M-Type of 1929 was the first of the Midgets and the first sports car to come within reach of a mass market.

MG TCs (foreground) and Y-type saloons roll off Abingdon production line in the 1940s. Kimber moved MG production to Abingdon-on-Thames in 1929, where MG was registered as a limited company the following year. There it remained until the MGB's sad demise in 1980.

Trial, winning a 'Gold'. This car was the real prototype MG, rather than the famous, pointed-tail two-seater which appeared in 1925 and is now known as "Old Number One".

A year later, in 1924, Kimber took a new, 1.8 litre, six-cylinder Oxford and turned it into the MG Super Sports, with a lightly-tuned engine, improved handling and a handsome aluminium body. Backed by Morris reliability and service, the MG was a great success.

At the 1928 Motor Show the first true production MG Six made its debut, with the 2.4 litre, 60 bhp engine. Based on the Morris Six, Kimber designed for it a completely new cylinder block and head, gave the car a light body and a high axle ratio and called it the MG Mk1 18/80hp. The result pleased the customers in numbers large enough to warrant building an additional factory. Around 2,000 had been turned out by 1929 when the MG Car Company moved to Abingdon, its home until sports car production ended as it closed in 1980.

During the first year at Abingdon, MG introduced the Midget, based on the 847cc Morris Minor with very little alteration other than lowering the suspension and improving the steering. The little fabric-bodied, pointed-tail, two-seater M-Type, with its engine tuned to provide 20 bhp, good acceleration and a top speed of 65 mph, was Britain's first really cheap and practical sports car.

MG went racing in 1930, the competition cars using superchargers and various other special parts, but retaining many components from the road cars. Development began with the Double-Twelve M-Type, named after the factory M-Types that had won the team prize at the Brooklands Double Twelve Hours race in 1930. The following year, a special MG became the first 750cc car to exceed 100 mph and although the works programme was abruptly cut short in 1935 privateers continued to race and rally MGs until 1939, while among record breakers 'Goldie' Gardner was outstanding.

It is difficult, in these days of commonplace 100 mph plus family saloons, to image what great fun these early MGs provided. Though their maximum speed was not much more than 70 mph, at least one was allowed to use it and they were essentially *drivers'* cars with excellent driving positions, stubby, remote-control gear levers, only a couple of inches from the driver's left hand, extensive instrumentation and well-placed controls. Somehow, they represented a piece of machinery, as distinct from mere transport; the styling, and details like a strap round the bonnet, wire stone guards over the lamps, aero screens and such-like, underlined their sporting character.

In the 1930s the ubiquitous MG enabled many hundreds of ordinary enthusiasts to get into all forms of motor sport, very often bringing them success against far more expensive opposition. One saw on the roads every kind of MG, from the sporting saloons to out-and-out racing cars like the K3 Magnettes. They were, somehow, the very personification of the fun and competition of motoring.

A brief introduction such as this does not allow space for the whole story, but the staff of *Autocar* have

Striking EX-E (top) was a sensational project car, but the realistic return to MG sports car production came with the RV8 (above, posed with a 1962 MGB).

described and tested MG sports cars throughout the company's life, while also covering much of the marque's competition and record-breaking activity and conveying something of the appeal of an MG. There is the original M-Type Midget – "An Extraordinarily Fascinating Little Car: Comfort at Speed" – which obviously appealed to the magazine's staff in 1929, who also described it as "the infant phenomenon". Then comes the beautifully businesslike Montlhéry Midget of 1931, and the famous J2 Midget of 1932 which went much faster than it ought to have done – to the embarrassment of its makers.

There are the post-war Ts, the first MGs produced after Kimber's departure, and the arguably tardy launch of the first modern MG, the A. But then in the tradition of "maintaining the breed" this followed on from a forerunner proved in racing. Then there were the Bs, with timeless lines and for a while with a V8-engined version, which were the most popular of all MGs, and the Midgets that fulfilled the functions of their 1930s forebears…

The end of MGB production in 1980 seemed to mark the end of the MG sports car line, and there was little affection for the badge-engineered variants of Austin-Rover models that

carried the badge through to 1991, although in earlier decades saloons had honourable places in MG ranges.

The EX-E in mid-decade was exciting, but it was not shown as the forerunner of a forthcoming production model. Then late in the 1980s, British Motor Heritage started making MGB body shells again, using the original press tooling rescued from the scrap merchant in the nick of time. In the eight years after the 1988 introduction, some 2500 bodies were made, and that presumably meant that a similar number of MGBs was restored. Beyond that, there have been shorter runs of other MG bodies of the recent past.

Then there was the RV8, not universally admired, perhaps, but a sales success in some markets – and with its 'B' lines and potent V8 engine a sports car following an old MG tradition. It was followed by a genuinely new MG, the F, a fascinating two-seater to carry the magic initials into the 21st century.

The reputation of MG was built up through decades, when so many other marques have disappeared, and it should serve the new cars well. The strength of the marque clubs testifies to the popularity of past MGs, perhaps the most popular British sports cars and among the most popular in the world.

A SIX-CYLINDER M.G.

Sports Car with Many Interesting Mechanical Features.

2½-Litre Model with Special Box Girder Frame.

THE latest model M.G. is an entire departure from previous practice in a very interesting manner. The engine is the Morris six-cylinder of 69 × 110 mm., which has a capacity of 2,468 c.c. It has an overhead camshaft, which, by the way, is an interesting point for this type of engine, designed to be produced in considerable quantities, forced lubrication, and an immense crankshaft held by massive bearings in a cast-iron crank case, the whole being just about as stiff as can be imagined; stiffness in these parts is three-quarters of the secret of success of the modern six-cylinder engine.

The clutch, the gear box (with its central control), and the transmission as a unit are also Morris, but—and this is where the interest of the latest M.G. arises—these units are assembled in a new frame of M.G. design.

Now the M.G. is a sports car, and the difficulty hitherto has been to adapt for this special purpose units and details of a chassis designed originally for a totally different purpose. Obviously the high performance necessary for a sports car, as distinct from a touring model, involves a lot of detail alteration, and detail alteration is hampered considerably by the necessity of using already existing parts.

Accordingly, for next year the frame has been designed entirely for sports car work, and, as the illustrations show, the side members are not only massive in themselves, but are very rigidly tied together by cross-members, of which one, near the centre of the frame, is a four-sided box girder—probably the stiffest type known.

Either side of the box girder

SPECIFICATION.
ENGINE: 17.7 h.p., six cylinders, 69 × 110 mm. (2,468 c.c.). Tax £18. Overhead valves and camshaft, detachable head, coil ignition.
TRANSMISSION: Three-speed and reverse gear box in unit with the engine.
SUSPENSION: Half-elliptic springs.
BRAKES: On all four wheels.
WHEELS: Wire detachable. Tyres 28 × 4.95 in.
WHEELBASE: 9 ft. 6 in. **Track,** 4 ft.
WEIGHT: 24 cwt. 2 qr.
PRICE (provisional): £425, Four-seater.

the frame is extended by wide webs, and there are additional webs also on either side of the front cross-member just below the radiator, while the forward cross tube between the dumbiron is splined at each end into bosses. Thus the frame has been made rigid, and by its rigidity prevents movement between the components, the other method of dealing with the same problem being to allow the frame to whip, but to isolate the power unit so that the effect of such whip is not apparent.

Then the brake mechanism is also of new design, and every care has been taken to prevent lost motion and to make the brake pedal feel as though it were directly attached to the cams without whip or delay. To do this the two brake cross tubes are of large diameter, and the levers in the brake actuation are triangular, instead of being the usual comparatively thin stamping, which in itself is liable to whip.

Of compensation there is none, the designers believing that the most effective form of brakes has the minimum number of parts, and an independent adjustment for each pair of shoes, as well as a single adjustment below the floorboards to take up all four sets of shoes simultaneously. Servo shoes—that is, shoes which tend to put themselves on further when applied to the brake drum, are used for the front axle, the axle beam being really stiff and strong. Extra shoes in the rear drums are operated by a lever on the right-hand side of the driver; this lever stays in position only if the trigger is depressed, an idea that has come from racing practice, and possesses great advantages.

The chassis, showing the box girder construction.

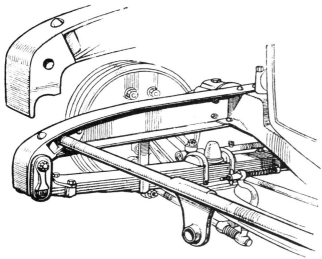

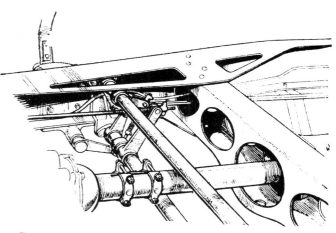

The method of steadying the spring shackle on the dumbirons.

B-ake cross-shafts and box section cross-members of the frame.

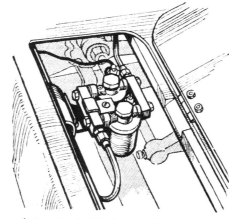

Auto-pulse fuel feed pump located under the rear seat.

Marles steering gear is standard, the steering gear box being held on the frame by two bronze blocks, of which the upper is rigid and the lower can be adjusted by two bolts, so as to grip the steering gear effectively at the frame end, the upper end being secured by a bracket from the dashboard a little below the spring-spoked steering wheel. Castor action for the steering, which is an important point in a sports car, is obtained by canting the front axle through the medium of adjustable wedges.

The springs are wide, and in front are canted to slope from the front dumb irons towards the rear, another interesting feature being that the dumbirons act as guides to the side plates of the shackle, the shackle being in front of the spring, thus assisting greatly in preventing side sway. The shackle in front brings the centre of movement of the front axle, which is the rear anchorage of the front spring, nearer to the drop arm, and therefore reduces the automatic movement of the steering wheel as the tyres pass over inequalities in the road.

A new radiator of unusual design is mounted on trunnions in front of the frame, and between the rear cross-members is a big fuel tank with two vent pipes and its filler on the right-hand side, free from interference from luggage, and at the same time out of the way of the exhaust pipe running along the left side of the chassis. Above the tank is a tool box, and over that again on the finished car, either open or closed, is the fabric suitcase carrier.

Fuel is fed to the two S.U. carburetters by an electrically operated diaphragm pump combined with a glass bowl filter, and placed near the fuel tank itself, so as to deaden the clicking noise noticeable when the pump is operating. Both pump and filter can be reached after raising the rear seat cushion.

On the dashboard is a two-gallon spare fuel tank feeding by gravity when required, together with a tank for spare oil and the apparatus for upper cylinder lubrication, that feeds oil through the carburetters to the combustion space. In the latest engines the two carburetters are mounted on the left side, just above the exhaust branches.

There are two standard bodies, a fabric saloon and an open four-seater. The saloon has adjustable front seats, a one-piece windscreen that opens entirely, and an armrest between the two rear seats, sufficient leg room for the rear passengers being provided by sinking wells in the floorboards, which pass slightly underneath the front seats.

The new car is a great improvement on the old one, is beautifully sprung, holds the road well, has very powerful brakes, and, by reason of the six-cylinder engine, is quiet and very smooth. At the moment the provisional price of the saloon is £525, and of the four-seater £425.

The new M.G. chassis is exceedingly handsome and clean in design.

Published *The Autocar,*
28 June 1929

"THE AUTOCAR" ROAD TESTS

No. 61.—M.G. MIDGET TWO-SEATER
An Extraordinarily Fascinating Little Car: Comfort at Speed.

NOT only has the M.G. Midget a fascinating appearance, but it goes so exceedingly well. Sixty to sixty-five miles an hour with it are not adventure but delight. It sits down on the road like a thoroughbred and at high speed feels more like a big car than a tiny one. Nor does it fuss when travelling quickly.

All cars seem to have a speed to which a sensitive driver settles down automatically. Some call it the "cruising speed," others the "kindest" speed. On the Midget this speed is 50 m.p.h. However, too much stress must not be laid upon the upper end of the performance scale, although for its size the car is decidedly fast, for there is plenty of flexibility, and on top gear it is possible to crawl along in traffic behind a slow-moving vehicle and get away quite smoothly again. In this respect the redoubtable S.U. carburetter and the battery ignition play their

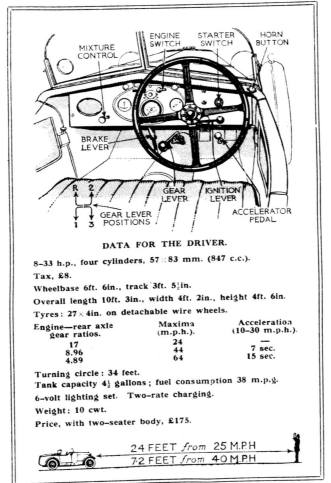

DATA FOR THE DRIVER.

8–33 h.p., four cylinders, 57×83 mm. (847 c.c.).

Tax, £8.

Wheelbase 6ft. 6in., track 3ft. 5½in.

Overall length 10ft. 3in., width 4ft. 2in., height 4ft. 6in.

Tyres: 27×4in. on detachable wire wheels.

Engine—rear axle gear ratios.	Maxima (m.p.h.).	Acceleration (10–30 m.p.h.).
17	24	—
8.96	44	7 sec.
4.89	64	15 sec.

Turning circle: 34 feet.

Tank capacity 4½ gallons; fuel consumption 38 m.p.g.

6–volt lighting set. Two-rate charging.

Weight: 10 cwt.

Price, with two–seater body, £175.

24 FEET *from* 25 M.P.H
7.2 FEET *from* 40 M.P.H

parts. Acceleration on top gear from very low speeds is notable for its smoothness more than for its rapidity, though the latter is pretty useful.

From 25 m.p.h. onwards on top gear acceleration is very brisk, while on second gear the little car fairly leaps away, as the figures in the table show. The gear change needs knowing. Changing is not difficult to accomplish after a little practice, but at first the shortness of the gear lever and the short travel of the clutch pedal are disconcerting. The clutch takes up the drive smoothly, and at the end of an hour one is accustomed to the process.

The speeds claimed by the makers for the various gears are, on first 20, second 40, and top 60 m.p.h. The claims are modest and the car will exceed these figures quite easily, though at 25 on bottom gear and at 45 m.p.h. on second there is a period of valve bounce. Although the exhaust has

" THE AUTOCAR " ROAD TESTS

a fairly healthy crackle when the throttle is wide open, the car itself is not unduly noisy; there are no annoying mechanical sounds, and the indirect gears do not shout about their work.

When the car is bowling along at 20 or so in the streets of a town the wary policeman is more interested in the look of the car than in the noise it is making. In confined spaces the Midget is very easy to manœuvre, for the steering is light and quick, and one can twist and turn rapidly through traffic. At high speed on the open road the car can be steered comfortably with one hand. It is very steady even over poor surfaces, really remarkably so in view of its small size.

Where the Infant Shines.

It is perhaps on hills that this infant phenomenon really excels. It will shoot up a straight 1 in 10 grade on top gear. One particular hill of this kind was approached at 52 m.p.h. and crested at 33 m.p.h. on top. Another 1 in 10 gradient, with a sharp turn at the foot which quite precludes a rush being made, was very nearly climbed on top. Steeper hills of the type which reach a maximum of 1 in 6 served to show up a surprisingly vivid second gear. They were surmounted on second at speeds varying between 32 and 38 m.p.h. This car is most excellent at hill-climbing.

Petrol consumption on a car of this nature depends very largely upon the way in which it is handled and the speed at which it is driven. The makers claim that the consumption lies between 37 and 45 m.p.g., according to circumstances. Over a run of 60 miles, including one or two hills, and driving fairly fast, the consumption worked out at 38 m.p.g., which is an economical figure in view of the liveliness of the car.

Not the least satisfactory feature is the brakes. They are effective, do not require a lot of force on the pedal, and do not show any tendency to lock an odd wheel. Also they are smooth unless applied with extreme

Front view of the M.G. Midget.

Over the whole top of the tail is a hinged lid.

The driving compartment.

violence. Each brake has an adjustment for its cable, and these are fairly accessible. There is also a single main adjustment for all four brakes under the floor boards, beneath the driver's feet. This adjustment is not very accessible.

As regards other matters of accessibility: the battery is below the driver's legs and is quite easy to reach. The engine oil filler and dipstick are on the off side and, with the ignition coil, the make-and-break a n d the distributor, as well as a drain-cock at the base of the radiator, are quite accessible. The sparking plugs, which are at a slight downward angle, can easily be tackled with a spanner, except that nearest the dashboard, this one being screened by the coil. On the near side of the engine is a detachable oil filter; on this side also lies the electric starting motor, while the cut-out and junction boxes of the electrical system are attached to the forward side of the dash.

Smart and Up to Date.

Outwardly the car is smart and up to date, with its striking radiator, fat filler cap, detachable dumb-iron shield, cycle type wings, and side valances. Actually the wings are carried on the car, not on the axles, and are rigidly attached. The two doors are extra wide, and it is easy enough to enter or leave the car. The screen is a fixed V type.

Pneumatic upholstery is employed and the seat is adjustable; also the back squab is movable, not only fore and aft, but can be set as to angle as well. Just behind the seat is a compartment in which the hood stays are carried when out of use. Over the whole top of the tail is a hinged lid, and in the compartment beneath is stowed the spare wheel, whilst above it is fair space for luggage.

Altogether the M.G. Midget is an extraordinarily fascinating little car, both to look at and to handle on the road.

1930 M.G. PROGRAMME

New Four-speed Six-cylinder Chassis to Supplement Existing Range. Midget Sportsman's Coupé.

AMONG those to whom a high performance as regards acceleration and speed particularly appeals the M.G. range has become extremely popular. For 1930 a new model has been introduced, the 18-80 h.p. Mark II Six, which supplements the existing 18-80 h.p. Mark I Six, and the range is completed by the M.G. Midget, now available as an open two-seater and as an attractive sportsman's coupé.

For the new chassis the same engine as used in the Mark I model is employed, but the frame is stiffer throughout, a four-speed gear box is fitted, the front axle and steering are more robust, and very powerful brakes with 14in. diameter drums are standardised. These are the major differences between the two six-cylinder-engined chassis, but minor points of variance also exist, such as in the layout of the half-elliptic rear springs, the provision of central chassis lubrication, and the method of brake operation.

Exceptionally Smooth Running.

As regards details of the engine, the bore and stroke are 69 × 110 mm. (2,468 c.c.), the R.A.C. rating being 17.7 h.p. The cylinders and crank case form a single casting in iron of great strength and rigidity, and in this the robust and carefully balanced crankshaft is mounted in four large bearings. It is largely due to this construction that the engine has achieved an excellent reputation for its smooth, vibrationless running. In the detachable head are mounted the inclined valves, operated through rockers from the overhead camshaft, the latter being chain-driven from the crankshaft, with the drive so arranged that the head can be dismounted, complete with the valve gear, without disturbing the timing.

Two S.U. carburetters, each with its own float chamber, are fitted on the near side, each supplying three cylinders, and ignition is by coil, the distributor being driven by a vertical shaft on the off side at the front of the engine. The lower end of this shaft actuates the gear-type oil pump, which delivers oil under pressure to main and big-end bearings, to the camshaft and valve gear, and to the distribution gear. Also, on the off side and driven from the front of the engine is the 12-volt dynamo, while the water impeller is driven in tandem from the dynamo, being situated towards the rear of the cylinder block.

On the near side are the exhaust manifold, with its connection to the exhaust pipe at the front end, the water outlet to the radiator, the large oil filler, and the dipstick oil gauge for the sump. A new type breather is fitted to the aluminium valve gear cover, and leads oil fumes away from the vicinity of the dash and body.

With the engine the five-plate clutch, having cork inserts and running in oil, and the four-speed gear box form a compact unit. The gear box is especially interesting, as helical teeth are used for the constant-mesh and third-gear pinions, engagement being by dog clutches. Thus not only is a quiet third speed obtained, but the change from top to third, or from third to top, is very easy. Another point is that a central division in the gear box carries intermediate bearings for both main and lay shafts, so that the shafts are supported close to whatever gears are transmitting power. An extension rearwards from the lid of the box carries a short, stiff gear lever with a ball joint, a gear lock being incorporated. The ratios are 14.58, 8.5, 5.58, and 4.27 to 1.

A Well-braced Frame.

At the rear of the gear box is the spherical joint at the head of the torque tube, enclosing the split-ring type universal joint at the head of the propeller-shaft. The final drive is by spiral bevel, and the rear axle is of stronger construction than that formerly used.

While the main frame members are similar to those of the Mark I chassis, except for minor modifications to give additional strength, being upswept at front and rear, they are united by a

M.G. Six saloon, Mark II.

box girder section cross-member just behind the gear box and by stronger front and rear cross-members. Stiffer tie bars are also fitted between front and rear dumb irons. Incidentally, use is made of the large central cross-member to carry the two batteries, one on either side of the torque tube.

The half-elliptic front springs are shackled at their forward ends, the shackles being fed by the Tecalemit automatic chassis lubrication system, which also attends to the steering pivots and joints, and to the trunnion bearings of the half-elliptic rear

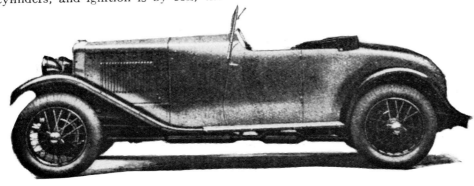

The two-seater 18-80 h.p. M.G. Six.

springs on the axle casing. The rear springs are wider than those of the Mark I chassis, and are mounted at the side of, and not beneath, the main frame, Silentbloc bushes being used for the shackles. There are thus no points · needing attention with the grease gun, and there are only the engine, gear box, back axle, steering box, and chassis lubrication tank to be attended to at fairly long intervals of time.

For the front axle a straight H-section beam with stiffened, upswept ends is employed. Marles steering is used, the column being adjustable for rake and carrying an 18in. Bluemel spring-spoked wheel with throttle and ignition levers in a neat mounting above it.

One of the advantages of the brake gear of the new chassis is that it leaves the body builder full scope for fitting foot wells. It is also extremely simple, for there is only one cross-shaft, carried by stainless steel cones received between three bronze rollers, so that lubrication is not necessary, and there is no possibility of the shaft binding owing to frame flexion. On each end of this cross-shaft are double-ended levers to which the operating cables are connected.

The brake drums are ground internally and have ribbed aluminium bands shrunk on them. Orthodox two-shoe expanding brakes are used, with Halo linings, giving a total braking area of 208 sq. in. The brake

lever is straight and is mounted on the frame, and it has the pawl and ratchet brought into engagement only when the knob is depressed, a reversal of normal practice and one which is favoured for sports and racing cars.

Petrol and Oil Supplies.

In the dash is mounted the auxiliary 2½-gallon fuel tank, which is fed by an Autovac from the 12-gallon main tank at the rear. A two-level tap for the auxiliary tank provides a reserve supply of 1 gallon. A Jaeger electrically operated gauge on the instrument board gives an indication of the state of the main tank, which has a 3¼in. diameter quickly detachable filler cap. A reserve oil supply of 1 gallon is also afforded by this tank, and the sump can be replenished merely by turning a tap.

The wiring has been made very neat, and a junction box on the dash carries the fuses and an inspection lamp. On the compact instrument panel are mounted clock, speedometer, revolution indicator, oil pressure gauge, and petrol gauge. Large Rotax head lamps are carried by stays, bracing radiator and wings. Rudge-Whitworth racing-type wire wheels are shod with 29in. × 5in. Dunlop Fort tyres, and the wheelbase and track are identical with those of the Mark I chassis—9ft. 6in. and 4ft. 4in. respectively. Accordingly, the coachwork is identical with that of the

Mark I range, the complete 1930 programme being as follows:—

Mark I.—Chassis, £445; two-seater, £510; tourer, £515; sports salonette, fabric £550, coachbuilt £555; four-door saloon, fabric £560, coachbuilt £570.

Mark II.—Chassis, £550; two-seater, £625; tourer, £630; sports salonette, fabric £655, coachbuilt £660; four-door saloon, fabric £660, coachbuilt £670.

Midget.—Two-seater, £185; sportsman's coupé, £245.

In producing the 8-33 h.p. Midget sportsman's coupé the M.G. Car Co., whose address is now Pavlova Works, Abingdon-on-Thames, Berks, have aimed at providing a really comfortable and well-finished small car, as well as one capable of a high performance. It is possessed of good lines, but is also roomy, and has wide doors which assure ease of access, and a sliding sunshine roof in which are let lights, so that, even when the roof is closed, the occupants of the rear seat do not feel shut in.

The front bucket seats are adjustable and have pneumatic cushions, while the rear seat has both pneumatic cushion and squab. The doors are recessed to give additional elbow room and carry useful pockets. Triplex glass is fitted throughout as standard, and the rear luggage trunk has the spare wheel mounted on the hinged lid. The oval instrument panel is sunk into the facia board, which provides a very useful locker at each end.

A sectioned drawing of the Mark II Six saloon appears in the photogravure pages.

Amy Johnson, whose solo flight to Australia in 1929 in her D.H. 60G Gipsy Moth "Jason" made world news (as did her many other flights, and later those with her husband Jim Mollison), is presented with an M.G. Six Mark I saloon by Sir William Morris, later Lord Nuffield. The radiator mascot is a model of the Gipsy Moth, and alongside Amy Johnson is her mother.

THE 1930
M.G. SIX
MARK II.

An addition to the range of an increasingly popular Sports Car. Its features include a strong and very rigid frame, a high-efficiency engine and four-speed gear box with constant mesh helical gears for third speed.

MAX MILLAR

 January 24th, 1930.

RACING AND THE M.G.

THE AUTOCAR is informed that there is no truth in the rumour that Sir William Morris has authorised the M.G. Car Co. to enter for races during the coming season. However, there are private entries for the "Double-Twelve-Hour." L. G. Callingham and H. D. Parker are driving an M.G. Six Mark II, and a privately organised team of three Midgets, probably under the leadership of C. J. Randall, will run in the same race.

INEXPENSIVE SPEED.

THE directors of the M.G. Car Co. in general, and Mr. Cecil Kimber in particular, are to be congratulated warmly on the fine plant, at the Pavlova Works, Abingdon-on-Thames, for production in considerable numbers of M.G. sports cars, which was formally opened on Monday last. At a very largely attended lunch Sir William Morris, Bart., made a characteristic and vigorous speech on the outlook for the motor industry and for M.G. sports cars in particular. He emphasised that very shortly enthusiasts would be able to obtain, in either the three- or the four-speed types, high-efficiency cars moderate in running cost, distinctly attractive in price, and with an efficiency comparable to that of any rivals. Sir William paid warm tribute to the keenness and loyalty of the staff and workmen engaged in the production of the cars, and uttered a powerful plea for a common-sense attitude on the part of the Government towards the British motor industry.

The works themselves are admirable—new, large and airy, and already the M.G. Midget and the Mark I and Mark II Sixes are coming through in routine production on assembly lines. It is obvious that M.G. products will be well to the fore in the sporting events of 1930 and onwards.

Fun-cars in the making, and a few dreams about to come true—the late F. Gordon Crosby's impression of the M.G. factory at Abingdon, with an M-type Midget coming off the line to the right, and what might be a six-cylinder chassis on test on the rolling-road dynamometer.

THE M.G. MARK III

Designed to Conform with International Racing Regulations and Turned Out Prepared for Racing.

BY reason of a certain silken swiftness of running and an appearance indubitably elegant, the M.G. Six Mark II has gained many ardent admirers. As a result, a demand arose for a model with which to race, and hence the 18-100 h.p. M.G. Six Sports Mark III Road Racing Model made its début.

Some twenty-five of the new cars form the first batch, and are on sale in the perfectly ordinary way at a price of £895 complete, and ready for racing without need of further preparation. Only one style of coachwork will be supplied, a four-seater body conforming to existing International Racing Regulations.

Bore and Stroke.

In actual size, namely, 69 mm. bore and 110 mm. stroke, giving a capacity of 2,468 c.c., the six-cylinder engine is the same as that of the Mark I and II models, this being for manufacturing reasons, but in other respects the differences are considerable. The crankshaft, which is carried in four bearings in a particularly rigid monoblock crank case, is bored out in the crank pins and has the webs fined down so as to reduce the load on the bearings. Connecting rods which are machined all over are employed in conjunction with a special piston of the waisted type, and all reciprocating parts are balanced individually, whilst the crankshaft is balanced statically and dynamically.

Within the water jackets the cylinder barrels are specially ribbed to prevent distortion; moreover, the water circulation is maintained by a centrifugal pump instead

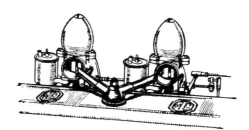

Breather pipes are taken to both the carburetter intakes.

On the M.G. Mark III the axle ends and steering arms are polished to facilitate inspection for flaws.

above the engine, and work on the down-draught principle. It is noticeable that the down-draught pipes are not arranged in bends, but in a series of angles.

On the opposite side of the cylinder head the exhausts are arranged to issue in three pairs to a triple pipe which blends into a Brooklands-type expansion chamber, having at each end a breather joint that allows for expansion and contraction. On this engine the overhead valves are operated by an overhead camshaft, which is driven by chain and spur gears from the front. A new type of camshaft is used, giving considerably more over-lap, whilst the valve springs are compounded.

Dry-sump lubrication is adopted. As compared with the normal M.G. engine it is noticeable that the vertical shaft which normally drives the pump has been moved from the right side of the engine at the front to the centre, and the drive for the verticle spindle passes from the chain gear to the extra stout spindle of a special high-duty dynamo.

Water and Oil Pumps.

Beyond a skew gear which drives the vertical shaft is mounted the water pump. At the base of the vertical spindle is a special twin pump. The upper of the two gear pumps draws oil from the sump and delivers it to an oil tank carried between the front dumb irons, flexible pipes being used for the purpose. The lower pump draws its supply from this tank, and delivers it under pressure to the engine bearings. There is a filter on the main suction pipe. There are no separate

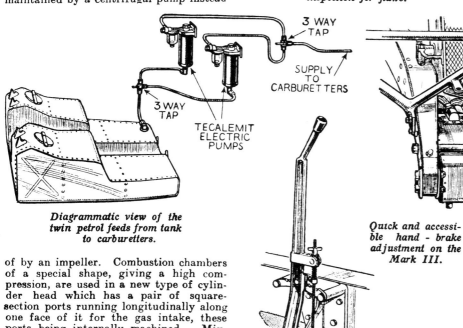

Diagrammatic view of the twin petrol feeds from tank to carburetters.

3 WAY TAP

SUPPLY TO CARBURETTERS

3 WAY TAP

TECALEMIT ELECTRIC PUMPS

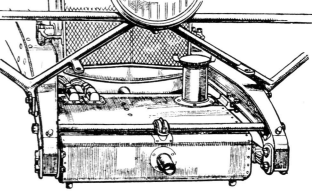

A large oil tank is located between the front dumb irons, through which the axis of the starting handle passes.

Quick and accessible hand - brake adjustment on the Mark III.

of by an impeller. Combustion chambers of a special shape, giving a high compression, are used in a new type of cylinder head which has a pair of square-section ports running longitudinally along one face of it for the gas intake, these ports being internally machined. Mixture is fed to these two separate ports from a pair of S.U. carburetters of an exclusive design, which are carried high

oil pipes in the engine, cast-in galleries being used instead. It is particularly interesting that there are two breather pipes in the top of the cover for the valve gear, and these permit oil mist to be drawn in through the carburetters to give top-cylinder lubrication. The oil pressure is set for 90 lb.

A double-ignition system is used, there being two sparking plugs in each cylinder.

The hand brake, with its quick adjustment, and the four wheel brake adjusting handle project through the body.

At the top of the vertical shaft of the oil pumps is mounted an electrically synchronised dual distributor, so arranged that the sparks of the two plugs occur simultaneously. Battery ignition is employed and the twin coils are neatly mounted saddle-wise over the dynamo.

Engine and four-speed gear box unit are carried in the frame from a cross-member in the front and from bearer arms extending from a new type of cast-iron banjo casing around the flywheel and clutch. Rubber pads are used in the engine mounting to give a small degree of flexibility.

For the purpose of racing, which demands quick gear changing, a new type of clutch has been designed. It is a single-plate design with highly compressed cork inserts. The clutch is toggle-operated, and has a compressed-graphite thrust race for the pedal fork.

The frame has channel-section side members which are up-swept at front and rear. Aft of the engine and gear box unit comes the keystone of the design. It consists of two very wide and deep channel-section cross members which are jointed together in the centre by a large-diameter tubular member, and through the centre of this the forward end of the propeller-shaft casing passes. Cradles formed by the cross-member on each side of the big tube are utilised to carry the batteries.

The top flanges of the frame are very wide between the spring anchorages, and again from the engine rear bearer arm right back to the front anchorages of the rear springs. Between the main double cross-member and the rear axle there is suspended, mainly below frame level, a 28-gallon petrol tank. In plan view this follows the shape of the frame, but the upper portion is shaped suitably to give a tunnel for the propeller-shaft case, and to allow room for the feet of rear-seat passengers. The tank is very firmly supported from three points, but at the same time is free from frame distortion. It is carried low and between the axles so as to give a good distribution of weight with as little variation as possible, whether the tank is full or nearly empty.

Half-elliptic springs are used both back and front, but the front springs are pinned at their rear ends and shackled at the front in boxes which prevent side play. The spring pin and shackle bearings are automatically lubricated from a central lubrication system, which will be described later. For the half-elliptic rear springs Silentbloc bushes, which need no lubrication, are employed. Large double Hartford shock absorbers are fitted to the front axle, whilst the rear axle has two pairs of double Hartfords, the units of each pair being set at right-angles to one

another. Also, the axle has check straps and rubber buffers, so that the spring travel is suitably limited.

Practical simplicity is a feature of the four wheel brake gear. From the pedal a tie-rod runs back to a lever mounted on a very stout cross tube carried in bearings in brackets hanging below frame level. These bearings are large in diameter and narrow, so that any twisting of the frame is not likely to cause binding of the cross-shaft. At each end of

The M.G. Mark III viewed from the rear.

the cross-shaft is a double lever, one arm pointing up, the other down.

From the upper lever on each side a rod runs forward to terminate in a thimble connection to the end of a stranded steel cable. The cable passes through a slide attached to a frame bracket, and then through a flexible cable covering, passing on to an anchorage on the hub bracket. The cable terminates in a steel slide which embraces the end of the lever, and is adjustable by means of a wing nut pin and a lock nut. From the lower lever on each side a cable runs back to a bracket by the front anchorage of the rear spring, and then passes through a flexible casing to a rear hub in the same way as at the front.

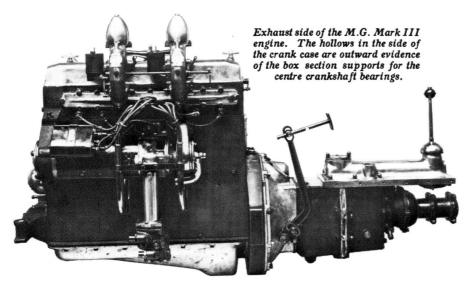

Exhaust side of the M.G. Mark III engine. The hollows in the side of the crank case are outward evidence of the box section supports for the centre crankshaft bearings.

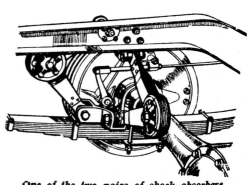

One of the two pairs of shock absorbers fitted to the rear axle.

There is a very ingenious method of taking up the main adjustment, which is situated on the end of the tie-rod that couples the cross-shaft lever to the brake pedal. A V-ended thimble screws on to the end of a tie-rod, and this thimble is attached to a flexible cable which is swept round at right angles and passes out through the frame to an adjustable wheel. When the wheel is turned the cable twists with it, and thereby rotates the sleeve on its screw thread.

Deep-valances cover the frames and help to increase the sturdy appearance of the car.

Viewed from the front the most striking feature of the M.G. is the powerful third head lamp.

These caps are very large and of the quick-action variety, and the idea is that both caps would be removed when filling so that a large quantity of fuel can be poured in at one orifice whilst the other makes a large vent for the escape of air. At the left-hand forward corner of the tank is the delivery stand-pipe. This is sheltered by a tube attached to a cap screwed in from the bottom; the tube has various large holes in it and is covered with fine-mesh gauze.

There are two separate fuel-delivery systems. From the stand-pipe and its union a flexible petrol-resisting tube goes forward to a two-way tap, and from each of the tap leads a pipe runs forward to a separate electrically operated pump. From each pump a pipe runs up to a two-way tap concealed under the dash. From this tap a flexible pipe then runs forward to the two carburetters. The two electric Tecalemit petrol pumps are controlled by separate switches. Thus, a leak in one pipe will not affect the other.

Another interesting feature is the automatic central chassis lubrication. It is a Tecalemit design, wherein a glass-bodied container attached to the front of the dashboard carries in its head a special form of automatic vibratory pump, the inertia of a bob-weight being used to build up oil pressure at between 60lb. and 90lb.

The car carries three head lamps, besides side and tail lamps. All electrical circuits throughout the vehicle are wired separately, and each line of wiring has its own separate fuse, a large fuse box being carried on the engine side of the dash. The idea of this is to localise faults as far as possible.

Very strong support is given to the three-head-lamp system and to the front wings, there being a double triangulated structure of streamline section steel tubing right across the front of the car.

All the vital points in the steering, by the way, are filed and polished to make sure that no hidden flaws exit.

The intention is to turn the car out absolutely run-in, with the bearings free, the brakes bedded in, all nuts split-pinned and wired, with racing tyres on racing rims, and, in fact, everything tuned up to the degree where there is no need for further work on the machine. It is hoped to guarantee a speed of 100 m.p.h.

The instruments include speedometer, rev counter, stop clock, oil gauge, ammeter, radiator and oil thermometers.

The body is a simple and sturdy metal-panelled four-seater, with a single shallow door on the near side, and it has a considerable portion of the off side cut away. The car carries a windscreen which can be folded flat forward, and there is, of course, a regulation hood.

Outside the body, and well forward, is a long hand-brake lever with the customary racing-type ratchet, and this lever operates all four brakes independently of the pedal by means of a trip lever attachment to the cross-shaft. Adjustment at this point is made by means of a large set pin. The brake drums are of very large diameter, with wide shoes, and the drums are also heavily ribbed so that they should stand up to prolonged hard work. Incidentally, the brake cam spindles are cadmium plated, and work in roller bearings which are packed with grease.

Reverting now to the fuel system. First, the big tank has two filling caps, one on each side of the floor of the car.

Two down-draught carburetters are fitted to the Mark III M.G. Six. Note the arrangement of the dynamo drive and vertical spindle drive with double ignition distributor at the top.

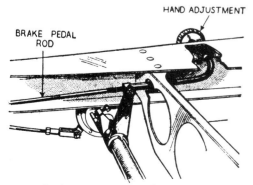

An ingenious hand adjustment is provided for the foot brake.

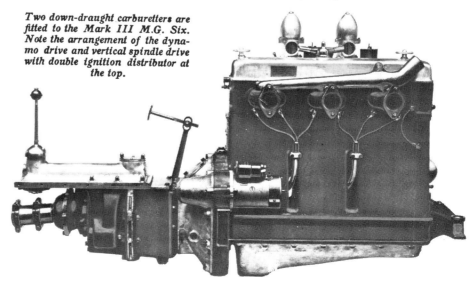

OUTLINE OF
SPECIFICATION.

Bore 69 mm.   Stroke 110 mm.
Capacity 2468 c.c.
R.A.C. Rating 17·7 h.p.   Tax £18.
Wheelbase, 9ft. 6in. ; Track 4 feet.

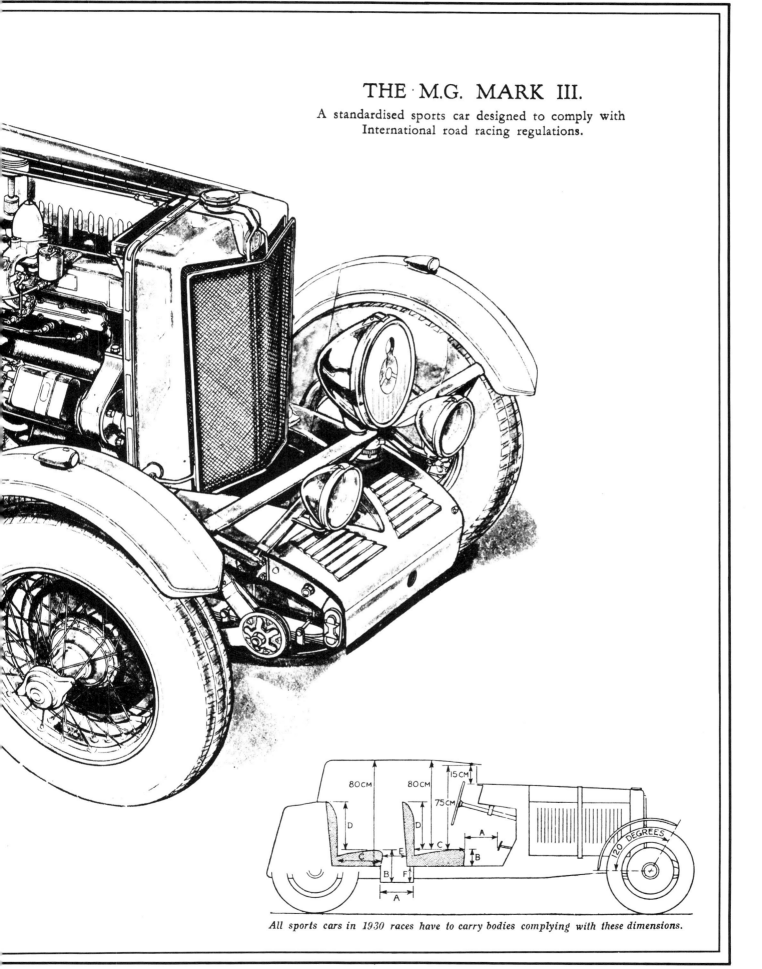

THE · M.G. MARK III.

A standardised sports car designed to comply with
International road racing regulations.

All sports cars in 1930 races have to carry bodies complying with these dimensions.

October 17th, 1930.

M.G.   (16)
Country of Origin: Great Britain.

M.G. CAR CO., LTD.,
PAVLOVA WORKS,
ABINGDON-ON-THAMES.

8-33 h.p., 4-cyls., 57×83 mm. (847 c.c.), tax £8. coil ignition, thermo cooling, single disc cl., 3-sp. unit gear box, spiral bevel, ½-E. front and rear springs, 27×4.00in. tyres on wire wheels, four wheel brakes. Prices: 2-seater touring car, £185; 2-seater coupé. £245.

SUCCESSFULLY and definitely built as sports cars, the M.G. range has become famous for speed, refinement and beauty of line. To the Midget no special alterations have been made, but the sportsman's coupé now has a panelled body and cleaner roof lines. Just as the two-seater is an ideal type of small specialised speed car, so the coupé is an extraordinarily smart and cleverly arranged little town carriage, with a remarkable amount of room inside, despite the compactness.

18-80 h.p., 6-cyls., 69×110 mm. (2,468 c.c.), tax £18, pump cooling, multi-plate cl., 29×5in. tyres, four wheel vacuum servo brakes. Prices: Chassis. £445; 4-seater touring car, £525; 4-seater saloon. £565.

Other details as in 8-33 h.p.

Remarkable for the fact that its six-cylinder engine is marvellously smooth running for all its power and flexibility, the M.G. Six is a much-appreciated car. There are two types, Mark I and Mark II, the latter having a four-speed gear box and other refinements. An example of the Mark I chassis shows individuality of design and sturdy build. There is also a two-door four-seater close-coupled light saloon with deep footwells in the rear compartment, and a new edition, a speed model with a four-seater open body. The Mark II sports saloon de luxe is another new type of coachwork, very smart and up to date, with close-fitting wings, novel, curved running boards, and Pytchley sliding roof; the price is £699. Tasteful paintwork and upholstery are another feature of this exhibit.

A really sporting appearance is imparted by the lines of the M.G. Six Mark I Speed Model

Two-door, four-seater close-coupled M.G. Six Saloon

An M.G. Six Mark III with special sports coachwork by Carbodies

INTO BATTLE   1933

*M.C.C. EXETER TRIAL 1931: H. S. Linfield's M.G. Speed Model, with its crew of four, completes an observed section. Then a staff member of **The Autocar**, Linfield was later to become editor of the journal. This is the same car that had been the subject of a Road Test report in the issue of 14 November 1930 (see opposite page)*

"THE AUTOCAR" ROAD TESTS

M.G. SIX SPEED MODEL.

Fascinating Car with an Excellent Performance, which Handles Very Well Indeed.

The illustration above indicates the size of the M.G. Six Speed Model compared with a 40-50 h.p. Rolls-Royce.

UNTIL recently the buyer wanting a real four-seater sports type car of medium size has been limited in scope by the fact that the majority of sports machines are, by their nature, relatively expensive. The M.G. speed model, which is a new type on the latest Mark I six-cylinder chassis, admirably fills this need, and, into the bargain, is a remarkably fascinating motor car to handle and own.

It is a very big asset that the engine is exceedingly smooth, devoid of all fierceness sometimes associated with this kind of car in the ordinary driver's mind, and in fact, the vehicle is capable of being driven for the greater part of a day's running on top gear alone. In a sense, this extreme smoothness is deceptive, for, although the engine can be throttled down so as to run without jerk at 5 m.p.h. on top, there is in reserve that extra liveliness of performance which is the very essence of a sports model.

Without using the indirects at all, except, of course, in starting from rest, the acceleration is very good, and a cruising speed which can be as high as 60 m.p.h. is quickly reached, and maintained, if the driver wishes, for as long as road conditions permit. On the other hand, second gear of the three-speed box is a relatively close ratio and exceedingly useful, in that a speedometer reading of 61 can be obtained on it. Obviously, therefore, the man who buys this type of car, who, as a rule, finds gear changing an art instead of an annoyance, can very materially improve the performance by judicious use of second, the change itself handling exceptionally well.

On a long run the M.G. is most satisfying, the high cruising speed—in almost complete silence, only the rush of air and the sound of the tyres on the road surface showing that the machine is travelling fast—and the performance on second gear already referred to, being just what are wanted. As illustrating the ability of the car to maintain a good speed, it was taken through an officially observed trial on Brooklands, in which, driven continuously for one hour, it covered 69.75 miles in the sixty minutes. The maximum is, obviously, excellent, and 80 is attainable on the road in conditions not unduly favourable to the car. The car handles most satisfactorily,

too; the control is light, and the brake action, with the vacuum servo now added, extremely good. The hand brake lever outside the body is of racing type, and the brake itself will hold the car on a steep gradient.

Steering is light, positive, and does not transmit road shock to the steering wheel itself—which has a thin rim and spring spokes —though it is possible that even more definite caster action than is provided at present, with consequent automatic sense of direction, would help a car of these speed capabilities, and is not difficult, by the way, to introduce. The suspension is exactly right, it being possible, of course, to set the big double-acting friction shock-absorbers so as to make the springing comparatively hard at low speeds, but giving the car an extraordinary stability that is essential for fast corner work.

A most interesting point is that the back seat is really comfortable, the occupants experiencing no direct shock, a thing not altogether common with a sports four-seater. The way in which the car can be taken round corners absolutely accurately, with not the slightest sway, contributes not a little to the success of the machine. It is interesting that the car is quiet, which is a very big point indeed, with just the right note in the exhaust to distinguish it from that of an ordinary touring car; while, in passing, the obvious possibilities of the car for competition work are worth mentioning.

The driving position is excellent, the bucket front seats holding one, as it were, in just the right position, the driver's seat being adjustable; the other front seat swings forward so as to make access to the back compartment more convenient, there being one door at each side of the car. The upholstery is very good indeed and comfortable; while as to detail, the instruments are grouped, panelled, and well lighted by two neat lamps giving a green-tinted light, among the dials being a rev. counter, fuel tank gauge, trip-type

speedometer, engine thermometer, and a clock. At either side of the instruments is a deep cubby hole, there are three pockets in the sides of the body, and the single panel windscreen, which has an electric wiper with dual arms, folds right down flat on the scuttle—a feature really worth having.

The engine is extremely neat, with all the sparking plugs very accessible indeed; the overhead-valve gear is easily reached when the cover secured by two hand wheels is removed; while the ignition distributor and coil, and the junction box for the electrical connections, are also well placed. On the other side of the engine, the carburetter, which is a dual type with a single float chamber, is also very accessible indeed, fuel feed being by an electric pump; and the oil filler is big, combining in its cap the dipstick.

The head lamps, by the way, are powerful, the dimming device is controlled by a convenient switch on the steering column, and with all the lights on there is a surplus of 3 amperes at normal speeds.

The chassis is well laid out for maintenance, the floorboards being held down by locks which are operated by an ordinary carriage key, which arrangement allows them to be removed with unusual ease. In the scuttle are separate spare tanks holding respectively a gallon of oil and two gallons of fuel.

Racing-type wire wheels give the right touch, and the hood is very neat, held securely when furled, and has a good cover. An interesting point was that during a particularly heavy rainstorm, with the hood up but none of the side curtains erected, practically no water at all came inside the car.

The appearance of the car as a whole is obviously just right for the type of machine; the general finish, too, is excellent.

The M.G. speed model is an exceedingly pleasant car to drive—in short, an enthusiast's delight—and should have a bright future.

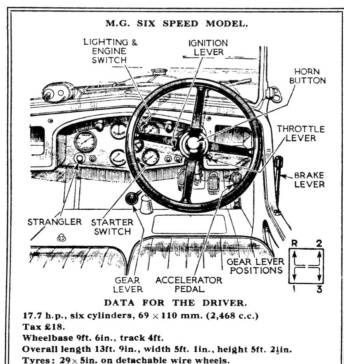

M.G. SIX SPEED MODEL.

LIGHTING & ENGINE SWITCH — IGNITION LEVER — HORN BUTTON — THROTTLE LEVER — BRAKE LEVER — GEAR LEVER POSITIONS — STRANGLER — STARTER SWITCH — GEAR LEVER — ACCELERATOR PEDAL

DATA FOR THE DRIVER.
17.7 h.p., six cylinders, 69 × 110 mm. (2,468 c.c.)
Tax £18.
Wheelbase 9ft. 6in., track 4ft.
Overall length 13ft. 9in., width 5ft. 1in., height 5ft. 2½in.
Tyres: 29×5in. on detachable wire wheels.

Engine—rear axle gear ratios.	Acceleration from steady 10 to 30 m.p.h.	Timed speed over ¼ mile.
13.2 to 1	—	
6.58 to 1	7¾ sec.	79.64 m.p.h.
4.25 to 1	11 sec.	

Turning circle: 43ft.
Tank capacity 12 gallons; fuel consumption 18-20 m.p.g.
12-volt lighting set cuts in at 12 m.p.h., 12 amps. at 30 m.p.h.
Weight: 22 cwt. 3 qr.
Price, with speed model four-seater body, £525.

31 FEET *from* 30 M.P.H.

The colour of speed

Above: Twenty-four years apart—the little M-type Midget, which started it all 'way back in 1929, seen through the screen of the infinitely more refined TF, still unmistakably MG

Below: Stark, functional and more typically MG Midget than any other body style—the sports-racing J4, of which only nine were produced, with its supercharged 746 c.c. 4-cylinder engine.

Overleaf:- TF Midget (October 1953 to October 1955)—last of the true Midgets·and by far the most stylish and civilised with its faired-in headlamps and gracefully curved radiator

Responsible for starting the MG sports car cult in the States—the TC Midget (1945 to 1949) which endeared itself to hundreds of American servicemen stationed in Europe, and accompanied many of them back across the Atlantic when the war was over. In the background, the latest MG BGT-V8

The M.G. Magna close-coupled coupé.

THE 12-70 h.p. M.G. MAGNA

Further Details of a High-performance Small Six of the Most Interesting Character

FOLLOWING the preliminary announcement which appeared in last week's issue of *The Autocar*, it is now possible to give a detailed description of the new M.G. Magna 12-70 h.p. small six-cylinder car. It is a design which must inevitably fascinate those enthusiasts to whom a sporting performance is the true zest of motoring, in whom there is an æsthetic ability to appreciate beauty of line, and by whom refinement of running is admired and enjoyed.

To look first at the low-built and utterly workmanlike chassis of the Magna, and then at the finished clean-cut car, is to experience a feeling of insular gratification that this job is British. Emanating as it does from a firm whose 750 c.c. Montlhéry Midgets have handsomely won this year the three most important international races held on British and Irish soil, the Magna is definitely something more than a mere new model: it is a car of latent possibilities.

Simple and Light

Possibly the outstanding feature is the simple directness of the design. The car is light, because it is devoid of complication. The frame, for example, follows the principles adopted for the successful Montlhéry Midgets; that is to say, the channel section side-members are arched over the front axle, and thereafter drop low down and parallel with the ground, and pass some five or six inches below the rear axle. Steel tubes form all the cross-members, and the springs, which are of the half-elliptic type and almost flat, are attached with the ordinary spring eyes at the front, and rollers at their rear ends in place of shackles, so that the possibility of side-play due to wear is brought down to a minimum, a point which considerably affects lateral stability. Hartford shock-absorbers are fitted back and front. At the extreme rear of the frame is a cradle in which a long, narrow battery is supported.

One of the reasons why the chassis looks so clean is that the brake-operating mechanism is so simple. In a heavily ribbed drum on the hub of each wheel is an expanding shoe brake provided with an individual adjustment. The brakes are operated by means of flexible steel cables, which pass through armoured casings, and the cables run to the centre of the car, where they pass over grooved pulleys on the ends of a cross-shaft. The mechanism is so arranged that the pedal operates all four brakes, while the centrally placed lever separately operates four brakes. By the base of the central lever is a fly nut master adjustment within easy reach of the driver's hand, whilst below the floorboards is another master adjustment for the pedal. One of the points about the brake mechanism is the fact that it is unaffected either by steering movements or spring movements of the axle. Care is taken to make sure that the cables do not rust, and that they can move freely in their casings, by providing a proper system of lubrication, and a grease gun applied to one of the nipples grouped in sets just in front of the dashboard pillars forces grease through the cable casings. Rudge-Whitworth detachable hub wire wheels are fitted.

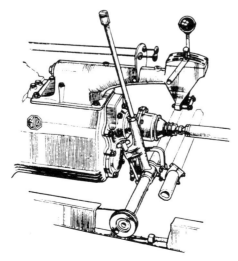

Layout of gear and brake mechanism on the Magna chassis. Note the position of the strangler and throttle controls.

Sitting fairly well back in the front of the frame is the engine and gear box unit. It is mounted with a three-point form of suspension, and an extension of the centre bracket at the forward end is arranged to carry the radiator, so that this component is unaffected by torsional movements of the frame. Naturally, the greatest interest attaches to the engine. This is a six-cylinder design, 57 by 83 mm. (1,250 c.c.). The cylinder block and the greater part of the crankcase are formed in one casting, in which an exceptionally stiff crankshaft is carried in four main bearings. From the front end of the crankshaft a spiral-bevel gear conveys the drive through a vertical shaft, and via the spindle of a vertically mounted dynamo, to a second gear above the cylinder block, and through this agency an overhead camshaft is driven. The camshaft actuates the overhead valves through light fingers having adjustable fulcrum points.

Lubrication

At the front of the engine is a gear pump which draws its supply of oil from a large aluminium sump with cooling fins containing 1¾ gallons of oil, and delivers it through an easily detachable filter to the main bearings, the big ends, and upwards to the camshaft and rockers. On the left side of the engine is a special induction pipe, fed by a pair of S.U. carburetters, and on the same side a large separate exhaust manifold is coupled up to an exhaust pipe situated by the front of the engine, and thus out of the way of the floorboards.

Aluminium pistons with three rings are employed in conjunction with steel connecting rods, and it may be mentioned that the crankshaft, reciprocating parts, valves, and so forth of this engine are specially prepared with a view to giving a sustained high performance.

Between the engine and the gear box is a large-diameter single-plate clutch. Four speeds are provided by the gear box, and the three top ratios are fairly close, the overall ratios being: First 19.6, second 9.79, third 6.65, and fourth 4.89. These close ratios give every possible opportunity for obtaining the best advantage from the gear box for acceleration, hill-climbing, and fast cornering. On the top of the box is a

The 847 c.c. M.G. Midget with Montlhéry-type frame and four-seater body.

cast aluminium tunnel which proceeds backwards to a point convenient to the driver's left hand, and here there is mounted a short and comfortable little gear lever working in a normal gate. A plate just in front of the gear lever carries a mixture control, and a control for throttle setting.

Drive from the gear box passes to a three-quarter floating spiral-bevel-driven rear axle through an open propeller-shaft of not excessive length, and having a Hardy Spicer metal universal joint at each end. One particularly interesting point about the design is the way in which the front driving compartment is insulated from heat and smell from the engine by using the circular casing around the flywheel as a bulkhead to carry a large rubber sealing ring which, in turn, fills up the circular hole at the point where the dashboard crosses the engine and gear box unit. Mention has been made of a grouped lubricating system. Under the bonnet in front of the dashboard on each side is a group of three nipples, through which all the bearings of the chassis can be lubricated, with the exception of the front spring parts, and the joints on the front axle and steering gear which have their own individual grease gun connections. For the steering a worm and wheel gear is used. The drag link from the gear passes transversely across the car, as the column is considerably raked so as to give a comfortable position for the steering wheel, which is a 16in. celluloid-covered spring-spoke type. The water cooling system of the engine is of the thermo-syphon system, and the effectiveness of the radiator is increased by a belt-driven fan. The radiator itself is of a special design, in shape somewhat similar to the well-known Midget,

but deeper from back to front, and provided with a sloping front, in which a stoneguard is incorporated.

Accessibility in the design has been very carefully studied, and to that end the bonnet is very long and is arranged so that when opened it discloses both sides of the bulkhead, dashboard, and

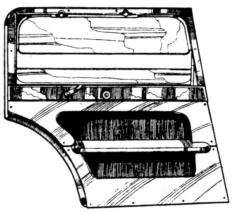

Window mechanism and arm-rest on the door of the Magna coupé.

also the back of the instrument board, besides the pedals and part of the gear box. There is room, therefore, not only to get at the engine, but many of the other important parts of the chassis as well.

Before turning to the coachwork, the following details of the chassis will be of interest. The Treasury rating of the engine is 12.08 h.p., and the tax £12; the track of the car is 3ft. 6in. and the wheelbase 7ft. 10in.; the wheels are shod with 27in. by 4in. tyres, and the chassis weighs approximately 9¼ cwt. The over-

Redesigned front engine mounting and radiator support on the Midget Occasional Four.

all width is 4ft. 2in. and the overall length 10ft. 6½in., whilst the overall height of the close-coupled saloon is only 4ft. 5in. One other chassis point demands mention: the petrol tank contains six gallons, and is carried at the rear of the frame, and is provided with a conveniently placed two-way tap which retains two gallons in reserve.

Now as regards coachwork. There are two bodies available; the first is a sports four-seater, priced at £250. This is a low-built, two-door, close-coupled design with plenty of room in the front seats, but with rear seats intended for occasional use. Alternatively the rear compartment can be used for the con-

(Right) The chassis of the Midget Occasional Four and (left) that of the Magna compared.

veyance of a good deal of luggage. This is a metal-panelled body of very attractive lines, and has at the front a single-panel windscreen which can, when desired, be folded flat forwards out of the way. Packed flat and partially in a recess at the back of the body, is a hood which will cover the whole of the interior of the car. All-weather side-panels are included in the equipment. Leather upholstery is used, and the front seats are of the adjustable bucket

type. Being low-built, the body has no running boards, whilst the wings are of the close-fitting, deep-sided type.

In appearance the closed edition of the Magna is particularly striking. The body is a close-coupled coupé with a sliding roof, and has been christened the Foursome. It has two wide doors to give access to the interior, and the pneumatically upholstered back seats are reached when the backs of the front seats are tilted forwards. Wells in the rear floorboards give increased room. Although the car as a whole cannot be described as a large one, every possible inch has been utilised in the width of the body, which swells out nearly to the full width of the rear wheels. Additional elbow room is given to the front seats by recesses in the doors in which are arm-rests, whilst below each arm-rest is a deep pocket for occasional packages.

Pleated leather upholstery of extra fine finish helps to render the interior very attractive, and another feature is that in the sliding portion of the roof is a series of celluloid windows which not only allow vision upwards, but also make the interior of the car bright. The price of this model is £289. For both cars the stock finish is ebony black with apple green, tudor brown, deep red, or Cearulean blue or suède grey leather upholstery. Other colours that can be obtained if desired at an extra charge of £2 10s. are biscuit, British racing green, russet brown, nile blue or rich red and white. Any other colours

The dropped frame from the rear showing the method of attachment of the rear springs.

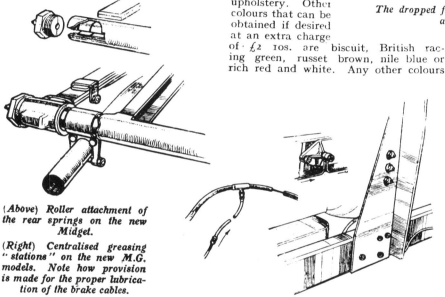

(Above) Roller attachment of the rear springs on the new Midget.

(Right) Centralised greasing "stations" on the new M.G. models. Note how provision is made for the proper lubrication of the brake cables.

than these may be had at an extra charge of £4 10s., whilst a deviation from the five leathers that have been standardised costs an additional five guineas.

The Midget Occasional Four

Finally a few notes may be added to the information already published about the 8-33 h.p. M.G. Midget Occasional Four. This is a new addition to the Midget range, and has an open four-seater body very similar to that of the

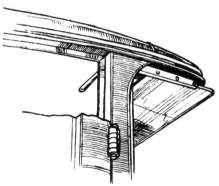

The sun visor on the Magna coupé can be conveniently operated from the interior of the car.

Magna. The chassis is also of the underslung frame type, with flat springs and slides instead of shackles. Most of the detail can be seen in the accompanying illustrations.

Special points of the model are that the gear lever is mounted at the end of a rearwardly projecting bracket on the top of the gear box, a grouped nipple system of chassis lubrication is provided, and the use of a long bonnet makes it possible to secure immediate access to the scuttle as well.

It is possible, additionally, to obtain this model with a four-speed box instead of three speeds. The chassis is very similar to the Montlhéry type, but the engine is the normal four-cylinder 847 c.c. type. This car has the petrol tank situated at the back, and Rudge-Whitworth racing type wire wheels are fitted. It is priced at £210.

The M.G. Magna has twin carburetters.

THE M.G. MAGNA.

A NEW SMALL SIX-CYLINDER SPORTS CAR.

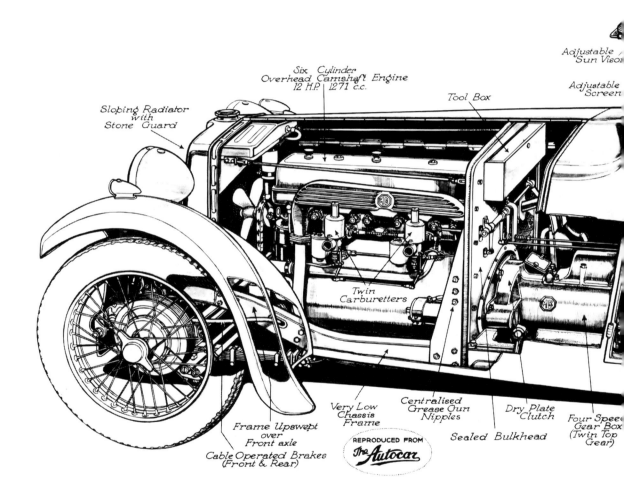

SALIENT FEATURES.

1271 c.c., o.h. camshaft engine, four-speed gear box with silent third. Frame underslung at rear. The engine is entirely separated from the passenger accommodation by an aluminium bulkhead and undershield.

Tax £12.   Wheelbase, 7 ft. 8 in.   Track, 3 ft. 6 in.
Overall length, 10 ft. 4½ in.   Overall width, 4 ft. 2 in.

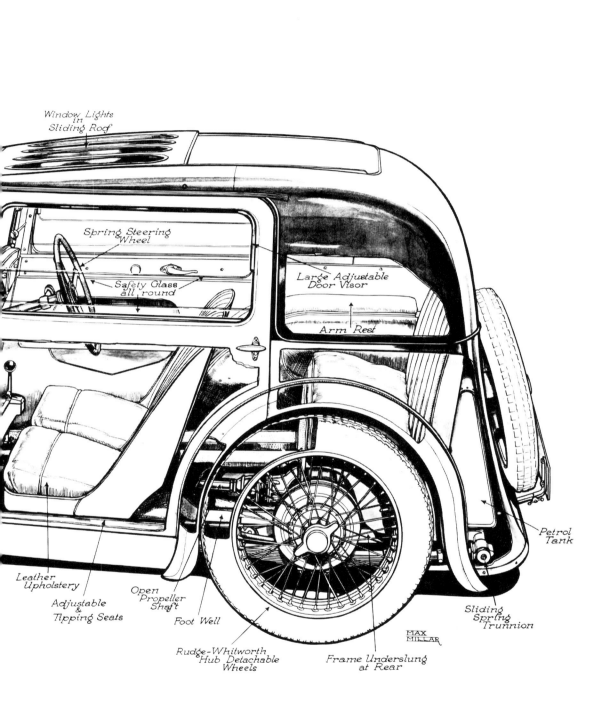

Window Lights in Sliding Roof

Spring Steering Wheel

Large Adjustable Door Visor

Safety Glass all round

Arm Rest

Leather Upholstery

Adjustable & Tipping Seats

Open Propeller Shaft

Foot Well

Rudge-Whitworth Hub Detachable Wheels

Frame Underslung at Rear

Sliding Spring Trunnion

Petrol Tank

MAX MILLAR

This little car is based on the design of the racing
M.G. Midget, which has been so successful this
year at Brooklands and in the two big Irish events.

Published *The Autocar,*
20 November 1931

The illustration above represents the size, in feet, of the Montlhéry M.G. Midget two-seater

No. 678 $\binom{Post-War}{Séries}$.—MONTLHERY M.G. MIDGET TWO-SEATER

WHATEVER one's experience of cars may be, there is a new thrill in handling the Montlhéry Mark II M.G. Midget, especially the supercharged model. It is not a question of how extremely well this small car goes, but, by contrast, how extraordinarily good is this car among cars as a whole. Apart altogether from the personal interest, great as that is, there exists as a background the fact that this particular model has become famous in about the shortest possible time on record, and has to its credit the winning of the three classic British races in 1931—two of them without being supercharged—as well as averaging over 92 m.p.h. for 500 miles in the last big race of the year. Few cars have achieved success so rapidly.

The point of the machine is that it is produced to be a competition car, and to that end is complete with every imaginable specialised fitting, and each machine is built individually and with an amount of painstaking hand workmanship of which the price of the complete car is a reflection.

The dimensions of the two-seater body conform to the international regulations, and one glance round the machine suffices to show that nothing need be added to enable one to take the car at once into a race. The instrument board has every conceivable gauge, the brakes can be adjusted while the car is moving, the back shock absorbers also; clip fillers are used for the radiator, fuel tank, and oil tank, the rear fuel tank is really usefully big, the bonnet has not to be lifted for oil replenishment since the tank in the scuttle supplies the engine as required, the wire mesh screen folds flat, there is a stone guard for the radiator, the wire wheels are of racing type, and the hand brake has a racing pawl mechanism.

It is extraordinarily interesting, first of all to test the car on Brooklands

track for maximum speed and other data, and then to take it on the road for a long run. This impresses one forcibly with the fact that so many of the features at present regarded as racing practice are actually the best and most efficient for everyday work. For instance, nothing could be better than the big fuel tank, with its touring range of over 350 miles, the quick-acting filler caps, and the method of brake and shock absorber adjustment.

In spite of the fact that this is a proper competition car, there is nothing which makes the machine unsuitable for touring. The car, in fact, constitutes a concrete instance of the value of the developments that are encouraged by modern racing. The exhaust note means that one has to be careful in going through towns, but no trouble need be experienced with the authorities. One would not expect the slow running on top or even third gear to be good; but, in fact, no one interested in a car of this nature would want to make it run slowly on the higher ratios.

With touring plugs in the engine, all the speed that can be ordinarily used on the road is obtainable, and there was no suggestion of any plug oiling up, racing plugs being used only for the fast work on the track. As to the timed speed figure for the half-mile, it is obviously outside everyday requirements, yet is by no means a limit for the car as a type. It may be mentioned that the actual machine tested was one that ran unsupercharged in the Double-Twelve, and was a practice car for the Tourist Trophy, being an early example, used a good deal by all sorts of people. Something close on 90 m.p.h. is an amazing speed for a 750 c.c. car that is also a practical vehicle on the road; and for all its power the engine is remarkably smooth.

Apart altogether from the maximum, the car has

fascination beyond the measure of cold words, for it handles beautifully, is as steady as the proverbial rock, is comfortably sprung as well, possesses a gear change that is a delight in consistency, meaning that the same treatment produces similar results each time, has brakes which recorded the shortest stopping distance during the past twelve months, steers literally to an inch, almost irrespective of road surface, and has terrific acceleration.

Acceleration figures have not been taken for top and third gears for the reason already indicated, and that on second from 10 m.p.h. gives but the slightest impression of the capabilities. It is over the middle range of speed, say from 20 to 50, or 30 to 60, that the car literally shoots away, of course using the indirects, and in the circumstances something rather unusual may be introduced as conveying an idea of what the car can do. From a standing start, going through the gears, it is possible to reach 60 m.p.h. in 20⅘ sec.

A normal limit for the engine is 5,500 r.p.m., and at that the equivalent road speeds on the indirects are 20 on first, 40 on second, and 60 m.p.h. on third. Far higher revs are possible, and during the test the engine held 5,750 r.p.m. on top gear, going actually to 6,200 when entering the timed section.

The car is compact, meaning that it can be slipped in and out of traffic with the greatest of ease, but the impression gained from the solid, steady feel is of a machine far bigger than the actual dimensions. The performance is a combination of opposing qualities. With the car once under way at a steady pace it is possible to climb most main-road hills on top gear, even accelerating up them, so considerable is the power developed; but the real joy of the machine lies in employing the indirects to the proper extent, and on a long run one finds one is maintaining in this way a steady speed, whether the road happens to be level, downhill, or ascending, all of which helps in giving a good average.

Of mechanical noise there is remarkably little, and except at quite low speeds the blower can scarcely be heard at all, while the exhaust possesses a remarkably satisfactory crackle to delight the ear of the enthusiast. Perhaps the most striking thing of all is that the car feels safe, so absolutely steady is it under all conditions, taking corners with very little diminution in speed, answering at once to the wheel, and never deflecting from the straight even when the brakes are applied hard. As another aspect of this machine—one able to win races, as has been amply demonstrated, and a practical touring car as well—there is the further point that it is perfectly capable of shining in a reliability trial, since first gear is low and there is sufficient power to take the car up the fiercest gradients. Further, the engine runs very cool.

The equipment has already been mentioned—in fact, it is this which appeals, next to the performance. The instrument panel is entirely free from unnecessary decoration, and carries a most imposing array of dials and push-and-pull switches. Both ignition and fuel supply systems are duplicated. In view of the way in which the car can be used, it should be worth providing a speedometer and lighting for the instruments.

The bucket type seats give support exactly as they should, that for the driver being adjustable; accessibly behind the passenger's seat is the battery; behind the driver's seat is space for oddments and small baggage, whilst in the tail, where the spare wheel is carried, there is additional space. There is a hood of the type fitted to the larger-engined Midgets, which, with its supports, is also stored in the tail.

Starting from cold is easy when the carburetter has been flooded; the fuel used is an 80-20 per cent. mixture of benzole and petrol. Unsupercharged, the machine costs £490.

Using a much misused word, the Montlhéry Mark II M.G. Midget is unique—and is a development that is essentially British.

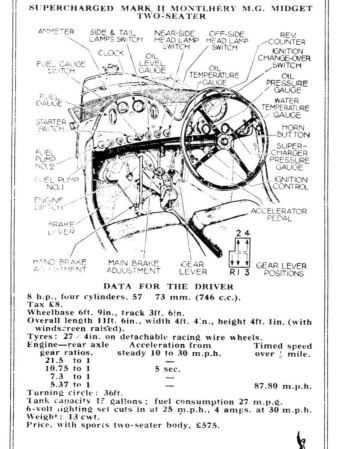

SUPERCHARGED MARK II MONTLHÉRY M.G. MIDGET TWO-SEATER

DATA FOR THE DRIVER

8 h.p., four cylinders, 57 × 73 mm. (746 c.c.).
Tax £8.
Wheelbase 6ft. 9in., track 3ft. 6in.
Overall length 11ft. 6in., width 4ft. 4in., height 4ft. 1in. (with windscreen raised).
Tyres: 27 × 4in. on detachable racing wire wheels.

Engine—rear axle gear ratios	Acceleration from steady 10 to 30 m.p.h.	Timed speed over ½ mile.
21.5 to 1	—	
10.75 to 1	5 sec.	
7.3 to 1	—	
5.37 to 1	—	87.80 m.p.h.

Turning circle : 36ft.
Tank capacity 15 gallons ; fuel consumption 27 m.p.g.
6-volt lighting set cuts in at 25 m.p.h., 4 amps. at 30 m.p.h.
Weight : 13 cwt.
Price, with sports two-seater body, £575.

26 FEET from 30 M.P.H.

USED CARS ON THE ROAD

No. 51.   M.G. Six Mark I Saloon   No. WL7125

PERFORMANCE DATA

Price, new - - - £545		Timed speed over measured	
Second-hand - - £225		mile - - 69.77 m.p.h.	
Acceleration - 10-30 m.p.h.		Brake test figure from	
Second gear - - 6⅛ sec.		30 m.p.h. - - - 42ft.	
Top gear - - 11 sec.		Speedometer records	
Fuel consumption 19½ m.p.g.		35,000 miles.	
Oil consumption 400 m.p.g.		First registered 1929.	

IT is a real pleasure to test a car like the M.G. Six saloon, submitted by University Motors, Ltd., Brick Street, W.1, which demonstrates how little effect 35,000 miles need have on a well-made car. Barring the oil consumption, which, even so, was no heavier than on many cars of a lesser mileage, and which was partially accounted for by really hard driving, there were no signs of mechanical wear. The engine was smooth and quiet, free from any mechanical knocks and noises. It started readily from cold in the morning, and required little warming up.

Once warm, its performance was excellent. The car could be driven at a walking pace on top gear without snatch, and then, by due manipulation of the sensitive ignition control,

accelerated to a speedometer reading of 73 m.p.h., which was not more than 3 m.p.h. optimistic. This corresponded to about 3,600 r.p.m. Above this speed—and 4,000 r.p.m. could be reached on the gears—the engine became more noisy, and valve bounce set in. The timed speed was taken over a full mile against a distinct breeze.

The ignition control needed handling with discretion, if "pinking" was to be avoided, but otherwise the engine was as docile as any touring design.

The gears were reasonably quiet, and 50 m.p.h. was a comfortable maximum on second. On the first ratio Brooklands test hill was surmounted from a standing start at 23 m.p.h. Road-holding was, perhaps, not up to the high standard otherwise set by the car.

The suspension was a little bumpy and could probably be improved by adjustment of the shock absorbers. If really fast cornering was attempted, the car tended to "judder" outwards—not to skid.

Externally, the condition of paint and fabric was good, except for naking on the off-side rear mudguard. Internally also there were no faults to find, all the instruments working well, the roof light and rear blind being in good order, and the leather upholstery not in the least shabby. The dynamo charged at eight amperes—sufficient to supply all the lights.

The head lamps were quite adequate, though not superlative, but the pneumatic-type dipper was out of action.

The seats were comfortable, and the driving position was good. A certain amount of resonance was noted, but one soon became accustomed to the low booming noise.

The brakes were adequate, and, though requiring a fair pressure, did not pull the steering to either side. In the course of the brake test the front off-side cable broke, but this has now been renewed. Even with the cable broken, the car was under perfect control, though naturally there was a pull to the right.

The M.G. was definitely a good car—gentle, yet with a sporting performance. It was sound, reliable, and smart, and no faults beyond those mentioned could be detected.

INTO BATTLE   1931

FEBRUARY 1931 - the first-ever meeting of the newly-formed M.G. Car Club, a half-day trial in the High Wycombe-Oxford area in which 60 members entered their cars. Here, Viscount Curzon, son of Earl Howe, sets off on the standing-start acceleration test up Waterworks Hill, near Tring.

MONTE CARLO RALLY 1931: Norman Black's Speed Model, which led the John o'Groats starters, put up fourth fastest time in the Acceleration and Brake Test (15·8 sec to Donald Healey's Invicta's 15·0 sec, outright winner of the Rally), and finished 16th in the Over 1,100 c.c. Division - winning the Barclay's Bank Cup. Of 149 starters, 62 finished, 25 of them British.

The Autocar Road Tests

The illustration above indicates the size, in feet, of the M.G. Six Mark II saloon

No. 681 ($\binom{Post-War}{Series}$)—M.G. SIX MARK II SALOON

AS from time to time acquaintance is renewed with the M.G. Six, the feature which impresses itself most vividly upon the mind is the amazing smoothness of the engine. This is a car which has many admirable qualities; it has power, it has performance, it handles very well indeed, it appeals at once to the enthusiast, yet is suitable for a driver who prefers to run for a great part of the time on top gear.

It is not too much to say that this particular engine is one of the smoothest and least obtrusive in existence, irrespective of price of car. This in itself, desirable as it is, would not be so attractive if the rest of the car did not make the driver feel that it is a machine responsive at once to all the controls, which amply repays intelligent handling, and is the kind of car for which the possessor soon comes to feel real pride of ownership. Moreover, it is one on which high average speeds are maintained without sense of effort.

Why one car should produce this effect, yet another, perfectly good in its way, remain to the discriminating motorist as chiefly a means of conveyance, is elusive.

But to start with, the M.G. has steering which is accurate and gives just the right amount of caster action. Further, the car can be cornered fast without sway or roll, and feels safe at speed. As might be expected, the springing has necessarily to be on the hard side, which is noticeable at low speeds, but even as far as back-seat passengers are concerned there is no suggestion of direct discomfort. Friction shock absorbers are employed, and with these set fairly tight the road-holding is all that can be desired, the springing smoothing itself out, as it

were, as the speed increases. The general stability for what is a comfortable saloon car is very good indeed.

Then the car could not be what it is if the brakes were not entirely adequate to the speed. They have proper progressiveness, so that light pressure produces the amount of slowing required in ordinary circumstances, whilst fairly heavy pressure on the pedal is needed to effect an emergency stop. At no time is it easy to lock wheels, nor is there any deviation from the straight. The hand lever is of racing type, which is actually the best type of hand brake for any car.

Of the several excellent features appealing to a driver who takes any interest at all in driving for its own sake, the gear change, with the short, stiff lever coming to hand at exactly the right point, is, again, one of the most delightful in existence. The movement of the lever from gear to gear is comparatively short; third speed is a silent ratio, and, incidentally, has been found to be quieter on other cars of this model previously driven. The change is perfectly straightforward, very quick for anything bar a machine of racing type, and changing from top to third is especially easy, the ratios being quite close. The clutch takes up its work smoothly, and the pedal action is light.

Top is a well-chosen ratio, though there is every reason, from the interest point of view, why third should be employed frequently to good effect. On the indirects, speedometer readings of 20 on first, 36 on second, and 65 on third are possible without forcing the engine to the point where it becomes even slightly harsh.

As to the limit on top, the great merit of this remarkable engine is that it

remains smooth almost to the very maximum, and is entirely happy to cruise at a speedometer reading as high as 65. During the timed speed test the speedometer went to a reading of 84 m.p.h. and the rev counter recorded 3,750 r.p.m. The speed, as an average over a measured distance, is excellent for a saloon of this engine capacity.

In studying the car from the point of view of maintenance and convenience, the feature which emerges strongly is that, much more than most, the M.G. has been laid out by practical motorists whose aim has been to make the owner's task as easy as possible, with full appreciation of the kind of difficulty that usually arises. For instance, in detail, the floorboards are arranged in sections, each section being held by locks operated by an ordinary carriage key, so that the floorboards are very easily removed.

Again, the luggage container at the back, which is built very neatly into the body, is capacious in itself, but should an unusual amount of luggage be carried, the lid hinges down, and is already provided with straps so that extra suitcases can be attached to it. Under the bonnet, too, on the cover for the overhead valve gear, is a metal plate inscribed with all manner of information. That alone may be a small thing, but it goes to show something of the attitude of those responsible.

The four-door saloon body has plenty of leg room, there being wells in the floor for the back-seat occupants; and though there are only two windows at either side a point upon which passengers comment is the unusual sense of light and spaciousness in the interior, as well as upon the lack of any drumming effect. The ventilator in the roof, which is provided with glass, helps materially in making the interior light, yet does not detract from the appearance of the car outwardly.

The upholstery is very good, being of durable leather; the bucket-type front seats are immediately adjustable, their backs sloping rearwards rather more than is usual for this type of seat, whilst at the rear there are arm-rests at either side and a central folding arm-rest, as well as neatly recessed companions.

Glass of the safety type is fitted to all the windows, including that at the back; the blind for the latter is controlled from the driving seat, there being a proper catch to hold it in the raised position. A blind is provided for each of the side windows; the screen opens fully and has an electric wiper with two blades, the mechanism being mounted very sensibly on the near side, out of the driver's line of vision. The instrument panel carries an engine thermometer as well as an electric fuel gauge, a clock, and a revolution counter, the dials being very nicely balanced and beautifully lighted at night by two direct lamps with green-tinted bulbs. On either side of the instruments are cubby holes with lids; and, in addition, there is a pocket in each of the rear doors, and a roof net.

The engine is very neat indeed; each of the sparking plugs is easily accessible, the coil also, there being the advantage that it is in a protected position. Carried in the scuttle, with their filler caps accessible under the bonnet, are containers for a spare gallon of oil and a gallon of fuel.

The engine starts remarkably easily, it being unnecessary during warm weather even to employ the mixture control when starting from cold. A special type of automatic chassis lubrication is fitted, the container for the oil being under the bonnet. This is operated by the movement of the car itself actuating an oscillating weight, and so a small plunger pump, with no other mechanism.

The head lamps give a very good beam indeed; the charging rate of the dynamo is sufficiently high to provide a surplus of current with all lights on.

This is a car with a definite personality, most fascinating to drive.

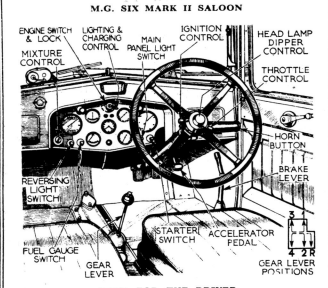

M.G. SIX MARK II SALOON

ENGINE SWITCH & LOCK — LIGHTING & CHARGING CONTROL — MAIN PANEL LIGHT SWITCH — IGNITION CONTROL — HEAD LAMP DIPPER CONTROL — MIXTURE CONTROL — THROTTLE CONTROL — HORN BUTTON — BRAKE LEVER — REVERSING LIGHT SWITCH — FUEL GAUGE SWITCH — GEAR LEVER — STARTER SWITCH — ACCELERATOR PEDAL — GEAR LEVER POSITIONS

DATA FOR THE DRIVER

17.7 h.p., six cylinders, 69 × 110 mm. (2,468 c.c.).
Tax £18.
Wheelbase 9ft. 6in., track 4ft. 4in.
Overall length 13ft. 1in., width 5ft. 5in., height 5ft. 7in.
Tyres: 29 × 5in. on detachable wire wheels.

Engine—rear axle gear ratios.	Acceleration from steady 10 to 30 m.p.h.	Timed speed over ¼ mile.
14.58 to 1		
8.5 to 1	6¼ sec.	
5.58 to 1	9 sec.	
4.27 to 1	12¼ sec.	74.38 m.p.h.

Turning circle: 38ft.
Tank capacity 12 gallons, fuel consumption 20 m.p.g.
12-volt lighting set cuts in at 13 m.p.h., 12 amps. at 30 m.p.h.
Weight: 29 cwt.
Price, with four-door saloon body, £670.

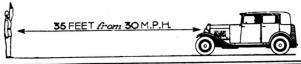

35 FEET from 30 M.P.H.

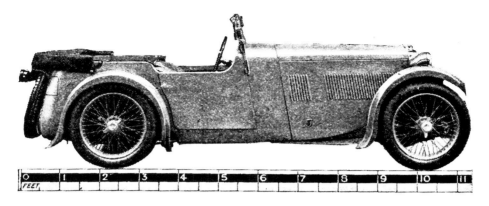

No. 692 (Post-War Series).—M.G. MAGNA FOUR-SEATER

THERE are some few cars, not necessarily of any one type, destined to be a success from the commencement. The new model which has inspired this remark is the M.G. Magna. This is definitely a car of the moment, and there are two sharp divisions at present—those who have tried the Magna, and those who have not. The former may almost be said to be equivalent to wanting to own one.

The Magna should be to the economical six-cylinder sports car class what the Midget has come to be in the smaller four-cylinder world. For £250 what one gets is this: A six-cylinder machine, noticeably but not freakishly low built, with a four-speed gear box, obviously laid out with sports car ideals in mind, yet giving the things that practically every driver wants, or would appreciate if he knew.

Add to this a trim little four-seater body—it being the open car that has been tested—with an imposing length of bonnet and scuttle, yet a perfectly clear view forward, and not the slightest suggestion of unwieldiness. In fact, one of the most marked points is the extreme ease with which the car can be handled on crowded roads, and the lack of effort associated with manœuvring it.

The strongest first impression is that the machine feels solid and rigid in the right way, suggesting a strong chassis properly built, and can be taken round curves and corners just as one pleases, the position of the steering wheel and other controls, coupled with this stability, making for confidence and accuracy right from the beginning, as nothing else can.

The Magna can maintain well above a genuine 70 miles an hour, as the timed speed in the accompanying table shows. That is excellent when one is in a hurry or feels like speed, for there is no particular sense of effort even at the limit; but the great charm of the car lies not at all in this maximum, good though it is to have in reserve. It is utterly fascinating to drive the car even in traffic, with its bright acceleration, or to cruise for mile on end at never more than 50 or 55, a speed which is reached very quickly, the engine running smoothly and quietly with just a pleasing but subdued note from the exhaust, simply because the "feel" of the car is exactly right—thoroughly satisfactory to an unusually enthusiastic driver, or subtly removing some of the doubts and difficulties of a possibly less experienced or less interested driver.

Five miles an hour is feasible on top gear without jerk or snatch, and hills are taken in the car's stride. But for those who like to use it there is what is probably the most delightful gear box fitted to a car of moderate price: four speeds with three close ratios, meaning that 60 can be reached on third and 40 on second, with a low first that will take the machine, fully loaded, up a hill of the trials order with power in hand, controlled by a short, stiff lever working in a visible gate, and with a really easily operated catch to guard reverse. The positions of the lever for the various ratios are different from what is normal, but that is a thing to which one is quickly accustomed; third and second gears run quite quietly, first being noisier by comparison, though it

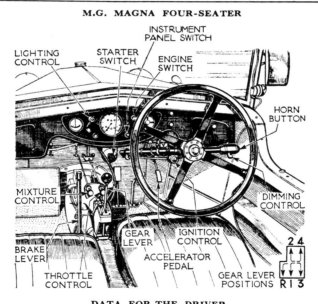

M.G. MAGNA FOUR-SEATER

INSTRUMENT PANEL SWITCH
LIGHTING CONTROL
STARTER SWITCH
ENGINE SWITCH
HORN BUTTON
MIXTURE CONTROL
DIMMING CONTROL
GEAR LEVER
IGNITION CONTROL
BRAKE LEVER
ACCELERATOR PEDAL
THROTTLE CONTROL
GEAR LEVER POSITIONS

DATA FOR THE DRIVER

12–70 h.p., six cylinders, 57 × 83 mm. (1,270 c.c.).
Tax £12.
Wheelbase 7ft. 10in., track 3ft. 6in.
Overall length 11ft. 6½in., width 4ft. 2in., height 4ft. 6in.
Tyres: 4 × 19in. on detachable wire wheels.

Engine—rear axle gear ratios.	Acceleration from steady 10 to 30 m.p.h.	Timed speed over ¼ mile.
19.2 to 1	—	
9.56 to 1	6 sec.	
6.3 to 1	8½ sec.	
4.78 to 1	11½ sec.	72.58 m.p.h.

Turning circle: 35ft.
Tank capacity 6 gallons, fuel consumption 26 m.p.g.
12-volt lighting set cuts in at 15 m.p.h., 8 amps. at 30 m.p.h.
Weight: 19 cwt. 1 qr.
Price, with sports four-seater body, £250.

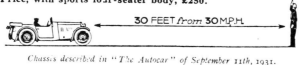

30 FEET *from* 30 M.P.H

Chassis described in "The Autocar" of September 11th, 1931.

M.G. MAGNA FOUR-SEATER

is seldom used for more than a few yards. The steering is very light, but not to the point of being indefinite, and the spring-spoked wheel has a nice thin rim, whilst the clutch works lightly, too, and takes up the drive smoothly. The brakes have plenty of power and, what is more, do not make the car swerve when they are put on hard. The hand-brake lever is of what is termed racing type, and is excellent in every way, besides having at its base an adjustment that can be taken up by hand.

As has been mentioned, the car holds the road very well indeed, helped by big double-acting friction shock absorbers front and rear, so that it might be expected that at quite low speeds, with the shock absorbers tight, the effect would be hard. That, however, is largely a question of adjustment to taste. Even the back seat is comfortable by sports car standards; there is good leg room for one tall passenger, and reasonable space for two normal people.

The separate front seats have pneumatic cushions and backs, the latter sloping rearward rather more than is usual in the interests of firm support for driving, though this is a point that comes rather to be liked. Each seat is quite easily adjustable, but a more rapid action might be preferable; the hood goes up easily and there are good side screens to make the interior snug, whilst a tonneau cover normally fits over the back seats. The front seats tilt forward to give access to the back compartment, the two doors being wide.

In each door is a wide pocket, above which is a small

arm-rest on each side. The grouped instruments —speedometer, ammeter, and oil feed indicating dial, in place of a normal pressure gauge—are brightly lit indirectly. A fuel gauge and an engine thermometer would be welcomed. The single-panel screen folds flat on the scuttle, if wished, and has a twin-blade suction wiper, which works at as much as 50 m.p.h.

A great thing is the instantaneous starting of the engine at all times. The accessibility of the engine, the tools— carried in a locker beneath the bonnet —the clutch housing and gear box, as well as the interior of the driving compartment for cleaning-out purposes, is excellent, because what is usually the scuttle is included in the hinged portion of the bonnet, and therefore opens up.

With its polished valve cover, and nicely red-painted cylinder block, the engine looks pleasing, and, on the practical side, the sparking plugs are eminently accessible, also the coil, distributor, and the electrical fuse box. Even with the fan belt removed the engine does not run hot. Also beneath the bonnet are two groups of lubricators, facing outwards ideally, which feed oil from the usual pressure gun through pipe lines to most of the chassis bearings, leaving very few to be dealt with individually.

An unusual point is the concealment of the filler for the fuel tank by a hinged lid in the side of the body tail; this is undeniably neat, but not too convenient.

The head lamp beam is good, and either the dimming switch or the horn button can be operated without removing the right hand from the wheel.

AN UNUSUAL BODY ON AN M.G.

November 20th, 1931.

THE M.G. Six Mark II, illustrated here, has a body by the Carlton Carriage Co., built to the special requirements of University Motors, Ltd. It is unusual in that the cant rails, from the rear pillars of the doors forward, fold inwards, and the canopy can then be rolled back and secured, thus converting the body into a modified coupé de ville. The hood can also be folded down to form a fully open car. In the tail is space for a considerable quantity of luggage. The chassis is a standard Mark II with four speeds, and the price of the complete car is £750.

December 25th, 1931.

The Earl Howe and the M.G. Magna he has just had delivered. It is finished in the Earl's racing colours.

The Autocar

PUTTING IN THE PEP

The Inner Meanings of " Faster than Most " and " Safety Fast "

by

MAURICE SAMPSON

Illustrated by F. GORDON-CROSBY

ON a nasty bleak morning early in 1931—February 16th, to be exact—Mr. G. E. T. Eyston, as is now well known, drove a British motor car with an engine of less than 750 c.c. at 103.13 m.p.h. over five kilometres. He kept up the remarkable speed of over 100 m.p.h. for ten miles, over which distance he averaged 101.86 m.p.h. He was attacking International Class H records at Montlhéry track, near Paris.

Eyston did more than annex the record on that occasion; he was the first man to attain a speed of over 100 m.p.h. with an engine of less than 750 c.c. He achieved this with an M.G. Midget.

The whole effort—car, driver and organisation — was purely British. This record had been the goal of designers and makers of what the public love to call baby cars for a long time. Whatever may be done in the future it must never be forgotten that this achievement, perhaps one of the most remarkable in the latter-day history of motoring, was accomplished by the Midget. Since then, on October 17th, 1931, Eldridge covered five kilometres on a 750 c.c. Midget at 110.28 m.p.h., a speed exactly equal to that of Kaye Don on the water with Miss England II.

M.G. cars hail from about as unlikely a spot to house a motor car factory as any I can imagine. I always regard Oxford as an unlikely spot wherein to find motor cars being pro-

duced; but, as all the world knows now, that always surprising person, Sir William Morris, and his associates, manage to turn out quite a number from the ancient city of learning. But if Oxford is unlikely as a motor car centre, how shall we regard Abingdon-on-Thames? Yet, tucked neatly away in this little Berkshire town of just over 7,000 inhabitants, is a modern, beautifully equipped, and marvellously clean factory, from which at least one hundred or more sports cars can be produced weekly.

The history of what is now known as the M.G. Car Co., Ltd., is interesting because it shows how a single individual with a single mind fired with great enthusiasm, and backed by a sympathetic and encouraging director, can from nothing, as it were, step right into the forefront of motor car constructors who matter.

Magna frames.

About seven years ago there was no such thing as an M.G. car, but soon afterwards it was very much alive, and this is how it came about. In Oxford, in addition to his great and growing establishment at Cowley, Mr. (now Sir William) Morris owned one or two garages. These were, and still are, known simply and appropriately as the Morris Garages. The bright, shining light in charge of them was one Cecil Kimber, who had already spent many years enthusiastically making fast motor bicycles faster and doing the same to cars when he got the chance. He prevailed upon his employer to let him get to work on the round-nosed Morris-Oxfords of the period, and he put the 'fluence on them to such purpose that they outdistanced every other Morris-Oxford on the road.

The first year's production of these hand-made cars—and do not forget they were produced only in the intervals of running busy garages, and more or less with the aid of the necessarily limited tool equipment available, Cowley merely supplying the chassis—amounted, I believe, to six in all. But those six were seeds that took root to some purpose, and next year things began to get busy. Then came the time when the round-nosed radiator of the Morris models gave way to the present rectangular type, and more ambitious plans were conceived.

The result was that only the essentials, such as the engine and its components, the gear box, and the back axle, and main frame, were obtained from Cowley. These were then "specialised," and the M.G. car began to take on an entity of its own. They began to be recognised in trials and became a usual mount for the sporting driver.

So things continued in a steadily growing volume until a little over two years ago, when an opportunity came

to purchase a very excellent modern factory, and a transfer of activities was made from Oxford to Abingdon, half a dozen miles along the Thames.

A new company was formed, Cecil Kimber placed in command, still, of course, with the sympathetic backing of Sir William, and a completely new line of cars evolved. There are three types of M.G. cars made at Abingdon —the six-cylinder of 17.7 nominal h.p., the Midget of 8 nominal h.p., and the Magna. The last was one of the greatest popular attractions at Olympia.

Safety Fast.

Their designer and maker has hit upon what I think are two of the cleverest and most apposite of slogans yet used in the motor industry. He boldly labels his cars "Faster than Most," and adopts the motto of "Safety Fast." I do not think a truer and more concise description could possibly be found. The M.G. Six, although not the fastest two-and-a-half litre, or thereabouts, sports car in the world, is certainly faster than most.

Appearances DO Count

What sort of an establishment do we find at the prettily named Pavlova works at Abingdon? Although assembly lines in the most modern style are used, every car is essentially handmade. Indeed, so completely is handwork carried out that almost the first thing I saw was two men busily filing and finishing the dumb-irons of an unpainted chassis frame of an M.G. Six, and apparently imparting such a gloss that one might have thought they were trying to convert the dumbirons into mirrors.

"Why that?" I asked. "It seems a funny way to spend money."

"Yes," said C. K., "but it makes the cellulose look nice and smooth at the front of the car, and I believe in appearance as much as in performance." Incidentally, the works have their own frame-building department, wherein the very rigid frame of the Magna is the biggest centre of interest.

This little incident is typical of the whole establishment, and, indeed, it

---

PUTTING IN THE PEP
(continued)

is typical of the designer, for not only does he conceive his working mission in life to be to provide ever better, and more efficient, speedy cars, but to do something worth doing towards making motor cars more beautiful and artistic objects than most of them are at present. "C. K." will unite with any Royal Academician in allowing that the average motor car is not yet a thing of beauty. You may arrange it so that, viewed sideways, it is very attractive, but seen from the front, or from the back, or from a three-quarter angle, ten to one something has gone wrong. So he spends hours plotting and planning and devising new lines which in due course may be incorporated in the finished article for which he is responsible.

A Chassis to Fit the Seats

Hitherto the bodymaker has been handicapped by the chassis maker. The chassis maker presents his structure and expects the bodymaker to render the whole symmetrical, and very often this is desperately difficult. After all, the only constant thing in a car is the seats. We all take up much the same space unless we happen to be very outsize or small size, but on the average we all require about the same head-room, leg-room, and elbow-room.

So I was not at all surprised to find some little experimental work proceeding whereby a set of seats had been arranged and drawings were

Midgets.

---

being made to design a chassis to go under the seats, thus reversing the principle of designing the seats to go over the chassis, and I thought how coachbuilders would, if such a millennium, from their point of view, came to pass, bless the name of Cecil Kimber, and raise statues to him in such places where they make motor car bodies.

Now it is a desperately difficult thing to make a fast car at all, and it is even more difficult when it has to be made more or less conventional. Yet the M.G. people have done it. Let us step right into the Pavlova works and see how it is brought about.

The first impression is one of spaciousness. No one is cramped; everyone has ample elbow room. The concrete floors are spotlessly clean. There

Faster Than Most.

are lines of Midgets, Magnas, and M.G. Sixes moving slowly from nothing to complete cars.

In a sense it seems incongruous that assembly lines are used for cars built so slowly and meticulously. But the lines ensure orderliness; they keep everything and everybody in their places, as it were. Now and again, from a high-up overhead gallery, a chain lowers an engine or a gear box to its appointed place.

Time Means Money

I need not follow the chassis bolt by bolt, so to speak. It is at length finished. Not to-day, perhaps, or even to-morrow. Time is expensive in a motor car factory, especially in one where the labour is necessarily very skilled. That is why the Magnas and the others are not cheap. They are never likely to be. They are made with two main objects in view: to run far and fast and to look attractive. It may be that a car here and there is a "special"; it has to embody certain little details to its future owner's desires. It will take an extra long time to get this one out of the works. Never mind! It is not a matter for worry or grumble; rather of pride. Here will be an M.G. which will go a bit faster than its fellows, or look just a little more *soigné*.

It is in touches like this that a sports car is judged. Sports cars are made for those who want "something different." As a pronounced and unrepentant individualist, I rejoice that there are such cars and people with the means and inclination to buy them. Many firms do not like people who have special ideas for their cars. Quite reasonably, from their viewpoint, they call the ideas fads, and discourage them. Their business is to make a lot of one sort. Probably very good cars, but each a twin of the last. It is because of this "like each other" method of production that we get such good cheap cars to-day. But a man who sets out to make and sell sports cars resembles some world-famous dressmaker; he must create exclusive models.

So if you say you want an M.G. differing in appearance and details and even faster than the one that insufferable young sportsman who lives down your road owns, you can have it—if you can pay for it and do not mind a little delay in delivery.

This is one of the reasons why people making sports cars are always enthusiasts. They have to be, they are for ever meeting enthusiasts. If I hadn't my own work to do I'd rather make sports cars for sporting men and women than do anything else. The whole atmosphere at Abingdon is keen, alert and enthusiastic. It is the sports car atmosphere. I noticed just the same air at Molsheim when I was there, and, I doubt not, would find it at a certain place in Milan, if I went there.

Of International Importance

Sports cars are really and truly international affairs. The keen amateurs of France and Italy and England, and of many other countries, know and appreciate and respect the sports cars and their makers of countries other than their own. Believing this, I believe in motor car racing. It is not only good for cars; it is good for humanity, which is more important.

Forgive this jump off the assembly line; we will go back there.

Behind the line, in a near-by bay, but visible through the narrow steel pillars, is a line of bodies, and as, at last, the chassis is complete and finally tested, its appropriate body steps forward to meet it.

Properly joined up, the complete M.G. car, no matter of what sort, goes

Black magic.

through three kinds of tests on machines I have not seen in operation under one roof before. Let me explain.

One of the difficulties confronting manufacturers of extra fast and necessarily rather costly cars is the matter of thoroughly testing them on the road. As I have just indicated, every M.G. chassis is properly tested, and every complete M.G. car is also taken on the road, and it is taken out to discover any lurking rattles or noises from chassis or body before delivery.

Safe Testing

There are several very potent reasons why road testing alone is not advisable for cars of the M.G. types. First of all it is far better, however experienced the tester, to have tests conducted under the eye of the principal factory officials. This cannot be the case when the car is miles out in the country. It is also difficult to ensure that highly finished coachwork does not acquire some small blemish however carefully washed after road tests at speed.

More serious still, there is the possibility of accident to be avoided No

manufacturer wants any of his employees to run any unnecessary risks, and it is evident that risks are involved in testing a fast car on the road if the test is to be a real test and is to do anything more than discover and rectify a rattle.

The Testing Apparatus

So at the Pavlova works three extremely clever and interesting mechanical installations are employed to obviate these drawbacks. These are respectively the Bendix-Cowdray brake tester, the Comparator, or high-speed tester, and a machine for checking any misalignment of the front wheels and indicating, while the adjustment is being made, the exact moment when accuracy is achieved.

The brake-testing apparatus consists of four sets of two small rollers, each of which receives a wheel of the car. Once the car is on the rollers the front axle is anchored to the machine by a chain; driving each of the four sets of rollers are electric motors, and connected to each of the roller sets is a torque resistance indicator. If the brakes are applied, the amount of braking resistance on each wheel is indicated on four dials, and each individual wheel can have the brakes adjusted so that resistance shown on the dials is equal; or, if desired, a greater resistance is shown on the front than on the back dials. While all this is taking place the head lamps are focused on a screen set at the correct height and distance from them.

On the wash.

Thus time is saved and accuracy in brake setting ensured without the car leaving the shop.

The brakes having been adjusted, the car is taken to the wheel tracking machine, which consists of two strips of steel let into a hollow platform and arranged on ball bearings so that they can be moved inwardly or outwardly, the motion being parallel. This motion is transmitted to a large dial on a pedestal, and all that is necessary is for the tester to drive the car over the two strips of steel, and if the alignment is correct the plates are not moved either inwards or outwards. If the wheels are "in-toed" the plates are forced outwards and the dials record the degree of "in-toe"; and conversely if "out-toe" is present. Adjustment of the track rod can then be made with the car on the machine, the dials registering all the time the exact position of the wheels. Compared with the old-fashioned trammels, the time saved and the accuracy attained are remarkable.

The Comparator

Our M.G. now having its tracking correct and its brakes perfectly adjusted, is taken to the Comparator, a device mainly composed of two sets of large-diameter rollers upon which the rear wheels of the car rest. When the engine has been started and top gear engaged the wheels drive the rollers. These are coupled to a brake fan, the size and resistance of the fan being adjustable so that the speeds obtained on this device are comparable with the speeds obtainable on the road, the resistance of the fan representing the resistance of the air.

PUTTING IN THE PEP
(continued)

Every Midget must show a genuine speed of 60 m.p.h. on this device, and if it fails the necessary engine adjustments and carburetter timing are made until the desired figure is reached.

The "once over."

Thus, without risk to anyone and with no possibility of damage to the car, high-speed tests are carried out in the privacy of the works.

Every engine, of course, has undergone long and strenuous bench tests before it has ever reached the chassis, and it can be said without possibility of contradiction that an M.G. car is a thoroughly tested machine the instant it is in its owner's hands.

Perhaps one of the most interesting corners in the works is that railed off and screened from prying eyes and de-

---

AUTHOR'S NOTE.

Since writing the foregoing, George Eyston has run a 750 c.c. Midget for 10 miles at Montlhéry at 114·46 m.p.h. For 5 km. he averaged 114·77 m.p.h. Some Pep!

---

voted to experimental work. Here the cars destined to compete in races are got ready, new ideas are tried out, and much experimental designing work is engaged in.

Adjoining this experimental department is the drawing office, and nothing more clearly conveys the amount of work involved in the production of sports cars than the fact that over 3,000 drawings have been made relative to the putting into production of the last two models.

I have deliberately tried to convey the atmosphere of these works rather than detail the processes of construction overmuch. A sports car must be made and manufactured—the two terms are *not* synonymous if you think about it—just like any other car.

By the way, what *is* a sports car? It used to be one which was fast and/or noisy and/or uncomfortable. But the M.G. is only fast; it fails dismally in the other characteristics. It is quiet and it is comfortable. Therefore it cannot, according to some people, be a sports car. But it is; most emphatically Yes!

What is a Sports Car?

My own idea of a sports car is a car which, once tried, makes ordinary cars feel ordinary when previously they felt remarkable. Certainly the M.G. models go a long way on this errand, and I take off my hat to them. What is more, I rehearse the "Come by" signal when I see the radiator of one in my driving mirror. Yes, although my own very good car is no slug. 114 m.p.h. (see author's note) with a 750 c.c. engine! Some of our quiet, old-fashioned English towns do produce rather wonderful things sometimes.

INTO BATTLE 1932

INTER-CENTRE RALLY. L. F. Robson's M.G. Magna skidding a corner at Ledbury during the J.C.C. Inter-Centre Rally. Liverpool Centre were the winners.

The new Abbey coupé on the M.G. Magna chassis.

S W E E T   A N D   L O W

WITH the ever-increasing number of standard type cars on the road the demand for special bodies increases in like proportion. Among the several firms meeting the needs of this market are Abbey Coachworks, Ltd., of Minerva Road, Chase Estate, North Acton, and their most recent design is a coupé on an M.G. Magna chassis, which particularly lends itself to special designs in coachwork on account of its low frame, long bonnet, and attractive radiator. These features provide the coachbuilder with plenty of scope for producing something really smart and out of the ordinary in the way of either open or closed bodywork.

Ample Comfort

This two-seater all-panelled coupé is of interesting design and is certainly striking. The unusual treatment of the wings and tail is the most outstanding feature of the body, coupled with a total height of only 4ft. 1½in., notwithstanding which there is ample headroom for even a tall passenger, while the width of the body is such that ample elbow room is provided for both passenger and driver. It will be seen, therefore, that comfort and practicability have not been sacrificed for appearance. Behind the two adjustable bucket seats, the squabs of

A Smart and Roomy New Special Coupé on the M.G. Magna Chassis, with Overall Height of Only Four Feet One and a Half Inches

The figure is admittedly tall and slightly over-emphasises the extremely low overall height of the car.

which fold forward, is space for two or three large suitcases.

At first sight it might appear that the narrowness of the single panel screen, which, incidentally, opens out fully,

restricts the driver's view, but such is not the case. The view from within the car is remarkable when one thinks of the dimensions from ground to roof. Tandem electric screenwipers are fitted, and wipe nearly the whole area of the glass, which makes for increased safety and comfort of mind in wet weather. The eight-gallon rear fuel tank is provided with a special quick-action cap, and is handily placed for refueling from a pump or can.

Easy to Enter

Ease of entry and exit is assisted by the wide doors opening from their forward edges. Winding windows are provided, that at the rear being in two halves. Tools are housed in a locker beneath the bonnet, which is standard practice on the Magna, and in every other respect the chassis is unaltered. The performance of the car is too well known to need any reference. It is sufficient to say that that performance, coupled with coachwork such as is illustrated on this page, is all that can be desired in the way of distinctiveness.

The price of the complete car is £345, so it cannot be considered a cheap car. On the other hand, it is good value in view of the general excellence of the workmanship and the high grade of finish.

The style of the panelling, which is well carried out, together with the unusual treatment of the wings and tail, are seen in these two "three-quarter" views of the little car.

**Published *The Autocar*,
5 August 1932**

THE AUTOCAR ROAD TESTS

No. 739
(Post-War Series)

M.G. MIDGET TWO-SEATER

7′2″

10′4″

THERE is every reason to suppose that the new M.G. Midget will be a great success. The latest car, described in detail elsewhere in this issue, is a direct and logical development from the experience gained by the firm in competition work of all kinds, yet its appeal is not based solely on performance, tremendous though that is for the engine size and the price of the complete car. Comfort has been studied so carefully that it is a remarkably pleasant car to ride in, quite apart from what it is able to do.

It would naturally be expected from the mechanical modifications in this latest car that the performance would be improved as compared with its predecessor, the ordinary Midget. What is not so much expected is that the performance should have gone up to a genuine 80 m.p.h., the car still retaining tractability and flexibility at low speeds. After testing the machine for sheer performance on Brooklands track, and then observing on the road how it behaves in comparison with other much bigger vehicles, there is every reason for the driver to feel amazed at what has been achieved, and to be led into the impression that the engine must be bigger than it actually is.

Apart from speed, not only on top gear but on the indirect gears, the things that matter most about a sports car are the driving position and controls. The new Midget has a driving position which is exactly right, the back rest of the seat being sloped at a natural angle, while the pneumatic cushions for driver and passenger are separate.

The steering wheel comes within easy reach, is bigger than it was formerly, and, of course, is spring-spoked; the short, stiff gear lever is of the remote control type, with a visible gate; the racing type central hand-brake lever is where it should be; in front of the driver is a big, clear dial, consisting of a combined speedometer and rev. counter, the latter applying to top and third gears, and each of the controls works with a minimum pressure of hand or foot.

The charm of the car to the enthusiast, again, is in the ability, in fact the eagerness, of the engine to turn over at extremely high revs., 5,800 r.p.m. being well within its capabilities. This means that though second and first are comparatively low gear ratios, the car gets going very snappily indeed, for it can be run up to 20 m.p.h. on first, 36 on second, and easily to 60 on third, in which connection it may be mentioned that on the cars delivered second gear will be a higher ratio, which should be a considerable improvement.

A highly commendable feature is that the speedometer read slow throughout

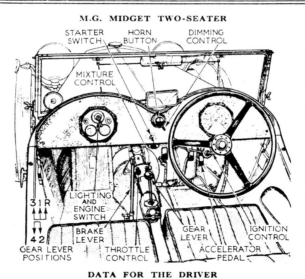

M.G. MIDGET TWO-SEATER

STARTER SWITCH — HORN BUTTON — DIMMING CONTROL

MIXTURE CONTROL

LIGHTING AND ENGINE SWITCH

BRAKE LEVER

GEAR LEVER POSITIONS — THROTTLE CONTROL

GEAR LEVER

IGNITION CONTROL

ACCELERATOR PEDAL

3 1 R

4 2

DATA FOR THE DRIVER

8 h.p., four cylinders, 57 × 83 mm. (847 c.c.).
Tax £8.
Wheelbase 7ft. 2in., track 3ft. 6in.
Overall length 10ft. 4in., width 4ft. 3½in., height 4ft. 4¾in.
Tyres: 27 × 4.00in. on detachable wire wheels.

Engine—rear axle gear ratios.	Acceleration from steady speed.			Timed speed over ¼ mile.
	10 to 30 m.p.h.	20 to 40 m.p.h.	30 to 50 m.p.h.	
19.24 to 1	—	—	—	
11.50 to 1	5¼ sec.	—	—	
7.31 to 1	9¼ sec.	9¼ sec.	10¼ sec.	
5.37 to 1	14¼ sec.	13¼ sec.	16 sec.	80.35 m.p.h.

Turning circle: 34ft.
Tank capacity 12 gallons, fuel consumption 35 m.p.g. (approx.).
12-volt lighting set cuts in at 12 m.p.h., 7 amps. at 30 m.p.h.
Weight: 11 cwt. 1 qr.
Price, with sports two-seater body, £199 10s.

27 FEET *from* 30 M.P.H.

"THE AUTOCAR" ROAD TESTS

the range, and even during the timed test did not go above 78. The maximum speed and acceleration figures were taken with the windscreen folded down flat on the scuttle.

The new Midget swings along beautifully anywhere from 30 to 60 m.p.h., as conditions permit. Yet immediately the driver wishes to increase the performance still more there is the extraordinarily valuable third gear which is not noisy, the change as a whole being delightful, allowing quick upward changes, though with the higher second gear the change from second to third—an important one—will become more rapid.

There is obviously speed in plenty—to a degree, in fact, which means that for the greater part of the time the car will be driven well within itself. What can be called the secondary appeal of the machine is very strong, too, because there is not that fierceness which, while it may be pleasing to the driver, is not, perhaps, regarded in the same way by a passenger.

The occupants sit well down in the car, the cushions and back rest are deep, the doors are wide and make getting in and out easy, and the real abilities of the car are still further disguised because a particularly effective form of silencer makes the exhaust note at ordinary speeds as quiet as that of many normal touring cars.

On the comfort side, again, the car is good at low as well as at high speeds, with the frictional shock

absorbers not too tightly adjusted. The steering is beautifully light and has a little caster action, the brakes are well up to their work, and the clutch takes up the drive smoothly. On top gear with the ignition retarded the engine will pull down to 8 m.p.h., which is an illustration of its flexibility, but is obviously not a thing which the owner of a car of this nature would wish to do.

From a standing start on first gear the Brooklands test hill, with its average gradient of 1 in 5, was climbed at 17 m.p.h., the speed being maintained steadily all the way up the 1 in 4 section. First gear is a low ratio on which there is an immense reserve of power for this kind of work.

Such points as pockets in the doors, a space for small luggage in the tail, and an easily erected hood and side screens for bad weather have not been neglected; it does not follow that an owner who wants high performance does not also require comfort and convenience in one and the same car. The hood is permanently secured, but is stowed out of sight in the tail beneath a neat cover held by quick-action fasteners; the big rear fuel tank is clearly most valuable, giving a range of something like 400 miles without need for replenishment, and there is a reserve supply of three gallons.

At the back the spare wheel is held securely, and the sensible mountings for the wings and head lamps are noteworthy.

MG Midget J2

Remarkable value for £199 10s, the J2 Midget was announced in August 1932, with its 847 c.c. engine based on the design of the successful Montlhéry Midget derivative of the original M-type. From the start, the little cars represented everything that was "right" in sports car design, embodying rear-mounted slab-tank, quick-action filler cap, centre-lock wheels, spring-spoke steering wheel, fold-flat screen, remote control gear-change—and, if you liked, radiator and headlamp grilles, and a strap over the bonnet . . . such things as Le Mans cars were made of! *The Autocar* staff achieved a mean maximum of 80 mph during the road test—from, it must be confessed, a somewhat non-standard car (though the road test staff were ignorant of the fact). In attempting to emulate this performance, one or two owners discovered the disadvantages of a two-bearing crankshaft! This model was announced in August 1932.

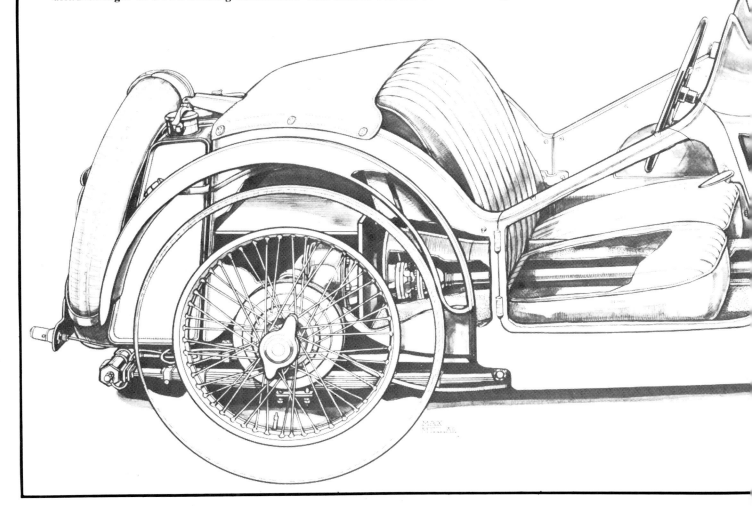

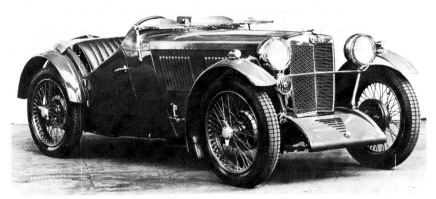

THE SUPERC

Impressions After a Day W
Drove in the Mannin B

S. C. H. Davis at
the wheel of G. E. T.
Eyston's Magnette
at Brooklands.

THE Magnette, with its 1,100 c.c. supercharged engine, is one of the most interesting cars that has been produced for some time, and is really one of the direct results that come from the Tourist Trophy type of race as opposed to the more spectacular but far more expensive product of Grand Prix racing.

Whether a supercharger is actually required for ordinary everyday use, whether, in fact, we should be better or worse if the supercharger had never been adopted for competition work, are questions it is not in the least necessary to discuss or to decide; but this at least can be said, that there is something alive, almost animal-like, wholly desirable, about the small, very fast little car with a supercharged engine, especially when it is being used for racing, and the very "feel" of the car, its tremendous pulling power, and its general fascination alone justify the existence of the type for anyone who realises that a car is something more than just a collection of machinery to carry one from place to place.

Individualism

So long, therefore, as there are enthusiasts in the land, cars of this type will be developed and their development will lift motor car manufacture a little out of the set, and rather tiring, routine which is governed almost entirely by analyses of the cost of production. Be it noted that the Magnette is not, strictly speaking, a racing car, but will give you the joy of a racing car without the latter's expense, for a racing car of the true breed is designed on the drawing board from the very commencement and in every detail for one thing, and one thing only, speed, speed un-

limited by considerations of expenditure, unhampered by the necessity of making the machine reasonably suitable for numerous purchasers. As it is, the speed that is possible with the Magnette varies with the purpose for which it is intended, but what can be done is shown by a lap speed of 115 m.p.h. recorded for one of these machines during a recent race.

The actual car which I drove had been Eyston's in the Isle of Man race, was, in fact, in the condition in which it was prepared for that race, with a low top gear of 4.89 to 1, with a starting motor, but without the battery and most of the other electrical equipment, since the starting motor was arranged to allow the battery to be in the pit and the connection to be made between it and the starting motor in the same fashion that we used to employ with old No. 1 six-cylinder Bentley in the "500."

"Not Easy to Handle" Rumours

Even without this equipment the car is not very light, a material fact when its performance has to be judged, and the performance was interesting, bearing in mind certain rumours that the car was not easy to handle and must necessarily be kept high on the banking. This proved so little true that, at its lap speed of 104.8 m.p.h., the car could be kept almost anywhere on the banking above the sixty-mile-an-hour line, and would actually cross the fork with ten or fifteen feet between it and the near side

of the blue line without pulling out of a natural course.

Actually, the maximum reading on the rev counter, which, because of

wheel slip, is optimistic, meant 114 m.p.h., the probable actual maximum being between 108 and 110 m.p.h., at which speed the engine had the perfect note of a machine going easily at its best, which, at 6,200 r.p.m., is, to say the least, interesting.

Now, it is curious how cars differ, for not ten years have passed since a car of 1,500 c.c. felt, when lapping at over 100 m.p.h., a he-man's job, and

HARGED MAGNETTE

he Car Which George Eyston
Race in the Isle of Man

by

S. C. H. DAVIS

it is a bare three since a lap at 110 with 1,100 c.c. was certainly like hard work, yet here was a car which seemed relatively as though it were lapping at 90 m.p.h. Unfortunately, a small difficulty with the revs-speed chart made it impossible to get some of the figures that I had wanted, for taking stop-watch readings from the rev counter of a racing machine is an extremely difficult job, and the faster the car the worse it becomes, with the result that the 10-30 m.p.h. acceleration times were obviously inaccurate.

This had its point of interest also, for the moment the engine really got

with the lever, one can select second while the car is ready to move off on first, and the run from gear to gear is altogether happy and beautiful.

Changing down brings in the controversy as to whether the effect of the self-change box is devastating for the transmission, and from what I tried I should say it might be if the driver took the drastic liberty of using second or first as an exceptionally violent transmission brake by engaging either gear at impossible engine revs. Anyhow, if one uses the throttle with the heel of the right foot while braking with the toe of that foot, and obeys the ordinary rev limit, the change down is not only lightning quick but quite smooth.

Advantages for Racing

I have not the slightest doubt that the gear has great advantages for racing, and the only criticism I would make is an old one, in that I want the gear lever in a gate and not in an ordinary quadrant, especially when the lever has to be used quickly and often. That the brakes stopped the car in 20ft. from 24 m.p.h. speaks for itself. I got the impression, which may be

quite wrong, that for road racing the car is a little heavy in front, and the steering slightly on the springy side, but that is an opinion given without being thoroughly accustomed to the machine, a thing which is necessary for accurate judgment.

Altogether it is a most fascinating little car, and I should think exceptionally interesting on a very twisty circuit. It is easy to drive, easier than most cars, and, because of the very smoothness of the engine, probably quite easy to over-rev.

Constant Performance

Certainly it is the sort of car which one would like in a long race most of all, and there's something to think about when you come to realise what reaching 75 m.p.h. from a standstill in under 15 sec. really means, remembering also that it is easier to repeat that performance on this car than on most, because of the gear change.

The ordinary version of the car, of course, includes lamps, wings, proper upholstery, and such-like touring requisites; obviously, also, that type has a performance which does not require frequent changes from soft to hard plugs, but such a machine should be immense fun in, say, the Land's End, and, anyhow, it is a car the joy of possessing which is great.

hold on first the rev counter needle moved at such a pace that accurate timing on first gear was impossible, but on second, to give you some idea of the car's powers, it took 12⅕ sec. to change from 26 to 66 m.p.h. on third, while the most convincing run of all was from zero to 75 m.p.h. in 14⅗ sec. That showed where the self-changing gear comes in, for, by a little trick

Part sectioned view of the supercharged Magnette as sold to the public

51

MONTE CARLO RALLY
and
Mont des Mules Hill Climb

Two firsts
Two seconds

M.G. Magnette makes second fastest time ever recorded for the Mont des Mules Hill Climb, only 10 seconds slower than the 8-litre supercharged car which holds the record.

Also—Fastest time of the day, winning the Automobile Club of Monaco Cup.

Mont des Mules
Hill Climb
results—

1st	500 - 750 c.c. class	- -	M.G. Midget (s) *Mr. W. C. Platt*
1st	750 - 1,100 c.c. class (record for class)	- -	M.G. Magnette *Mr. G. Wright*
2nd	1,100 - 1,500 c.c. class	- -	M.G. Magna *Mr. M. Lacroze*

Monte Carlo
Rally results—

2nd	Braking & Acceleration test	M.G. Magnette *Mr. G. Wright*

(Subject to official confirmation)

SAFETY FAST !

The M.G. Magnette, driven by Mr. G. W. J. H. Wright, which put up the fastest time in the Mont des Mules Hill Climb.

The badge of the M.G. Car Club.

THE M.G. CAR CO. LTD., ABINGDON-ON-THAMES, BERKSHIRE
EXPORT DEPARTMENT - - - - STRATTON HOUSE, 80, PICCADILLY, W.1

SPORTING COLOUR

Previous page: 18/80 Mark II two-seater with dickey—coachwork by Carbodies of Coventry. Only 13 Mark IIs were built with this particular bodywork, of which only four are thought to survive—this car, one in the Doune collection, and two in the United States

Left: One of the most handsome sporting cars of their time—the Speed Model 18/80 which was available on the Mark I and Mark II chassis of 1929 and 1930. This example is owned by Sid Beer

Below: Somewhat non-standard, lightweight version of the MGC, one of those built up by John Chatham from factory parts, using triple Weber carburettors in place of the standard twin S.U.s. Built closer to factory specification than Chatham's other cars, this example was run in the 1970 Targa Florio. **Right:** The standard 6-cylinder Austin engine of the production cars, with twin S.U.s.

LEFT: MONTE CARLO RALLY: Wright's supercharged K3 Magnette started from John o'Groats, completed the Rally successfully, and put up fastest time on the Mont des Mules hill-climb

BELOW: MILLE MIGLIA: One of the three works K3 Magnettes entered for Lord Howe, H. C. Hamilton, Sir Henry Birkin, George Eyston and Count "Johnny" Lurani. The Eyston/Lurani car took first place in the 1,000 c.c. Class, with an average speed of 56·89 m.p.h., followed by the Howe/Hamilton car, 1 min. 30 sec. behind after 1,000 miles

ABOVE: INTERNATIONAL TROPHY RACE, BROOKLANDS: "Bill" Wisdom's K3 Magnette, which took third place in what was referred to as "... the most gruelling event ever staged at Brooklands"

RIGHT: LIGHT CAR CLUB RELAY RACE, BROOKLANDS: Left to right, C. E. C. Martin's, G. W. J. Wright's and A. C. Hess' Magnas win the Team Prize

BELOW: MANIN BEG: Cluster of cars headed by Kaye Don's (No. 18), S. A. Crabtree's (No. 19) Magnettes, F. W. Dixon's Riley (No. 7), and Hamilton's (No. 16) and Eyston's (No. 15) Magnettes at Greenshill's Corner, Douglas, Isle of Man. Of the 14 starters, only two cars finished - Dixon's Riley and Mansell's M.G. Midget

M.G. CARS FOR 1934

Slightly Modified J.2 Midget, Continental Coupé Added to Magna Range, Magnette With Greater Engine Capacity, and Pre-selector Gear Box Combined With Plate Clutch

M.G. Midget J2. Two-seater, £199 10s.

VERY little change is being made in the M.G. series of cars for the coming season, for they have been brought to a state of development where extensive modifications are not considered necessary. Prices also are practically unaltered, save for slight variations in the Magnette. The complete range of cars and their prices are as follows:—

M.G. Midget: chassis £160, two-seater £199 10s.

M.G. Magna: chassis £245, open two-seater £285, open four-seater £299, salonette £345, Continental coupé £350.

M.G. Magnette: chassis £340, open two-seater £390, open four-seater £399, pillarless four-door saloon £445.

It will be noticed that there is a departure in the Midget range, inasmuch as the car is now offered as a two-seater only, other bodies being discontinued. The lines are similar to the previous model, but the appearance has been distinctly improved by fitting a modern type of flared wing, and also the addition of running boards makes sure that the car and its occupants are kept clean in bad weather. In order to preserve and improve the snappy and sparkling performance which these exceedingly attractive little cars possess on the road—the four-cylinder engine is capable of turning over at pretty well 6,000 r.p.m.—one or two modifications have been introduced, for example, the connecting rods now have fully floating gudgeon pins, and pistons with controlled expansion skirts included, and the compression ratio also has been slightly raised.

Midget Specification

It is interesting to review the specification of the Midget. It has a four-cylinder overhead-valve and camshaft engine, 57 × 83 mm. (847 c.c.), tax £8. Twin S.U. semi-downdraught carburetters are fitted, and the fuel from the 12-gallon rear tank is fed through an S.U. petrol pump. The engine is cooled on the thermo-syphon system, and in order to avoid waste of power a Burgess straight-through silencer is used. The gear box is a four-speed twin-top type

M.G. PRICES FOR 1934.		
M.G MIDGET.	**£**	**s.**
Chassis	160	0
Two=Seater	199	10
M.G. MAGNA.		
Chassis	245	0
Open Two=Seater	285	0
Open Four=Seater	299	0
Salonette	345	0
Continental Coupé	350	0
M.G. MAGNETTE.		
Chassis	340	0
Open Two=Seater	390	0
Open Four=Seater	399	0
Pillarless Saloon	445	0

provided with a particularly neat remote control which brings the gear lever close up to the driver's left hand. The clutch is a single plate, and the open propeller shaft has Hardy Spicer joints at both ends. Final drive is by spiral bevel, and the road wheels are of the Rudge racing type, fitted with Dunlop tyres. A feature of the car is, of course, the underslung frame, which is responsible for the low centre of gravity, and hence the road-holding qualities. The Midget has a wheelbase of 7ft. 2in. and a track of

3ft. 6in., and the semi-elliptic springs are damped by Hartford shock absorbers.

Marles-Weller steering with a transverse drag link is fitted, and the four wheel brake set is operated through a system of fully enclosed cables provided with proper means of regular lubrication. To handle a Midget on the road is always a pleasure, for the car is fascinating in every way and is not only fast, but has quite a different feel about it from most vehicles. The engine is particularly willing, and also notably smooth for a four-cylinder, and it has a very exhilarating way of going about its work, especially if proper use is made of the gear box.

If a gathering of motor enthusiasts was asked to make a choice out of the M.G. range, the majority would undoubtedly go for the Magna two-seater, for it is a car with just exactly the right balance of bonnet length to body, it sits down to the ground so compactly, and has a distinctly thoroughbred air. That the Magna is capable of doing a great deal more than look well is obvious from the success which it has scored during the recent season—for example, winning the L.C.C. Relay Race, and also the Manufacturers' Team Prize in its group in the International Alpine Trial. Elsewhere in this issue will be found an account of road impressions of one of the current "L" type Magnas.

Magna Revisions

Practically the only alteration to record for 1934 is that larger and more effective head lamps have been fitted. A new type of body, however, is now in production—the Continental coupé. This is a very striking-looking design of two-door four-seater with a large luggage trunk at the back. The interior of the body is most attractively furnished, and there are numerous special points, including elbow rests to the front seats, a sliding roof with windowlets in it, and recessed elbow room. This new body can be finished in black and yellow, in all-black, or various other colours, and is likely to become popular because it is very individual.

Magna Continental coupé.

It will be remembered that the Magna specification includes a six-cylinder engine, 57 × 71 mm. (1,087 c.c.), tax £12, with o.h.v. and camshaft, twin S.U. carburetters, external oil filter, separate dynamo and starter, an Elektron sump holding 1¼ gallons of oil, floating connecting rods, and special pistons with controlled expansion skirts, a gear-type oil pump, and pump water circulation.

Magna Details

Transmission is through the two-plate clutch and four-speed gear box, of the twin-top type, with a remote control gear lever. An open Hardy Spicer propeller-shaft with metal universal joints conveys the drive to a spiral bevel gear, contained in a three-quarter floating design of rear axle. Rudge racing-type wire wheels are fitted and are shod with Dunlop tyres 4.5 × 19in. Jaeger instruments are standardised and include a 5in. diameter speedometer and revolution counter. De luxe equipment is available on all Magna models at an inclusive cost of £11 extra. On the closed cars a No. 5 Philco radio set may also be had at an additional charge of £21, and, incidentally, the salonettes and Continental coupés have, as a part of the standard equipment, an invisible aerial, in case the owner at any time wishes to instal a radio set.

It is in the M.G. Magnette that the most notable changes are to be observed. Following the process of development to which the Magnette has been subjected in the course of racing and other experience, a new type of engine has been evolved for the normal models. The design of this follows very closely on the racing engine, with modifications to make it suitable for the needs of the sporting motorist. The new engine has the same horse-power rating and pays the same tax as the old ones, but its dimensions are 57 × 84 mm. (1,286 c.c.). It has, of course, the usual M.G. type of overhead valves and camshaft, but is fitted

M.G. Magnette K2. Two-seater, £390.

the gear box and the engine a single-plate Don-Flex clutch has been added. This clutch is so arranged that the first movement of the pedal operates the single-plate clutch, and the further movement is then applied to the busbar of the pre-selector gear striking mechanism. Between the pedal and the two systems is an ingenious balancing arm which ensures that the plate clutch shall always work first.

A Smooth Take-up

On the opposite side of the clutch pit to the pedal is a clever tripping cam which again makes certain that when the gear is in neutral position the plate clutch is held out of engagement, but is automatically released ready for use when a gear is being engaged. The object of fitting a plate clutch is to give a perfectly smooth and even take-up when starting from rest or when engaging the lower gears. Also, when the engine is running and the gear is in neutral, the gear box is entirely idle and therefore cannot make a noise. The clutch also makes sure that, should too low a gear be engaged inadvertently whilst travelling at a high speed, the plate clutch is able to slip, and this relieves the rest

of the transmission from what might be excessive stress and strain.

A short run on one of the Magnettes fitted with this device showed that a much more smooth and pleasant take-up is the result when starting from rest and gear changing. The Magnette is made in two lengths of wheelbase, the short being 7ft. 10in., and the long 9ft. The frames of both cars are underslung, and the half-elliptic springs have special slides at their rear ends in place of shackles. To ensure rigidity on the long wheelbase models, a cruciform type of cross bracing is fitted in the centre between the side members, in addition to the usual tubular cross-members. The wheel track of the Magnette models is, by the way, 4ft. For the steering a Marles-Weller gear is used, but the car has a special M.G. patented divided track rod, and this is very effective in practice.

Another minor modification to the Magnette is the provision of a felt-lined tool box in the top of the scuttle, underneath the back of the bonnet.

An Attractive Saloon

Particular interest attaches to the four-door saloon mounted on the Magnette chassis. This body is particularly attractively proportioned, and not only looks well, but allows extreme ease of entry, as it is of the pillarless construction, so that if both doors are open on one side there is nothing in the way of getting in or out. The rear panel of this body can be folded outwards to form a useful luggage carrier, whilst at the same time the spare wheel may be retained in position behind the petrol tank instead of adding to the weight of overhang, as would be the case if the spare wheel were attached to the lid.

Triplex glass is standardised all round on all M.G. models.

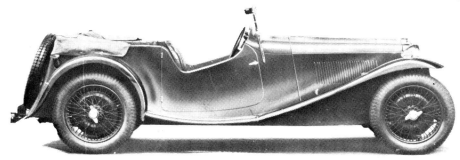

The Magnette K1. Four-seater, £399.

with 14 mm. instead of the more usual pattern 18 mm. sparking plugs.

It is equipped with triple S.U. carburetters and has a special coil and automatic distributor designed to meet the high engine speeds which are obtainable. "H" section floating connecting rods are used, the pistons are of the controlled expansion type, and the same features of Elektron sump, pump water circulation, and external oil filter are employed. The water temperature is controlled by an R.P. Thermostat.

There is a particularly interesting change in the transmission of this car. The four-speed pre-selective self-changing gear box is standardised, but between

Magnette four-door pillarless saloon.

THE M.G. MAGNA FOR 1934.

The Magna
two-seater

The Salonette. One of the close body types on the Magna chassis

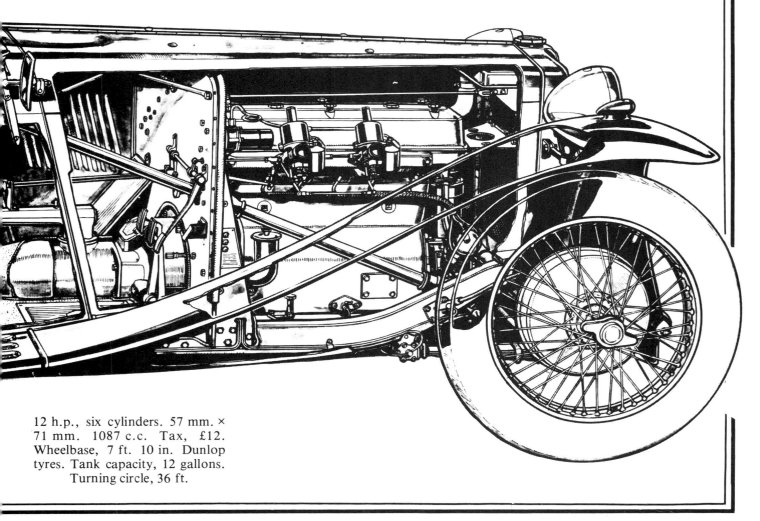

12 h.p., six cylinders. 57 mm. ×
71 mm. 1087 c.c. Tax, £12.
Wheelbase, 7 ft. 10 in. Dunlop
tyres. Tank capacity, 12 gallons.
Turning circle, 36 ft.

Road Impressions of New Models

The M.G. Magna Two-seater

IT is for ever a refreshing experience to change over from the every-day sort of saloon to a piquant and intensely alive little car like the M.G. Magna type "L." The road is no longer a mere highway from place to place, but a path of adventure, as the sea must be adventure to the man who handles a trim sailing craft. There is appeal in the very lines of the Magna, with its long bonnet promising speed, its workmanlike stern view, and long, graceful mudguards. To sense the appeal and try the car is to appreciate in full the very real qualities which are there.

Sitting well down in a deep cockpit, rendered comfortable by pneumatic upholstery, the driver starts the engine, finds a steering wheel tucking itself into his hands, notices the freedom for his arms and elbows, and, looking over the curved scuttle along the shapely snout of the car into the distance of the road, drops his left hand instinctively to the little close-up gear lever. A little light footwork, a snick of the gear lever, a flick of the accelerator, and he is away off the mark with the engine note rising.

Smoothness Outstanding

This modern six-cylinder 1,086 c.c. engine in the Magna is a fine design, and it runs with notable smoothness right throughout its range, from a comfortable toddle on top gear right up to nearly 6,000 r.p.m. when all out. Its flexibility and its freedom from vibration or mechanical noise are remarkable, when taken in conjunction with a big power output in relation to size. It responds instantly to the movements of the accelerator pedal, and, as the acceleration figures show, maintains its liveliness right up through the speed range. The car can be depended upon to reach its maximum on the level without hesitation.

There is a great fascination in driving the Magna. The steering is light and quick—at first grasp disconcertingly so—with a strong caster action, but, as soon as it is realised that the wheel is best held with a light grip, the car can be placed neatly, or taken round curves at speed, in an elegant fashion. Although the car is light and lively, the steering has no apparent vices such as incipient wheel tramp, and the radiator and head lamps do not dither about on bad surfaces. Because of the low build and special form of spring anchorages, the car holds the road excellently, and can be driven anywhere with confidence.

DATA FOR THE DRIVER

12 h.p., six cylinders, 57 × 71 mm. (1,086 c.c.) Tax £12.
Wheelbase 7ft. 10in., track 3ft. 6in.
Overall length 10ft. 10in., width 4ft. $3\frac{1}{2}$in. height 4ft. 2in. Hood up.
Tyres: 4.5 × 19 on detachable Rudge-Whitworth wire wheels.

Engine-rear axle gear ratios.	Acceleration from steady speed. 10 to 30 m.p.h.	20 to 40 m.p.h.	30 to 50 m.p.h.
19.21	—	—	—
11.49	$6\frac{4}{5}$	$6\frac{3}{5}$	—
7.31	$10\frac{2}{5}$	$10\frac{3}{5}$	$10\frac{1}{5}$
5.375	$14\frac{4}{5}$	$15\frac{2}{5}$	$17\frac{3}{5}$

Timed speed over $\frac{1}{4}$ mile, 75 m.p.h.
With screen down 77.59
Turning circle 32ft. 6in.
Tank capacity 10 gallons; fuel consumption 22-24 m.p.g.
12-volt lighting set.
Weight: 16 cwt.
Price, with two-seater body, £285.
Acceleration from rest through the gears to 50 m.p.h. 18 sec.
Acceleration from rest through the gears to 60 m.p.h. $24\frac{2}{5}$ sec.
15 yards of 1 in 5 gradient from rest $3\frac{2}{5}$ sec.

One of the features is the four-speed twin-top gear box with remote control. A long extension on the top of the box brings a short gear lever close to the hand, and the gear change is a simple and effective one to handle, whilst the indirect gears are quiet. The ratios are well chosen and the car will reach 40 m.p.h. on second gear, which is pretty useful. The clutch is sweet and light, and is well up to its work. It may be noted that the cockpit of this two-seater does not become uncomfortably hot, due no doubt to the metal facings of the dashboard and the rubber sealing around the clutch pit and the steering column, which prevents hot air from blowing through.

Another point which contributes to the general attractiveness of the car is that the large diameter brakes are smooth and progressive, and may be used to pull the car up from high speed without trepidation. Because of the smoothness, they are deceptive in that they pull the car up more quickly than they appear to do, which is always a hall-mark of good brakes. They are armoured-cable operated, but proper provision is made for regular lubrication of the cable sheathing. Except at low speeds, when the shock absorbers can be felt to be doing their work, the comfort of riding is very good, and the stability of the car at any speed of which this model is capable on the track is all that could be desired.

Special Points

There are certain points to attract special attention. The large fuel tank at the rear of the body has a gauge visible on the top, and there is a two-way control which enables some two gallons to be held in reserve. The windscreen is arranged so that it can be folded down flat forwards when needed, and incidentally there is surprisingly little wind when the screen is down, owing to the shape of the dash "humps" and the way that they deflect the wind over the heads of the occupants. It may be mentioned that the maximum speed figure given in the table was an average obtained with the screen down; with it up the maximum was 75 m.p.h.

The speedometer on the car gave a reasonably accurate reading. This instrument is, by the way, a combined speedometer and revolution indicator, for it has separate calibrations showing the engine revolutions equivalent to various road speeds on the different gears. The various controls of the car are well placed and simple to handle; mounted on the tunnel just forward of the gear lever are knobs for the jet adjustment and the slow running setting of the twin S.U. carburetters, the ignition advance is automatic, the lights are controlled from the instrument board, and thus the steering wheel is left quite free of encumbrances.

Taken all round, the open two-seater Magna is a most delectable car with the manners, as well as the air, of a thoroughbred.

The Magna L2 two-seater.

GILDING THE LILY

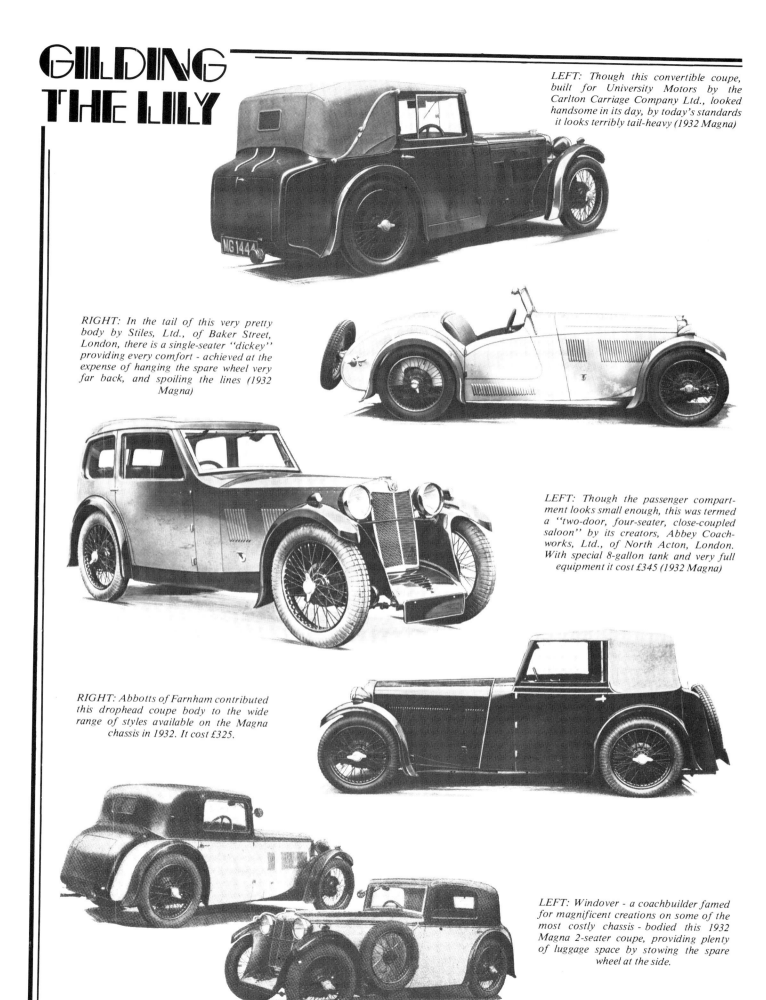

LEFT: Though this convertible coupe, built for University Motors by the Carlton Carriage Company Ltd., looked handsome in its day, by today's standards it looks terribly tail-heavy (1932 Magna)

RIGHT: In the tail of this very pretty body by Stiles, Ltd., of Baker Street, London, there is a single-seater "dickey" providing every comfort - achieved at the expense of hanging the spare wheel very far back, and spoiling the lines (1932 Magna)

LEFT: Though the passenger compartment looks small enough, this was termed a "two-door, four-seater, close-coupled saloon" by its creators, Abbey Coachworks, Ltd., of North Acton, London. With special 8-gallon tank and very full equipment it cost £345 (1932 Magna)

RIGHT: Abbotts of Farnham contributed this drophead coupe body to the wide range of styles available on the Magna chassis in 1932. It cost £325.

LEFT: Windover - a coachbuilder famed for magnificent creations on some of the most costly chassis - bodied this 1932 Magna 2-seater coupe, providing plenty of luggage space by stowing the spare wheel at the side.

NUMBER ONE

Romance of the First Born in the M.G. Magnette Family

by

BARRÉ LYNDON

Author of "Combat," "Speed Fever," etc.

NOW and again the world of motor racing produces a car destined to unusual adventure. It was for such a machine that, at two o'clock in the morning, thousands of enthusiastic Italians waited in an avenue, gazing down a smooth, black road which shone glassily under the stark light of brilliant arc lamps. The spectators were held back by ropes and planking stretched between flag-poles set at the edge of the highway, and the ceaseless, high-pitched drone of their voices maintained an atmosphere of tension and expectation.

Officials hovered beneath a banner strung high above the road, its chequered edging silhouetted against the shadowy trees. Ever and again they looked to where a slender arch straddled the avenue, so placed that it formed an entrance from the deep darkness of the countryside beyond the town.

Without warning a brilliant glare burst from the black distance, rushing towards the arch. The grouped officials broke up, and above the noise of their stirring came the blare of a trumpet sounding a long-drawn call, while the blaze of white light rushed nearer. As the trumpet-note died it was echoed by the growing roar of a racing car travelling under full throttle.

Its head lamps caught the arch, silvering the structure's sides. They revealed the animated crowd, lit the scattering officials, and caught the stretched banner as the dark shape of the machine dived through the opening and pitched down the centre of the road. A flag fell in the moment that the car roared beneath the banner, then brakes went on, and men ran from all directions towards the slowing machine.

Proud Bearer of the Union Jack

Beneath its dusty flanks showed the green of England's racing colour. The Union Jack was painted on the bonnet, and on the curve of the scuttle was the Italian flag. Behind the wheel sat Captain G. E. T Eyston, with Count Lurani huddled at his side, both cramped and stiff. In eighteen hours they had covered one thousand and twenty-four miles, and were the first to finish the course for the 1933 Mille Miglia. They had broken all records for 1,100 c.c. machines, and the car they drove was the first of all racing Magnettes.

Such was the *début* of a machine which had been built in record time, and had then journeyed to Italy during twelve stormy days, surrounded by boxes in a vessel laden

Magnette No 1 in the Mille Miglia

The standing crowds swayed, and above the noise of their stirring came the blare of a trumpet sounding a long-drawn call, while the blaze of white light rushed nearer.

with china clay. By all precedent a car erected so rapidly, and of new design, should have been subjected to the trials and errors of a dozen events before it ran first past the chequered flag. Yet in its first race it achieved victory in its class, which is unusual.

The crowds swarmed close while Eyston and Lurani were lifted out, and the Italians remained staring at the *vetture Inglese* while other cars came in. They left it only when Tazio Nuvolari raced across the finishing line, but they might have remained could they have known that the future was to link Nuvolari with this dusty green machine

When the crowd had gone the M.G. Magnette was rolled away, returning to the factory to be prepared for the International Trophy at Brooklands. It was driven in this event by Mrs. T. H. Wisdom, who had shown her skill with other machines, including the giant Leyland Thomas. The 1,087 c.c. machine now responded under her hands. It ran faultlessly, stopping only once for fuel and a wheel change, touching 106 m.p.h. down the railway straight, and slipping handily through the turns, aided by its preselector gear box; the car was unique in the fact that it was the first road-racing machine ever to be given this fitment. The slim, black-overalled woman ran the machine into third place, ending a splendid event.

Other Drivers Interested

Mechanics returned the Magnette to the works, and for a month it was used by visiting drivers who wanted to get the feel of this new type of car. It served them on the roads around the factory, and, once or twice, showed its paces on the open track, lapping happily at 110 m.p.h., until George Eyston decided to test its prowess at Shelsley Walsh.

For the first time it met trouble. On the journey down, where the road was narrow, Eyston came fast through a curve to find the way barred by a car backing out of an orchard. The Magnette slowed, but not enough; it dented the tail of the baulking machine and bent its own front axle.

The car went back for repairs, and was soon again demonstrating its capabilities, persuading many to ownership of cars that were duplicates of itself, lacking only its growing tradition. June trailed away, and Eyston entered the machine for the Mannin Beg in the Isle of Man, a race which was something different from anything that the car had yet encountered. *Continued overleaf.*

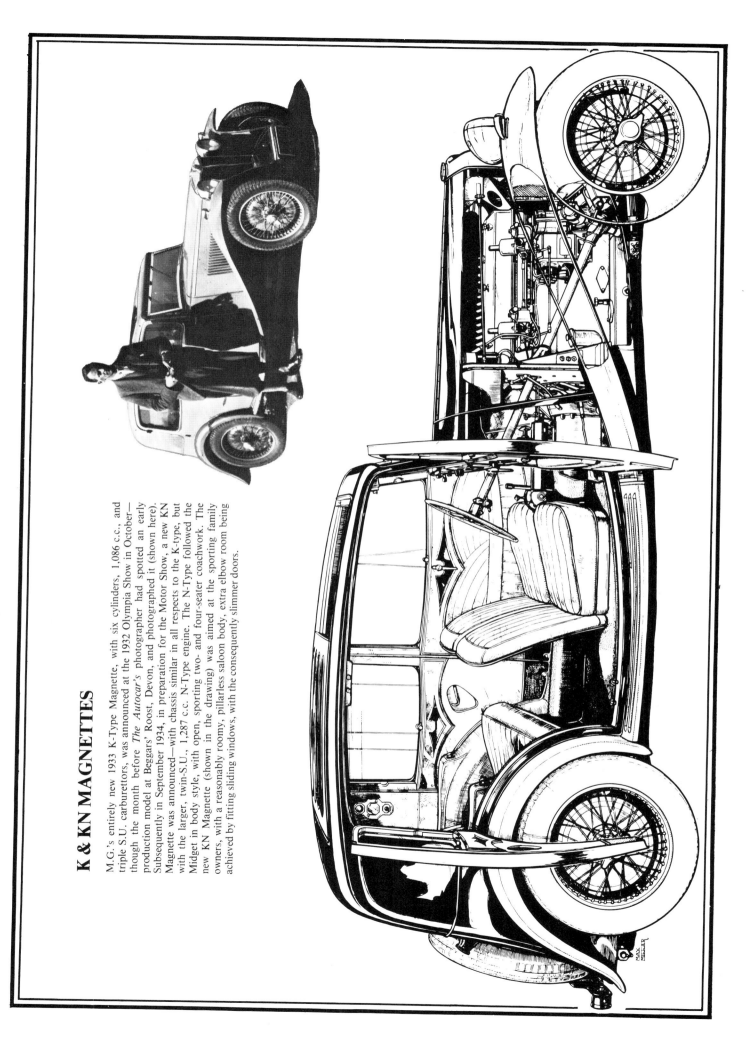

K & KN MAGNETTES

M.G.'s entirely new 1933 K-Type Magnette, with six cylinders, 1,086 c.c., and triple S.U. carburettors, was announced at the 1932 Olympia Show in October—though the month before *The Autocar's* photographer had spotted an early production model at Beggars' Roost, Devon, and photographed it (shown here). Subsequently in September 1934, in preparation for the Motor Show, a new KN Magnette was announced—with chassis similar in all respects to the K-type, but with the larger, twin-S.U., 1,287 c.c. N-Type engine. The N-Type followed the Midget in body style, with open, sporting two- and four-seater coachwork. The new KN Magnette (shown in the drawing) was aimed at the sporting family owners, with a reasonably roomy, pillarless saloon body, extra elbow room being achieved by fitting sliding windows, with the consequently slimmer doors.

INTO BATTLE

It was an event through house-hemmed streets, with sand-bags to protect spectators and shop windows, with a dozen abrupt corners and endless bends, with tramlines to offer hazards. When the flag fell Eyston let others make the pace, yet lapped only seven-tenths of a mile an hour slower than the leader. Three cars had fallen out before he began to open up; then, on his seventh lap, the engine faltered and went dead. The camshaft drive had fractured.

The car came home again, a little disgraced. It had done good work, but, it seemed, its work was ended. The gruelling of the Mille Miglia had, perhaps, taken too great a toll, and it seemed unwise again to trust its reliability in a race. Mechanics used it for running fast errands, and it was now employed for demonstration only when no newer Magnette was available.

Nuvolari as its Driver

It stood by while other machines were made ready for the Tourist Trophy race. At times it suffered the indignity of journeying to obtain parts that were needed for these cars, of which it was the forerunner. Then, in the midst of the preparations, news came that Nuvolari wanted a wheel for the T.T., and Eyston suggested offering him a Magnette. There was no machine available except the now worn-looking Number One, but there was fine history behind the car and it might respond in the hands of so fine a driver.

Work on the machine—which had descended to a factory hack—was begun at a time when the rest entered for the Belfast race were almost ready. It had less preparation than any, but it looked in fine trim when it came to the line, bearing No. 17, and rightful leader of the four Magnettes which had been entered. Nuvolari had not handled the car before he began practice, and he had never raced with a machine carrying a preselector gear box, but his practice laps were very fast, and he said that he liked the car long before he came to the starting line.

From the fall of the flag Nuvolari began tucking other machines behind his tail, and at the end of half an hour broke his class record with 77.6 m.p.h. After that he put his foot down, and, touching 115 mp.h. along the straight to Comber, lowered his own record on three successive laps, climbing up to third place. He followed Freddy Dixon's Riley, until Dixon lost time through his exhaust pipe coming loose, on which the Magnette again smashed the record on three consecutive laps, snatching the lead which H. C. Hamilton's M.G. Midget had held from the start.

Still the car's speed mounted. Man and machine formed a perfect combination, and Nuvolari broke the lap record yet again when he came round at 81 m.p.h. Two laps later he put up his fastest time, clocking 10 min. 4 sec.—a lap at 81.42 m.p.h. Then, as if to prove that this was no chance performance, the machine duplicated the effort next time round, and, at the end of the following lap, Nuvolari came home victor of the fastest Tourist Trophy race ever run.

The car had broken its class lap record eleven times, and had shown its mettle by finishing the long race at its highest speed.

Italy, Brooklands, Ulster

It had led the rest home in Italy's greatest event, it had taken third place in the International Trophy, and now it had won the finest race the British Isles had ever seen, handled by a man whom many believe to be the world's greatest driver.

THE 1933 TOURIST TROPHY

Driven by no less than the legendary Tazio Nuvolari, with Alec Hounslow of M.G.s as his riding mechanic, a supercharged Magnette won the 1933 Tourist Trophy, 12th in the series, - with H.C. Hamilton's supercharged 750 c.c. Midget in second place, only 40 seconds behind, the issue being in doubt right up to the last minute. But for a delay during one of his pit stops, Hamilton should have won. The race was run on handicap, a supercharged 750 c.c. car being credited with three 13⅜-mile laps before the start, and an unblown 1,100 with two.

AL Hounslow

A MAGIC MAGNETTE, JANUARY 1934: George Eyston's single-seater 1,100 c.c. Magnette under construction - a larger version of the famous Magic Midget, since the car was said to be too small for Eyston's increasing size! The new car had two bodies - one, the single-seater, very similar to the Magic Midget, for track work and records, and the other a road-racing body. This car proved the basis of a remarkable series of record-breakers, driven by Eyston and then by Col. Goldie Gardner.

MILLE MIGLIA, APRIL 1934: The team of supercharged K3 Magnettes entered for the 1,000-mile race, under the leadership of Lord Howe, who had his mechanic Thomas as co-driver; the second works car was driven by Lurani and Penn Hughes; the third, a private entry, was driven by Mr and Mrs E. R. Hall. Lord Howe crashed, the Halls retired, and Lurani and Penn Hughes took second place in the 1,100 c.c. class.

A NEW M.G. MAG

Very Interesting New Design to Take the Place
Four-seater

Following the introduction just recently of the new "P" type M.G. Midget, the progressive spirit of the M.G. Car Company is now responsible for the production of another new model, a six-cylinder Magnette, which is to fill the gap left by an exhaustion of the supply of the Magna two- and four-seaters. This latest new car, which is to be known as the Magnette N type, is every bit as interesting in design as the P-type Midget, and shows several features of new development.

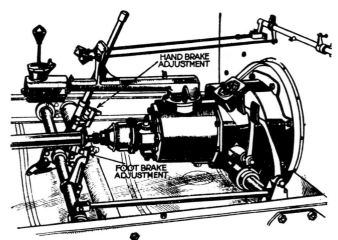

(Below) The rear end of the chassis, showing the special body supports.

FLEXIBLE SUPPORTS FOR BODY

HAND BRAKE ADJUSTMENT

FOOT BRAKE ADJUSTMENT

Details of the gear box and propeller-shaft drive. Both butterfly adjustments for the brakes protrude through the floorboards for accessibility.

Designed and constructed in the light of experience gained by continuous racing and competition work, the six-cylinder engine embodies the latest M.G. practice and has the same inclined overhead valves operated by a single camshaft and light rocker fingers as are incorporated in the new Midget, together with the special feature of ports on opposite sides of the detachable cylinder head, and of a special shape to give a free gas flow. The six cylinders are of 57 × 83 mm. bore and stroke (1,271 c.c.), tax £12.

Extra-rigid construction is a particular feature of the design, for the engine is intended to be able to stand up to heavy duty, and the crankshaft is carried in four bearings. The normal maximum to which this engine may be run is 5,500 r.p.m. on third equivalent to about 63 m.p.h. The engine can be revved as high as 6,000,

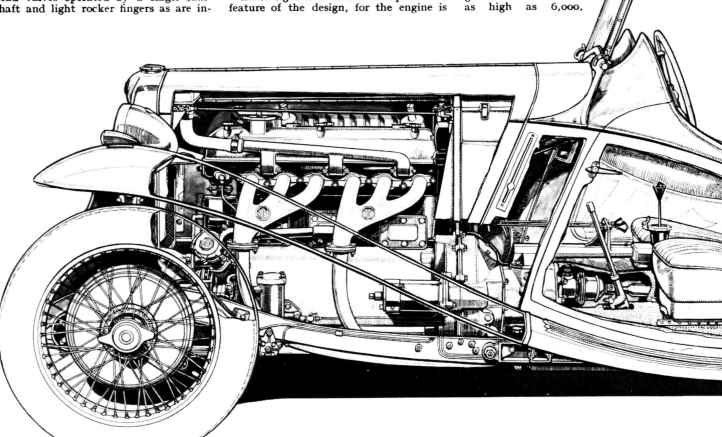

The Magnette four-seater shown in part-section.

NETTE

of the Open Two- and Magna Types

but if a regular practice is made of this the life will naturally be lessened.

It is interesting that this latest six-cylinder engine, which conforms to the same general design as the four-cylinder Midget, develops round about 47 per cent. more power than that of the Midget; that is to say, the two extra cylinders are adding nearly one-third more power, and this is distinctly an achievement in small six-cylinder engine design.

The result is secured by attention to many minor points, including valve design and combustion chamber shape, but also by the use of a special form of inlet manifold with twin carburetters. This has an S.U. carburetter, applied not in the middle of each half, but towards the outer end of each, whilst between the two portions is a very special form of balancing port which has been the subject of a considerable amount of research work.

Amongst other minor improvements in the engine design may be mentioned a large oil filler on the top of the valve cover, a breather at the side of the crank case, twin three-branch exhaust manifolds, a large elektron sump containing 1¼ gallons of oil, and ribbed underneath for cooling purposes, an improved type of dynamo in the vertical drive to the overhead camshaft, with a neat enclosed junction box for the wires, and a

The rear seat of the four-seater has been designed especially for room and comfort.

Tecalemit oil filter. Driven from the timing case at the front of the engine by skew gears is a centrifugal pump which attends to the water circulation.

The silencing of the engine is obtained by a Burgess silencer of exceptional length. At the back of the car is a ten-gallon fuel tank which holds two gallons in reserve by means of a special cock and two-level pipes controlled by a handle on the dash in front of the driver. Fuel from this tank is fed by an electric pump through Petroflex tubing to the two carburetters.

In unit with the engine are a four-speed twin top gear box and a new-type single-plate clutch with a laminated centre plate, fabric-faced finger ring, and a new type of grease-retaining thrust race. Mounted on the top of the gear box is the characteristically neat remote gear control with its short lever brought well back within reach of the driver's left hand. This control is of an improved type with a reverse stop on the gate, and a solid bracket formed integrally with the tunnel carries the mixture and slow running controls for the carburetter. The overall gear ratios are: first, 21.94; second, 11.9; third, 6.98; and top, 5.125 to 1. At an engine speed of 1,000 r.p.m. the speed of the car in m.p.h. on each gear is: first, 3.74; second, 6.75; third, 11.5; and top, 15.65.

To carry the engine unit in the frame a special type of mounting is employed which is slightly flexible, but not definitely free. At the front end of the engine a rubber sleeve in a metal housing surrounds the extension of the forward end of the crankshaft centre, whilst passing through the base of the bell housing of the flywheel and clutch, towards the back of the unit, is a stout tubular cross-member which supports the unit through the agency of a rubber bush on each side. The engine unit and the frame, therefore, assist one another as regards general rigidity.

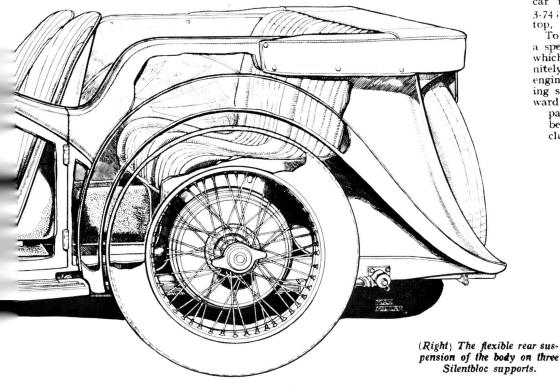

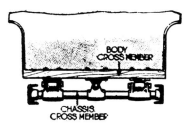

(Right) The flexible rear suspension of the body on three Silentbloc supports.

A New M.G. Magnette

This design is further interesting because of the M.G. method of front end assembly, for the radiator is carried as part of the engine unit assembly, and the radiator, front wings, and the head lamps are braced by tie-bars, so that the front end of the frame itself is relieved of the pendulum or inertia effects which the weight of these accessories would otherwise add. In practice, the front end of these new M.G.s remains perfectly steady even whilst travelling at high speed over bad roads.

Final drive is by means of a balanced open propeller-shaft with Hardy Spicer

Flowing lines are a pronounced feature of the new four-seater.

The tool case is in the scuttle under the bonnet. Note the position of the traffic signal.

joints, coupled to a spiral bevel drive with a four-star differential in the centre, all contained within a three-quarter floating type banjo rear axle. There are special oil seals to prevent oil from finding its way on to the brake surfaces, and also there is a dipstick in the rear axle centre to show the oil level.

The frame of the N type Magnette is a new one, and is notable for stiff side-members underslung at the rear, and eight tubular cross-members, including one right across the front end of the dumb-irons. One very neat portion of the design is to be found in the brackets which secure the front end of the rear springs to the frame, and which support a very strong tubular member, whilst a continuation of these brackets also carries one end of the special flexibly mounted body frame, which will be referred to later. The tail end of the frame is prolonged some way backwards, in order to give a really stiff support for the back end of the body, especially in the case of the four-seaters.

Wider and longer half-elliptic springs are used throughout and follow the special M.G. practice of having their

sliding ends arranged in roller trunnions in place of shackles, whereby side play due to wear is reduced to a minimum. The forward ends of the front springs have metal bushes, provided with lubricators, whilst the forward ends of the rear springs have Silentbloc bushes. The front springs are checked in their action by large Duplex Hartford shock absorbers, whilst the back springs are regulated by Luvax hydraulic shock absorbers of a special type, in which there

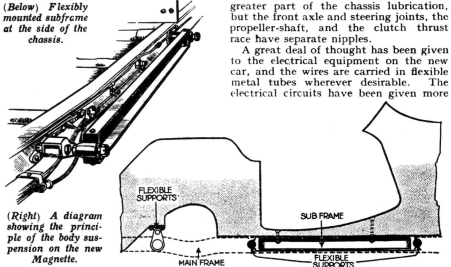

(Below) Flexibly mounted subframe at the side of the chassis.

(Right) A diagram showing the principle of the body suspension on the new Magnette.

is not only a thermostat control, but also a spring-loaded ball valve control which enables the shock absorber to deal equally well with slow movements as with quick ones. An entirely new Bishop type cam steering gear is employed.

Another interesting feature of the chassis design is that a long undershield protects the underneath part of the car from damage, and at the same time com-

pletely insulates the floorboards and continues the effectiveness of the seal which is made between the dash structure and the engine unit by means of a circular rubber ring round the bell housing. In this way special precautions are taken to keep heat and fumes out of the driving compartment.

Another point is that the batteries are divided into two, and are mounted on each side of the propeller-shaft, close to the rear axle. The system of grouped oil nipples on each side of the forward face of the dashboard attends to the greater part of the chassis lubrication, but the front axle and steering joints, the propeller-shaft, and the clutch thrust race have separate nipples.

A great deal of thought has been given to the electrical equipment on the new car, and the wires are carried in flexible metal tubes wherever desirable. The electrical circuits have been given more

fuses than before, there being a separate fuse for each head lamp, a fuse for the side and tail lamps, a fuse for the horn, and a fuse for the auxiliaries, such as the instrument board lamp, and the plug-in socket. These are in addition to the dynamo field fuse.

Other points in the electrical equipment are a twin electric screenwiper, concealed traffic indicators which are mounted in the scuttle sides, and a stop light. Incidentally, the fog light is a standard fitting, and is carried on a special bar, in front of the radiator, which also carries a horn, and provides a proper anchorage for badges. The windscreen is of Triplex Toughened glass.

The wheelbase of the N type Magnette is 8ft., and the track 3ft. 9in., which figures are slightly increased compared with the Magna, with the intention of giving more body space. Rudge-Whitworth racing-type wheels are fitted, and their 18in. rims carry 4.75in. tyres. The brakes are operated by means of cables enclosed in armoured casings.

The very smart and business-like Magnette two-seater.

TOURIST TROPHY, BELFAST 1934: C. J. P. Dodson driving George Eyston's 1,287 c.c. unblown M.G. Magnette, wins (at 74·65 m.p.h.) the 465-mile race on handicap from E. R. Hall's 3,669 c.c. Bentley after a long and close-fought struggle. The two cars were still so close at the finish that the officials had both Dodson's and Hall's number-boards ready, with the chequered flag. The previous year's Tourist Trophy had been won by a supercharged K3 Magnette, driven by Tazio Nuvolari, with Alec Hounslow as riding mechanic, at 78·65 m.p.h.

Into battle...

Above: 1931: The first 750 c.c. car to achieve 100 mph—the supercharged Midget of George Eyston at Montlhéry which Eyston (in car) and E. A. D. Eldridge (behind car) prepared specially

Below: 1931: MGs dominated the 1931 J.C.C. Brooklands Double-Twelve on handicap, frustrating drivers of the big cars. Tim Birkin, of Bentley fame, talked of a "scurrying kindergarten" of midgets

Below: 1932: Eyston in the specially-bodied, blown 750 Midget at Pendine Sands in February set new records, including a mean of 118.38 mph over the measured mile

Right: 1934: MGs made a great name for themselves in trials in the 'thirties. Here, over typical going, is R. A. Macdermid's PA ascending Hatherland in the Brighton-Beer trial

Above: 1933 supercharged 1,100 c.c. K3 Magnette — found on a scrapyard by Tom David, one of M.G. Specialist Maurice Toulmin's employees, and sold to Michael Elman-Browne, who rebuilt the car, finally selling it to Philip Bayne-Powell, who completed the rebuild to Mille Miglia specification. **Right:** The engine of another example of the K3, owned by Sid Beer and part of a fine collection

SPORTING COLOUR

Below: N-Type Magnette for 1936, first announced in August 1935, the principal external difference from the 1935 cars being that the doors were hinged on their forward edges, the hinges forming part of the styling, and the scuttle line was lowered slightly

Following page: Gordon Crosby captures all the atmosphere of Brooklands between the wars in this painting of the Leslie Callingham/Harold Parker 18/100 Mark III "Tigress", high on the banking in the Double-Twelve Hour Race of 1930

A NEW M.G. MIDGET

FEW cars have ever attained the achievements and the popularity amongst sporting motorists which stand to the credit of the M.G. Midget. This success proves that there is as much demand for a superfine quality in small cars as exists in the case of larger vehicles, wherein only the best is good enough for the critical owner. Therefore it is quite a special event when a new type is announced, the more so since the improvements incorporated in the latest design are obviously inspired by the experience gained in constant racing, and in the breaking of speed records for cars of the size. Christened the P type, the new model supersedes the well-known J, to which it bears only a resemblance in general layout, for the detail work of the components is altogether different.

Rated at 8 h.p., the four-cylinder engine is a new one, though the dimensions are retained at 57 × 83 mm. (847 c.c.). It is a monobloc design with over-

Redesigned Engine With Three - bearing Crankshaft, Many Important Improvements, and a Slightly Increased Price

head valves and an overhead camshaft carried in a detachable cylinder head. The cylinder block is noticeably massive so as to give a maximum degree of rigidity to the whole structure and render the engine capable of standing up to very high speeds of revolution.

Perhaps it is more correct to say that the rigidity is the feature which primarily permits high revolutions to be attained, since it is the enemy of small vibrations, which otherwise may " get into step " and cause all kinds of limitations on performance. Likewise, there is a great art in the disposing of the thickness of metal so as to avoid localised high temperatures and consequent distortion, for one of the limitations of ultra-high power output from a small engine is the difficulty of disposing evenly of heat.

Crankshaft and Lubrication

In this rigid cylinder block the large diameter balanced but not counter-weighted crankshaft is supported in three plain journal bearings. As the crankshaft is assembled into the block from the rear end, the centre bearing takes the form of a large, split cylindrical cage. Naturally, lubrication is a very important part of the design, and is provided by a large gear-type pump driven from the front end of the distribution system. This pump draws oil from a large rectangular sump at the base of the crank case, through a long, cylindrical filter. It delivers its supply at a fairly high pressure through a special Tecalemit filter to the main bearings, big ends, camshaft drive, and rocker gear. The whole supply of oil is obliged constantly to pass through the Tecalemit filter, and as a result it is stated that there is a considerable saving in cylinder wall and crankshaft wear. Incidentally, the oil filler

cap is a very special affair mounted in the top of the valve cover, and provided with a filter.

The connecting-rods are special steel stampings of generous section, in which the metal is disposed to the very best advantage to give support to the big-end bearings, the caps of which are stiffened with ribs. Pistons of aluminium alloy are used; they are the Aerolite type, with expansion joint skirts and three rings, of which the lower unit is a scraper.

It is perhaps in the cylinder head design that the greatest interest lies. The overhead valves are situated in combustion chambers of an oval formation, the major axis of each oval lying at an angle to the centre line of the cylinder block. The valves are not vertical, but are slightly inclined inwards, not outwards as is more usual. The valve ports are in opposite sides of the head, the exhausts on the right, the inlets on the left, and the passages are not horizontal, but incline upwards at a considerable angle, as they run from the valve heads to the manifold flanges. This inclination is

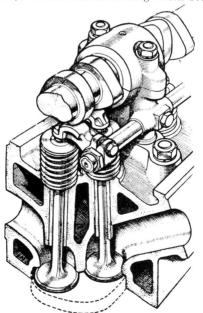

How the valves are inclined in the head. Note the large camshaft and rocker shaft support.

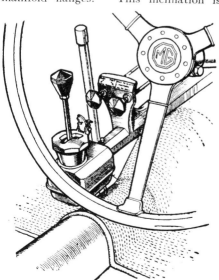

New mounting of the controls on a solid bracket on the gear-change tunnel.

(Left) Spare wheel carrier on the extended frame.

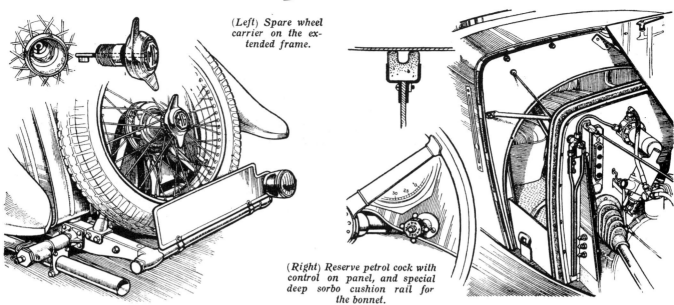

(Right) Reserve petrol cock with control on panel, and special deep sorbo cushion rail for the bonnet.

greater with the inlets than the exhausts. The valves themselves are carried in extra long guides, and are closed by compound coil springs. The inlet ports are left particularly clear of obstructions, to give a clean gas flow.

As on the earlier types of Midget engines, the overhead camshaft is driven by spiral bevel gearing and a vertical shaft at the front, which shaft is the armature spindle of the dynamo. There is a very particular reason for using this design on a high-speed, high-efficiency engine. The dynamo armature acts as a kind of flywheel, or damper of oscillations, and it smooths out the drive to the camshaft via the bevel gears in a very effective manner, whereby the valve springs and the cam contours are permitted to do their proper work without the likelihood of interference being caused by harmonic vibrations set up in the camshaft drive.

The camshaft of this engine is unusually large and stiff, also the hollow oil-fed shafts which form the rocker

fulcrums are very stiffly supported by several brackets. The engine is fed with mixture by twin S.U. semi-downdraught carburetters through a balanced inlet manifold which has an adjustment for the balance passage. On the opposite side the exhaust manifold is notable. It has a separate branch from each cylinder, and these branches merge at some distance from the head. This is a further result of racing practice, and is a method of disposing of what would otherwise be localised intense heat.

It may be evident from the foregoing description that the P type is a design possessing the essentials of a racing engine, and thus should be well suited to super tuning or to easy modification for running in conjunction with a supercharger. As fitted to the normal new Midget, this engine has passed off test developing 44 b.h.p. at 5,500 r.p.m. To cope with the extra power that is developed by the new engine, the trans-

mission, which follows the main lines of that of the J 2, has been considerably strengthened, an entirely new heavy-duty single-plate dry clutch adopted, the rear axle strengthened and provided with a four-star instead of a two-star differential gear in the centre of the spiral bevel final drive. To meet the requirements of owners who specialise in "the sport," the four-speed twin top gear box has been fitted with a specially low bottom gear. The ratios now are: Top, 5.375; third, 7.31; second, 12.46; and first, 22.5 to 1. Another but minor improvement is a bracket which forms a part of the casting of the remote gear control tunnel to carry the controls for jet setting and slow running.

As compared with the earlier model, the P type has a frame of deeper section and improved rigidity. This frame, which is slung below the rear axle, is extended an extra distance to give additional support to the tail of the body in the case of the four-seater model, or in the case of the two-seater to carry two spare wheels if needed, and also a very strong tubular steel luggage grid. The spare wheel carrier is a stout tubular construction, and it has a cunningly contrived central M.G. medallion which always remains upright in any position of the wheel-locking ring screw.

A very valuable feature of the new car is to be found in the size of the brake drums, which are now of 12in. diameter instead of 8in., and which are well ribbed. The brakes are operated by enclosed cables, and the master adjustment for the pedal operation is accessible through a small trap-door in the floor-

The P type four-seater showing, on the left, the amount of room in the body.

boards in front of the driver's seat. The hand lever has its adjustment at the bottom. Extra large Hartford shock absorbers are fitted to the front axle, and hydraulic, thermostatically controlled shock absorbers at the rear.

As in the design of the larger M.G., the Magna, a very interesting construction is to be found in the front end of the chassis. The engine unit is flexibly mounted—not floating—and the radiator is carried as part of the unit. The front wings are braced to the radiator structure by tie-bars, which carry the head lamps, and thus the front end of the frame is more free than is usual. Its natural frequency of vibration is high, and therefore the frame is free from the phenomenon usually called "front end dither." Another point is that shackles are not used at the ends of the road springs, but special roller slides take their place, eliminating side play due to wear.

On the new car the long bonnet is so arranged that when it is open entry is also given to the front part of the driving compartment, which is a good point for general accessibility. To prevent the long bonnet from sagging or squeaking the dash structure has a metal rim around its edge in which is situated a massive section of special sponge rubber, providing a supporting cushion.

Big Fuel Tanks

Several points must be mentioned about the fuel system. In the case of the two-seater a 12-gallon rear tank is fitted, and on the four-seater a 10-gallon tank. Petroflex piping is used to prevent vibration from causing any trouble. On the dash is a two-way tap which operates through twin piping and high- and low-level standpipes in the tank. This tap has a remote control mounted on the instrument board in front of the driver. The fuel pump is the S.U. electric device.

The instrument board, with its two humps, is finished with a special wood, sequea, with a grain like bird's-eye maple. It carries a large combined speedometer and revolution indicator, besides the usual instruments. Close to the driver's left hand are two plunger stops which operate Trafficators concealed in the sides of the scuttle. Where the engine unit passes through the dash there is a rubber-sealed bulkhead which prevents heat and smell getting into the car. On the new model there is also a carpet, arranged with an air space over the gear box, to neaten matters, and to keep unwanted heat away from the feet.

Three styles of coachwork are available, a two-seater at £220, a four-seater

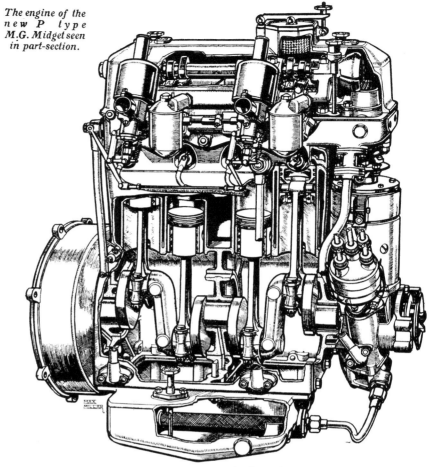

The engine of the new P type M.G. Midget seen in part-section.

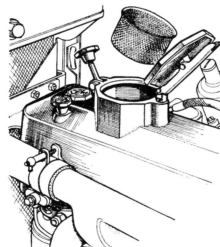

(Above) Special oil filler cap on the top of the valve cover.

(Left) An impression of the new Airline coupé model.

priced at £240, both of which are open cars, provided with hoods and detachable side panels for use in bad weather. Both bodies are new, with improved lines, better wings, and a modernised appearance. The two-seater has an improved method for adjusting the reach of the single-piece front seat. On the four-seater foot wells give extra leg room, and the tail portion has flowing lines which allow a long body with room in it to be used without appearing to have much overhang.

Then the third style is a closed two-seater, Airline coupé, a streamline design with a great deal of room for luggage. The price is £290. There will be the usual M.G. range of colour schemes. The Airline body has been designed from a performance angle, and is expected to be faster than the open models. It is light, has extra wide doors for ease of entry, and the windows are carried in steel slides. There are lights in the roof.

Pending facilities for a complete performance test of the new P type Midget, that is to say, the reopening of the Brooklands track, and the availability of a production model well run in, an opportunity was taken for a short spell on the road with one of the first cars off the line. There is no question but that the new type represents a big advance, and the various detail improvements total up in a very effective way.

Two features are outstanding: the new three-bearing four-cylinder engine is phenomenally smooth and sweet running —it might easily be mistaken for a six;

the second point is the suspension. The combination of frictional shock absorbers at the front with special preloaded hydraulic ones at the rear has given a remarkable suspension, and the car rides with the aplomb of one of much larger size. It is absolutely steady at its highest speeds, and takes minimum notice of bad surfaces. The radiator, lamps, and wings ride as much "in one piece" as the bow of a boat. These two factors, engine smoothness and steady riding, give the Midget almost a new character; it no longer feels like a small car.

Then the engine has a great capacity for "revving," it runs up to its 5,000 r.p.m. in no time, and on the lower gears has to be watched lest its eagerness to get away should persuade the driver to let it run up to the 6,000 or more r.p.m. of which it is capable, but which is really rather over-revving. There is no valve bounce to give audible warning.

The car is most fascinating to handle, the steering is light and quick, and the brakes are decidedly powerful and progressive, and by reason of the large drums and efficient layout they can be used at the higher speeds without introducing a tendency to wander. The neat remote gear change is excellent to handle, and the clutch quick and light, the pedal having only a short travel. One rather curious point is that the driving position seems to suit a tall man as comfortably as a short one. The engine has a very pleasant exhaust, and at about 3,000 r.p.m. emits almost an organ note, which quietens down to a hum as the revolutions rise further.

Warm to Ride in

Although the open two-seater was tried on a cold day, the cockpit is not cold, even to the feet, whilst the careful sealing of the dash around the clutch pit, and the carpet round the gear box prevent fumes and heat from being a nuisance. In front of the driver is a special instrument with a large dial which shows engine r.p.m., but a second smaller calibration indicates speeds in m.p.h. on top gear. Close to the driver's left hand is a group on the instrument board of horn button, head-lamp dipper, and a pair of push buttons for the Trafficators concealed in the scuttle sides. In this group is also a rectangular dial showing mileage.

When the new Midget comes into the hands of sporting private owners it is likely to achieve an even greater success than the models which have preceded it, for it has a character quite its own, and is notably a blend of performance, sweetness, and, withal, comfort.

The leading dimensions of the car are wheelbase 7ft. 3½in., track 3ft. 6in., overall length 11ft. 3in., width 4ft. 3in., height, with hood up, 4ft. 4in., and ground clearance 6in. The tyres are of 19 by 4.0in. on Rudge-Whitworth wheels; the weight of the two-seater is 14 cwt

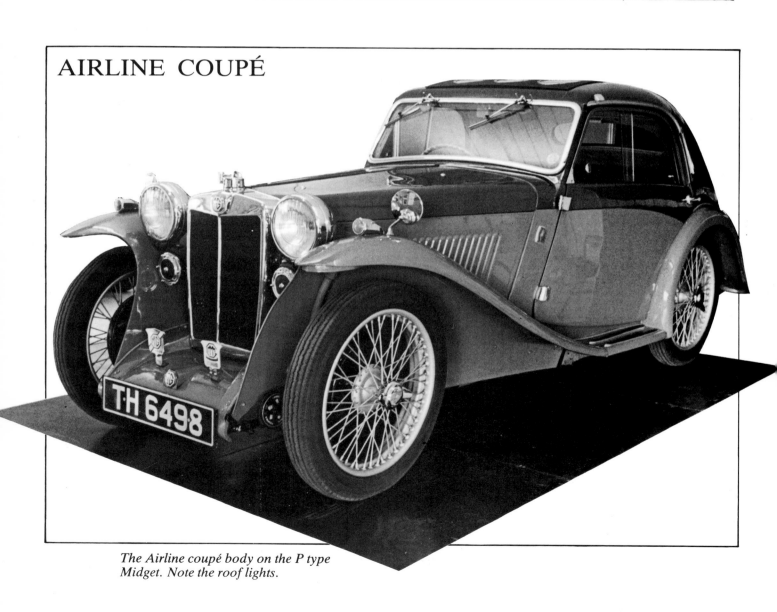

AIRLINE COUPÉ

The Airline coupé body on the P type Midget. Note the roof lights.

M.G. MAGNETTE TWO-SEATER

No. 886 (*Post-War Series*)

Latest N Model a Delightful Car to Handle

WHEN one has had a car in one's care for several days, driving it under the assortment of conditions represented by town traffic, pottering on by-ways, with an occasional steep hill or two, and leavened by sections of good, fast, main-road running, and then, finally, when one has taken the same car to Brooklands and tested it for maximum performance, there is a good basis for fair judgment to be passed. The opportunity is all the better when, as in the case of the M.G., it has been possible in the course of time to follow the successive stages of development through the various models, with plenty of practical experience of their behaviour.

So it is with the latest N Magnette that one comes to it knowing the characteristics of the marque, but naturally expecting to find the most recent model an improvement. Even so, one is not prepared for the very great advance which the N model shows as against earlier types of M.G.s of approximately the same size.

It is not just that the car is fast—its true potentialities in this direction are not easily appreciated until it comes to be taken to the track; it is that it *feels* so very much better. Speed is one thing, and a matter of importance, perhaps sometimes overrated, to some people; but vastly more important is the manner of a car's behaviour. For, as a rule, it is likely to be driven even by an enthusiastic owner at speeds nearer 50 m.p.h. than its maximum, and the greater part of the joy of owning a real sports car lies in the more normal handling of it.

Acceleration, certainly, is essential to this kind of car, to give which, with a not big engine, revs are the vital essence, and those revs must be maintainable without any suggestion that something is going to break. This engine seems veritably to delight in revs, yet it remains delightfully smooth and quiet, and feels so remarkably happy that the driver quickly gets into the habit of revving "for fun," thereby obtaining a vivid performance.

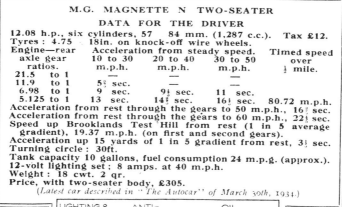

M.G. MAGNETTE N TWO-SEATER

DATA FOR THE DRIVER

12.08 h.p., six cylinders, 57 84 mm. (1,287 c.c.). Tax £12.
Tyres: 4.75 18in. on knock-off wire wheels.

Engine—rear axle gear ratios.	Acceleration from steady speed. 10 to 30 m.p.h.	20 to 40 m.p.h.	30 to 50 m.p.h.	Timed speed over ½ mile.
21.5 to 1	—	—	—	
11.9 to 1	5 3/5 sec.	—	—	
6.98 to 1	9 sec.	9 1/5 sec.	11 sec.	
5.125 to 1	13 sec.	14 3/5 sec.	16 1/5 sec.	80.72 m.p.h.

Acceleration from rest through the gears to 50 m.p.h., 16 3/5 sec.
Acceleration from rest through the gears to 60 m.p.h., 22 1/5 sec.
Speed up Brooklands Test Hill from rest (1 in 5 average gradient), 19.37 m.p.h. (on first and second gears).
Acceleration up 15 yards of 1 in 5 gradient from rest, 3 1/5 sec.
Turning circle: 30ft.
Tank capacity 10 gallons, fuel consumption 24 m.p.g. (approx.).
12-volt lighting set; 8 amps. at 40 m.p.h.
Weight: 18 cwt. 2 qr.
Price, with two-seater body, £305.

(*Latest car described in "The Autocar" of March 30th, 1934.*)

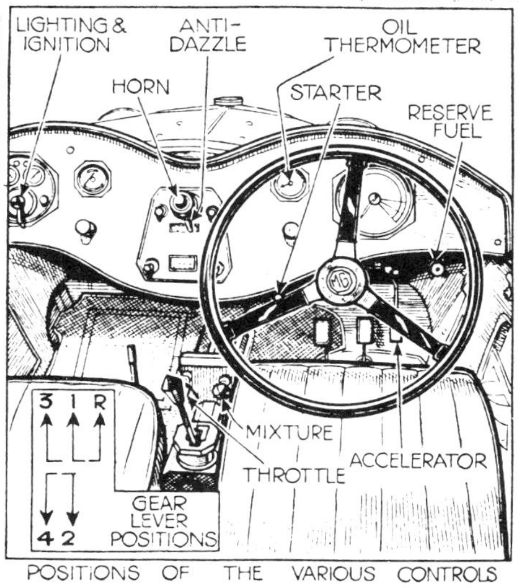
LIGHTING & IGNITION
ANTI-DAZZLE
OIL THERMOMETER
HORN
STARTER
RESERVE FUEL
MIXTURE
THROTTLE
ACCELERATOR
3 1 R
4 2
GEAR LEVER POSITIONS

POSITIONS OF THE VARIOUS CONTROLS

30 FEET
from 30 M.P.H

It must not be supposed from what has been said that it is a sixty- rather than an eighty-mile-an-hour car; the distinction lies principally in the road and opportunity available. It is not surprising that with the makers' knowledge of racing, and with the 1,287 c.c. engine that the N Magnette has, it should be capable of giving as high a speed as 80 m.p.h. What comes as a revelation is the ease with which on Brooklands that speed is reached and held, the rev needle hovering between the 5,000 and the 5,500 marks, the whole mechanism feeling as one, and with no sense of adventure attached to such speeds.

It is a sports car, yet it is not harsh in its riding, wherein the use of hydraulic shock absorbers for the back axle no doubt has some considerable effect, the frictional type being retained in front. It is not noisy, either mechanically or in the exhaust; with the same setting of shock-absorbers, the same tyre pressures, and without change of any kind being made anywhere, it is a car perfectly suitable for ordinary running about, for conveying, for instance, an elderly passenger around the country, yet immediately afterwards, and without factory experts being in attendance, the car can be put over the half-mile and record close on 82 m.p.h. (81.45 m.p.h. actually). This was given as the best figure on a practically calm day, with the windscreen lowered but with the normal full equipment in place, the driver only being on board. The best timed speed over a quarter-mile with the windscreen raised normally was 76.27 m.p.h.

On a suitable safe road, with the screen in position in the ordinary way, 75 m.p.h. is a speed which can be got up to with ease and considerable satisfaction. With quite ordinary methods, and changing up fairly early, 50 is registered almost automatically; the way in which the car runs at this speed makes it delightful to keep up, practically irrespective of bend and curve, so rock-steady is the car on the road.

M.G. MAGNETTE TWO-SEATER

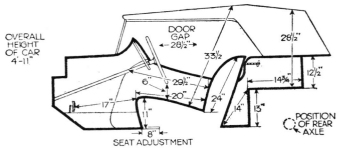

OVERALL HEIGHT OF CAR 4'-11"

DOOR GAP 28½"

28½"
33½"
6" 29½"
12½"
14¾"
20" 24" 14 13
17"
11"
8"
SEAT ADJUSTMENT

POSITION OF REAR AXLE

the maximum m.p.h. figure during the fastest timed run being 83 or so..

Apart from the performance, the most striking thing about the car is its feeling of solidity without, however, seeming "dead." One soon has the feeling of being able to do almost anything with the car on corners. This, and the acceleration, coupled with brakes having big drums of racing pattern, which do their job really well, yet never give the impression of being fierce, make high average speeds a matter of course when required.

An excellent angle has been given to the steering column, the wheel comes in an ideal position for power of control over it, both arms being inside the body of the car. Though very light, the steering is properly accurate. The seats themselves are very comfortable.

Behind the seat there is a genuinely useful-sized compartment for baggage. On the chassis one outstanding provision is a system of grouped lubricators which, communicating by pipe lines to various bearings, reduces lubrication almost to a pleasure.

But the difference compared with most ordinary cars is that, when it is wanted, there is instant acceleration available from that speed onwards on top gear ; or, better still, of course, with a quick drop down to third—a movement of sheer joy to the practised driver with the latest gear box, the revs being taken right round to the "five-five" mark if he so chooses—almost exactly 60 m.p.h. on third gear.

To pass, or to climb really fast, in this way is an experience in motoring which is difficult to excel ; the whole running of the car spells efficiency, and, a good point on this N model, there is no ostentation about the exhaust note. Actually, 6,000 is not by any means an unheard-of figure with this engine, but the red marking on the dial leads one to treat 5,500 r.p.m. as a usual limit, which gives 36 m.p.h. on second, and just over 20 on first gear.

The big dial in front of the driver is essentially a rev counter, an intelligent instrument for the owner of a car such as this, but there is an inner ring of readings on which are plotted the equivalent speeds on top gear. The instrument proved very close to accurate in its speed readings,

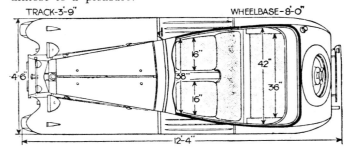

TRACK-3'-9"   WHEELBASE-8'-0"
16"
-4'-6"   38"   42"
16"   36"
12'-4"

INTO BATTLE   Manin Beg 1934

As the results show, this event proved a walkover for the supercharged K3 Magnettes! The two illustrations above - both taken at Promenade Corner in Douglas, Isle of Man - show (left) Norman Black (No. 22), the eventual winner, leading Hamilton's car, and (right) George Eyston's very non-standard bodied car.

RESULTS.

Pos.	Car.	Driver.	Time.			Speed.
			h.	m.	s.	m.p.h.
1	M.G. Magnette (S)	N. Black	2	34	37	70.99
2	M.G. Magnette (S)	C. J. P. Dodson	2	36	20	70.20
3	M.G. Magnette (S)	G. E. T. Eyston	2	36	57	69.93
4	M.G. Magnette (S)	C. E. C. Martin	2	41	5	68.11
5	M.G. Magnette (S)	R. H. Eccles	2	44	22	66.78
6	Riley	C. Paul	2	44	25	66.67
7	M.G. Magnette (S)	R. T. Horton	2	44	54	65.55
8	M.G. Midget (S)	W. G. Everitt	2	48	3	63.30

M.G. CONTINUITY

No Seasonal Changes, Improvements If and When Desirable

The new KN Magnette saloon, with 1,287 c.c. engine.

AS hard-won racing experience accumulates a fund of knowledge upon which to draw for the purpose of producing cars that are able to maintain with reliability a high performance in the hands of private owners, so does it become possible from time to time for the keen designers to incorporate improvements in existing models or to evolve altogether new ones. These periods of evolution are not governed by the weather, or by the season of the year, but by the state of knowledge, and by the production facilities of the factory, which always will run most economically when working full and regular time.

These are the reasons why the M.G. Company has no new programme announcement to make. New or improved M.G. cars have been introduced at intervals, and each one has marked a very real step forward. When further improvements are discovered, tested, and made commercial they will doubtless be incorporated, but it is definitely the policy not to make seasonal alterations, and thus the existing range of cars remains current. To write of them is an interesting subject.

Full credit must be given to the enterprise and the dogged hard work which

have eventually raised the M.G. racing stable to international fame. How many motorists realise that size for size, M.G. cars can race anything in the world and stand an odds-on chance of winning? Or that in Abingdon, England, they knew more about getting and holding stupendous horse powers out of the smallest of engines than anywhere else? Two hundred brake horse power per litre capacity would have sounded utterly incredible a few years ago, but it is an M.G. hope very near now to realisation. The 750 c.c. engine of the Q-type racer will hold round about 111 b.h.p., suitably tuned, and the car is capable of lapping Brooklands track at 111 m.p.h., and reaching 123 m.p.h. down the straight.

Racing Cars Purchasable

Types of M.G. racing cars can be purchased by anyone in the ordinary way; there are two sizes, the Q-type Midget, four cylinders, 57 by 73 mm. (746 c.c.), and the K3 Magnette, six cylinders, 57 by 71 (1,087 c.c.), the first priced at £550, and the second at £795.

In salient points the design of the two cars is similar. The engines have overhead valves, with straight ports on opposite sides, operated by an overhead cam-

shaft driven by spiral bevel gears through a vertical shaft, dynamo-damped to prevent oscillation. The combustion chambers are of a special shape, and a very special type of gasket is fitted to hand-scraped surfaces between cylinder head and cylinder block-cum-crank case casting. The large size balanced crankshaft is carried in three bearings on the four-cylinder and four bearings on the six.

Engine lubrication is a very important point in cars of this description. A large gear-type oil pump is driven from the crankshaft feeds all the bearings under high pressure through a fine Tecalemit filter. The pump draws through a strainer its supply from an elektron sump ribbed for cooling, and an automatic float feed maintains the oil at a set level from an auxiliary tank in the scuttle. Both engines are supercharged, the blower being driven from the front end of the crankshaft through universal couplings. On the K3 a Roots type is used, with a normal boost of 10 lb. per sq. in. and a maximum of 13 lb., whilst on the Q the compressor is a Zoller with a normal boost of 20 lb. and a maximum of 24 lb. The four-speed gear box is a preselector made under Wilson patents, and is operated from a very neat control in the centre of the cockpit.

The P-type M.G. Midget two-seater, which goes on without change.

The N Magnette two-seater, which also is unaltered.

of course, the absence of a supercharger. The Q-type machine has been developed from the P.

Materially, the four-cylinder engine of the P is the same, only the stroke is longer, 83 mm. instead of 73 mm., whereby the capacity is put up to 847 c.c. By reason of the rigid construction and the cylinder head and valve design, this engine is

Besides the clutch incorporated in the gear box, the Q has an additional two-plate inoperative clutch in the flywheel, with a pre-determined slip load. The frame of each car is underslung at the rear, and has tubular cross-bracing. An aluminium undershield is fitted flush under the bottom of the chassis to reduce air resistance, and scoops assist the cooling of the gear box and rear axle.

The half-elliptic springs are underslung and flat, and have bronze-lined trunnions at the rear, instead of shackles, to oppose side movement. They are taped and bound, and in the case of the front axles steel cables are carried to the frame to take the torque of heavy braking. On the K3 a very special type of braking is used, consisting of twin cam levers operated through cables and casings in such a way as to double the force of brake application for a given cable load.

The cars are fitted with two-seater bodies of extremely light construction in the form of a beaten aluminium shell, with the fuel tank concealed in a stream-lined tail of which the point is hinged. The wings are easily removable, and the body can be lifted without disturbing the mechanism of the car. The body dimensions conform to A.I.A.C.R. regulations.

(Right) Rear end of the Q racing model Midget, showing how access is gained by means of a hinged tail.

(Below) The supercharged 1,100 c.c. K3 Magnette in racing guise. It costs £795.

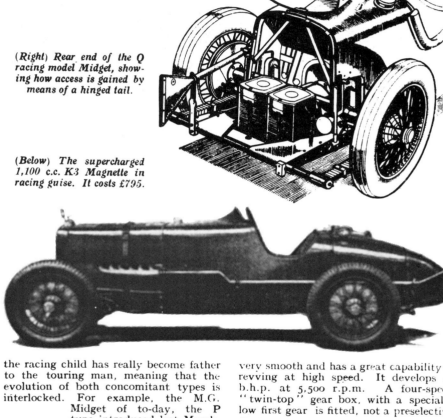

(Left) Cockpit of the Q-type Midget. The large-figure instruments, brake adjustment and fuel taps will be noticed.

BRAKE ADJUSTMENT

TWIN FUEL TAPS

That is an outline of the general design; there are, of course, numerous other points of special value for racing purposes.

It is perhaps natural for the pen to move first towards describing racing cars, but actually the M.G.s of touring type should have the premier position, because

the racing child has really become father to the touring man, meaning that the evolution of both concomitant types is interlocked. For example, the M.G. Midget of to-day, the P type introduced last March, has a very similar chassis to that of the Q type, except only in details, and,

very smooth and has a great capability of revving at high speed. It develops 44 b.h.p. at 5,500 r.p.m. A four-speed "twin-top" gear box, with a specially low first gear is fitted, not a preselective gear.

Remarkable at sight for its trim and alert appearance, the Midget has a number of attractive points apart from the particular qualities of all M.G. cars, namely, that they are designed for fast work and show their mettle best when the speed is high enough to illustrate the

The P-type Midget four-seater.

Interior of the new Magnette saloon.

engine by a metal-faced bulkhead, with a rubber annulus around the flywheel housing, and the cable-operated, large diameter brakes have an easy master adjustment. There are three coachwork models of the P type Midget: — two-seater, £222; four-seater, £240; and Airline coupé, £290.

Then come the six-cylinder models. First is the N type Magnette. This again follows normal M.G. practice and is very similar to the Midget, except that it is on a larger scale and has a six-cylinder twin-carburetter engine of 57 by 84 mm. (1,287 c.c.). One additional special feature is the method of mounting the body on flexibly attached side sub-frames and a flexible cross-member at the rear.

The two-seater is priced at £305, the four-seater at £335, the two-four-seater at £350, and the Airline coupé at £385.

Of other six-cylinder closed models there are the Continental coupé, a two-door four-seater of striking appearance with a large luggage trunk at the back, built on the Magna chassis, which has a 1,087 c.c. engine and a 3ft. 6in. track, priced at £350, and then a new model only just introduced.

This is the KN saloon, which has a K-type Magnette chassis, but the engine is the N type of 1,287 c.c. The KN saloon is likely to attract many purchasers, for it has all the typical M.G. roadworthiness and fast performance, but offers the comfort of a roomy saloon body.

The appearance is not extremist, but very graceful and well proportioned. The seating position is low, but the bonnet and scuttle are also low, so that an excellent forward view is obtained. There are four doors, arranged on the pillarless principle, so that access to the rear seats is extremely easy. In the rear panel is a luggage box, the lid of which can be used as a luggage platform. This car runs quietly and easily, and is very pleasant to handle. The arrangement of sliding windows gives extra elbow room, and altogether the interior is not confined or cramped for either head or leg room. The price is £399.

(A full description of the N-Type Magnette, with cutaway drawing, appears on pages 48 and 49.)

meaning of a perfect road hold, steadiness in quick curves, a sensitive steering, and brakes that can safely be used at high speed.

The gear control is brought well back into the cockpit, and has a short, stiff lever, the brake lever is of racing type, which is free until locked by the top catch; the instrument board is well arranged, and has a large diameter revolution indicator combined with a speedometer; the screen can be folded flat forward, and the long bonnet, when opened up, gives access also to the interior of the scuttle. The radiator, lamps and wings are mounted in a special way which relieves the front end of the frame of pendulum action, and avoids "front end dither." There is a reserve to the fuel tank with a control in reach of the driver's hand. The driving compartment is sealed off from the

Q-type M.G. Midget competition model, priced at £550.

INTO BATTLE 1935

M.C.C. EXETER TRIAL: S. E. H Bowyer (one of the 276 car competitors; there were solo motorcycles, sidecar outfits and three-wheelers as well!) climbs Ibberton in his M.G. Midget — last hill of the trial. M.G's of various types and sizes accounted for a substantial proportion of the entries for these pre-war, long-distance M.C.C. trials - the Land's End, Exeter, and Edinburgh, as well as the Club's Brooklands one-hour "blind".

"THE AUTOCAR" ROAD TESTS

M.G. MIDGET
P-TYPE
TWO-SEATER

No. 894 (*Post-War Series*)

Latest Model a Marked Improvement in All Important Respects Over Its Forerunners

THE P-type M.G. Midget is already very well known, but it so happens that only recently has there been an opportunity of carrying out the ordinary Road Test on it. Anyone who has had experience of the various preceding Midget models cannot fail to be struck by the very great improvement which this P-type shows in practically all respects over its forerunners.

One of the greatest things is that the latest engine, with its three-bearing crankshaft and other improvements, is an enormous gain in smoothness, so much so that it seems as happy at high engine speeds as it is lower down the range. This is very valuable indeed, for pre-eminently it is a car which depends upon revs for its performance. If it be driven gently on top gear and with early upward changes, then its performance is much like that of any ordinary small touring car; the gears are definitely there to be used, and thoroughly justify their use.

An excellent gear change, with remote-control lever, is provided, and the engine can be taken up as a regular thing to as much as 5,000 r.p.m., thereby obtaining a performance definitely superior to that of ordinary cars of small and medium size, and very pleasing to the enthusiastic driver because of the remarkable ease with which the engine turns over fast.

There is no doubt that the M.G. people have developed to a fine art the attainment of revs without fuss by engines of small capacity.

The car was driven hard, particularly during the tests on Brooklands, and for several hundred miles on ordinary roads, but at no time did it give any impression that anything was going to break. It seemed, in fact, to defy any such attempts.

On one occasion, on second gear, the revs were taken round to an indicated 6,000 r.p.m. on the instrument, yet still the engine was smooth and apparently contented.

The figure given in the table for maximum speed was taken with the windscreen lowered and with only the driver on board, and represents a

mean of several runs in opposite directions. As the best speed under such conditions, but with the wind following, 76.27 m.p.h. was recorded over the quarter-mile. With the windscreen raised a best speed of 69.23 m.p.h. was given over the timed quarter-mile.

It was not a good day for these tests, since a strong cross-wind gave no real help at any time, and was a handicap in one direction. The speedometer did not go above a reading of 78, and a rather remarkable thing about the maximum speed is that, though somewhere about 5,000 r.p.m. is being held, the engine feels perfectly happy. In fact, after several such runs it began almost to feel slow at this speed.

On the gears, using a limit of 5,500 r.p.m. on the combined rev counter and speedometer instrument, readings of 20 on first gear, 36 on second, and 60 on third are given, but there are still revs in hand, and a full 60 m.p.h. on third is possible. The speedometer had an optimistic error not above $2\frac{1}{2}$ m.p.h. at any speed.

Along with this most useful performance the handling of the car is excellent. The P-type feels more comfortable as a touring car, especially at the lower speeds, yet is steadier in the sports car sense at speed. It can be taken round corners with that feeling of rock-steadiness and absolute control which is altogether delightful, and the steering, though very light, is accurate. The brakes, too, are very good indeed. Their full power is not realised until one comes to tread hard on the pedal in making an emergency stop; then it is found that they pull up the car really decisively. The very good figure given was taken using the pedal alone:

With the hand lever as well, which gives an even more powerful leverage, 27ft. from 30 m.p.h. was recorded as the mean of two tests. For ordinary slowing they are really good brakes, too, as the action is smooth and progressive, and the pedal pressure need only be light.

A cruising speed cannot be quoted

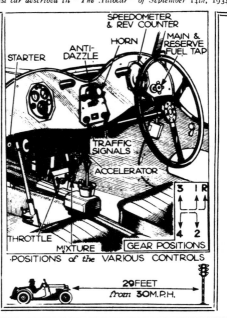

M.G. MIDGET P-TYPE TWO-SEATER
DATA FOR THE DRIVER

8 h.p., four cylinders, 57 × 83 mm. (846 c.c.). Tax £8 (1935, £6).
Tyres: 19 × 4.00in. on knock-off wire wheels.

Engine—rear axle gear ratios.	Acceleration from steady speed.			Timed speed over $\frac{1}{4}$ mile.
	10 to 30 m.p.h.	20 to 40 m.p.h.	30 to 50 m.p.h.	
22.50 to 1	—	—	—	
12.46 to 1	$7\frac{1}{5}$ sec.	—	—	
7.31 to 1	$12\frac{1}{5}$ sec.	$12\frac{3}{5}$ sec.	$13\frac{1}{5}$ sec.	
5.375 to 1	$19\frac{3}{5}$ sec.	$19\frac{3}{5}$ sec.	$26\frac{1}{5}$ sec.	74.38 m.p.h.

Acceleration from rest through the gears to 50 m.p.h., $20\frac{1}{5}$ sec.
Acceleration from rest through the gears to 60 m.p.h., $32\frac{1}{5}$ sec.
Speed up Brooklands Test Hill from rest (1 in 5 average gradient), 18.19 m.p.h. (on first and second gears).
Acceleration up 15 yards of 1 in 5 gradient from rest, $3\frac{4}{5}$ sec.
Turning circle: 36ft.
Tank capacity 12 gallons, fuel consumption 35 m.p.g. (approx.)
12-volt lighting set cuts in at 16 m.p.h., 8 amps. at 30 m.p.h.
Weight: 13 cwt. 2 qr.
Price, with two-seater body, £222.
(*Latest car described in "The Autocar" of September 14th, 1934.*)

SPEEDOMETER & REV COUNTER
HORN
MAIN & RESERVE FUEL TAP
ANTI-DAZZLE
STARTER
TRAFFIC SIGNALS
ACCELERATOR
THROTTLE
MIXTURE
GEAR POSITIONS
·POSITIONS of the VARIOUS CONTROLS

29 FEET
from 30 M.P.H.

"THE AUTOCAR" ROAD TESTS

M.G. MIDGET P-TYPE TWO-SEATER

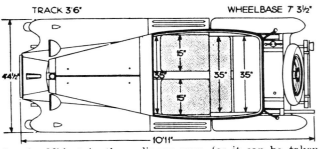

It is possible to say of this particular car, in a way not always feasible under the conditions of an ordinary test, that the oil consumption was exceptionally light.

The hood is easily raised and lowered, there are good side screens, and a fair-sized luggage space is provided under cover. The seats are very comfortable.

The fuel tank is of a sensible capacity; a noticeable point under the bonnet is the provision of a fuse to guard each circuit. The new oil filler in the top of the valve gear cover is a great convenience. The exhaust note is quieter than when the P-type was first produced, apart from a period of resonance at about 2,500 r.p.m.

A most desirable little sports car.

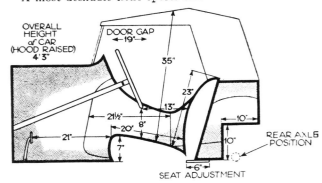

for the Midget in the ordinary way, for it can be taken along at whatever speed within its range the road permits; 60 m.p.h. is quickly attained on a good open stretch.

The gear change, especially between top and third, is a delight to use, third is barely distinguishable from top in sound; the upward changes, except between third and top, need a fair pause in neutral. The performance would be still better in acceleration were it possible to get through more rapidly from first to second and from second to third without crashing the gears.

The two-seater body is comfortable and adequately wide; the windscreen has a double-blade electric wiper, there are recessed traffic signals, and the head-lamp beam is good. An important point which has been noticed in all the normal M.G. models is the instantaneous starting from cold, with very little use indeed of the mixture control.

A four seater version of the P-type Midget was also available.

MG P~type Midget

Introduced in February 1934, the P-type replaced the
starker J. Available in two-seater form for £220, 4-seater
for £240, and as the stylish, closed Airline Coupé for
£290, the new model retained the 847 c.c. engine capacity
of the earlier car, though the engine was a new design
with a much-needed third bearing on the crankshaft.
Right: The car in two-seater form, and below, the
construction details of the 4-seater laid bare.

The Autocar Road Tests

12 h.p. M.G. MAGNETTE KN SALOON No. 913 (*Post-War Series*)

Accuracy of Control and a Feeling of Complete Safety Outstanding Features of a Fast 12 h.p. Car

ONE approaches an M.G. saloon in the expectation that it will prove to be decidedly above the average of cars of similar nominal size in regard to road behaviour. In this new KN pillarless saloon the market represented by those who appreciate performance and fine handling qualities in a car is better catered for, one can say, than by any previous closed model on a comparatively small chassis that the M.G. Company have put forward.

One very important underlying reason is that the N Magnette engine, which has been doing so well during the past year, provides ample power for the additional weight of a saloon body. To-day, the makers of these cars have a very varied experience in producing fast cars, that enables them to provide not only a powerful, willing and reliable engine, but to fit this engine in a chassis which as regards stability, braking, and steering, those all-important factors, is in every way excellent.

Experience of the KN saloon, which, incidentally, is on a chassis with a longer wheelbase and a wider track than that applying to the open Magnette models, has extended for purposes of this account over some hundreds of miles, taking in all kinds of conditions of fast motoring, byway pottering, and traffic use, as well as distinct variations in weather.

It happened that a car of this type was driven for some distance on two separate occasions. During the greater part of the time on the first occasion the roads were wet, and there was no opportunity of discovering how the car showed up on a dry road. From the very commencement, however, and this is the important point, a driver new to the car felt that he was able to handle this saloon on surfaces far from ideal almost exactly as though the roads had been dry, either in cornering or under braking, and there was no suggestion at any time that his faith in the road-holding qualities was misplaced.

With the greater confidence of even the experienced driver when eventually it was possible to drive on dry roads, it was found that almost anything could be done with the car on corners, bends being hardly noticed as regards need for conscious steering, whilst on sharper turns taken fast where there was vision ahead the car felt rock-steady.

This question of stability is stressed because in it lies much of the character of the car, and by it is emphasised the natural safety of a machine designed from the start to be driven fast where conditions permit.

There is that feeling about the steering which enables one to steer to the proverbial inch, at all events, to place the car exactly where one wishes on the road, and as to the brakes, with their large, businesslike-looking drums, they can be put on hard without thought on average roads as to whether the car will remain on a straight course. They are most satisfactorily progressive brakes in that light pressure on the pedal gives ordinary slowing down, and for maximum results heavier pressure is needed.

A rather remarkable feature of the springing is that in spite of the extreme steadiness the riding is not harsh. For all its accuracy, the steering is very light indeed, though not disconcertingly so.

The gear change remains of straightforward pattern; that is, there is no synchromesh or similar device, but third speed has helical-toothed pinions which run in constant mesh. Without being difficult, it is a gear change suited to the car, with its short, stiff remote-control lever, and it handles with exactness.

Third is a quiet gear, second and first are more noisy, but not markedly so. Limits of approximately 16, 35, and 62 m.p.h. are given on first, second, and third gears, up to a full 50 m.p.h. on third without appearing to stress the engine in the least.

---

12 h.p. M.G. MAGNETTE KN SALOON.

DATA FOR THE DRIVER

12 h.p., six cylinders, 57 × 84 mm. (1,287 c.c.). Tax £9.
Tyres: 4.75 × 19in. on knock-off wire wheels.

Engine—rear axle gear ratios.	Acceleration from steady speed.			Timed speed
	10 to 30 m.p.h.	20 to 40 m.p.h.	30 to 50 m.p.h.	over ¼ mile.
24.15 to 1	—	—	—	
13.40 to 1	6 sec.	—	—	
7.86 to 1	9¼ sec.	10¼ sec.	12½ sec.	
5.78 to 1	13¼ sec.	16 sec.	17½ sec.	75.31 m.p.h.

Acceleration from rest through the gears to 50 m.p.h., 18¾ sec.
Acceleration from rest through the gears to 60 m.p.h., 28¾ sec.
Speed up Brooklands Test Hill from rest (1 in 5 average gradient), 16.45 m.p.h. (on first and second gears).
Acceleration up 15 yards of 1 in 5 gradient from rest, 3¼ sec.
Turning circle: 38ft.
Tank capacity 10 gallons; fuel consumption 25 m.p.g.
12-volt lighting set; 8 amps. at 30 m.p.h.
Weight: 21 cwt.
Price, with pillarless four-door saloon body, £399.

(Described in "The Autocar" of September 14th, 1934.)

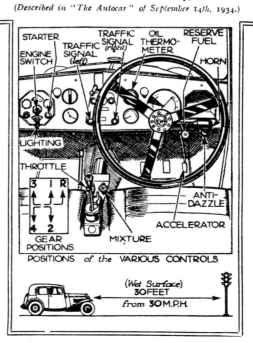

POSITIONS of the VARIOUS CONTROLS

STARTER / TRAFFIC SIGNAL (*right*) / OIL THERMOMETER / RESERVE FUEL / ENGINE SWITCH / TRAFFIC SIGNAL (*left*) / HORN / LIGHTING / THROTTLE / 3 R / 4 2 / GEAR POSITIONS / MIXTURE / ACCELERATOR / ANTI-DAZZLE

(Wet Surface) 30 FEET from 30 M.P.H.

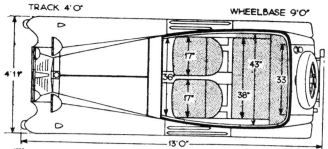

The manner of one's progression depends almost entirely upon the circumstances. If to go from one place to another is the object, the car responds beautifully, and will hold its 60 m.p.h. or more. On the other hand, it is happy in itself and pleasing to the occupants when running in the thirties and forties, though seeming to express a preference for somewhere about 50 m.p.h. on open roads.

Humming along in its purposeful stride it sweeps up the ordinary kind of hill, helped by the fact that top gear ratio is lower for the saloon model. Often, if slowed by other traffic, it will naturally make a faster climb on third; second, too, is a very valuable gear.

In acceleration the car exhibits a cleanness of carburation, with ready response to the throttle pedal, this on the gears especially, though on top gear, too, the pick-up is satisfactory and it is a machine that can still accelerate usefully from speeds of 40 m.p.h. or so.

For a 12 h.p. saloon which is not particularly light, though material has not been wasted, the speed figures show up outstandingly well. For the test at Brooklands conditions were bad, with a strong head wind against the car in one direction and a wet surface, but the mean speed of several runs, above a genuine 75 m.p.h., speaks well for the power. The best timed run over a quarter-mile with the wind following was at 78.26 m.p.h.

The standard combined rev counter and top and third gear speed instrument read high by 5 m.p.h. at 60.

The pillarless four-door construction of the body is an asset as regards convenience of getting in, and out where a car of comparatively small size is concerned. Pneumatic upholstery is used and is very comfortable, the back rest and cushion being in one, deck-chair style.

Elbow room is conserved for the occupants of the front seats by the use of sliding windows, which obviate winding mechanism in the doors. The driving position is particularly comfortable, with the spring-spoked wheel brought well back and set not too high. The rear view mirror, fitted externally, could be more effective. At the back a platform can be lowered to carry luggage.

A machine for an owner who appreciates a car as a car and not solely as a means of transport.

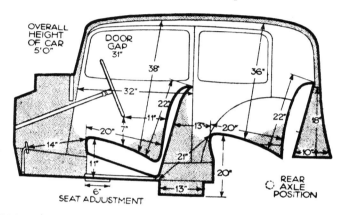

THE "CRESTA" MAGNETTE

Special Two-seater Model in Which Both Light Weight and Comfort Have Been Studied

A SPECIAL model of the M.G. Magnette, to be known as the "Cresta" Magnette, has just been placed on the market by the Cresta Motor Company, Ltd., of Worthing. The coachwork, which is shown in the accompanying photographs, has been carried out by E. Bertelli, Ltd., and the two-seater body is designed with a disappearing hood, an occasional seat, ample luggage accommodation, and a windscreen which, when in the raised position, has flanking screens that can be used as miniature windscreens when the main screen is horizontal. A cover is provided for the rear of the car and for the passenger's seat when necessary, there is a very large tool box under the bonnet, an Ashby or a Bluemel steering wheel is available, the fuel tank holds 11½ gallons, the seats are adjustable for angle as well as for position, and the detail work of the car is carried out very well indeed, weight being kept down by the use of a special grade of aluminium panel. The finish of the upholstery and paintwork adds very greatly to the attractiveness of the car.

The "Cresta" Magnette has a handsome aluminium-panelled body with many excellent features.

M.G.'s Quit Racing

THE decision that the M.G. Company is to cease racing forthwith has come as quite a bit of a shock to a lot of people. The announcement as worded says that the company is to cease building racing cars and concentrate solely on sports cars, but I think it means much more than that, for it affects all racing by the firm's cars, whether they are of the type we call sports cars or not. This is a pretty shrewd blow, but there's no getting away from the fact that racing can be overdone, and I maintain once more that, as far as the real racing machines are concerned, the best policy is to build and maintain one team and to concentrate on that. If the type is interesting and exciting it is bound to have teething troubles before success arrives, and teething troubles are far more serious if there are a great number of these machines in the hands of various people. It's a pity about the Tourist Trophy, though, as the team might have stood a very good chance of pulling it off again, but beyond question the wisest policy for the moment is to concentrate on making money.

TOP *The "Three Musketeers" team of Magnettes —and* Aramis *again—this time winning outright the first Welsh Rally, held in July 1935. The driver, as in the previous illustration, was C. W. Nash*

ABOVE *This illustration—taken on holiday in the I. of M.—of R. A. Yallop's K3 Magnettes seems to sum up all the sporting features and character of these famous cars*

LEFT *NUFFIELD TROPHY, DONINGTON 1935: Reg Parnell's offset single-seater Magnette finds unexpectedly strong opposition in Ian Connell's Vale Special—the Vale finishing the race, while the Magnette retired. The Vale, incidentally, was powered by Triumph Super Seven*

BELOW *Brooklands, Whit Monday 1936: Closely fought Mountain Circuit races were a feature of this meeting, in this case with R. C. Vickers' Type 35 Bugatti being chased by "Bira" and Reg Parnell in Magnettes.*

*Thought for many years to be the first-ever MG, this special
was driven by Cecil Kimber on the 1925 Lands End Trial*

Miss Betty Haig's immaculately preserved 1935 PB Midget

Gilding the Lily?

However goodlooking the production M.G. coachwork, there were always those who thought they could improve on it. Here (left and below) is the Sportsman's coupé version of the 1929 M-Type Midget, complete with unusual sunshine roof

1935: Elegant Airline coupé on the P-type Midget. On the PA chassis this cost £267 10s, and you paid £22 10s more for a PB version

The Midget

New M.G. Midget, The Series T : Bigger Engine, Longer

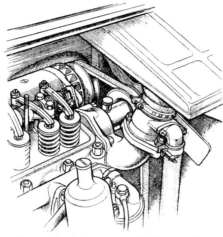

are regaining popularity even where engine size is increased. It may be noted that the new four-cylinder Midget has a larger engine than the existing six-cylinder Magnette, of 1,286 c.c.

Removal of the cover discloses valve gear. The water pump and dynamo are belt-driven; cooling is thermostat-controlled.

The Series T engine has push-rod-operated overhead valves, with double valve springs and a camshaft driven by duplex roller chain. The crankshaft has three main bearings, as on the "P" and "PB" types. An external oil filter is fitted between the pump and the bearings, as well as a float-type filter on the suction side. This float-filter rides on top of the oil in the sump, the suction pipe being pivoted, and thus avoids the possible collection of sediment or sludge from the base of the sump. The sump itself, of aluminium alloy, ribbed for cooling, holds 1½ gallons, and an accessible oil

filler is fitted on the top of the valve cover.

The engine consumes its own fumes, a pipe from the valve cover connecting with the large air cleaner for two semi-downdraught S.U. carburetters. There is also a fume-extractor from the crank case, with a pipe leading down below the engine to the rush of air.

On the former models cooling was by thermo-syphon action, but on the Series T there is a water pump and also a fan,

while the water temperature is regulated by a thermostat. The pump and fan are both driven by a triangular belt which also drives the dynamo, now mounted at the side of the engine instead of vertically in front as before. Ignition is by coil and distributor, with 14 mm. sparking plugs.

A single-plate clutch with cork insets running in oil is fitted, and the gear box is of the straightforward type, no synchromesh or other easy-change mechanism having been found necessary. There are four forward speeds, the ratios being 4.875 to 1, 6.92 to 1, 10.73 to 1, and 18.11 to 1. Reverse gear is 23.26 to 1. A new and massive-feeling remote-

Seats are adjustable for rake and distance from steering wheel.

SO outstanding have been the successes of the M.G. Midget, and so great its popularity amongst small car enthusiasts, that the announcement of a new and much improved production from this firm is of instant interest. The existing "P" and "PB" types, with the well-known 847 c.c. and 939 c.c. engines, are now to be superseded by a bigger model with an engine of 1,292 c.c., a longer wheelbase, and a slightly wider track, to be known as Series T. **Price, £222.**

In addition, the overhead camshaft design which has for so long been a feature of M.G. engines has been dropped in favour of push-rod-operated overhead valves, and many detail modifications of the chassis layout have been introduced, though the price remains unaltered, as compared with the "PB" type, at £222. The car is marketed as an open two-seater only.

The new engine unit is a four-cylinder, as before, and the bore and stroke are 63.5 by 102 mm., giving 1,292 c.c., rated **at** 10 h.p., with a tax of £7 10s. This is in keeping with the modern trend of design, in which four-cylinder engines

The familiar M.G. lines are comparatively unaltered.

Grows Up

Wheelbase, Improved Specification

control type of gear lever is fitted, with no external gate as hitherto. The final drive is by a Hardy Spicer balanced propeller shaft.

The wheelbase is now 7ft. 10½in., as compared with 7ft. 3½in. on previous

Extra light with the hood up is gained by having two transparent chromium-beaded panels.

models, and the track 3ft. 9in. compared with the former 3ft. 6in. The frame follows the same lines as before, and is underslung beneath the rear axle; there is now a box section extending from the front engine mounting to the gear box stays, thus stiffening the side members where torsional stresses are greatest. Both sets of springs are half-elliptic, as usual, but the rear springs are now mounted on Silentbloc bearings at their forward ends, with sliding trunnions at the rear. Luvax hydraulic shock absorbers are fitted at both front and rear, instead of only at the rear, as previously.

In a deep locker at the back are stowed the side screens. The filler cap is of quick-action design.

Another interesting modification is that Lockheed hydraulic type brakes are used instead of the cable-operated pattern on former M.G. Midgets. These have 9in. drums, which are of smaller diameter than the old type, but this is counter-

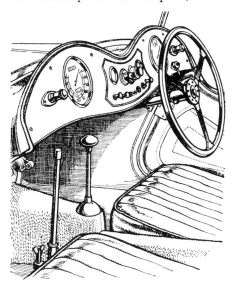

The air filter also extracts fumes from the valve cover.

acted by wider braking surfaces, giving a similar frictional area.

The petrol tank is wider, and now holds fifteen gallons instead of twelve, three gallons of which can be trapped as a reserve. There is a dual petrol line leading to a neat two-way switch on the

instrument panel. The spare wheel is carried at the rear of the tank.

The longer wheelbase has rendered a very generous luggage compartment possible, a big point on a small sporting two-seater. It should be possible to get three or even four quite large suitcases in the space behind the front seats, which is protected by a tonneau cover. The front seat cushions are separate, but their back squab is in one piece, which

There is no longer the external gate for the remote-control gear lever. A 30 m.p.h. warning light is included among the instruments.

makes the seats more secure, and the squab is sufficiently high to support the shoulders comfortably. A neat adjustment is provided for the squab.

Easily Operated Hood

The hood folds down into the rear compartment, without unduly curtailing the luggage space, and is exceptionally easy to operate. The supports consist of full irons and a rigid bar at the front, fixing to the screen pillars by thumb-nuts. When erected, together with the side curtains, its easy lines give a smart appearance, and the side curtains themselves are well made, with a chromium bead all round. There are two side curtains on each side, each with mica windows—an unusual feature on a two-seater—so the car is light and pleasant to sit in with the hood up, while there is plenty of head room even for a tall person.

Ample leg room has also been provided, and the driving position gives comfort and a feeling of control. The instruments include a separate Jaeger rev counter as well as a speedometer, both with specially finished white dials, and there is a 30 m.p.h. warning light, indirect dash lighting, and an exterior map-reading lamp. A badge bar is now standard, as well as a fog lamp.

Generally speaking, the new, larger M.G. Midget should have much-improved facilities as a touring machine, but should have lost none of its sporting characteristics, whilst a good performance is certain to be provided.

Not much changed, but wider and perhaps more solid in appearance—the latest Midget.

Marshall Supercharger Fitted to PB-type M.G. Midget

The new Marshall supercharger installation available for various types of M.G.s was described in *The Autocar* of December 13th, 1935, and an opportunity has now arisen for a short test run on a PB-type M.G. Midget with this supercharger fitted.

The car tested by a member of *The Autocar* staff was one owned by Mr. D. L. Briault, of Northern Motors, Ltd., of Harrow, where the actual fitting of the supercharger was carried out. It is stated that the only material difference from standard was that a higher axle ratio of 5.1 to 1 instead of 5.3 to 1 had been adopted, this being in many cases a desirable alteration when a blower has been fitted, owing to the increased power of the engine. This car was originally one of last year's Le Mans team, a P-type now fitted with the larger "PB" engine.

The car ran smoothly in traffic, and pulled exceptionally well at low speeds on top gear. The engine speed was allowed to drop as low as 1,000 r.p.m., and the car would still accelerate away. There was no undue pinking unless the throttle was abused very violently, a 20 per cent. benzole mixture being used. No tendency to oil or soot up plugs was noted, even after several miles of top gear work at purposely low speeds. It was not until open stretches were reached and the engine speed rose considerably that one could detect any noise at all from the blower, and the faint whine that could then be heard was almost entirely pneumatic and quite pleasant to the ear.

There was a slight rain falling at the time, but the car was timed at 86 m.p.h. over a flying quarter-mile with the screen flat and aero screens erected, the maximum reading by calculation from the rev counter being 89 m.p.h. This was with the assistance of a slight wind, over 80 m.p.h. being attained in the other direction. Acceleration figures taken were: 0-50 m.p.h., 10⅕ sec.; 0-60 m.p.h., 14⅗ sec.; standing quarter- mile, 21⅖ sec.

The manufacturers of the supercharger are Marshall, Drew and Co., Ltd., 140, Clarendon Road, London, W.11, and the price of the set for the "PB" has now been reduced to £29, the sets for the N Magnette and the Magna remaining at £33.

Supercharging a Popular Sports Car

Trial of a P-Type M.G. Midget Fitted with a Centric Blower

Interest has undoubtedly been growing lately in the application of supercharging to existing cars, not with the object of raising the maximum speed excitingly, but as a method of improving acceleration and all-round performance. This can often be achieved by the use of a supercharger set to work at a mild pressure sufficient to give a forced induction effect, but not strong enough to lead to over-revving and consequent stress on the components beyond the limits of the original design.

An example is a 1935 P-type M.G. Midget converted by the well- known firm of Jarvis and Sons, Ltd., of Wimbledon, Distributors of M.G. cars for south-west London, who have applied a Centric supercharger to one of these cars.

This machine was driven some 150 miles by way of a test, including a good proportion of traffic use, main road running and checking performance at Brooklands. The maximum speed was found to be 78 m.p.h. with the windscreen folded down, and 75 m.p.h. genuinely with the screen erected, but more interesting were the acceleration figures, which from rest through the gears to 50 m.p.h. worked out at an average of 18⅕ sec., and from rest to 60 m.p.h. at 26⅕ sec., these being good figures for a car nominally of 8 h.p.

Improved Top-gear Acceleration

The acceleration on top gear, too, was interesting, averaging out from 10 to 30 m.p.h. at 14⅗ sec., from 20 to 40 m.p.h. at 15⅘ sec., and from 30 to 50 m.p.h. at 17⅖ sec. Also, the 1 in 5 Test Hill was climbed from a standing start, using first and second gears, at 20.02 m.p.h., a much faster climb being made by changing up than on first gear only.

A fuel consumption test was taken, using two gallons of fuel for the purpose. Including the Brooklands test mentioned, employing maximum speed for some distance, full use of the gears, and also bringing in conditions which would correspond to town use, and some main road motoring, the figure worked out at the very creditable average of 29 m.p.g. The enging oil level did not alter.

A striking point about the car from the supercharger angle was that it had not been made noisy mechanically; at low speeds only a faint whirr from the blower was audible, and in spite of several experiments to see whether the sparking plugs would oil up with the engine left ticking over slowly, no such difficulty was experienced. Neither was there spitting back or missing at any time, whilst starting from cold was as easy as it usually is with M.G. cars, which is saying a lot.

The use of the supercharger gives the car definitely improved acceleration from the lower and middle speeds, and there is a useful reserve for top gear acceleration from 55 or 60 m.p.h. onwards, which is valuable. When cruising at about 60 with the throttle partly open no "blow" is indicated, however, on the gauge, and in any case the maximum supercharger pressure is 5 lb. per sq. in. Provided that this degree of supercharging is not exceeded it is understood that the M.G. Company approve of the conversion, which can be undertaken by the firm of Jarvis at £32, including fitting, for the P-type M.G. At 50 m.p.h. and onwards the exhaust was barely noticeable, and the car settled down beautifully, whilst its safe, steady handling was greatly appreciated; at lower speeds, around 2,500 r.p.m., there was a conspicuous exhaust note.

The Centric supercharger fits in quite neatly on the off side of the engine, and is driven by a belt from the existing pulley on the nose of the crankshaft, with a jockey pulley interposed. This drive, besides being dead silent, appears to be perfectly positive.

An important point is that oil does not have to be added to the fuel, nor is there a separate oil tank for the supercharger. A pump embodied in the blower ensures a supply automatically. Accessibility of the engine in general does not seem to be impaired.

The Autocar

Published *The Autocar*, 17 January 1936

The Autocar Road Tests

The Midget taking a mud section, part of the old Pilgrim's Way, near Wrotham, Kent.

No. 991 (*Post-War Series*)

M.G. MIDGET PB TWO-SEATER

A Fascinating Small Sports Car : The Latest Model Shows Marked Improvements in Several Important Points

SOMETIMES the truest expression of opinion upon a car which one has tested in the usual way is to say it is a machine one would like to own oneself. Any such statement is naturally dependent upon the views of the individual expressing it, but, since the M.G. Midget is to be considered as a sports car, appealing to the more enthusiastic type of driver, it is at all events fair comment from someone who tries all manner of cars.

The PB Midget now tested is the model that was introduced just before the last Olympia Show, differing from the earlier P type in having a slightly bigger engine capacity, of 939 c.c. against 847 c.c.—a size retained for what is known now as the PA type. Besides the larger engine there are other points of difference in the PB Midget which contribute towards making it an appreciably improved car.

It would be difficult for anyone free from prejudice and at all capable of being enthused by the performance of a small sports car not to be quickly attracted to this M.G. It does so much for so little. It is almost as fast as can be used reasonably; certainly on either a long or a short journey it covers the ground just about as quickly as any type of car can, and in some circumstances more rapidly than is possible to a bigger, faster but less handy vehicle. Its acceleration is good, and it runs happily at 50, 55 and even 60 m.p.h., for the engine is smooth and will go up to a limit of as much as 5,500 r.p.m. on the indirect gears.

The acceleration shows a distinct gain as a result of the increased engine size—on paper as well as on the road. Not only is the pick-up better from the lower speeds on top and third gears, but in the middle range too, and, if recollections serve, there is a decidedly superior feeling of power in reserve.

Those are points of far more importance than the actual maximum speed. In regard, to speed figures, the state of Brooklands at present, undergoing repair as it is, prevented the proper maximum being developed in the available distance. The best that could be managed as a timed speed over a quarter-mile with the windscreen lowered and two up was fractionally below 71 m.p.h.—very definitely that is not the car's limit of speed.

This particular machine was fitted with a speedometer which showed no measurable error at 40, 50, 60 and even 70, and which was slightly *slow* at 30. It is therefore possible to say from the indications the car gave on Brooklands and its subsequent behaviour on the road that the maximum would lie around 75 or 76 m.p.h., given space in which to attain it. That is remarkable for a 9 h.p.-rated car which is flexible, tractable, and thoroughly pleasant for by-way pottering, for instance, and for the slower kind of motoring which often appeals.

Reference has already been made to the high speeds the Midget is capable of keeping up; indeed, about 50 m.p.h. seems a natural speed on open roads. Even without ever driving it faster than that there is a charm about the car it is difficult to express, but which no doubt partly arises from the undeniable efficiency of the small overhead camshaft four-cylinder engine.

DATA FOR THE DRIVER

M.G. MIDGET PB TWO-SEATER

PRICE, with two-seater body, £222. Tax, £6 15s.
RATING : 8.9 h.p., four cylinders, o.h.v., 60 × 83 mm., 939 c.c.
WEIGHT, without passengers, 15 cwt. 2 qr. 16 lb.
TYRE SIZE : 4.00 × 19in. on knock-off wire wheels.
LIGHTING SET : 12-volt ; 9 amps at 30 m.p.h.
TANK CAPACITY : 12 gallons ; fuel consumption, 35 m.p.g. (approx.).
TURNING CIRCLE : (L. and R.) 34ft. GROUND CLEARANCE : 6 in.

ACCELERATION

Overall gear ratios.	From steady m.p.h. of 10 to 30	20 to 40	30 to 50
5.375 to 1	$15\frac{1}{5}$ sec.	$16\frac{3}{5}$ sec.	$18\frac{2}{5}$ sec.
7.31 to 1	$10\frac{3}{5}$ sec.	11 sec.	$11\frac{1}{5}$ sec.
11.50 to 1	$6\frac{3}{5}$ sec.	—	—
19.24 to 1	—	—	—

From rest to 50 m.p.h. through gears $16\frac{2}{5}$ sec.

From rest to 60 m.p.h. through gears, $27\frac{3}{5}$ sec.

25 yards of 1 in 5 gradient from rest, $5\frac{2}{5}$ sec.

SPEED

	m.p.h.
Mean maximum timed speed over ¼ mile	—
Best timed speed over ¼ mile...	—
Speeds attainable on indirect gears—	
1st	22
2nd	37
3rd	55-60
Speed from rest up 1 in 5 Test Hill (on 1st gear)	18.47

Performance figures of acceleration and maximum speed are the means of several runs in opposite directions.

(Latest model described in "The Autocar" of August 30th, 1935.)

This unit has been developed to a fine pitch of performance and generally pleasing behaviour. Not only does it give a remarkable power output for its size, but it has been kept quiet mechanically and smooth for an engine of this description.

A good compromise has now been reached in the matter of the exhaust note; just sufficient remains to indicate that this is a sports and not a perfectly normal touring car, and the peak of the note is reached at about 2,500 r.p.m. No sign of pinking was evident from the engine at any time.

The PB Midget does well in running about slowly in speed-limit areas; indeed, its slow-running capabilities on top gear are extremely good in relation to the performance. Also, it shows a good ability to climb comparatively slowly on top gear on those occasions when it is not desired to rush a gradient or to rev on the gears.

An excellent point is the provision of an amber-tinted warning lamp on the instrument board, which lights up at about 20 m.p.h. and then automatically switches out at 30 to attract the driver's attention. Especially at night this is a prominent warning, and removes any perhaps captious criticism there might be that the "30" range of the centrally mounted speedometer is apt to be obstructed from view by the steering wheel. The separate rev counter now fitted is, however, immediately in front of the driver, and thoroughly visible. Whilst on this same subject of driving in built-up areas, it may be mentioned that, even after adjustment, the view given in the external driving mirror is not all it might be.

It is the handling of the car which gives it much of its appeal. The M.G. is low-built, of course, and it feels in "one piece"; the controls are exact, and very soon the driver is at one with the car. The driving position is right, vision is excellent, both wings being seen from the driving seat, and the big-diameter spring-spoked steering wheel comes in just the right place.

Though most satisfactorily light even when manœuvring, the steering feels firm as well in a way which is remarkably good for fast work. It is by no means unduly low-geared steering, either, for approximately one and a half turns take the front wheels from full lock on one side to full lock on the other side. There is a delightful sense of having absolute control over the car, and, within reason, the road surface, whether wet or dry, makes practically no difference to the driver's handling of it. It rides so firmly, so safely, takes bends to the proverbial inch, and is able to respond completely to the judgment of an experienced driver.

The brakes do all they should do, too, giving an excellent, regularly achieved emergency test pull-up in less

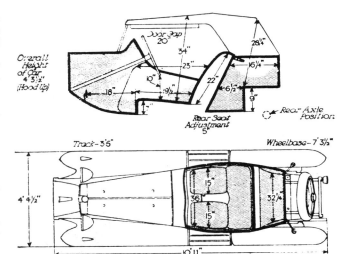

29 feet (Dry Surface) from 30 M.P.H.

Positions of the Various Controls

than 30ft. from 30 m.p.h., yet with little actual feeling of brakes having been applied, and without the least pull to either side. The fly-off racing-type hand lever is excellent for holding the car firmly on the steepest gradient.

One of the improvements concerns the gear change. A lighter clutch driving plate is now used, and, in conjunction with appreciably higher first and second gear ratios, the result is a gear change which can be handled really quickly on the upward movements with no more than mild noise from the teeth, or dead silently with a brief, single-clutch pause. Top and third gear ratios remain as before. This is indeed a gear change that handles beautifully as a whole.

The springing is firm to give the stability that has been mentioned, but not really harsh at any time on surfaces which are at all reasonable. There is at times fairly hard movement, this being principally noticeable in towns, but for a car of this description the riding is comfortable and at its best over the middle range of speed.

The hood, which disappears into the body, is raised or lowered and secured really easily. It is not a very natural position for the driver to have his right arm entirely inside the body. There is fair room for small luggage.

The engine has an extremely good oil filler in the top of the valve gear cover; starting is immediate. Grouped "long range" lubricators serve chassis bearings which otherwise would be awkward to reach.

A fascinating, satisfying little car.

The trim appearance of the Midget is not lost when the hood is raised.

The Autocar Road Tests

THOUGH there are many changes noticeable in the latest Series T M.G. Midget by anyone who has been well acquainted with its extremely popular forerunners, in character the car remains of the same type. That is, it gives an unusually good performance for its engine size, handles in a distinctly better manner than the ordinary touring vehicle, and possesses those touches in the *tout ensemble* that endear it to the owner with sporting tendencies. In fact, as regards the last-mentioned point, the new car achieves a more "solid" and impressive appearance, the wheelbase being longer and the track slightly wider, with a greater length of bonnet, and the further important practical advantage of a wider and more roomy two-seater body. It will be remembered that the design of the latest car embodies a four-cylinder engine, with push-rod-operated overhead valves, of appreciably larger capacity than the previous model of the Midget possessed.

The M.G. has as background a remarkable hedge, some twenty-five feet high, near Chichester.

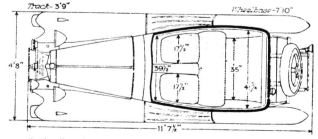

No. 1,058.—10 h.p. M.G. MIDGET SERIES T TWO-SEATER

New Bigger Model, Although Considerably Altered, Remains Essentially of the Same Likeable Style

On the road the "feel" of the car has undergone a change; the new Midget is softer, quieter, and more flexible at low speeds from the ordinary touring car angle. No car, even a sports machine, is driven fast all the time, and to be able to potter really satisfactorily is a quality worth having. That the sheer maximum possible is extremely creditable with the new engine is shown by the figures in the table, and it is certain, too, that the acceleration has been improved for ordinary purposes, in overtaking and in getting away from low speeds. It was odd to be without the familiar exhaust burble, for there was no real sound from the tail pipe. Ideas in this respect

have considerably altered latterly, but it is understood that slightly more of an "M.G. note" is to be restored; indeed, the same car was tried a second time with this change effected.

It is in itself a tribute to the success and popularity attained by the Midget that in driving this new model one is inclined to be more analytical than usual; in other words, to take more than average interest in the car. Really, of course, it has to be judged as a new car.

Probably the biggest advantage of the larger engine is that it needs to be less highly tuned to give a good all-round performance, is therefore not so sensitive to both fuel and ignition, and gives about as much performance as can be used, with reduced stress upon the mechanism. A good power output is obtained — superior over a normal r.p.m. range even to that of the N-type Magnette—and higher gear ratios are used, which have a notable effect as regards ease of performance, for engine revs are kept lower. In consequence of these points it should be a better machine for the ordinary owner to maintain.

It is still a car which seems to revel in being held at a speed between 50 and 60 m.p.h., and which, given any chance, will run easily up to a good deal more when wanted. The new engine will rev freely on the indirect gears, too, and as a result, coupled with the handy size of the car, its cornering capabilities, and hydraulically operated brakes that are fully capable of dealing with the performance, a very good average can be made, even over roads that give little assistance. This car does more than may be suspected until actual measurement of the performance comes to be made.

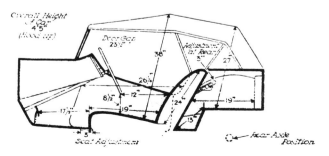

General handling is good, for though the springing is a shade softer, and hydraulic shock absorbers are now fitted all round instead of at the back only, the Midget can be put into a fast curve confidently and be swung round an acute turn with a most satisfactory feeling of stability. The steering is firm, more so than formerly, without becoming actually heavy for manœuvring, and has definite

"The Autocar" Road Tests

caster return action; the latest steering gear ratio is higher, rather less than 1½ turns being needed from lock to lock. The suspension avoids shock to the occupants except in really severe conditions, though on a wavy surface there is sometimes a good deal of motion apparent. The brakes give a most potent power for an emergency pull-up, which can be regularly repeated, and the braking tests were made immediately after 300 miles of road work.

Synchromesh is employed for the gear changes to top, third, and second; there is a new well-placed rigid remote-control lever. Some people may disagree with the use of synchromesh on the Midget, there again indirectly paying tribute to the esteem in which the car has been held by enthusiasts, but there is no getting away from the fact that for general purposes this box handles easily, and at the same time satisfactorily to anyone who takes a pleasure in using the gears of a sports car. Changing up quickly is greatly facilitated, and rapid, quiet, downward changes can be made by speeding up the engine exactly as would be done were there no synchromesh. At lower speeds the synchromesh engages very

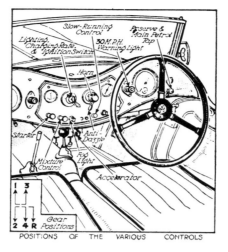

POSITIONS OF THE VARIOUS CONTROLS

26 feet (Dry, Concrete Surface) from **30 M.P.H.**

vision, being able to see both wings, whilst a decided improvement is that there is more room for the left foot when off the clutch pedal. The clutch action is light and at the same time smooth in taking up the drive. Quite apart from comparing actual measurements, there is the definite impression of more room inside the body, particularly as regards elbow clearance, and the driver can bring his right arm entirely inside the car.

To warn the driver a green-tinted lamp is illuminated as long as the car's speed remains below 30 m.p.h. When this flashes out, he knows that he has gone past the legal limit. This is an excellent idea, but for night work this lamp is a little over-powering. It is understood that the necessary modification has already been incorporated. The instruments are indirectly illuminated with a soft green effect at night. There is also a direct lamp, useful for map reading and so forth. The speedometer proved to be 1.6 m.p.h. fast at 30, 4.8 at 50, and showed a highest reading of 90-91 when the car was being timed in the favourable direction with the windscreen lowered. Tests were made also with the windscreen raised normally, and the car covered a timed quarter-mile thus at 73.77 m.p.h.

The latest hood goes up and down easily and secures quickly to the windscreen frame, whilst the all-weather protection is good, there being two screens at each side which render the interior light with the hood up and at the same time snug. Also, the luggage space behind the seats has been considerably increased. Although there is a straight-across, one-piece back-rest, easily adjustable for angle, separate adjustable seat cushions are fitted. They are very comfortable seats.

There are door pockets, ventilators in the scuttle sides, a twin-blade electric screenwiper, dip and switch head lamps, a fog lamp out in front with a separate switch, and, an extremely good feature, a control on the instrument board to bring a reserve supply of fuel into use, three gallons being trapped.

A "different" Midget, admittedly, but one with some distinctly practical features embodied, and giving plenty of performance in an interesting way.

DATA FOR THE DRIVER.

10 h.p. M.G. MIDGET SERIES T TWO-SEATER.

PRICE, with open two-seater body, £222. Tax, £7 10s.
RATING : 10 h.p., four cylinders, o.h.v., 63.5 × 102 mm., 1,292 c.c.
WEIGHT, without passengers, 17 cwt. 1 qr. 3 lb.
LB. (WEIGHT) PER C.C. : 1.50.
TYRE SIZE : 4.50 × 19in. on knock-off wire wheels.
LIGHTING SET : 12-volt ; 7 amps at 30 m.p.h. ; three-rate charging.
TANK CAPACITY : 15 gallons ; fuel consumption, 27-29 m.p.g. (approx.)
TURNING CIRCLE (L. and R.) : 37ft.   GROUND CLEARANCE : 6in.

ACCELERATION

Overall gear ratios	From steady m.p.h. of 10 to 30	20 to 40	30 to 50
4.88 to 1	13.2 sec.	15.2 sec.	17.2 sec.
6.46 to 1	9.9 sec.	10.6 sec.	11.5 sec.
9.85 to 1	6.4 sec.	—	—
16.50 to 1	—		

From rest to 30 m.p.h. through gears, 6.1 sec.
From rest to 50 m.p.h. through gears, 15.4 sec.
From rest to 60 m.p.h. through gears, 23.1 sec.
25 yards of 1 in 5 gradient from rest, 5.0 sec.

SPEED

	m.p.h.
Mean maximum timed speed over ¼ mile ...	77.59
Best timed speed over ¼ mile ...	79.65

Speeds attainable on indirect gears :—

1st	...	...	...	17-23
2nd	...	...	...	29-39
3rd	...	...	...	50-61

Speed from rest up 1 in 5 Test Hill (on 1st and 2nd gears) 18.91

Performance figures for acceleration and maximum speed are the means of several runs in opposite directions.

(Latest model described in "The Autocar" of June 19th, 1936.)

---

well unassisted, and a sure drop can be made to third or second for extra acceleration or a steep gradient. The gears, more particularly second, are on the noisy side, judged by this particular car. The hand-brake lever is of the familiar fly-off type, operating in the rear drums, and powerful to hold the car on a hill.

The driving position has not been in the least spoilt, again making mental comparison, as seems inevitable with this car; the spring-spoked wheel is set well down in a position that gives the driver power over it, and he has very good

Front or rear, the new Series T Midget is typically an M.G. in lines. The body is wider, and the rear petrol tank is now of even greater capacity than before.

New Cars Described —

Four Types of M.G.s

Prices and Models to Remain Unchanged : A New Larger 2.6-litre Model to Come : New Midget Drop-head Coupé Described

SOME time ago the M.G. Car Company dropped the announcement of a "programme" each year, and, instead, adopted the plan of introducing new series, or editions, of models whenever improvements had been found desirable. Thus the following notes are not a programme announcement, but indications of some new things to come, and a review of current affairs.

Next week's issue of *The Autocar* will contain a description of an entirely new M.G. car of larger size, with body styles similar to the 2-litre, and with a 2.6-litre engine. Meanwhile, a new item to be described is a drop-head coupé on the Series T Midget chassis. Of the current cars the prices and specifications remain unchanged, and the range is as follows :—

RANGE AND PRICES OF M.G. CARS.

Series T.

Midget two-seater	£222
Midget coupé	Price not fixed

Series V.

1½-litre chassis	£215
1½-litre four-seater	£280
1½-litre four-door saloon	£325
1½-litre foursome coupé	£351

With Jackall equipment the above prices for the 1½-litre are raised by £5

Series S.

2-litre chassis	£260
2-litre four-seater	£399
2-litre four-door saloon	£389
2-litre foursome coupé	£415

These prices include Jackall equipment.

The folding-head foursome coupé coachwork is built on the Tickford principles by Salmons and Sons, Ltd., of Newport Pagnell, and the open four-seater tourer body of the 2-litre by Charlesworth of Coventry.

Despite the decrease in general registration figures, 1938 has beaten the M.G. record for previous output.

Deliveries of the new Midget coupé are scheduled to commence in September. This is a most attractive little two-seater and a genuine drop-head coupé without makeshifts or compromises. It can be used as a completely closed car, when the well-padded head with its toggle irons presents a smart appearance, and the solid construction should make it draught-proof, without wind noise, and free from rattles. The car has a windscreen which can be opened right up into the horizontal position (a valuable asset if one is driving through a thick fog) and locked into place by outriggers. Also the windows are of full size and operated by winding handles.

Besides the fully closed position there are two alternatives. In a few seconds the taut peak of the head can be undone, and rolled neatly back to form a coupé de ville. Finally, the cant rails may be undone at the front end, folded back laterally, the toggle irons "broken" and the head folded flat down to open the body completely to the sunshine and fresh air.

To accommodate drivers of different stature, besides the other adjustments, a neat form of telescopic mounting is provided for the spring-spoked steering-wheel.

The direction indicators are concealed in the sides of the scuttle, and are operated by a switch with a red warning light in its centre. Another feature is that the fuel tank, placed at the back, contains no less than 13½ gal. Various small changes have gradually

A new model is the coupé body on the Series T M.G. Midget.

taken place in other M.G. models since the cars were last described. For example, there is now an extremely wide choice of colour schemes, inside and out, for all models. No fewer than eight cellulose exterior finishes are available, and seven interior leather colours. The exterior colours are blue, red, green, duo green, maroon, black, grey, and metallic grey, whilst the choice of leather colours is biscuit, green, brown, maroon, grey, red and blue.

Quick control lever for the adjustable steering wheel.

Any combination of the above colours may be selected for any model except the new Midget coupé, without extra cost, and, furthermore, the body, if desired, can be finished in one of these colours and the wings and fairings in another.

Actually, the metallic grey finish is applied to the body only, the wings being painted to match, but without the metallic lustre. The reason for this is that if "the other fellow" should damage the wings in a cramped parking place it is more easy to repaint them to match. On the Midget coupé the complete range of exterior colours is available, but the leathers are limited to the standard shades of biscuit, maroon, brown and grey.

2-litre Refinements

Of recent times considerable improvements have been effected in the interior finishes of the 2-litre saloon, chiefly in regard to the woodwork. Also the "engine room" has come in for some extra refinement, and, amongst other things, the metal scuttle structure is now painted grey instead of black. Another feature of the 2-litre is that trap-doors in the bonnet sides will be abandoned in favour of louvres.

In conclusion, the specifications of the three chassis may be summarised. The Midget has a twin-carburettor, four-cylinder engine rated at 10 h.p. (tax £7 10s.) of 63.5×102 mm. bore and stroke (1,292 c.c.). The overhead valves are operated by push-rods, and the crankshaft is carried in three bearings.

The folding-head foursome coupé on the 2-litre is a real dual-purpose body.

a remote gear lever carried on the chassis, and a single-plate clutch. The unit is mounted flexibly on rubber. Transmission is by open propeller-shaft to a spiral-bevel gear. Lockheed hydraulic brakes are fitted. The springs are half-elliptic back and front. Wheelbase is 9ft. and track 4ft. 2in. Centre-lock wire wheels are used and shod with 5.00 × 19in. tyres.

The saloon is of the four-door, four-light style with a luggage boot at the back, in the lid of which the tools are recessed in a tray. This body is notable for large and comfortable seats, neat trimming, large-dial instruments, and a system of no-draught ventilation.

In unit with the engine are a single-plate clutch and four-speed gear box, with synchromesh on third and top, and a remote gear-lever control. The unit is flexibly mounted on rubber. Transmission is by an open tubular propeller-shaft to a spiral-bevel gear in a pressed-steel rear axle casing.

Of box-section, with a forward diagonal bracing and tubular cross-members, the frame is underslung at the rear. Half-elliptic springs are used back and front, and are damped with hydraulic shock absorbers. The wheelbase is 7ft. 10in., track 3ft. 9in., and the tyre size 4.50 × 19in. Lockheed hydraulic brakes are fitted.

The Midget is not sold as a chassis, and, in addition to the new coupé, the standard coachwork is a smart two-seater with all-weather equipment, having space for luggage in the back behind the seats.

The 1½-litre Model

Next in size, and somewhat different in type, though basically similar in mechanical principle, the 1½-litre M.G. is a sporting style of car rather than a sports car. In short, it is intended to suit those who choose a car for the sake of motoring and not as a humdrum means of transport. So the 1½-litre is typically British and typically specialist, with its long, low bonnet and compact, shapely bodywork. It has been designed for driving fast and in safety, with a weight of experience behind it to ensure that it is up to its specified work. Rated

Most popular of the 2-litre range is the smart four-door, four-light saloon at £389

at 12 h.p. (tax £9), the engine has four cylinders, 69.5 × 102 mm. (1,548 c.c.), with push-rod-operated overhead valves, twin S.U. carburettors, high-pressure lubrication with a "top feed" oil float, full filtration, and an air-cooled sump. It is in unit with a four-speed gear box, having synchromesh on third and top,

The larger M.G. cars, by the way, have a special bulkhead interposed between the engine and the scuttle to prevent undue heat from reaching the interior of the bodywork.

Much that has been said of the 1½-litre applies equally to the 2-litre model, which is a larger car on the same lines, but provided with a more powerful six-cylinder engine. This is rated at 17.97 h.p. (tax £13 10s.) and has six cylinders of 69.5 × 102 mm. (2,322 c.c.). The wheelbase is 10ft. 3in., track 4ft. 5in., and the centre-lock wire wheels carry 5.50 × 18in. Dunlop Fort tyres. The frame is of deep box-section side-members, plentifully cross-braced with stout tubes, whilst the rigidity of the forward end is increased by extra diagonal runners, also of box-section, which form a cradle for the flexibly mounted engine unit. The M.G. 2-litre is a striking and attractive car in its various styles of coachwork.

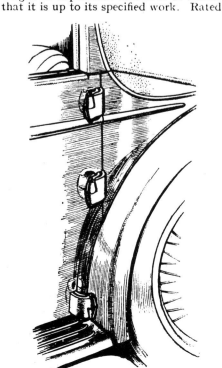

(Above) Fabric tensioning device on the Midget coupé.

(Left) The door of the little coupé is supported by three substantial hinges.

(Right) The rear of the Midget coupé is given up to providing good luggage space for driver and passenger.

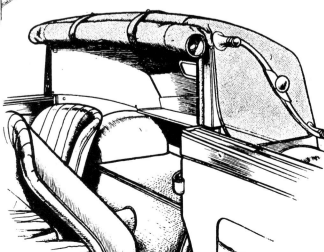

Intermediate M.G. Model

New 1½-litre Four-cylinder Car, Between the Midget and the 2-litre, for Open and Closed Four-seater Bodywork

This view of the chassis gives a satisfying impression of sturdiness.

(Illustrations of the complete cars appear in the Photo-gravure Section.)

AN intermediate M.G. model is now announced, supplementing the 10 h.p. Series T Midget lately introduced, and replacing the 12 h.p. six-cylinder Magnette. This new model is a 12 h.p. four-cylinder to be known as the 1½-litre. It is intended to fill the gap in size and price between the Midget, offered only as a two-seater, and the six-cylinder 2-litre M.G., a model which carries roomy saloon, convertible, and open tourer coachwork.

The 1½-litre thus rounds off the range of models and, with a useful wheelbase of 9ft., is to be provided with four-seater bodywork, both an open tourer and a four-door saloon being standardised, at £280 and £325, respectively. The chassis price is £215. Promise of a very good performance in the M.G. manner is given, and, at the same time, this newcomer is aimed at providing quiet, comfortable travel and ample seating accommodation.

In general layout it has a number of items in common with the 2-litre M.G., on a scaled-down version, of course, and certain points of similarity to the latest Midget, though the frame, for instance, is quite different from that of the smaller car. It is not simply and wholly a larger Midget. The four-cylinder engine has push-rod-operated overhead valves, the crankshaft runs in three bearings, there is a ribbed aluminium sump, and mixture is supplied by two semi-downdraught S.U. carburetters, to the intakes of which is attached a large air cleaner

▲25

and silencer unit; the pipe connecting this to the carburetters runs transverse to the engine, passing over the valve gear cover. Ignition, of course, is by coil and distributor, the distributor being accessible on the near side, and there is a hand-operated vernier adjustment to enable the timing to be rapidly altered to suit different fuels. The sparking plugs are of the small 14 mm. size, recessed at an angle in the near side of the cylinder block, but readily accessible.

There is thermostatic control of the water temperature, the water when cold, with the thermostat closed, being short-

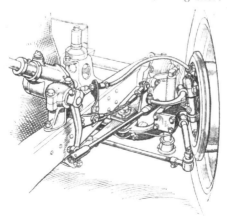

Steering gear layout, also showing the brake reaction steel-rope link.

circuited through a by-pass system until temperature is gained, when gradually the whole quantity comes into circulation. There is a fan, belt-driven from the crankshaft, in conjunction also with an impeller type of pump to assist the water flow; the same belt drives the dynamo, which is placed fairly high up at the front of the unit on the near side, affording an easy means of adjustment for the tension of the belt. This dynamo is of the ventilated type. In the engine lubrication system is a filter of the renewable element type, conveniently placed for periodical cleaning and eventual renewal.

The bore and stroke of this unit are 69.5 by 102 mm., giving a capacity of 1,546 c.c., the rating being 12 h.p. and the tax £9. A compression ratio of 6.5 to 1 is employed, and maximum engine revs are 4,500 p.m.

In unit with the engine is a single-plate clutch of the cork insert kind, running in oil, together with a four-speed gear box having synchromesh on top and third, and a neat remote-control lever extended back to an excellent position for the left hand. This lever works in an open, visible gate with a positive stop against reverse gear position. Top gear ratio is 5.22 to 1, third is 6.92, second 10.54, and first 18.01 to 1.

Alongside the gear lever, to the right, is the hand-brake lever. This is not of the fly-off type, engaging with its ratchet only when the knob at the top is depressed, but of normal press-down-the-knob-to-release design, though of neat construction, similar in appearance to the previous type of lever.

This ensemble of engine and gear box is mounted flexibly on rubber at four points in the frame—two in front and two at either side of the gear box, a considerable thickness of rubber bonded to the metal being employed. Transmission is by an open propeller-shaft with needle bearing universal joints to a normal pattern of spiral bevel rear axle. At both front and back the suspension is by half-elliptics, and these have the special feature at the shackle ends of side plates which should minimise the

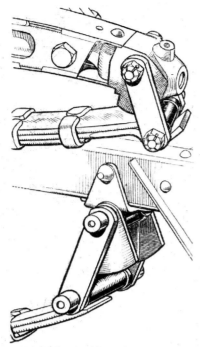

(Left) The spring shackles have special end plates.

(Right) Arrangement of the frame members at the centre of the chassis.

(Below) There are two S.U. carburetters, with air intake silencer and cleaner.

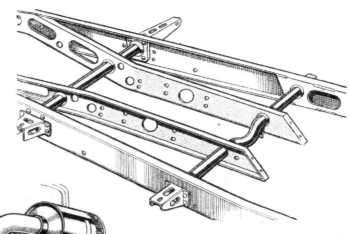

effect of wear in the pins in the later life of the car. A Burman Douglas worm and nut steering gear is employed, the column is well raked, and there is a steering wheel of the spring-spoked kind, with a telescopic quick adjustment.

Both axles have Luvax double-acting shock absorbers of large size; the front axle is nicely laid out and looks sturdy, besides having a special braking torque member. The brake gear is Lockheed hydraulic, with independent control of the rear wheel shoes by cables operated from the hand-brake lever. Dunlop knock-off wire wheels are fitted, and carry 19 by 5.00in. Fort tyres. The chassis wheelbase of this 1½-litre M.G., as already stated, is 9ft., and the track is 4ft. 2in.

The frame merits separate mention.

In distinction from the Midget design, the rear members are upswept over the back axle, and from the rear extremity to a point approximately at the centre of the car a latticed box section is given to the side-members. Then, starting from the front of the frame, there is a similar construction, but the extra member which forms the box section layout in front is swept inwards at a point corresponding to about the gear box, the two members in question leaving the side-members and approaching one another at the centre of the frame, where they are welded to cross-members. The tubular cross-members look generous.

There is the familiar M.G. shape of radiator, with its neat name badge and vertical-slatted shell in front of the block, a finishing touch being given by the familiar octagonal cap, which remains in the external position. Carried amidships in the frame is the 12-volt battery. A centrally mounted pass light is provided in front, having a separate switch on the instrument board, and, in common with the layout recently adopted on the 2-litre, separate fuses for the different electrical circuits are provided.

As already indicated, this 1½-litre chassis is destined to take a sports four-seater open body, with a neat hood and complete all-weather equipment, of which a feature is the particularly large area of celluloid material, making for a light interior when this is in use. The saloon is a full four-seater of four-door construction, resembling to some extent a scaled-down version of the most attractive present 2-litre M.G. saloon. A departure for this make is the carrying of the spare wheel in the near-side wing, it being enclosed in a cellulosed metal cover. The body is very well appointed.

This model will be seen at Olympia.

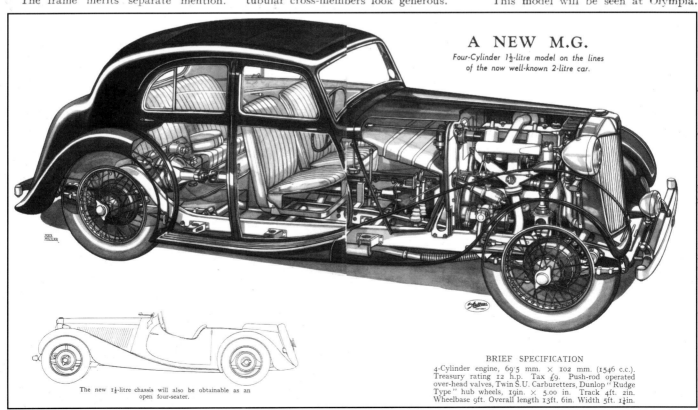

A NEW M.G.
Four-Cylinder 1½-litre model on the lines of the now well-known 2-litre car.

The new 1½-litre chassis will also be obtainable as an open four-seater.

BRIEF SPECIFICATION
4-Cylinder engine, 69.5 mm. × 102 mm. (1546 c.c.). Treasury rating 12 h.p. Tax £9. Push-rod operated over-head valves, Twin S.U. Carburetters, Dunlop "Rudge Type" hub wheels, 19in. × 5.00 in. Track 4ft. 2in. Wheelbase 9ft. Overall length 13ft. 6in. Width 5ft. 1½in.

The M.G. Programme

Improved Engine for the Midget and Other Modifications to Attractive Range

A handsome foursome coupé the 2.6-litre, priced at £475.

Midget has gone through a regular system of evolution which has kept it in the forefront. The present model, known as the Series T.B., is a development from the Series T, and it is interesting that the Midget, from being at first an 8 h.p. car, has stepped up in engine size until it now has a rating of 10.97 h.p. The engine of the T.B. is different from the T, having four cylinders 66.5 × 90 mm. (1,250 c.c.), whilst the T engine was four cylinders 63.5 × 102 mm. (1,292 c.c.).

From this it will be seen that the improved engine of the Series T.B. has a larger bore, a shorter stroke, and a slightly smaller capacity, and these features have in this modern design secured a considerable increase in power output, accompanied by a greater smoothness of running. This latest engine has a stout balanced and counterweighted crank,

CONCEIVED and built around the ideal of a compact type of car entirely suitable for fast travel, M.G. cars have secured an enviable reputation for success in this country and abroad. The latest and the most amazing M.G. feat was accomplished recently by Major Gardner, who put up the mile record in the 1,100 c.c. class—or about 10 h.p. rating—to the fantastic figure of 203.5 m.p.h. It is with the knowledge and experience of such successful feats as

The 1½-litre saloon is smart in appearance and performance. It costs £335.

Behind the hinged bumper badge is the hole for the starting handle.

these that the M.G. normal range of cars is produced. There are four sizes, priced as follows :—

M.G. Midget, series T.B. Open two-seater £225, drop-head coupé £270.
M.G. 1½-litre. Open four-seater £295. Four-door saloon £335. Folding-head foursome £360.
M.G. 2-litre. Four-door saloon £393. Folding-head foursome £425.
M.G. 2.6-litre. Four-door saloon £450. Folding-head foursome £475.

One of the most successful small fast cars ever made in this country, the M.G.

shaft carried in three main bearings, steel H-section connecting rods and aluminium alloy pistons of the controlled-expansion type with three rings, the lowest of the set being an oil-control ring.

Cast monobloc, the cylinders are carefully designed and water-jacketed to prevent distortion under heat, the water circulation being by pump, and having a thermostat temperature control. A fan is also fitted. In the detachable cylinder head the valves are placed overhead. They have triple springs, and are operated by rockers and push-rods from a camshaft driven by duplex chain. Lubrication is force fed and the oil is contained in an aluminium sump ribbed for cooling.

Two S.U. semi-downdraught carburettors supply the mixture through short ports coupled by a balance pipe, and the carburettors draw their air through a large cleaner and filter via a balanced-end type of air intake.

Being essentially a sports car, the Midget has many special features to render it self-supporting on prolonged journeys; for example, the fuel tank at

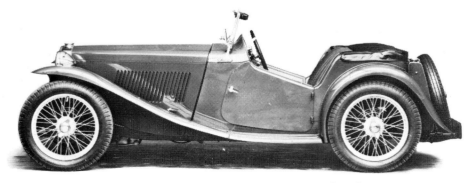

This is the famous T.B. Midget two-seater, costing £225.

Fast and adequately powered is the 2.6-litre saloon, costing £450.

wheels are centre-lock wire type, and the tyres Dunlop 4.50 by 19. The instruments include a large-dial speedometer, revolution indicator and clock. The wheelbase is 7ft. 10in., and the track 3ft. 9in.

Turning next to the larger cars of the M.G. range: the 1½-litre, although it has built into it the results of great experience with fast cars, is aimed more at luxury high-speed travel than at being a sports type pure and simple. The coachwork is well finished and equipped, and enough room is provided without losing the compactness and the low centre of gravity which are valuable to high performance.

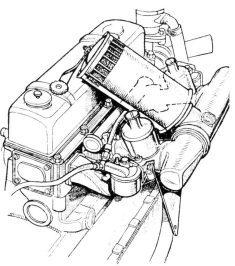

Twin carburettors are fitted to the new M.G. T.B. Midget engine.

the rear is of extra large size, holding 13½ gal., enough for 400 to 500 miles, according to circumstances. A two-way tap operated from the dash retains three gallons in reserve. The carburettors are fed from the tank by an S.U. fuel pump and flexible piping.

In unit with the engine are the clutch and four-speed gear box. The clutch is also of improved type—a heavy-duty Borg and Beck single dry-plate, in place of the cork insert clutch running in oil which was used on earlier models. Also the gear box has synchromesh on second, third and top. The overall ratios are: first, 17.32; second, 10; third, 6.92; and top 5.22 to 1.

grouped nipples. High-geared cam steering is fitted and a valuable addition is the provision of a telescopically adjustable steering wheel with spring spokes.

The four-wheel brakes are Lockheed

Telescopic steering is an M.G. feature.

hydraulic, and the quick-release racing-type hand brake lever applies the rear brakes by independent cable. The

The 1½-litre has also received various improvements. The engine is fitted with a counterbalanced crankshaft, a new type of camshaft, and a dry-plate clutch. The latest Luvax piston-type hydraulic shock absorbers have been adopted, and the Jackall inbuilt jacking system is now standard on all types, as also the new Lund bulb head lamp dipping system in place of the conventional system hitherto used.

Another item is that the interior of the folding-head foursome has been designed to give added accommodation.

How the spare wheel is mounted on the 2.6-litre foursome coupé.

The gear change has a short lever mounted on an extension to bring it conveniently close to the driver's left hand. Transmission is by a Hardy Spicer balanced propeller-shaft to a spiral drive in a three-quarter floating rear axle.

Box-section side members cross-braced with tubes form the frame, which is underslung at the rear. Half-elliptic springs controlled by hydraulic shock absorbers are employed back and front, and, instead of shackles, sliding trunnions are employed to prevent side play. Chassis lubrication is by a system of

The 1½-litre drop-head foursome coupé, which costs £360.

Here is the M.G. 1½-litre open four-seater tourer, which costs £295.

This is a particularly attractive style of coachwork, as it offers three distinct changes, fully closed, fully open, or partly open as a coupé de ville. The compact low build of the saloon is emphasised by a very clean-cut contour, there being no mouldings on the outside of the body. The rear seating position comes within the wheelbase.

Leading features of the specification of the 1½-litre M.G. are: engine, four cylinders 69.5 × 102 mm. (1,548 c.c.), push-rod-operated overhead valves, single-plate clutch, unit four-speed gear with remote control and synchromesh, rubber unit suspension, twin semi-down-draught S.U. carburettor, 12½ gal. rear fuel tank, high-pressure engine lubrication with constant-level float and 100 per cent. filtration, pump water circulation and thermostat control. The wheelbase is 9ft. and the track 4ft. 2in., and the 5.00 by 19 tyres are mounted on centre-lock wire wheels.

Having the success of several years to its credit, the M.G. 2-litre has reached a stage in development which leaves room only for minor improvements. Recently the externals of the six-cylinder engine have been tidied up, and Luvax piston-type hydraulic shock absorbers have been standardised, also screw-type bearings have been adopted for the spring shackles. A rear bumper has been added to the equipment of all types. On the foursome the spare wheel is now recessed into the near-side front wing.

In the arrangement of the saloon coachwork the underlying principle has been to provide for comfort in the front and back seats throughout the wide range of speed of which this car is capable. To this end the centre of gravity is kept low, the seats are within the axle compass, and the suspension is carefully arranged to give complete stability. The coachwork is panelled in steel on hardwood framing, and is as light as is consistent with proper durability.

Features are: leather upholstery, inlaid walnut fillets, winding windows to all four doors, no-draught ventilating system, adjustable bucket front seats, centre folding arm rest and head cushions in the rear seat, sliding roof, and a luggage boot with a capacity of 11 cubic

The rear seating of the 2.6-litre drop-head foursome coupé.

feet, and a lid which may be used as an extra platform.

Rated at 17.97 h.p., the engine has six cylinders 69.5 × 102 mm. (2,322 c.c.). The wheelbase is 10ft. 3in. and the track 4ft. 5in., the tyres being 5.50 by 18 on centre-lock wire wheels.

Largest of the M.G. range, the 2.6-litre model has met with a marked success since its introduction last year. It is built on similar general lines to the 2-litre, but has coachwork of increased capacity. No changes are being made.

Amongst the special features of this "Safety-Fastest" M.G. model the following may be cited:—Visors, draughtless ventilation by means of triangular panels in each of the four drop windows, folding arm rest and head-rests in the rear seats, and a metal shroud carried by each rear door which keeps the rear wings clean, and prevents clothing from being soiled on wet days.

The luggage boot is of large size, and the lid, which can also be used as a platform, contains a tray into which all the tools are neatly recessed. The spare wheel does not obstruct luggage accommodation as it is mounted in a recess in the front wing.

From the mechanical angle attention is drawn to the high efficiency six-cylinder engine with its twin carburettors, and overhead valves. This engine is able to develop over 100 h.p. The rating is 19.8 h.p. six cylinders 73 × 102 mm. (2,561 c.c.).

Amongst many excellent points it has a constant oil-temperature control operating in conjunction with the water cooling system. Another feature is the use of a "kick shackle" on the off-side front spring, also special cables connecting the front axle to the frame, to take the torque reaction of the brakes. Yet another point is that the electrical wiring is carried out in a manner to avoid interference with a radio set, for on M.G. cars provision is made to render radio installation easy.

The car has a 16½ gal. fuel tank. The wheelbase is 10ft. 3in., front track 4ft. 5¾in., and rear track 4ft. 8¾in.

Instrument board and controls of the 2.6-litre M.G.

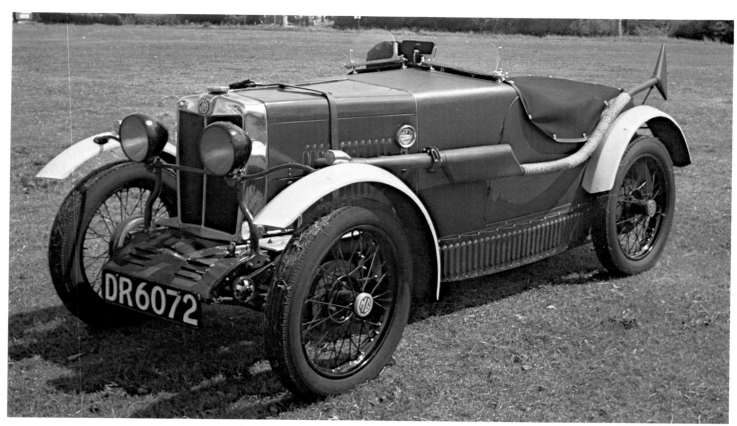

*Dave Cooksey's M-Type Midget, a replica of the team cars
which won the 1930 Double-Twelve Hours Race at Brooklands*

*Two generations of racing MG: Syd Beere's 1933
K3 Magnette (top) and the interior of a 1950s Le Mans
MGA*

Published *The Autocar,* 28 June 1940

Still a

by

H. S. LINFIELD

IT took the mind back over several years, flicking the dust off a certain chromium-plated radiator surmounted by an octagonal cap. The car it belonged to was due to go back to its birthplace the next morning. I remembered doing the same thing, and checking over the oil level, topping-up the radiator, and having a last look round many of its predecessors on similar occasions, and then often starting back to the factory with them early on a summer morning just such as we have had during this sadly troubled June.

Still, I start at the wrong end of the story. The car, of course, was an M.G., one of the last of the current series TB Midgets to come out of the factory before car production had to dry up, for the present, in favour of more urgent calls upon the resources.

Unless you are lucky enough to find one in stock somewhere you cannot now just order an M.G., but there is interest from the road-behaviour angle, and some day these representatives of the British sports car will be in production once again on the old or even a bigger scale.

There is something about the modern M.G. that "gets you," just as perhaps years ago, as in my own case, the earlier models "got" you. An open body always helps, for it is more than a die-hard attitude of mind to consider that open-car motoring has that something in its "fresh-airness" and maximum visibility that no closed body can provide—no, not even a closed M.G. (There is a drop-head coupé Midget model.) One must always qualify this opinion with the proviso—in the right sort of weather.

I will be honest and say I was unusually fortunate with the weather on this recent test run. The petrol position being what it is, there is now none of the opportunity of other days of piling large mileages into a short time, so I took the Midget over for quite a spell, and motored as I could, running it in from practically brand new. It was a fortnight before I had to put up the hood, and as the car was on the road on every day of the fortnight, if sometimes only covering eight or ten miles, it was exceptionally lucky for this country.

But there is more than the appeal of the open car. An unroadworthy M.G. has never been put out—they have always built into these cars an inherent stability, accuracy of steering and power of stopping which make them safe to drive fast. The familiar slogan has more point than most of its kind.

The Series T Midget instituted a new type of Midget, it will be remembered, back in 1936, and the smallest M.G. then became a 10 h.p.-rated machine instead of an 8 h.p. The latest of all, the TB, has a slightly *smaller* engine capacity than the first of the Ts—strictly the type TA. The bore was increased from 63.5 to 66.5 mm., and the stroke shortened from 102 to 90 (1,250 c.c. against 1,292 previously), giving a more nearly "square" engine, and, in conjunction with a slightly lower final-drive ratio, correspondingly more zip for low-speed acceleration.

Keeping to 3,000 r.p.m.

Owing to the running-in process I kept the engine speed on this occasion within 3,000 r.p.m. until the speedometer showed between 800 and 900 miles total. This allowed rather less than 45 m.p.h. on top gear and thirtyish on third. Yet it was not irksome driving, largely because the car handled well and allowed the corners to be taken without slackening appreciably below the self-imposed limit. Again, the clearer roads help, for if, as is now possible on even main-road routes, 40 to 45 m.p.h. can be maintained steadily it seems a respectable pace and gets you over the ground.

Once, without exceeding 43 m.p.h., I covered 36 miles in an hour, yet it seemed—and was—leisurely motoring, and because of the rev limit adopted on all gears there was no question of gaining anything by rapid bursts of acceleration or fast climbing.

With the mileage eventually approaching the 1,000 mark I began to give the engine some throttle. It was pleasant to go briefly up to the 60 mark and to use second and third more as they are intended to be used. The engine never felt really stiff from the first, but there was that slightly hot smell of new paint after a run, and its freedom after

Midget

M, 12, P, PB, T, and Now TB—M.G.'s Have Run Through the Alphabet! : The Latest Model on the Road in Wartime

1,000 miles or so was distinctly noticeable in contrast with the earlier stages.

During the last two days before the final scene with which this account opens I discovered something of what the Midget could do, though never in these times does one feel justified in holding full throttle for any appreciable distance when 45 or 50 will do just as well. There was, however, a rather joyous mile or two of by-pass, a perfect surface, clear of traffic, and with a beautifully radiused right-hand bend that you can take hard over to the right-hand kerb since it is a twin-track road. For that short time and one other brief section the M.G. came to life for the first time in its career, which I hope will be a satisfactory one, and never allow it to be said that this was a car that was "beaten" when it was young! My conscience is clear.

There is no sideways "give" when cornering fast, and the steering, though light, is nicely accurate and firm, but the springing is a great improvement for comfort over the old types. You notice the difference between various kinds of surfaces, and feel fairly appreciable movement over the less good, but never real shock.

Praise for the Hydraulic Brakes

I liked the Lockheed hydraulic brakes a lot. All through the run the linings must have been bedding down from the new condition, but the brakes did not become soft and always had a reserve. In the last fifty miles a quick stop was necessary at traffic lights on a de-restricted road that I had not been watching closely enough, and the M.G. pulled up right on the line, dead straight. The hand brake is still the fly-off pattern, that you pull on to release without touching the knob, always the best kind when restarting on a gradient. The synchromesh gives really nice "slicing" changes up and down, and covers the useful second gear. The steering wheel is telescopically adjustable over a useful range.

The car came to me first of all with all the side screens in position but the hood down, and though I think I have never previously driven an open car for more than an hour or two in this rig I found it a good one—and one's wife appreciates it! It stops nearly all draught. These particular screens are metal-framed, with a big clear area, and if securely clamped on to their clips do not rattle.

There *is* a flap in the right-hand one for signalling, but its use I found a little irksome. As a matter of fact, I got into the habit of watching the useful external mirror more even than usually and gave up signalling except on the most obviously important occasions! I do not necessarily advocate the plan and never felt really easy about it, but it brings home to you how much of the signal-flapping and hand-waving is strictly superfluous. The hood is an easy enough one-man affair and is neat when down, besides allowing plenty of head-room when up. There is handy luggage space beneath the "tonneau" cover, of leather material rubberised on the inside, which conceals it.

The "Thirtilite" that M.G.s have had for a long while proved a blessing. Consisting of a small green lamp in front of the driver, it was set to light up at 20 m.p.h. and go out at 30. Thus, when driving slowly at night, striving for a level 20, you know that if there is no green tell-tale you are O.K., and that in 30 m.p.h. stretches if there *is* a green light you are below 30 m.p.h. Altogether an excellent thing, now doubly useful, though for driving on really dark nights I should experiment with a view to somewhat reducing the brightness of the green illumination.

In the practical M.G. style a rev counter is fitted, and the red line on its dial is placed at 4,800 r.p.m. In the later stages of the run I found that this gave 72 or 73 by speedometer, but that it could be exceeded without apparent distress. Limit recommended revs mean a comfortable 50 on third, but 60 can be seen by winding things up.

When you come to driving it fast you realise what a reserve the car possesses, and it can obviously hold 55 or thereabouts all day on a suitable road without fussing itself. Shades of the past and hopes for the future!

Highly Satisfactory M.P.G. Figures

A 13½-gallon tank is a grand feature of the Midget—if you can legitimately get it filled these days. For driving in the wartime manner, but by no means crawling about, a full tank means a mileage approaching 500. I made a number of successive tests by quart tank over different routes and the average of six checks worked out at 37.6 m.p.g. The conditions included 20 and 30 m.p.h. driving in town areas, steady 30 m.p.h. runs for a specific purpose, and 50 to 60 m.p.h. work with fair use of the gears, *but* always taking advantage of coasting possibilities without letting the speed come down so much as seriously to slow the general rate of progress.

I should regard the all-round average as being 36 m.p.g. in normal conditions. At 30 m.p.h. steadily held the figure was 39.6 m.p.g. I devoted one quart of petrol to a test in the full-throttle style of driving that has been forgotten for the moment—pedal hard down wherever possible, second and third gear used at roundabouts on a by-pass and for accelerating away from them, and generally reverting to pre-war style when in a hurry. Even then the Midget gave 30.4 m.p.g., which is remarkable. All this was done as part of necessary journeys, not as special test runs.

It would be difficult to find a car of similar liveliness and all-round performance—interesting performance—that would be as economical, and this was with a barely run-in engine that had not had any special settings. I came to agree with the makers' policy on the Midget of fitting a reserve petrol tap, but not a gauge. There is the big tank to start with, and the reserve system traps the exceptional quantity of three gallons. The control tap is on the instrument board, right in front of the driver. You can go a long way—several days of running around—without having to think about petrol, and then when the S.U. pump begins to "tick" you turn over to reserve and have 90-110 miles in hand.

Especially on a car that has as good a consumption as the Midget's I would personally sooner have the reserve supply and no gauge, than a gauge and no reserve. I found one other thing about this arrangement, that it avoided the plaguey gauge-watching habit one has got into since a gallon of petrol came to mean so much—a practice which does no good in any case, and is irritating, yet almost impossible to avoid nowadays.

This engine proved to be another example of the fairly high compression sports type that takes no violent exception to the present-day petrol. A certain amount of pinking occurred when accelerating, but never excessively. I think that the alleged evils of Pool were overrated at first, though probably it is desirable to decarbonise more frequently than in the past.

No. 1339

TC M.G.

MIDGET

TWO-SEATER

The Autocar ROAD TESTS

DATA FOR THE DRIVER

TC M.G. MIDGET.

PRICE, with open two-seater body, £412 10s, plus £115 6s 8d purchase tax. Total, £527 16s 8d.

RATING : 10.97 h.p., 4 cylinders, overhead valves, 66.5 × 90 mm, 1,250 c.c. **TAX** (1947), £13.

BRAKE HORSE-POWER: 54.4 at 5,200 r.p.m. **COMPRESSION RATIO:** 7.25 to 1.

WEIGHT, without passengers : 16 cwt 19 lb. **LB. PER C.C. :** 1.45.

TYRE SIZE : 4.50 × 19.0in on knock-off wire wheels.

LIGHTING SET : 12-volt. Automatic voltage control.

TANK CAPACITY : 13½ gallons : approx. fuel consumption range, 28-34 m.p.g.

TURNING CIRCLE : 37ft (L. and R.). **MINIMUM GROUND CLEARANCE :** 6in.

MAIN DIMENSIONS : Wheelbase, 7ft 10in. Track, 3ft 9in (front and rear). Overall length, 11ft 7½in ; width, 4ft 8in ; height, 4ft 5in.

Labelled diagram

SCREEN WIPER · CHOKE · HORN & ANTI-DAZZLE · 30 M.P.H. WARNING LIGHT · LIGHTS & IGNITION · STARTER · SLOW RUNNING · FOG LAMP · HAND BRAKE · FUEL WARNING LIGHT · THROTTLE · GEAR POSITIONS

ACCELERATION			
Overall gear ratios	*From steady m.p.h. of*		
	10 to 30	20 to 40	30 to 50
5.125 to 1	12.1 sec.	13.5 sec.	14.9 sec.
6.93 to 1	8.9 sec.	9.5 sec.	10.3 sec.
10.00 to 1	6.2 sec.	6.6 sec.	—
17.32 to 1	—	—	—

From rest through gears to :—

30 m.p.h.	.. .. ..	5.7 sec.
50 m.p.h.	.. .. ..	14.7 sec.
60 m.p.h.	.. .. ..	22.7 sec.

Steering wheel movement from lock to lock : 1⅜ turns.

Speedometer correction by Electrical Speedometer : 10 (car speedometer)

7 ; 20 = 22 ; 30 = 29 ; 40 = 41 ; 50 = 50 ; 60 = 59.5 ; 70 = 70.

Speeds attainable on indirect gears (by Electrical Speedometer) :

		M.p.h. normal and max.
1st	.. ..	15—25
2nd	.. ..	32—40
3rd	.. ..	52—61

WEATHER : Dry, warm ; wind light.

Acceleration figures are the means of several runs in opposite directions.

Current model described in " The Autocar " of October 12, 1945.

IN a motoring world in which there is so much talk as there is today of rationalization, and in which cars tend more and more to resemble one another in appearance as well as in performance for a given size, the M.G. Midget two-seater stands unique. Yet an interesting point, as shown by recent public utterances on export subjects as well as by other sources of information, is that this car does not appeal only to the trials-minded and youthful fraternity of motorists in this country. On the contrary, it is gaining more and more of a following in other countries, including the U.S.A., and has reached a position where it can be regarded as one of our more exportable cars in terms of proportion of total output of the model.

Today it is certainly a class alone among cars made anywhere in the world as a sporting type retaining the conventional outward appearance of the " real " car dear to the hearts of enthusiasts in years gone by—that is, by displaying its radiator, or at all events a normal grille, and lamps, and in not having gone " all streamlined." It is a model, too, which more than most cars has evolved through the years, with its beginnings in that much smaller Midget of seventeen years or so ago that instantly registered a success. No car has done so much to maintain open-air

motoring and to support the demand that exists all over the world for sports car performance and characteristics in a car of not exorbitant first cost and at moderate running costs.

It offers a great deal in sheer performance, yet is not just a sports car with an appeal limited to special occasions; instead it is in every way a perfectly practicable car for all occasions where two seats are sufficient and the fresh-air style of progress is preferred. Actually, the all-weather equipment is good, the hood being easily erected and the side screens likewise, and they turn this car into a very reasonable imitation of a permanently closed car for bad weather use.

The Midget is in no way more difficult to drive than the ordinary family saloon, but given the type of driver who usually falls for such a machine—not necessarily a youngster—and who likes to use the gear box, the performance becomes quite vivid. That is not to suggest that the gear box has to be used in the manner of a pump handle whether the driver chooses or not; the 11 h.p.-rated engine that the TC Midget possesses has quite a range of flexibility on top gear, and the car is tractable in traffic. On the other hand, with an engine that will rev very freely without

Autocar ROAD TESTS

complaint much more can be made of the performance, of course, by using indirects that offer maxima as high as 60 m.p.h. on third and 40 on second.

Owing to the handy size of this car, its ability to pass safely where a bigger car would be held back, and the way in which it regains its cruising rate after it has been checked by other traffic, the Midget is almost as fast a car, over British roads, as can be found today. One feels, too, from its ability to take hard treatment and to hold speeds between 60 and 70 m.p.h., apparently for as long as roads in this country permit such motoring, that stretches of motor road offering far more opportunity of sustained speed than ever is found in this island would not "melt" a Midget engine.

The handiness of the car, the way in which it helps the driver in its manner of cornering, its "quick" steering, are big factors in giving it unusual average speed capabilities without an extremely high maximum speed being attained. The present car has been handled over a considerable distance in conditions which provided crowded roads, and also over routes on which traffic had been thinned by seasonal and petrol considerations. In both circumstances the average speeds were exceptional, a 40-miles-in-the-hour showing seeming always to be within its reach on a journey of any length, while, when roads are clear, figures such as 44 and 46 m.p.h. averages have been obtained. When the car was being timed by *The Autocar's* electrical speedometer to be travelling at 75 m.p.h., the car's speedometer showed only 73 an unusual state of affairs. In other more helpful road conditions subsequently the car's speedometer was seen at the 75 mark.

Sense of Accurate Control

Always one has the feeling of being able to make a fast run easily in the Midget, for it responds so readily to all the controls and is so quick—eager, it seems—to get moving. The biggest factor in this and other directions, apart from the actual performance available, is the complete sense of command which the driver feels he has over the car at all times, including the major features of brakes, steering and road holding on corners. The Lockheed brakes deserve special mention, for they deal most effectively with high-speed braking, and also are powerfully smooth in low speed applications.

Merits and demerits of normal versus independent suspension can be argued, in the main to the latter's marked

With a hinged-down-the-centre bonnet and normal wings it is easy to reach the engine, and accessibility of the individual components that require periodical attention is well above the average of presentday standards.

advantage, but there is no doubt of one fact in this connection. The normally sprung car, rather hard sprung, as in this instance, does let the driver gauge within close limits the speeds at which he can corner safely fast. After a little experience of it one finds oneself holding quite high speeds round bends in the Midget, and the car steering to a close course only a foot or two out from the near-side verge. Such a half-elliptic suspension has, of course, the counter-balancing feature that it is on the harsh side over poor surfaces, but on the Midget this tendency is by no means excessive.

It is a trim and appealing little car in its general arrangement and very practically laid out, besides offering a considerably higher accessibility factor than is usual today. One quickly comes to feel an affection for its efficiency and willingness, and in all respects, including performance, it is "man-size," with no suggestion of the tiny car about it.

Driving Position and Controls

Doubly important in a car of this type is the driving position. The Midget is provided with an adjustment for the seat back rest, which is in one piece, although there are two separate cushions, whilst also the spring-spoked steering wheel is telescopically adjustable and can be placed ideally for full power of control. A feature much appreciated or disliked, according to the point of view, is the fly-off type of hand brake lever—in *The Autocar's* view a form of control to be highly commended for its certainty and positiveness of operation. A more comfortable position for the left foot off the clutch pedal would be welcomed.

The gear change has synchromesh on second, third and top, and with a short vertical lever, which is well placed, this works very well for really quick upward and downward changes when the utmost is being made of the performance potential. The instruments include a rev counter, and the engine can be taken round to 5,500 r.p.m. with celerity, and it will readily go beyond that figure.

One does not think of this car in the usual way in terms of top gear climbing ability. Actually, however, the capabilities in this direction are good, for the power-to-weight ratio is favourable, but it is a delight to drop to third and fly over the gradients that bring the speed down at all appreciably on top. As to steeper gradients, second gear lets the car tear up a hill of 1 in 6½ calibre.

The head lamps are good for fast night driving. Starting from cold is immediate, and not much use of the mixture control for the twin S.U. carburettors is needed before the engine will pull properly. An excellent point, of value here, but still more so in territories where filling facilities are widely spaced, is the big petrol tank, giving a range of action of approximately 400 miles.

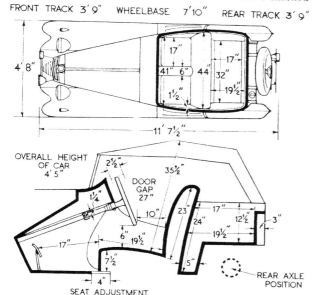

FRONT TRACK 3' 9"   WHEELBASE 7'10"   REAR TRACK 3' 9"

4' 8"

17"

41" 6" 44 32"

17"

19½"

1½"

11' 7½"

OVERALL HEIGHT OF CAR 4' 5"

2½"

35½"

DOOR GAP 27"

1¼"

10"   23"   17"

24"   12½"   3"

6"   19½"

19½"

17"

7½"

5"

4"

SEAT ADJUSTMENT

REAR AXLE POSITION

Measurements are taken with the driving seat at the central position of fore and aft adjustment. These body diagrams are to scale.

Published *The Autocar*, 15 May 1953

No. 1497 : M.G. MIDGET SERIES TD TWO-SEATER

Though the body is wider, nowadays giving ample elbow room for two passengers, the familiar lines of the Midget are preserved. Bumpers with substantial over-riders cater for the relatively large overseas market that the car enjoys.

The Autocar ROAD TESTS

FEW cars, if indeed any, can claim to have fostered enthusiasm for sports cars to the extent that the M.G. Midget has done. In April, 1929, the first of these cars, a Series M Midget, left the M.G. works and started a line of small sports cars which, under various type letters, but always with the suffix Midget, has continued unbroken to the present day. Many different models have made up this succession; some, notably the Montlhéry J4, Q and R types, were out and out racing cars, but their less stark and highly tuned counterparts, too, have been competing in races, rallies and trials ever since.

It is likely that a car with a lineage of this sort should possess qualities in handling and performance that are out of the ordinary; the relatively large market for the current model, the Series TD Midget, in America is evidence of this fact, and the car can claim to have played a fair part in the present rapid growth of enthusiasm for sports cars amongst the American public. That this model has continued virtually unchanged since it was introduced early in 1950, and has lost none of its popularity, is further evidence, if such were needed. It is interesting to try to analyse the points which, collectively, make the TD such fun to drive.

The feel of the car on the road inspires confidence and there is the impression that even an indifferent driver could make a good showing behind the wheel; however long the journey, the actual driving of the car is beguiling all the way. In traffic its small size and good visibility make it very manoeuvrable and the flexibility of the 1¼-litre engine is such that one can trickle along at 10 m.p.h. on top gear, using the lively acceleration on third and second gears to pass through comparatively narrow openings in the traffic. For the daily shopping it could not be more convenient; its small size and good steering lock make parking an easy matter.

The high-geared rack-and-pinion steering is light, accurate and sensitive, and small movements of the wheel produce a quick response. On the open road it is necessary only to hold the wheel very lightly, and long, fast bends are taken more by leaning the body into the corner than by steering round it. A slight tendency to oversteer at the recommended tyre pressures, particularly with a full tank, was cured by increasing the rear pressures to 20 lb. One of the few major departures from the design of the earlier cars lies in the front suspension, which is independent, using coil springs and wishbones; leaf springs are used at the rear, though not of the short, stiff variety on the Midget's forebears. In operation, the suspension is sufficiently stiff to reduce roll on corners to a minimum and it gives a comfortable ride over rough surfaces, though there is a certain amount of vertical motion over roads with undulating bumps.

Speeds up to 65 m.p.h. are reached easily and a cruising speed of 60–65 m.p.h. can be maintained whenever conditions allow. Above these figures, however, the increase is slower and to reach 75 m.p.h. on the slightly flattering speedometer requires a fair length of road. With the windscreen flat and only the driver in the car a true speed of 78 m.p.h. was reached on two occasions on level ground. Without unduly stressing the engine or the driver it is possible to put upwards of 45 miles into the hour in normal road conditions. Main road hills are taken easily on top gear and it is very seldom indeed that it is necessary to drop below third gear for gradient alone. For normal use the top gear ratio of 5.125 to 1 is about right, but for extensive main road driving, particularly on the long straight roads of Europe, one feels that a slightly higher gear would be useful.

The gear box, with synchromesh on second, third and top,

Accessibility at its old-time best. Regular maintenance of the auxiliaries and components of the 1¼-litre engine is encouraged by neat layout. Dipstick, oil filler, oil-bath air cleaner, distributor, sparking plugs, fuel pump, battery and tool boxes are all accessible.

and its short, remote control, central lever, are a joy to use—to such an extent that one tends to use third gear more than one needs. For normal purposes the synchromesh is adequate but, in the conditions of recording the performance tests where full use of the performance was made, it was quite easy to override it. In this connection, too, it was found that, in taking the acceleration figures, when full-throttle gear changes were made there was a tendency for the clutch to spin. In a car of this type which is bound to be used in competitions by many owners, stronger clutch springs would be an advantage; this would be particularly necessary in a car which had been subjected to the stage-by-stage tuning which can be carried out under the guidance of the M.G. company and which was fully detailed, with its results, in *The Autocar* of July 18 and 25, 1952.

The Lockheed hydraulic brakes, with two-leading shoes at the front and leading and trailing shoes at the rear, are amply adequate to the car's performance. Heavy pedal pressures are not required and, as a test, the brakes will stop the car in a straight line from 50 m.p.h. with the driver's hands off the wheel. There was no sign of fade in the arduous conditions of the test, and after extensive use both while taking the performance figures and during many miles of normal motoring, they did not deteriorate nor did the pedal travel increase to any great extent.

Noise Levels

Mechanically, the engine is agreeably quiet and the exhaust note is subdued and pleasant; even on the intermediate gears between high buildings there is no back echo. Inevitably there is a certain amount of wind noise in an open car at high speeds, but this is not worrying and conversation can be maintained without the need to shout; gear noise is confined to a pleasant whine on the intermediates. The engine starts easily from cold and the mixture control is required only for the initial start. It is sensitive to fuel and, on a low-grade diet, it pinks readily. At speeds not exceeding 50 m.p.h. maintained over a long run, the fuel consumption worked out at a little under 30 m.p.g.

The driving position is good and the seats are adjustable —together, not separately, because of the one-piece back rest—to an extent to suit drivers of widely different heights; the steering column, too, is adjustable for individual reach. Space is rather cramped round the pedals and there is barely enough room for the left foot when it is not on the clutch pedal. Both front wings are visible from the driving seat,

Still undisguised, the radiator has changed little since the days of the first series M Midgets; the flat, octagonal filler cap is functional, not just ornamental.

though the left wing view is in line with the driving mirror. The 5in speedometer and revolution counter dials are directly in front of the driver, though it is felt that they could both be moved over to the right, as the higher readings on the speedometer are hidden by the rim of the steering wheel. On a panel in the centre of the facia are grouped the remaining instruments: a combined radiator thermometer and oil pressure gauge, ammeter, horn button, lighting and starter switches, mixture control, rheostatically controlled facia lighting switch, ignition warning light and a green light which warns the driver when the level of fuel in the tank drops below $2\frac{1}{2}$ gallons; a fuel gauge is not fitted. There is an additional switch for a spot lamp if one should be fitted, though such a lamp is not standard. There is a deep cupboard in front of the passenger, though its lid is not lockable; upholstery and interior trim are in leather and the seats are comfortable, well padded, and give ample support to the extent that, after a long drive, no signs of stiffness are felt. The windscreen wiper motor is placed at the top of the fold-flat windscreen, in front of the passenger, and the twin blades clear a wide area of the screen. At high speeds, with the blades in the parked position, and occasionally when they are in operation, the blade on the driving side disappeared above the screen; a stop to prevent this would be valuable.

The weather equipment, once in position, is excellent and free from draughts and rattles, and the side screens are rigid and fit well; soon after raising the hood the interior becomes almost as warm and comfortable as that of a convertible. At high speeds the canvas of the hood vibrates and produces a fair amount of noise, but the side screens remain well

All the attributes of an enthusiast's car: a good driving position with the pleasant, long bonnet stretching away in front of the driver, accessible spare wheel, external slab tank with quick-action filler cap, and adequate luggage space. In closed form the car is proof against the worst weather, and is warm and comfortable.

fitting and they do not flap. The hood and side screens take a fair time to un-stow and erect; against this, however, must be balanced the pleasant thought that, in fine weather, one has the joy of driving along in the sunshine and, given warning of the weather's more obscure moods, one has first-class protection available against them. Adequate luggage space for two large suitcases is provided behind the seats and it is fully protected by the hood.

The double-dip head lights give a good beam which is adequate for any speeds within the car's range; a conveniently placed dip switch lies to the left of the clutch pedal. In general, the finish of the car is first-class and in keeping with the better traditions of British craftsmanship and quality-built British cars. A minor criticism in this connection is that the washers under the chromium-plated screws on the apron in front of the radiator are inadequately plated, if indeed at all, and rust very quickly.

From the point of view of the owner who carries out his own maintenance, the accessibility of the engine and its auxiliaries could not be better. The gear box has a dip-stick which is reached through an inspection cover in the floor above the gear box; the rear axle, too, is easily checked for level and replenished by removing the floor of the luggage compartment.

The Midget is a survival of what, in the opinion of many people, is the right sort of small sports car. It caters for those who look upon motoring not as a means to an end, but as an end in itself. Many thousands of these little cars are succeeding admirably in providing their owners with something that will, at one moment, journey forth and do the shopping and, at the next, take part in serious competitive events or tackle a 400-mile journey with zest; and this at a price which, in modern times, amounts to a very modest outlay.

M.G. MIDGET SERIES TD TWO-SEATER

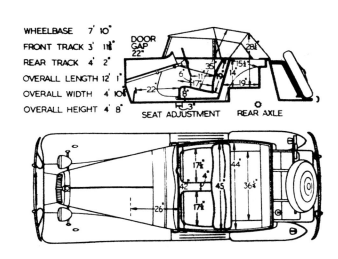

WHEELBASE 7' 10"
FRONT TRACK 3' 11½"
REAR TRACK 4' 2"
OVERALL LENGTH 12' 1"
OVERALL WIDTH 4' 10½"
OVERALL HEIGHT 4' 8"

Measurements in these ¼in to 1ft scale body diagrams are taken with the driving seat in the central position of fore and aft adjustment and with the seat cushions uncompressed.

DATA

PRICE (basic), with open two-seater body, £530.
British purchase tax, £221 19s 2d.
Total (in Great Britain), £751 19s 2d.

ENGINE: Capacity: 1,250 c.c. (76.28 cu in).
Number of cylinders: 4.
Bore and stroke: 66.5 × 90 mm (2.62 × 3.54in).
Valve gear: Overhead; push rods.
Compression ratio: 7.25 to 1.
B.H.P.: 54.4 at 5,200 r.p.m. (B.H.P. per ton laden 50.8).
Torque: 63.5 lb ft at 2,600 r.p.m.
M.P.H. per 1,000 r.p.m. on top gear, 14.5.

WEIGHT (with 5 gals. fuel): 17¾ cwt (1,995 lb).
Weight distribution (per cent) 50.2 F; 49.8 R.
Laden as tested: 21¼ cwt (2,395 lb).
Lb per c.c. (laden): 1.9.

BRAKES: Type: F, Two-leading shoe. R, Leading and trailing.
Method of operation: F, Hydraulic. R, Hydraulic.
Drum dimensions: F, 9in diameter, 1.5in wide. R, 9in diameter, 1.5in wide.
Lining area: F, 52.5 sq in. R, 52.5 sq in (98.1 sq in per ton laden).

TYRES: 5.50—15in.
Pressures (lb per sq in): F, 18. R, 18 (normal).

TANK CAPACITY: 12¼ Imperial gallons.
Oil sump, 10½ pints.
Cooling system, 12 pints.

TURNING CIRCLE: 31ft 3in (L and R).
Steering wheel turns (lock to lock): 2¾.

DIMENSIONS: Wheelbase, 7ft 10in.
Track: 3ft 11½in (F); 4ft 2in (R).
Length (overall): 12ft 1in.
Height: 4ft 8in.
Width: 4ft 10½in.
Ground clearance: 6in.
Frontal area: 16.6 sq ft (approx), with hood erected. 13.0 sq ft (approx), with hood and windscreen down.

ELECTRICAL SYSTEM: 12-volt; 51-ampere-hour battery.
Head lights: Double dip, 42–36 watt.

SUSPENSION: Front, Independent; coil springs and wishbones.
Rear, Half-elliptic springs.

PERFORMANCE

ACCELERATION: from constant speeds.
Speed, Gear Ratios and time in sec.

M.P.H.	5.125 to 1	7.098 to 1	10.609 to 1	17.938 to 1
10—30	11.7	8.6	6.1	—
20—40	12.4	8.9	—	—
30—50	12.6	9.8	—	—
40—60	15.1	—	—	—
50—70	22.6	—	—	—

From rest through gears to:

M.P.H.	sec
30	6.3
50	15.6
60	23.9
70	39.6

Standing quarter mile, 23.4 sec.

SPEED ON GEARS

Gear		M.P.H. (normal and max.)	K.P.H. (normal and max.)
Top	(mean)	73.5	118.3
	(best)	75	120.7
3rd		48—59	77—95
2nd		30—38	48—61
1st		16—20	26—32

TRACTIVE RESISTANCE: 26 lb per ton at 10 M.P.H.

TRACTIVE EFFORT:

	Pull (lb per ton)	Equivalent Gradient
Top	179	1 in 12.5
Third	257	1 in 8.5
Second	390	1 in 5.6

BRAKES:

Efficiency	Pedal Pressure (lb)
96 per cent	130
78 per cent	95
35 per cent	53

FUEL CONSUMPTION:
25 m.p.g. overall for 320 miles (11.3 litres per 100 km).
Approximate normal range 23–29 m.p.g. (12.3–9.7 litres per 100 km).
Fuel, First grade.

WEATHER: Dry surface, light wind.
Air temperature 55 degrees F.
Acceleration figures are the means of several runs in opposite directions.
Tractive effort and resistance obtained by Tapley meter.
Model described in *The Autocar* of January 20, 1950.

SPEEDOMETER CORRECTION: M.P.H.

Car speedometer	10	20	30	40	50	60	70	80
True speed	10.5	19.8	29	38	48	57.5	67	77.5

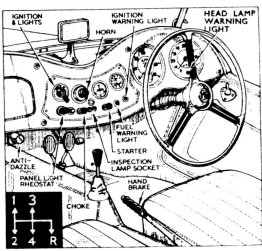

LOWERED BODY LINE FOR MIDGET

THE M.G. Midget is a car that, probably, has changed less in outward appearance than any other model over the same period of time, and it is this feature that makes the car contrast so sharply with the production models of overseas countries such as the United States of America, where the Midget is particularly popular. By these remarks it is not meant to imply that design has remained static since the first M.G. Midget was produced very many years ago; nothing could be further from the truth. Over the years, the model has been developed to improve its performance, handling qualities and general comfort. However, in spite of this, the main external features have remained more or less unchanged and even now the recently introduced TF model shows that the bodywork has been restyled to produce a much cleaner external appearance though retaining the M.G. Midget characteristics.

In detail, the centre of the scuttle has been lowered slightly, while the radiator grille height has been reduced by over 3½in, so that the bonnet now has a marked forward slope. The front wings have also been re-styled and the head lamps are faired into the main wing pressings, instead of being bolted to the wing stay as on previous models. The general style of the rear end has also received attention. Modifications have been made to the fuel tank and spare wheel mounting to help to tidy up the overall appearance.

The overall height is reduced by 1½in and this should help to reduce the wind resistance and further to improve the performance of the new TF.

Although no major modifications have been made to the basic design of the mechanical components, a number of modifications have been made to the engine which is, in effect, now similar to stage 2 of the makers' tuning recommendations for TD Midgets. It will be remembered that the results of stage-by-stage tuning were tested by *The Autocar* and described in the issues of July 18 and July 25, 1952, together with performance figures.

The modifications to the engine include raising the compression ratio to 8 to 1, fitting larger valves and stronger valve springs, and using 1½in diameter twin S.U. carburettors. The reduction in radiator grille height has also reduced the height of the radiator core and, to prevent any possibility of overheating, the core thickness has been increased.

In keeping with the external alterations, the cockpit layout has also been modified, and in place of a one-piece back rest, two adjustable seats are now fitted. The facia panel has been completely redesigned to provide two useful lockers, one on each side of the central instrument panel, and the top of the swept scuttle is padded with leather-covered rubber. The previously screen-mounted windscreen wiper motor has been replaced by a cable-rack unit with the motor housed in the engine compartment. The wipers can be individually parked by means of knobs in the glove lockers. Other items of equipment include a map reading light and flashing direction indicators. The car is supplied with steel disc wheels as standard, although centre lock wire wheels can be supplied at extra cost. Other optional extras include a badge bar, fog lamp and luggage carrier.

M.G. T.F. MIDGET

SPECIFICATION:

Engine.—4 cyl, 66.5 × 90mm (1,250 c.c.). Compression ratio 8 to 1. 57 b.h.p. at 5,500 r.p.m. Maximum torque 65 lb ft at 3,000 r.p.m. Three-bearing crankshaft. Inverted "bath tub" combustion chambers. Overhead valves operated by push rods and rockers. Single side camshaft.

Clutch.—8in diameter dry single plate. Six springs. Mechanical withdrawal mechanism.

Gear Box.—Overall ratios: top 4.875; third 6.752; second 10.09; first 17.06 ; reverse 17.06 to 1.

Final Drive.—Hypoid axle (8:39). Ratio 4.875 to 1. Two-pinion differential.

Suspension. — Front: independent, coil springs and wishbones. Rear: half-elliptic. Suspension rate (at the wheel): front, 74 lb per in; rear, 139 lb per in. Static deflection: front, 6.45in; rear 3.4in.

Brakes.—Front: hydraulically operated two-leading shoe. Rear: leading and trailing shoe. Drums: front, 9in diameter, 1½in wide; rear, 9in diameter, 1½in wide. Total lining area: 105 sq in (52.5 sq in front).

Steering.—Rack and pinion.

Wheels and Tyres.—4.00—15in tyres on 4—15in rims. Steel disc wheels (centre lock wire wheels, optional extra).

Electrical Equipment.—12-volt; 51 ampère-hour battery. Head lamps, 42-36 watt bulbs.

Fuel System.—12-gallon tank. Engine sump oil capacity 10½ pints.

Main Dimensions.—Wheelbase 7ft 10in. Track (with disc wheels): front, 3ft 11⅞in; rear, 4ft 2 in; (with centre lock wire wheels): front, 4ft 0$\frac{3}{16}$in; rear, 4ft 2$\frac{13}{16}$in. Overall length 12ft 3in. Width 4ft 11in. Height 4ft 6½in. Ground clearance 6in. Frontal area 16.1 sq ft approximately (hood up). Turning circle 31ft 3in. Weight (with ½-gallon fuel) 17¼ cwt. Weight distribution: 51.4 per cent front; 48.6 per cent rear. Basic price £550, plus British purchase tax £230 5s 10d. Total £780 5s 10d.

The latest M.G. Midget, with lowered radiator and built-in head lamps.

Ready for Le Mans III

BACK IN CIRCULATION

An example of the 1934 Magnette in the racing trim of that era

The classical grille and emblem have been skilfully blended into the new body form

IT is indeed good to contemplate the return of the M.G. Car Company to competitive racing and to look forward once more to seeing the magic octagonal emblem on the circuits. The reappearance is to be at Le Mans, on the same circuit as a works-sponsored team last raced just 20 years ago. On that occasion in 1935, the team (all women—Miss Joan Richmond and Mrs. G. Simpson, Miss Doreen Evans and Miss Barbara Skinner, Miss Margaret Allan and Mrs. C. Eaton) drove strictly to schedule, finishing 24th, 25th and 26th respectively in classification and qualifying for the Biennial Cup. Alas, the firm's decision soon afterwards to retire from racing meant that this qualification was not to be taken up in the following year.

The name of M.G. has been associated with sports car racing since 1923 when Cecil Kimber, at that time general manager of Morris Garages, prepared a very special version of the then current Morris-Oxford. Taking an 11.9 h.p. Hotchkiss engine from the production Morris Cowley, he converted this standard side-valve unit to o.h.v. with push-rod operation, and as a result of careful building and preparation, the car put up a most creditable performance.

In 1928 the M.G. fortunes were really founded with the introduction of what has become perhaps the most famous sports car of all, the M.G. Midget. It was constructed almost entirely from Morris Minor components and set the standard for small sports cars over many years, giving a high performance with reliability and low upkeep costs. During its development over the years its competition successes were legion, though perhaps the most outstanding lay in the performance of record-breaking cars for

Goldie Gardner and for George Eyston.

In classes F and G, M.G.s registered speeds of 204 and 203 m.p.h. respectively for the flying kilometre as long ago as 1939. The culminating model, EX179, built for George Eyston, last year set up a new 10-mile record in class F (1,100 to 1,500 c.c.) at Utah, U.S.A., when it achieved 153 m.p.h.

Throughout its history, the policy of the M.G. company has been to compete with cars developed from their standard production models, and the 1955 Le Mans car, designated EX182, is a further example of this policy.

The car has been built to provide information for a production version. Thus the general design, materials, and method of construction could be reproduced in quantity and the resultant

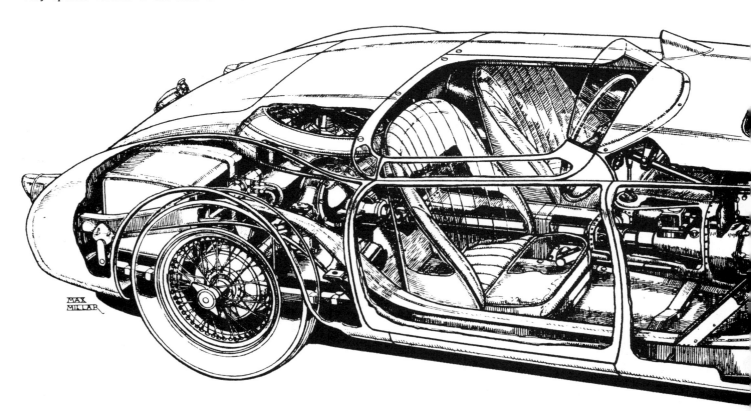

The box section frame is noteworthy for the method used to transfer front suspension loads to the deep scuttle cross-member. There is a considerable increase in the section of the frame where it diverts from a straight line. The driver and passenger seats are placed each side of the central tunnel between the frame side members

1½-litre M.G. will carry the famous name round the Sarthe Circuit

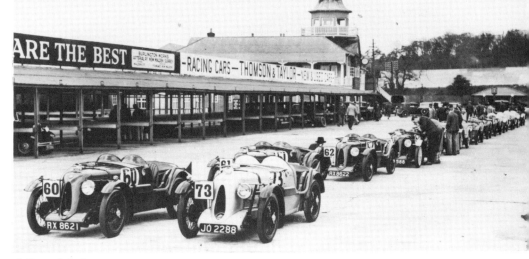

A fleet of M.G.s arrives at Brooklands in pre-war racing days

vehicle would sell at a reasonable price. Responsible for the design and development is Sidney Enever, M.G.'s chief engineer, who has grown up with the company since his schooldays. Having learned the hard lessons as a racing mechanic in earlier days, his thorough practical knowledge and experience on such a project must be invaluable.

The four-cylinder o.h.v. engine, with a bore of 73.025 mm and stroke of 89 mm, has a three-bearing crankshaft and is basically the B.M.C. B-type unit, but the white metal bearings of the connecting rods and big-ends have been replaced by the lead-bronze types necessary for the higher speeds and loads imposed. The compression ratio has been raised to 9.4 to 1, and the speed range extended upwards by approximately 40 per cent.

Although the cylinder head retains the same basic shape of combustion chamber, it is new, and the valves are of larger diameter. Improvements to the gas flow have been undertaken by the Weslake company, and a certain amount of scooping out of the combustion chamber around the valves is evident. The inlet ports are siamesed. Balance between the

cylinders is provided by extending the inlet ports through to the sparking plug side of the head, and connecting with an external fabricated pipe. This is claimed to give much better results under part-throttle conditions than the more normal pipe between the induction stubs. It also opens up all sorts of possibilities for multi-carburettor arrangements if required.

The basic B-type engine was designed as a very short unit in the production version and the connecting-rod bearings are, therefore, offset from the cylinder centre line. The lands between the cylinder bores are rather narrow and there is no water space between the exhaust valves. To reduce the possibility of gasket troubles with the increase in compression ratio and, therefore, cylinder pressures, the cylinder head gasket has been eliminated and the mating faces of the head and block scraped and lapped;

this method has proved very satisfactory during extended bench tests.

Twin 1¾in diameter S.U. carburettors of semi-downdraught type are fitted. Valve lifts and opening periods have been increased and, in its present form, the engine delivers 82.5 b.h.p. at 6,000 r.p.m., with a peak brake mean effective pressure of 142 lb per sq in at 4,500 r.p.m.

Fuel is fed by twin S.U. high-pressure fuel pumps to the carburettors from the 20-gallon tank, which is mounted at the rear between the chassis side members. The pumps are located on a rear cross member. The full-flow oil filter has been removed from the engine and is placed on the chassis, just behind the oil cooler in the nose of the car.

Close Ratio Gears

The B.M.C. B-type gear box and combined clutch housing is mounted to the cylinder block at the rear engine plate, and the drive is through an 8in single dry-plate Borg and Beck clutch. Special close-ratio gears are fitted, having synchromesh on fourth, third and second. The ratios are: top direct, third 1.268, second 1.62, and first 2.45 to 1. A centrally mounted, remote gear change linkage extends rearwards from the main box with a short vertical shift lever.

From the extended tail bearing of the gear box, a Hardy Spicer double universal shaft carries the drive to the orthodox, three-quarter floating hypoid rear axle. Again, this is a standard production B-type unit which has been provided with a special crown wheel and pinion to give the ratio of 3.7 to 1.

Half-elliptic rear springs are used, and the axle movements are damped by Armstrong piston-type dampers bolted to the inside of the chassis frame and connected with the normal arm and drop link. Rubber bump stops are fixed to the underside of the swept-up frame side members, and rebound is checked by canvas web straps anchored between the frame and spring-mounting saddle.

The front suspension assembly is standard, as used in the TD and TF models, and consists of unequal length wishbones and coil springs. Short upper wishbones are attached at their inner ends to the operating shafts of the Armstrong piston-type spring dampers. Manufactured as two identical forgings, the wishbone arms are linked by two bolts running fore and aft, the outer one passing through the upper king pin post. The lower wishbone is a three-piece steel pressing, the channel-section arms being identical. They are bridged by, and bolted to, a central section which also forms the lower abutment of the helical coil spring. The upper abutment for the

Autocar
COPYRIGHT

The new shape departs completely from traditional M.G. lines and its contours are a clever compromise between design for aerodynamics and eventual production

Developed from standard production units produced in large quantity, the engine is fitted with a modified cylinder head and twin carburettors. The obverse balance pipe for the induction system is apparent. Special close ratio gears are fitted in the otherwise standard production gear box

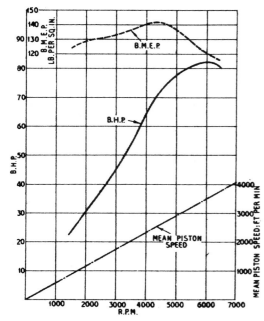

With modifications to the induction side of the engine and increased compression ratio, a peak power of 82 b.h.p. has been achieved

spring is the top-hat section of the frame, to which is also bolted the conical rubber bump stop.

Steering is by pinion and rack which extends across the full width of the frame. It is connected to the wheels by a short shaft at each side, through a forward-facing steering arm forged in steel and bolted to the stub axle. A single universal joint is placed in the shaft connecting the rack and pinion assembly to the steering wheel. Two bearings are provided in the steering column, one at the main bulkhead and one from a pendant bracket behind the instrument panel.

The box section frame sweeps upwards over the rear axle. Each side member consists of two channel sections with turned-out flanges, placed together and welded throughout the length at its mid-section. This frame is a direct development of the one used in the record-breaking EX179, and an outstanding feature is the method of bracing the main scuttle section with box-section struts to the side members. In this manner the front suspension anchorages are made extremely stiff, with little likelihood of deflection. Six cross-members are provided, the front one being very deep in section and of top-hat form. Arc welded

joints are used throughout the structure.

Although the chassis frame must be adjudged rather heavy, it will undoubtedly stand up to the very hard work it will be called upon to do in trials and competitions. Furthermore, it permits the use of very light bodywork, since the body is not relied upon for stiffness.

Hydraulic Brakes

Lockheed hydraulic brakes are fitted, having an effective size of 10in diameter by 1¾in wide. At the front they are of two-leading shoe construction, while at the rear, leading and trailing shoes are used. Operation is by a pendant pedal mounted on the scuttle and connected to the master cylinder by a short operating rod. This unit also contains the master cylinder for clutch operation, connected to a similar pedal placed alongside on a common bracket. With a car dry weight of 14½cwt and cast iron drums, the brakes appear small for a race such as Le Mans, and an increase in diameter could be very beneficial.

The body is a complete departure from previous M.G. practice and can be described as fully enveloping, with extremely beautiful lines. Constructed of

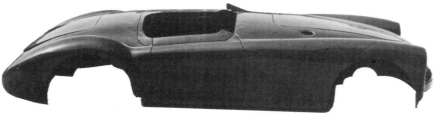

The chassis frame has been designed with ample inherent stiffness in order to provide a self-contained body of low weight. The box section frame permits the use of normal opening doors

A view from underneath the chassis reveals the chassis-mounted oil filter and flexible pipes connecting to the oil radiator

18-gauge aluminium alloy, the panels are secured to the body framework by countersunk rivets. The orthodox type of chassis frame permits normal opening doors, hinged at their forward ends, and the bucket-type seats are situated low down in the section formed between the propeller-shaft tunnel and frame side-members. A sheet metal tonneau cover is fastened with Dzus fasteners over the passenger seat to reduce wind drag.

Among The Classics

A lift-up type bonnet, hinged at the scuttle end, provides access to the top of the engine compartment. The film block type of radiator is mounted vertically on the front cross-member and the oil cooler is situated much farther forward, low down in the nose with a separate air entry. In days gone by the radiator was the pride of many car owners, and the M.G. design was certainly among the classics. The designers are to be congratulated on providing an extremely attractive grille, retaining the classical M.G. appearance, yet blending so well into the streamline form.

The underside of the car is covered completely with a light alloy pan, and low drag figures are claimed for the models which have been air-tunnel tested. At the rear, the spare wheel is mounted horizontally above the rear axle and attached by a dummy hub to a chassis cross-member. Access to the spare wheel is gained through a hinged lid in the tail. A quick-action filler of Monza type protrudes through the rear panel.

Dunlop centre-lock wire wheels of Rudge pattern have light alloy rims. At the front, 5.50-15in tyres are fitted and at the rear 6.00-15in. A 12-volt positive-earth electrical system is fed by a lightweight 37 ampère-hour battery, mounted at the rear.

Prime Object

This, then, is the vehicle which will hail the return of the M.G. company to the competitive field, and the lessons learned undoubtedly will have great influence on the type of car marketed for the public in the future. It is obvious that no attempt has been made to produce a car intended to win its class regardless of cost, and with little resemblance to a normal road vehicle. This year the qualifying speed in the 1½-litre class is a little under 80 m.p.h., and the prime object of the company is that the cars should finish at this speed.

Two entries have been accepted for this year's Le Mans race, the cars to be driven by R. W. Jacobs and J. J. Flynn, and Ken Miles and J. Lockett. A third car has been nominated in the reserve list, and at present stands fourth in that classification, with a good chance of completing a triple entry should there be withdrawals between now and June 11.

This transverse section through the cylinder head shows how the siamesed induction ports are extended to the sparking plug side for fitting an external balance pipe.

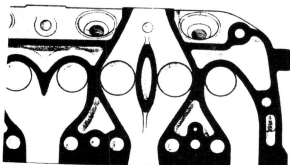

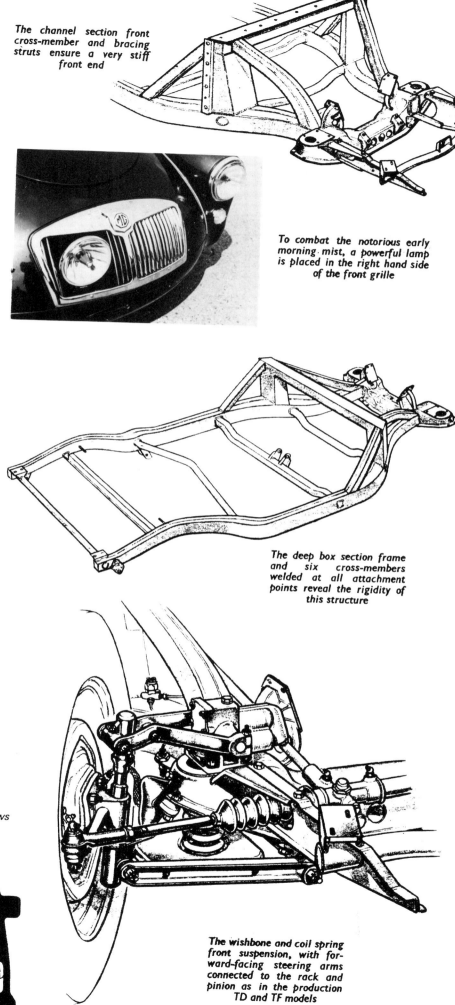

The channel section front cross-member and bracing struts ensure a very stiff front end

To combat the notorious early morning mist, a powerful lamp is placed in the right hand side of the front grille

The deep box section frame and six cross-members welded at all attachment points reveal the rigidity of this structure

The wishbone and coil spring front suspension, with forward-facing steering arms connected to the rack and pinion as in the production TD and TF models

BACK IN CIRCULATION . . .
. . . . continued

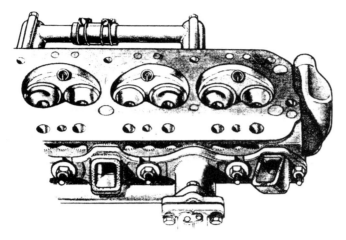

An inverted view of the cylinder head with the heart-shaped combustion chamber resulting from the work carried out by Weslake and Co.

LE MANS M.G. SPECIFICATION

Engine.—4 cyl, bore 73.025 mm, stroke 89 mm (1,489 c.c.). Compression ratio 9.4 to 1. Three-bearing crankshaft, lead indium bearings. 82.5 b.h.p. at 6,000 r.p.m. Maximum b.m.e.p., 142 lb per sq in at 4,500 r.p.m. Heart-shaped combustion chamber with vertical valves operated by rockers and push rods from single side camshaft.

Transmission.—Dry single plate 8in dia. Ball type clutch withdrawal race. Gear box, four forward speeds and reverse, with synchomesh on second, third and top. Remote control gear change. Hypoid rear axle with bevel gear-type differential. Overall gear ratios (with 3.7 axle ratio), top, 3.7; third 4.712; second 5.994; first 9.065 to 1. 21 m.p.h. per 1,000 r.p.m. of engine, with 6.00-15in rear tyres, in top gear.

Suspension.—Front, independent, wish-bones and coil spring, piston-type dampers. Rear, half-elliptic leaf springs, piston-type dampers.

Brakes.—Lockheed hydraulic, two-leading shoe front, leading and trailing shoe rear. Drums 10in diameter by 1¾in wide.

Steering.—Rack and pinion.

Wheels and Tyres.—Dunlop wire wheels with light alloy rims. Rudge type hubs. Tyre sizes, front 5.50-15in; rear, 6.00-15in.

Electrical Equipment.—12-volt positive earth; 37 ampere-hour battery.

Fuel System.—20 gallon tank. Twin high pressure S.U. electric feed pump.

Main Dimensions.—Wheelbase, 7ft 10in. Track, front 3ft 11⅞in, rear 4ft 0¾in. Overall length, 12ft 6in. Height, 3ft 5in (excluding screen). Ground clearance, 6in. Dry weight, 14¼ cwt (1,596 lb).

SAFETY—FASTER STILL!

ROAD IMPRESSIONS OF THE 1½-LITRE LE MANS M.G.—EX. 182

IT is not often that the opportunity arises to put a prototype car through its paces, but *The Autocar* was recently given such a chance when car No. 64 in the Le Mans programme was placed at its disposal by the M.G. company. This car finished 17th in general classification, after suffering damage to the left side front bodywork as a result of a bump during the seventeenth hour of the race. A full technical description was given in *The Autocar* of 3 June, 1955.

When the car was collected from Abingdon it bore no trace of its 24-hour ordeal, and one could again admire the graceful lines of the body. It is also obvious that grace has been allied to efficiency in view of the 119.5 m.p.h. achieved along the timed kilometre of the Mulsanne straight.

Since its debut at Le Mans, the car had been prepared for participation in the Alpine Rally as a further stage in its development for a new production version. It was in this form that the car was tested, and several changes had taken place. The 3.7 to 1 axle had been replaced by a lower one of 4.3 to 1 ratio, and a standard Magnette gear box was fitted, having ratios of top 1; third 1.374; second 2.214; and first 3.64 to 1.

The single, small Perspex windscreen had been replaced by a metal framed one of full width, equipped with twin wipers. Also discarded was the metal cover over the passenger's seat, and a fabric one was provided in the equipment but not used during the tests. The powerful fog lamp had been removed, enabling the radiator grille to be completed on the right-hand side. A hood, folding away behind the rear seats, had been added to complete the touring equipment.

There is a quite extraordinary feeling of comfort and safety with ample covered-in elbow-room in taking up station in the driving seat. Positive location is provided by the bucket seats, with the squab having the right degree of flexibility for comfort yet able to follow the contours of the human frame and support the lumbar regions—most important if long journeys are to be achieved without fatigue. Similarly the seat has sufficient fore and aft depth, with a roll over form at the front edge to give support to the distal end of the thigh.

Even for a person of more than average height, the top rail of the windscreen does not impair vision. There is ample room for the feet around the pedals, although these could be repositioned with advantage. On this particular

The view from the rear is as graceful as that from the front. A neat feature of the windscreen is a combined grab handle and stiffening member at each corner

from the wheel. This adds to the sense of control one has in the driving seat, although the steering wheel is rather close to the knees. It could well be raised—and without impairing vision over the wheel rim.

A short, stiff change-speed lever is ideally placed, and it is easy to move it from third to top for a leisurely change with the fingers doing the work and thumb around the steering wheel. During a fast change the synchromesh could be beaten into top gear, and the change down from third to second was stiff, but this could have been owing to the fitting of the new gearbox.

For optimum performance on a production version the gear ratios appear to be a little wide, particularly between second and third. With a three-quarter full tank and two people on board it is possible to spin the wheels in the get-away on a dry road; similarly in changing from first to second the tyres will tweak with a rapid change, which indicates that the indirect gearbox ratios could be raised and closed with advantage. An examination of the chart show-

Developed from the B.M.C. B-Series unit, the four-cylinder engine is fitted with two semi-down-draught S.U. carburettors with flared inlet pipes to assist ram, and develops 82.5 b.h.p. at 6,000 r.p.m. with a 9.4 to 1 compression ratio and premium fuel

The EX 182 M.G. provides ample space in the driving compartment and engine heat escapes through the louvres near the windscreen

With the hood erected there is no sense of feeling cramped inside the car; externally it harmonizes well with the general body lines

car the pendant type pedals had been lengthened, and there was a tendency for the brake pedal particularly to escape the toe of one's shoe at full travel, unless the foot was lifted and placed high on the pedal at the outset.

The driving position has been improved compared with that of previous M.G. models, the driver now sitting farther

The bonnet opens at its forward edge, where there are two straps to supplement the interior catch. The driving lamp used at Le Mans has been removed and the grille completed

ing the engine r.p.m. set against road speed, with the torque curve superimposed, makes it plain that a normal upward gear-change drops the engine speed to a point where the torque is still rising. This indicates that there is plenty of acceleration in the higher engine speed range which is one of the outstanding features of the car.

All performance figures taken were with a passenger aboard, the hood down and approximately sixteen gallons of fuel in the tank. Under these far from ideal conditions a maximum speed of 103 m.p.h. was recorded on the clock, which against calibration was extremely accurate above 40 m.p.h.; this corresponds to approximately 5,720 engine r.p.m. on the 4.3 axle. Similarly the standing starts were 0–40 m.p.h. 6.2sec, 0–60 m.p.h. 13.8sec, and 0–80 m.p.h. 25.8sec.

The suspension and road holding are of a very high order. As the car was still fitted with the additional friction dampers used at Le Mans, the ride was fairly harsh over cobbled streets at low speeds. But as the speed rises the suspension is remarkable—pleasantly firm but very comfortable—and there is a complete absence of any tendency to roll.

Two factors would seem to contribute to this—first, the low centre of gravity and consequently the smaller roll moment at the front end, and secondly, the mean track is 4ft, which is wide for such a size of car, but has undoubtedly contributed much to the superb handling.

The directness and accuracy of the steering enable the car to be placed exactly as desired. Such technical terms as oversteer and understeer appear to have no place in its handling, as it seems to corner without conscious movement of the steering wheel. The steering wheel has 2⅓ turns from lock to lock, combined with a low turning circle of 28ft, which makes for very good manœuvrability in congested towns, particularly as the steering is still light at very low speeds.

On a journey from Coventry to Bourne in Lincolnshire taking the road through Lutterworth, Market Harborough, Corby and Stamford, it was possible to complete the journey of 67 miles in 1 hour 14 minutes, which represents a little over 53 miles in the hour. Although there was not a lot of traffic on the road, there are very few straights where speeds much over 80 m.p.h. could be achieved. Under such conditions of short straights and frequent fast, sweeping bends the car was in its element.

The Lockheed brakes were superb and entirely free from fade, when driven over a particularly arduous route during the afternoon heat of the recent hot spell.

Fuel consumption worked out at 23.8 m.p.g. over a period in which the car was driven hard, and which included the maximum speed and acceleration tests. Under more normal driving conditions it would appear that something around 28 m.p.g. would be a reasonable figure to expect.

At no time did the water temperature rise above 160 deg F (71 deg C) on the open road and, in traffic, the highest recorded was 182 deg F (83 deg C). The car is flexible in town use, and there were no adverse indications of the high compression ratio (9.2 to 1) except a tendency to run on slightly when the engine was switched off after a hard run.

Despite the provision of a fresh air intake to the cockpit from the nose of the car, the heat to the driver and passenger was rather excessive. It must be remembered, however, that this was a prototype car without any sort of insulation, and undoubtedly this matter will receive the necessary attention before a production version appears.

With empty fuel tank but containing the full quantity of oil and water and including touring equipment and tools, the car weighed 16 cwt and 25 lb. Weight distribution was 54.5 per cent front and 45.5 per cent rear under these conditions; with the full twenty gallons of fuel aboard this became almost exactly 50 per cent at each end.

When the car was parked in Leamington during the recent *concours d'élégance* of the V.C.C. Rally, it created enormous interest among competitors and spectators. It seems quite evident that the production version is eagerly awaited.

If the engine can be offered without too much detuning, and the weight kept down to around present level, this delightful car will be a serious contender in the small high performance class, and should have a ready sale in home and overseas markets. Some thought will need to be given to luggage space, but a reduction in tank capacity and a slight closing up of the exceptional length of leg room could accommodate this.

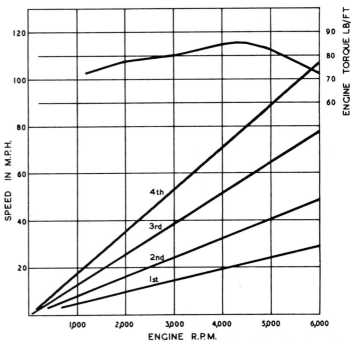

The speeds available in the various gears with the 4.3 to 1 axle ratio are in accordance with this chart. The torque curve peaking at approximately 4,500 r.p.m. explains the good acceleration in the higher engine speed range

The panel layout was dull though thoroughly functional as a prototype for Le Mans, but could be restyled with advantage, particularly with the export market in view.

BRIEF SPECIFICATION

Engine.—4 cyl, 73.025 mm bore, 89 mm stroke (1,489 c.c.) Compression ratio 9.4 to 1. Overhead valves operated by pushrods and rockers. 82.5 b.h.p. at 6,000 r.p.m.

Transmission.—Borg and Beck 8in dia dry single plate clutch. Four-speed gear box with synchromesh on all but first gear. Central remote gear change. Hypoid rear axle (4.3 to 1). Overall ratios: top 4.3; third 5.908; second 9.520; first 15.652 to 1.

Chassis.—Box section frame. Independent front suspension with wishbones and coil springs. Rack and pinion steering. Live rear axle with half-elliptic springs. Racing type wire wheels with light-alloy rims fitted 5.50 × 15in racing tyres.

Brakes.—Lockheed hydraulic 10in diameter 1¾in wide. Two leading shoes front, leading and trailing shoe rear. Central fly-off handbrake.

Main Dimensions.—Weight without fuel but with oil, water, spare wheel, hood and tools, 16 cwt 25 lb. Wheelbase, 7ft 10in; front track, 3ft 11⅞in; rear track, 4ft 0¾in. Overall length, 12ft 6in; overall width, 4ft 10in; height with hood raised, 4ft 2in; ground clearance, 6in.

Seen in company with a Magnette saloon, the grille of the Le Mans model shows how the classical M.G. radiator shape has been restyled and blended into the streamlined form

Strong bumpers follow the contours of the new M.G.'s front and rear wings and radiator. The curved windscreen can be replaced by a shallow screen for competitions

M.G.—*The Breed Improved*

NEW MODEL A PROFITS BY RACING EXPERIENCE

WHEN the M.G. Car Company announced its participation in the Le Mans 24-hour race, after a lapse of 20 years, the three cars entered were acknowledged to be prototypes for a possible new production car. Two cars out of three finished (one crashed), and came 12th and 17th in the classification on distance covered; the totals during the 24 hours were 2,084 and 1,961 miles respectively. Nobody will deny that this performance of the model, after the company's long absence from racing, was impressive.

From these Le Mans cars, known as the type EX 182 (a full description of which was given in *The Autocar* of June 3), has been developed the production series M.G. A. It is apparent that the experiment of Le Mans was considered successful, as the car shows no basic changes from those cars which took part in the race, but detail modifications have been made for normal road use.

Equipped with the 4.3 to 1 axle ratio, the car is capable of nearly 100 m.p.h. in touring trim with hood and sidescreens erected. At the moderate price of £884 0s 10d, including purchase tax, it becomes a serious challenger in the 1½-litre sports car class. Its appearance, with its wind-cheating body, is a complete departure from the shape of previous models from the Abingdon factory.

The four-cylinder engine is basically the B.M.C. B-Series unit, as used in the Magnette saloon. It is equipped with two semi-downdraught 1½in S.U. carburettors and the compression ratio has been raised to 8.3 to 1, with a peak output of 68 b.h.p. at 5,500 r.p.m. Maximum torque is produced at 3,500 r.p.m., at which speed the b.m.e.p. is 128.8 lb per square inch.

Siamesed inlet ports are used and the short induction manifold for the two carburettors is bolted direct to the face where these merge into a common bore; a balance pipe connects these two short induction stubs. This is different from the Le Mans cars, wherein the induction ports were connected through to the opposite side of the head and an external balance pipe was used on the other side from the manifold. Presumably this extra complication did not give a worthwhile improvement in power output on the production version.

The overhead-valve engine, with a bore of 73.025 mm and stroke of 89 mm (1,489 c.c.), has a sturdy three-bearing crankshaft which runs in white metal thin wall bearings, this type also being used for the big-ends. A heart-shaped combustion chamber is used in conjunction with in-line vertical valves operated by rockers and push rods from the side-mounted camshaft. This is driven from the front end of the crankshaft by a duplex roller chain. Lubricant is supplied by an eccentric rotor pump driven by the camshaft and this feeds the oil through a full-flow filter to the main oil gallery, from which the drillings to the main bearings are taken.

Each carburettor is fitted with a wetted gauze-type circular air filter and cool air is ducted to these from a large-bore flexible pipe with its entry placed to the left-hand side of the front grille. A high-pressure S.U. electric fuel pump is mounted on a chassis cross-member behind the driving seat and draws fuel from the 10-gallon tank. The tank, which has an external filler, is placed below the floor of the luggage locker between the chassis frame members.

From the engine the drive is taken through an 8in Borg and Beck single dry plate clutch with six pressure springs and hydraulic withdrawal mechanism.

SPECIFICATION

Engine.—Capacity: 1,489 c.c. (90.88 cu in). Number of cylinders: 4. Bore and stroke: 73.025 × 89 mm (2.875 × 3.5in). Valve gear: overhead, push rods and rockers. Compression ratio: 8.3 to 1. B.H.P.: 68 at 5,500 r.p.m. Torque: 77.4 lb ft at 3,500 r.p.m. Max. b.m.e.p.: 128.8 lb per sq in at 3,500 r.p.m. Speed on top gear at 1,000 r.p.m. with 4.3 rear axle ratio, 17.0 m.p.h.

Clutch.—Borg and Beck, 8in single dry plate.

Transmission.—Overall ratios, top 4.3, third 5.908, second 9.520, first 15.652, reverse 20.468 to 1. Synchromesh on second, third and top.

Rear Axle.—Three-quarter floating with hypoid drive. Standard ratio 4.3 to 1 (4.55 to 1 ratio available if required).

Brakes.—Lockheed hydraulic. Front, two-leading shoe; rear, leading and trailing. Drum dimensions: F, 10in dia., 1¾in wide. R, 10in dia., 1¼in wide.

Tyre Size.—5.60-15in on disc wheels. Pressures, front, 17 lb per sq in; rear, 20 lb per sq in.

Steering Gear.—Cam Gears. Rack and pinion. Turning circle L and R, 28ft.

Electrical System.—12-volt by two 6-volt batteries. 51-ampère-hour capacity.

Tank Capacity.—10 Imperial gallons. Oil sump, 6½ pints. Cooling system, 10 pints.

Dimensions.—Wheelbase: 7ft 10in. Track: F, 3ft 11½in; R, 4ft 0¾in. Length (overall): 13ft. Height: 4ft 2in with hood raised. Width: 4ft 10in. Ground clearance: 6in. Frontal area (hood raised): 13.77 sq ft (approx). Weight, depending upon extras fitted, 1,900 to 2,000 lb.

Price (Basic).—With two-seater body, £595. U.K. purchase tax: £249 0s 10d. Total price in U.K.: £844 0s 10d.

Optional Extras.—Provision has been made for fitting H.M.V. car radio. Wire wheels are available as an extra if specified with order. Other optional extras are heater, white wall tyres, 4.55 to 1 axle gears, twin horns, external luggage carrier, fog lamp, overall tonneau cover, radiator blind, chromium-plated wheel rim embellishers and telescopic steering column.

M.G.—The Breed Improved . . .

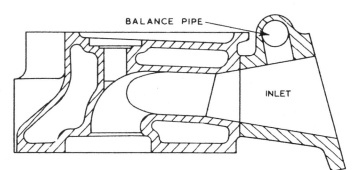

A standard B.M.C. B-type gear box and combined clutch housing is mounted on the cylinder block at the rear engine plate. It is a four-speed unit with synchromesh on second, third and top. The ratios are: top direct, third 1.373, second 2.21 and first 3.64 to 1. From the top of the gear box casing above the selector forks, a separate casting extends rearwards and contains the mechanism of the central remote control. A short vertical lever rises from this extension and is well placed in relation to the steering wheel. The travel of the change speed lever knob is short, a desirable feature for rapid changes. An oil filler cap, with dipstick, is placed on the left-hand side of the gear box casing and is reached through a hole in the tunnel which surrounds it.

The gear box casing is extended to reduce the length of the Hardy Spicer propeller-shaft which connects the drive to the three-quarter floating hypoid spiral bevel rear axle. The standard crown wheel and pinion give a ratio of 4.3 to 1, but an alternative ratio of 4.55 to 1 is offered. An orthodox bevel gear differential with two pinions is used.

The front suspension is identical with that of the previous TD and TF models, and was also used on the Le Mans cars. It is conventional in layout, using coil springs in conjunction with unequal

The balance pipe on the M.G. A is on the carburettor side of the head. On the Le Mans engine the ports went across the head to a balance pipe on the other side

length wishbones. No anti-roll bar has been found necessary, and this is undoubtedly because of the low centre of gravity of the car and its mean track of 4ft, which is wide for its size.

The top wishbone consists of two forgings attached at their inner ends to the cross-shaft of the Armstrong piston-type spring dampers and bolted at their outer ends to the king-pin post. The lower wishbone is a steel pressing consisting of two identical arms bridged by a centre section which forms the seat for the helical coil spring. The upper end of the coil spring fits into a housing formed by an extension of the main front cross-member, to which is also bolted the conical rubber bump stop.

In common with other M.G. models, rack and pinion steering gear is used, mounted ahead of the suspension unit and connected to the steering arms by a short track rod at each side. A single universal joint is incorporated in the shaft between

the steering wheel and the rack and pinion. Like several cars nowadays, the M.G. has, strictly speaking, no steering column, the shaft rotating where a column remains stationary. It is customary to shroud the top end of such a shaft with an extension pressing from the facia.

Half-elliptic springs are used at the rear, mounted directly beneath the frame side members. They are shackled at their rear ends and controlled by vertical piston-type Armstrong dampers bolted to the inside of the frame members. Check straps control rebound and rubber bump stops are mounted on the underside of the frame where it sweeps up over the rear axle.

Disc wheels with ventilation holes and four-stud attachment are supplied as standard, but wire-spoked centre-lock wheels can be obtained as an optional extra. Dunlop 5.60—15in tyres fitted on 4.00—15in well-base rims are used with both types of wheel.

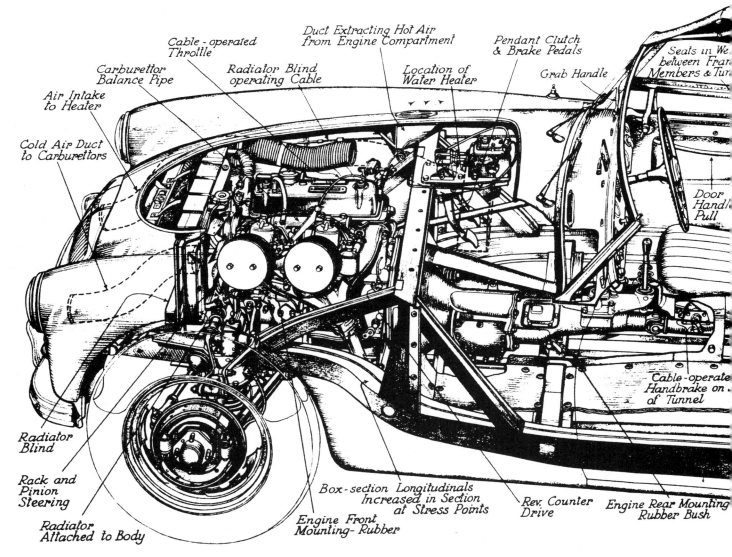

Lockheed hydraulic brakes with 10in-diameter drums and 1¾in-wide shoes are fitted. Two-leading shoe operation is used in the front drums and leading and trailing shoes at the rear. Actuation is by a pendant pedal mounted on the scuttle and connected to the master cylinder by a short operating rod. The master cylinder is a duplex unit with a similar pedal for clutch actuation. Mounted in this position, the two master cylinders are accessible for topping up with fluid. The fly-off type hand-brake lever is located between the seats close to the propeller-shaft tunnel and is connected to the rear brakes by cable.

The chassis frame is based on two side members boxed throughout their length and spaced to the full width of the body, which gives a low seating position because the floor is flush with the underside. At the front end they sweep in to give the necessary wheel clearance for the good turning circle of 28ft, which the designers have provided for easy manoeuvrability. The frame is given extra rigidity by extensive bracing at the scuttle structure over the clutch and gear box; stiffening of this section is further increased by a tubular cross-member placed under the transmission at the same point. Although it is rather heavy, the frame possesses very good torsional rigidity, which is reflected in the outstanding road-holding qualities of the car.

The body is panelled in steel and the doors in aluminium. Much research work has gone into the design of the body to reduce the wind resistance, and because of this it is a complete breakaway from the traditional lines which have been associated with this make for so many years. At the same time, the traditional M.G. character has somehow been retained, and the front grille is so styled that its classical origin is at once apparent.

Lucas double-dipping head lamps with pre-focused bulbs and blocked lenses have been blended into the contours of the front wings so that they rise above the falling bonnet line. Separate side lamps are placed immediately below the head lamps, just above the swept-round bumpers, which also carry overriders.

Separate bucket-type seats are placed low down between the widely spaced chassis side members and the propeller-shaft tunnel, to the top of which is fixed a permanent armrest. Good access is achieved by the use of forward-hinged wide doors at each side. They are hung on concealed hinges with no exterior handles, the opening being controlled by pull cables in the spacious door pockets. The hood folds away out of sight behind the rear seat, which area is also used for side screen stowage. The seat back-rests are hinged forward to allow easy access to this compartment. An overall tonneau cover can be supplied at extra charge.

Luggage space is provided above the petrol tank and access is from the outside of the car. The hinged lid to this compartment is released from inside the body

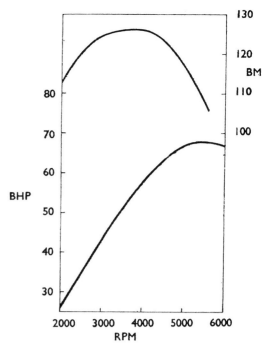

B.M.E.P. and B.H.P. curves for the engine fitted in the M.G. A

by a catch behind the passenger seat. The spare wheel is placed horizontally on the luggage compartment floor, and is canvas covered.

Twin six-volt batteries of 51 ampère-hour capacity are located beneath the locker floor, one on each side of the propeller-shaft.

A single-piece bonnet, hinged at its rear end and supported in the open position by a stay, gives access to the engine compartment.

The curved, one-piece, sloping windscreen is provided with grab handles at each corner which add considerably to the stiffness of this fitting and make it completely free from any vibration or other movement. The four sprung spokes of the steering wheel are arranged to give a clear view of the vital instruments in front of the driver. These consist of a 4in speedometer with dead-beat reading and incorporating a head lamp high beam warning lamp. To the left of the speedometer is a matching 4in revolution counter with ignition warning light. A combined oil pressure and water temperature gauge completes the range of essential instruments

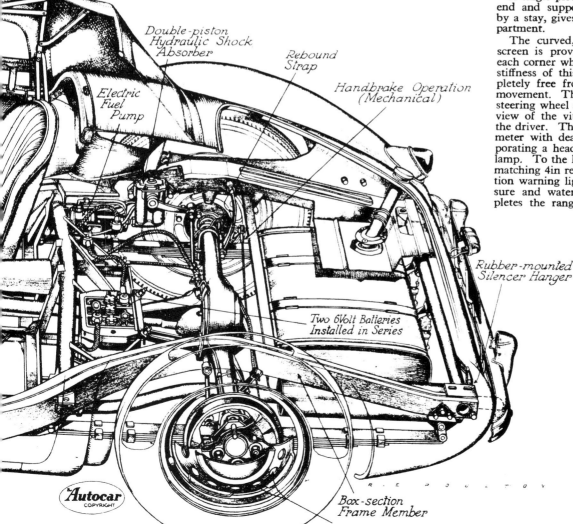

Double-piston Hydraulic Shock Absorber

Rebound Strap

Handbrake Operation (Mechanical)

Electric Fuel Pump

Rubber-mounted Silencer Hanger

Two 6-Volt Batteries Installed in Series

Box-section Frame Member

Brake Cooling Holes

LATEST of an illustrious line: Salient features of the M.G. Model A are annoted in this special cut-away drawing

M.G.—The Breed Improved . . .

immediately in front of the driver and a rheostat-controlled panel light, map-reading light and fuel indicator gauge, make up, with the normal range of switches, the functional yet attractive facia panel.

There is a wide range of optional extras if required. Provision has been made for the fitting of H.M.V. car radio, and others include white wall tyres, twin horns, an external luggage carrier, fog lamp and tonneau cover. In the same category are a radiator blind, wire wheels, telescopic steering wheel and the axle ratio of 4.55 to 1.

This new car appears to be a worthy successor to the famous and well-loved T-types, incorporating many lessons learned in racing. At its price it is a desirable car for normal road use, yet is still suitable for competition in the 1,500 c.c. class. In view of the increasing popularity of sports car racing, there is available from the factory both the information and the necessary parts for those owners who wish to increase further the performance of the A model, in the same way as they could its predecessors.

Frontal structure, rack and pinion steering and independent suspension of the new M.G.

The Autocar ROAD TESTS

Published *The Autocar*, 23 September 1955

THE NEW M.G.
ON THE ROAD

TO confound the critics who say that racing teaches no useful lessons comes the brand-new M.G. sports two-seater. Designated the model A—thus starting afresh after the long line of M, J, Q and R racing cars, and TA, TD and TF Midgets that rolled out of the Abingdon works—the new car is a very close development of the M.G.s that did so well in the 24-hours race at Le Mans this year.

There are naturally some differences between the racing car and the production model, but the road holding, braking and steering are unaffected and in these respects the M.G. A recalls very intimately the Le Mans car, road impressions of which were published in *The Autocar* of July 29, 1955.

The immediate impression on sitting in the driving seat was that the car had been tailored to fit, of which more later. Starting the 1½-litre B.M.C. engine presented no problems. A radiator blind, as fitted to the test car, is available as optional extra equipment and is easily operated by a control below the right-hand corner of the facia. This blind facilitates the warming-up in which any right-thinking enthusiast will indulge, although even without its use operating temperature was reached very quickly.

On opening the cable-operated throttle there came the familiar M.G. exhaust note. At no time did this become objectionable to others, and there was no annoying boom to be heard with the hood up. The car will drift along through residential areas on a whiff of throttle and with no unwelcome attention attracted.

There is immediate response to sudden pressure on the accelerator and the getaway from rest is very good, 70 m.p.h. being reached in just over 21 seconds. On wet roads, which were experienced during the taking of the acceleration figures, wheelspin was very apparent, and black lines can be left on a dry surface if the start is abrupt. At the end of the standing quarter mile the M.G. was travelling at very nearly 70 m.p.h., and this was very creditable with the load carried. Performance figures were taken with hood and sidescreens erected, except for some

runs to determine maximum speed, when a small racing-type screen was fitted.

With this small screen and a tonneau cover over the passenger seat, the best speed reached was 96 m.p.h., as against 99 m.p.h. with the hood and sidescreens in position. At such high speeds the M.G. A is very stable and the driver is able to concentrate on the rev counter needle as it climbs to the orange 5,500 r.p.m. mark on the dial, and the road shooting past him and away under the nose of the car. On Continental roads it was possible to cruise for mile after mile with the speedometer needle between 90 and 100 m.p.h. The oil pressure and temperature gauge needles remained steady in spite of a considerable amount of high-speed driving.

The M.G. A is, in fact, one of those cars whose cruising speed is determined by road conditions, and this became very evident after driving fast over the French and Belgian roads. But there is no feeling at the end of a hard day that the driver has been doing most of the work. Long, winding hillside roads are a joy to traverse; the car rockets to the top in third gear, and this gear is also extremely useful for overtaking other traffic and for town use. Yet it is possible to accelerate smoothly from 12 m.p.h. using the 4.3 to 1 top gear, and the car can be very pleasant when used in a gentle fashion. The engine is no temperamental unit, liable to behave only when it thinks it will.

Fuel consumption benefits from the body shape; driving at 50 m.p.h., with short periods at 70, resulted in a figure of 30.8 m.p.g., which was achieved on a give-and-take main road in Great Britain where to maintain the predetermined average speed the available acceleration had to be used.

The road holding and steering are of a high order. Even with the tyre pressures set for fast driving, there was no feeling of discomfort or pattering when on *pavé* and other poor surfaces. Fast cornering was a joy, the driver being able to position the car exactly where he wanted, and exit from a corner is also very satisfactory. On roads just wet after a sudden rainfall, the tail of the car would swing out slightly, but correction brought an immediate response and there was no lack of control. Suspension and damping is such that the whole car feels in one piece and the front end does not hop about.

The rack and pinion steering, with one of the æsthetically better types of present-day steering wheel, has a good, easy action with very little lost motion. There are two and three-quarter turns from lock to lock and the car proves to be guided by a slight motion of the hands rather than turning the wheel through a number of degrees.

Control is helped at all speeds by the excellent driving position previously mentioned. The seat is low down, below the level of the frame, and the driver's legs stretch comfortably to the pedals. The steering wheel (non-adjustable column) is at a good angle and there is plenty of room for the driver's elbows. The sight line of a tall driver is well below the top of the windscreen, and there is space for large feet in the neighbourhood of the pedals. The short remote control gear lever comes immediately to hand and the movements are precise and extremely satisfactory, the results being equally so! Occasional difficulty was encountered in engaging first gear from rest. The reverse stop spring on the car tested was also rather stiff, but experience of a similar gear box has shown that this stiffness wears off. The clutch is hydraulically operated and has a nice feel. It is capable of enabling very quick gear changes to be made without slip.

Racing experience shows in the M.G. A braking, which is all that could be required for very fast road work. Two-leading shoes in the front brakes, with leading and trailing shoes working in the rear, give the driver all the retarding power he is likely to need in normal circumstances. No fade was experienced during the test, and only when the brake performance figures were being obtained did any unevenness set in. The fitting of centre-lock wire wheels, an optional extra, would assist in cooling the drums as well as improving the already attractive appearance of the car. The hand-brake lever lies horizontally by the side of the propeller-shaft tunnel and has a fly-off action. It is easily reached and does not get in the way of the driver's leg.

Fast night driving is quite safe with the beam of the head lights, but the foot-operated dip-switch is placed rather high and is difficult to reach. It would be considerably better if it could be adjacent to the clutch pedal. There is a rheostat for the instrument lighting, and at one position of the switch the speedometer alone is illuminated. The only reflection in the windscreen comes from the tonneau cover studs immediately in front of the steering wheel. With the hood up and head lamp beams reaching away in front, the M.G. A is as comforting to drive at night as it is exhilarating by day.

Both seats have adequate adjustment and the back rest is at a comfortable angle. Some drivers would prefer more support for the thighs. The passenger has a grab handle and this also forms the windscreen frame support. As is to be expected, it is easier for two persons to erect the hood from its stowed position behind the seats, but the driver alone can manage it. The sidescreens, which have a spring-loaded flap, are simple to put into position and remove; they are each locked by one turnbuckle. Some

A new slant on the familiar M.G. front, successfully adapted

wet came in between the windscreen and front edge of the sidescreens when travelling fast, and in extremely heavy rain water dripped on to the driver's right leg from a point under the scuttle. There is a very reasonable amount of head room with the hood erect, and there was no instance of the driver's head hitting the hoop sticks when going over a bump. At speeds between 70 and 80 m.p.h. the hood

Seats tip forward if required. Instruments confront the driver but the horn is in the centre of the facia

For a sports car, luggage space is reasonable. Hood up, the new model loses nothing in smartness; the rear window is flexible

material vibrated on the frame but this noise was not experienced at lower speeds.

There is no cubby-hole in the facia; the space occupied by the radio fitted on the test car is blanked by a plate with an M.G. motif when there is no radio. A large pocket in each door is sufficient for maps, torch and the usual odds and ends crews require for a few days away from home. The pockets remain dry in rain when sidescreens are not fitted. The door handle cord is slung across the inside top of the pocket and can be reached by inserting a hand underneath the flap of the sidescreen. There are fitted envelopes behind the seats for the side curtains and these envelopes neatly conceal the hood when it is folded away.

The release handle for the luggage locker lid can be reached behind the passenger seat; there is room in the locker for a suitcase and small articles. Strapped on the rear bulkhead is the tool roll, containing the lifting jack and wheelbrace. The jack, surprisingly enough, is of the old-fashioned screw type. A starting handle is supplied and is clipped to the back of the locker. Nine points require attention with a grease gun every 1,000 miles and the twin six-volt batteries are housed beneath the luggage locker. They can be reached by removing the spare wheel.

A heating and demisting unit, available as an optional extra, was fitted to the test car. It worked well, and draws in fresh air via a long duct through the engine compartment. On the left side of the radiator, fresh air is ducted to the intakes of the twin S.U. carburettors. Hot air and fumes from the engine compartment are cleared by a vent on each side of the bonnet. As is usual with these B.M.C. engines, the oil filler is accessible, though it is difficult to see why the oil level dipstick could not be two inches longer, raising it clear of the sparking plug leads. Dynamo belt adjustment is not particularly easy with the standard tool kit.

M.G. TWO-SEATER (SERIES A)

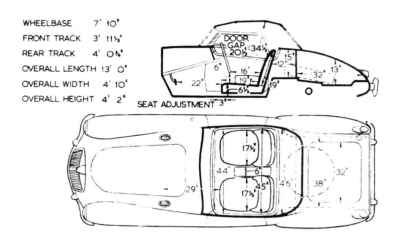

WHEELBASE 7' 10"
FRONT TRACK 3' 11½"
REAR TRACK 4' 0¾"
OVERALL LENGTH 13' 0"
OVERALL WIDTH 4' 10"
OVERALL HEIGHT 4' 2"

Measurements in these ¼in to 1ft scale body diagrams are taken with the driving seat in the central position of fore and aft adjustment and with the seat cushions uncompressed

DATA

PRICE (basic), with two-seater body, £595. British purchase tax, £249 0s 10d. Total (in Great Britain), £844 0s 10d.

ENGINE: Capacity: 1,489 c.c. (90.88 cu in). Number of cylinders: 4. Bore and stroke: 73.025 × 89 mm. (2.875 × 3.5in). Valve gear: o.h.v., push rods. Compression ratio: 8.3 to 1. B.H.P.: 68 at 5,500 r.p.m. (B.H.P. per ton laden 70.6). Torque: 77.4 lb ft at 3,500 r.p.m. M.P.H. per 1,000 r.p.m. on top gear, 17.0.

WEIGHT: (with 5 gals fuel), 17½ cwt (1,904 lb). Weight distribution (per cent): F, 51.5; R, 48.5. Laden as tested: 21 cwt (2,254 lb). Lb per c.c. (laden): 1.51.

BRAKES: Type: F, two-leading shoe; R, leading and trailing. Method of operation: F, hydraulic; R, hydraulic. Drum dimensions: F, 10in diameter; 1¾in wide. R, 10in diameter; 1¾in wide. Lining area: F, 67.2 sq in. R, 67.2 sq in (112.6 sq in per ton laden).

TYRES: 5.60—15in. Pressures (lb per sq in): F, 17; R, 20 (normal). F, 18; R, 23 (for fast driving).

TANK CAPACITY: 10 Imperial gallons. Oil sump, 6½ pints. Cooling system, 10 pints (plus 0.65 pints if heater is fitted).

TURNING CIRCLE: 28ft 0in (L and R). Steering wheel turns (lock to lock): 2¾.

DIMENSIONS: Wheelbase: 7ft 10in. Track: F, 3ft 11½in; R, 4ft 0¾in. Length (overall): 13ft. Height: 4ft 2in. Width: 4ft 10in. Ground clearance: 6in. Frontal area: 13.77 sq ft (approximately) (with hood up).

ELECTRICAL SYSTEM: 12-volt; 51 ampère-hour battery. Head lights: Double dip; 42-36 watt bulbs.

SUSPENSION: Front, independent, coil springs. Rear, half-elliptic leaf springs.

PERFORMANCE

ACCELERATION: from constant speeds. Speed Range, Gear Ratios and Time in sec.

M.P.H.	4.3 to 1	5.908 to 1	9.520 to 1	15.652 to 1
10—30..	—	8.2	5.0	—
20—40..	12.2	8.0	4.8	—
30—50..	12.3	8.4	—	—
40—60..	13.1	9.1	—	—
50—70..	15.0	10.7	—	—
60—80..	18.1	—	—	—

From rest through gears to:

M.P.H.	sec.
30	4.9
50	11.0
60	15.6
70	21.4
80	32.1
90	50.1

Standing quarter mile, 20.2 sec.

SPEEDS ON GEARS:

Gear		M.P.H. (normal and max.)	K.P.H. (normal and max.)
Top	(mean)	98.0	157.7
	(best)	99.0	159.3
3rd		58—70	93—113
2nd		38—44	61—71
1st		20—26	32—42

TRACTIVE RESISTANCE: 20 lb per ton at 10 M.P.H.

TRACTIVE EFFORT:

	Pull (lb per ton)	Equivalent Gradient
Top	203	1 in 11.0
Third	303	1 in 7.3
Second	455	1 in 4.9

BRAKES:

Efficiency	Pedal Pressure (lb)
85 per cent	100
77 per cent	50
58 per cent	25

FUEL CONSUMPTION: 27 m.p.g. overall for 672 miles (10.46 litres per 100 km). Approximate normal range 25—38 m.p.g. (11.3—7.4 litres per 100 km). Fuel, First grade.

WEATHER: Overcast, wet surface. Air temperature 68 deg F. Acceleration figures are the means of several runs in opposite directions. Tractive effort and resistance obtained by Tapley meter. Model described in *The Autocar* of September 23, 1955.

SPEEDOMETER CORRECTION: M.P.H.

Car speedometer	10	20	30	40	50	60	70	80	90	100
True speed:	11	20	29	38	48	58	68	77	86	96

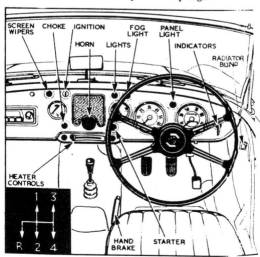

Published
The Autocar,
18 July 1958

The radiator grille bears the well-known M.G. octagonal motif. On each side of the bonnet are vents to allow hot air to escape from the engine compartment. Direction indicators are combined with the side lights

Autocar ROAD TESTS

M.G. Twin Cam MGA

OPEN TWO-SEATER

BY producing a high-performance model to partner the successful MGA two-seater, the M.G. Car Company, Ltd., has filled a gap which has been evident to overseas and competition-minded motorists; the new 1,588 c.c. twin overhead camshaft engine will enable the car to compete on equal terms in the 1,300-1,600 c.c. class with Continental-built cars. As described in preceding pages, this engine is a development of the special power unit used in the record-breaking M.G. EX 181.

The new model also has Dunlop 10¾in disc brakes, centre-lock steel wheels and Road Speed tyres, which are not fitted to the standard MGA. The road test car was an open model equipped with hood and side screens and all optionally extra equipment. A coupé version of the car is available.

Powered by the twin carburettor version of the 1½-litre B series engine, the standard MGA coupé is capable of slightly more than 100 m.p.h.; the new 1,600 c.c. unit gives the open car, with hood and side curtains in position, a maximum of 114 m.p.h. It is faster than the 1½-litre car by 1.7sec to 60 m.p.h., and by 15sec to 90 m.p.h.

The engine starts easily and quickly reaches working temperature. It revs freely, and the limit marking on the tachometer is 7,000 r.p.m.; it was taken up to this limit repeatedly during the test.

Engine vibration was noticed at 2,500 and 5,500 r.p.m.; at maximum speed in top gear the tachometer reading was 6,500 r.p.m., and this was held for approximately 5 miles on a level stretch of *autoroute*.

Power builds up noticeably after the engine tops 3,500 r.p.m.; by the time 4,000 r.p.m. is reached it really takes hold and the little car begins to show its potential performance. In first gear it gets very quickly to 30 m.p.h., and a fast change to second gear is needed to avoid exceeding the rev. limit. The comfortable minimum speed in top is 18-20 m.p.h., and in traffic, second and third gears are most used. In open road cruising, 80-90 m.p.h. can be held indefinitely, with plenty in hand for use when required. The car was quite happy at 100 m.p.h. for long stretches on Continental roads, although to maintain high engine speeds has a marked effect on the fuel consumption, of course,

and above 90 m.p.h. the driver has the feeling that the engine is working much harder.

There is a constant, rather obtrusive background of mechanical noise; most of this can be traced to the valve gear, particularly the tappets, which have a recommended clearance of 0.018in, but there is also a "ring" associated with the first stage of the timing gears. Nor can it be said that the engine is smooth or silky. Exhaust-wise, the car is not objectionable, and it can be driven through city traffic without attracting undue attention. This car had a loose silencer baffle. Carburettor intake noise is not noticeable, although only small flame-trap type air cleaners are fitted.

From the performance and maintenance angles, the MGA has an enthusiast's engine. Many of the ancillary units are not easy to reach, as the underbonnet space is filled by the engine itself. The distributor is located below a camshaft housing (it became covered in oil during the test), and the coil is tucked away under the heater trunking. The oil level dipstick would be easier to replace if its containing tube were a little longer. An oil cooler, which is an optional extra, was mounted in front of the radiator, but no oil temperature gauge was supplied.

All maximum speed and acceleration tests were carried

When the side curtains alone are used, the crew can enjoy fresh air motoring with some measure of protection from draughts. The Twin Cam insignia appears beneath the motif on the tail panel

The hood and side curtains are a snug fit and follow closely the contours of the body. There is no exterior door handle. Three large windows at the back of the hood are made of flexible Vybak. Bumper over-riders are standard

out with 100 octane petrol. With this, and Belgian premium petrol (89 research octane rating), the engine tended to "run on" after being switched off. It also used a considerable amount of oil; five pints were added to the sump during one journey of 800 miles, and an overall oil consumption figure of 1,020 m.p.g. was recorded—approximately one quart of oil each time the petrol tank (capacity 10 gallons) was refilled.

Once accustomed to the controls, an experienced driver can get off the mark with very little wheel spin, but it was felt that more suitable gear box ratios would give an even more sparkling getaway, without losing the benefit of easy fast cruising—there is a very noticeable interval between first and second, and between second and third. An owner using the car for circuit racing would, no doubt, prefer a gear box with closer ratios. A 4.55 to 1 axle ratio can be fitted in place of the standard 4.3 to 1 ratio at an extra cost of £10 2s 6d.

Apart from occasional difficulty in selecting first gear when the car is stationary, the gear box is generally pleasant to use. The short, remote control lever has precise movements between the ratios, and very fast changes can be made. One notices a slight difficulty—not uncommon in B-series gear boxes—in getting through the gate transversely, particularly when the gear box is hot. This sometimes makes difficult the change from third into second, and there is a risk that the lever may overshoot into the reverse quadrant. The top of the lever is close to the steering wheel when the latter is set near the facia; it is also well placed in relation to the driving seat. There was no vibration from the transmission, and the axle was silent.

Free from slip during full-bore gear changes, the clutch transmitted the engine power without judder under all conditions. Some adjustment was found necessary to take up pedal movement, but once attended to the need did not recur. Positioning of the pedals is good, although to clear the clutch pedal, the left foot has to be placed beneath it rather than to the left. The accelerator, which is connected to the throttle by a cable, works smoothly, and delicate, progressive control can be achieved.

Among the most delightful features of the MGA are its road-holding and cornering. The manufacturers' well-known motto—Safety Fast—is particularly pertinent to this new model. Changes in road surface have little effect on the manner in which the car sits firmly on the road, and its behaviour on a streaming wet road is equally good, although the tail will swing slightly if the throttle is opened suddenly when cornering. Power can be used judiciously to help the car round a corner, in fact progress on a winding road is all the better if this technique is applied.

There is strong self-centring of the steering, and there is no lost motion to impair its accuracy; from lock to lock requires only 2¾ turns of the wheel, and although the turning circle is greater by 4ft 6in than that of the 1½-litre-engined car, the Twin Cam model can be manoeuvred easily in narrow streets.

A slight heaviness in the steering was noticed with the tyres inflated to the normal recommended 18 lb front and 20 lb rear; when pressures were raised by 4 lb sq in, this

heaviness disappeared and the ride was not uncomfortable.

With full load, or with the driver only in the car, there is a satisfactory firmness about the suspension, which reaches an excellent compromise in a car which may be called upon to take the owner to work during the week, and yet be driven in races at the weekend. Stability is first class and there is no heeling-over on corners, although brisk progress is marked by excessive tyre squeal; the latest pattern Road Speed tyres were not fitted to the test car.

The driving position is well suited to most drivers, but a person of small stature would be happier with a higher seat cushion. The steering wheel can be set close to the facia, by a lock-nut and bolt fitting; in this position of adjustment the driver has fingertip control of the horn button and indicator switch. The thin-rimmed wheel is set at an ideal angle for control, being almost vertical; it does not obscure the instruments.

Fitted to the test car were the competition-type seats, which have a padded roll round the edge of the back rest, and long cushion; they proved most comfortable and provided firm support at a good angle. Driver and passenger are well held when cornering fast, and long distances can be covered without fatigue. The proximity of the engine and gear box can bring about an uncomfortably high temperature around the legs and feet; it is probable that owners in hot climates will call for separate fresh air ventilators. On the other hand, the warmth would be appreciated in winter conditions.

All the advantages which this car affords for fast motoring would be wasted if the braking system was not up to the same standards. It is becoming increasingly the practice for 100 m.p.h. cars, whether they are large saloons or agile two-seaters, to be fitted with disc brakes. The Dunlop 10¼in diameter discs fitted to the Twin Cam MGA are adequate to all they are called upon to do in wet or dry. The pedal has a good feel to it, being neither spongy nor too hard, though loads are rather high in normal traffic stops; this is normal with discs, which have no self-servo effect, and is noticeable

A cover encloses the spare wheel, on top of which is strapped the tool kit. The petrol filler has a quick release cap

132

M.G. Twin Cam
MGA . . . .

The polished aluminium covers of the camshaft housings dominate the under-bonnet view

when there is no external servo assistance, as in the case of the MGA. Maximum braking brought the car to a standstill all square, and the brakes could be applied hard when the car was being driven fast on wet roads. There was no noticeable increase in pedal travel after 800 miles of fast driving. The front discs did show signs of scoring, which has not been noticed on other cars.

The parking brake is controlled by a fly-off-pattern lever, in which the button is pressed to lock the brake on. The lever is placed between the transmission cover and the driving seat, and the hand falls readily on it.

At night reasonable use can be made of the car's performance, although more powerful head lamps would be appreciated for speeds close to 100 m.p.h.; the dipped beam did not inconvenience oncoming traffic. The Twin Cam MGA is one of the cars which really do require a hand dipper switch. When driving on the open road at night, one needs two left feet to operate the clutch and the foot dipper, for the driver always seems to need to change gear and alter the light setting at the same moment. The positioning of the pedal and switch are such that the changeover cannot be made on the instant.

Facia instruments are well lit, and the switch is fitted with a rheostat. There is a small map light, with a separate switch on the left side of the facia. Self-parking wipers are fitted, and although they are powerful and silent, they are up against an unusual handicap—in heavy rain, water is blown off the bonnet on to the screen and the wipers have difficulty in clearing it. An owner could perhaps prevent this by fitting a shallow Perspex deflector across the bonnet to deflect the air stream up and over the screen.

With the hood and side curtains erected, the car proved weatherproof except at speeds over 90 m.p.h., when wind pressure tended to lift the hood above the middle of the windscreen; rain found its way in there, and also through the scuttle on to the passenger's legs. Although there were gaps between the windscreen frame and the side screens,

rain did not penetrate here. The hood is comparatively simple to erect and can be folded away neatly behind the seat backrests. A plastic bag, secured to the bodywork behind the seats, provided stowage for the side curtains.

With the hood and side curtains erected, a tall driver has no difficulty in getting into or out of the car, and there is ample headroom. In this condition, the occupants find the interior rather warm, and it was not possible to obtain a flow of cool air through the vent above the gear box cover. A heater—part of the extra equipment—proved amply efficient in the moderate temperatures encountered during the test.

Accommodation for maps and small articles is provided by a deep pocket in each door, but as the doors cannot be locked, it is not advisable to stow valuables in these pockets if the car is left unattended. Only the Twin Cam models and the 1½-litre coupé are supplied with a leather-covered facia. A large proportion of the luggage compartment is occupied by the spare wheel and tool kit, and it is not easy to find room for a large suitcase, but a number of small bags and boxes can be stowed away. If coats and soft travelling bags are fitted in carefully, more can be carried than at first appears likely.

The tool kit includes a starting handle and, surprisingly, an old-fashioned, screw-type lifting jack. Two 6-volt batteries are located just forward of the rear axle; to service them the spare wheel and a panel in the floor behind the seats must be removed. The high-pressure electric fuel pump is close to the battery on the right side of the frame. Nine lubrication points require grease gun attention every 1,000 miles.

In the road test of the 1½-litre MGA coupé it was stated in summary that the car was capable of holding its own against more powerful vehicles; this applies even more markedly to the 1,600 c.c. Twin Cam model. The extra performance is matched by the road-holding, steering and brakes, and this car maintains the M.G. tradition of good looks coupled with a very fine performance.

Left: Competition seats, an optional extra, are contoured to give extra support in cornering, and under the thighs. Right: This is a functional facia, with neat, easily read dials. The main switches come quickly to hand. The steering wheel is shown in its nearest adjustment to the facia. The plated support on the left of the windscreen forms a useful grab handle for the passenger

SPECIFICATION

ENGINE

No. of cylinders ...	4 in line
Bore and stroke ...	75.4 x 88.9 mm (2.97 x 3.5in)
Displacement	1.588 c.c. (96.91 cu in)
Valve position ...	Twin O.H.C. Hemispherical combustion chamber
Compression ratio ...	9.9 to 1
Max. b.h.p. (nett) ...	108 at 6,700 r.p.m.
Max. b.m.e.p. (nett) ...	163 lb sq in at 4,500 r.p.m.
Max. torque (nett) ...	104 lb ft at 4,500 r.p.m.
Carburettors	Twin 1¾in dia S.U. type H.6
Fuel pump	S.U. high pressure
Tank capacity	10 Imp. gallons (37.8 litres)
Sump capacity ...	12 pints max. (5.7 litres)
	7¾ pints min. (3.6 litres)
Oil filter	Full flow
Cooling system ...	Pump, fan and thermostat
Battery	12 volt, 51 ampère hour

TRANSMISSION

Clutch	B and B. 8in dia single dry plate
Gear box	4 speeds and reverse, synchromesh on top, 3rd and 2nd. Central lever
Overall ratios ...	Top 4.30; 3rd 5.91; 2nd 9.52; 1st 15.65; reverse 20.47 to 1.
Final drive	Hypoid bevel, 4.3 to 1.

CHASSIS

Brakes	Dunlop disc. Hydraulic operation. Mechanical calipers for hand brake on rear wheels
Disc dia, pad width ...	10¾in outside dia (2⅛ x 1⅞in pads)
Suspension: front ...	Independent, coil springs and wishbones
rear ...	Live axle, half-elliptic leaf springs
Dampers: front ...	Armstrong in unit with wishbone pivots
rear ...	Armstrong lever arm, chassis-mounted
Wheels	Dunlop centre-lock steel disc type
Tyre size	5.90—15in Dunlop R.S.4
Steering	Rack and pinion
Steering wheel ...	16½in dia four spoke
Turns, lock to lock ...	2¾

DIMENSIONS

Wheelbase	7ft 10in (239 cm)
Track: front	3ft 11.9in (121 cm)
rear	4ft 0.87in (124 cm)
Overall length ...	13ft (396 cm)
Overall width ...	4ft 10in (147 cm)
Overall height ...	4ft 2in (127 cm)
Ground clearance ...	6in (15 cm)
Turning circle ...	31ft 4in (9.55 m)
Kerb weight	2,156 lb (19¼ cwt) (977 kg)

PERFORMANCE DATA

Top gear m.p.h. per 1,000 r.p.m. ...	17.3
Torque lb ft per cu in engine capacity	1.083
Brake surface area swept by linings ...	494.8 sq in
Weight distribution (dry)	F, 54.6 per cent R, 45.4 per cent

M.G. TWIN CAM MGA

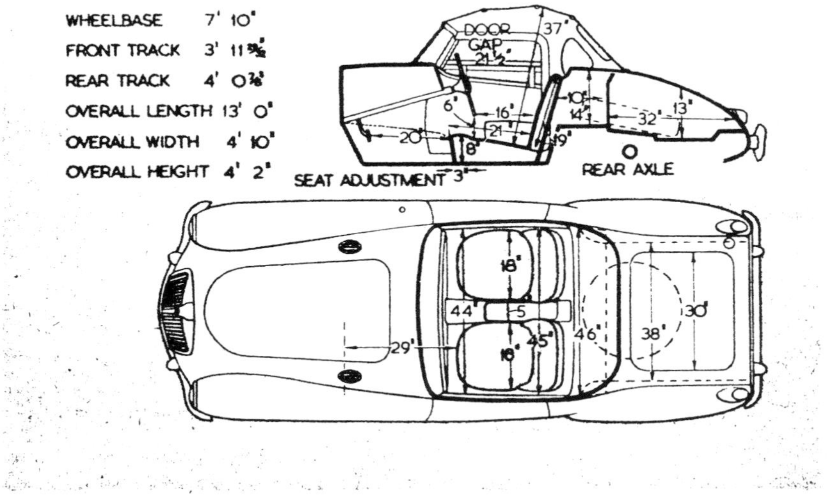

WHEELBASE 7' 10"
FRONT TRACK 3' 11 29/32"
REAR TRACK 4' 0⅞"
OVERALL LENGTH 13' 0"
OVERALL WIDTH 4' 10"
OVERALL HEIGHT 4' 2"
DOOR GAP 21½
SEAT ADJUSTMENT 3"
REAR AXLE

Scale ¼in to 1ft. Driving seat in central position. Cushions uncompressed

PERFORMANCE

ACCELERATION:

Speed Range, Gear Ratios and Time in sec.

M.P.H.	4.30 to 1	5.91 to 1	9.52 to 1	15.65 to 1
10—30 ..	—	—	4.5	3.3
20—40 ..	11.0	7.1	4.5	—
30—50 ..	10.2	7.4	4.9	—
40—60 ..	10.5	7.5	—	—
50—70 ..	11.7	7.6	—	—
60—80 ..	11.7	8.9	—	—
70—90 ..	13.6	—	—	—
80—100	18.7	—	—	—

From rest through gears to:

M.P.H.	sec.
30	4.3
40	6.9
50	9.4
60	13.3
70	17.3
80	22.5
90	30.0
100	41.1

Standing quarter mile, 18.6 sec.

MAXIMUM SPEEDS ON GEARS:

Gear		M.P.H.	K.P.H.
Top ..	**(mean)**	**113.5**	**182.7**
	(best)	**114.0**	**183.5**
3rd ..	.. ..	**86**	**138**
2nd ..	.. ..	**53**	**85**
1st ..	.. ..	**32**	**51**

TRACTIVE EFFORT:

	Pull (lb per ton)	Equivalent Gradient
Top	232	1 in 9.6
Third	315	1 in 7.0
Second	486	1 in 4.5

BRAKES (at 30 m.p.h. in neutral)

Pedal load in lb	Retardation	Equivalent stopping distance in ft
25	0.45g	67.2
50	0.62g	48.7
75	0.81g	37.4
90	0.92g	32.8

FUEL CONSUMPTION:

M.P.G. at steady speeds

M.P.H.	Direct Top
30	42.4
40	40.0
50	35.6
60	31.7
70	27.4
80	23.6
90	20.2
100	18.1

Overall fuel consumption for 1,117 miles, 21.8 m.p.g. (12.9 litres per 100 km).

Approximate normal range 18-30 m.p.g. (15.7-9.4 litres per 100 km).

Fuel: Super premium.

TEST CONDITIONS: Weather: overcast, raining. Slight breeze. Acceleration and braking tests on dry surface.

Air temperature, 55–65 deg F.

Acceleration figures are the means of several runs in opposite directions.

Tractive effort obtained by Tapley meter.

SPEEDOMETER CORRECTION: M.P.H.

Car speedometer:	10	20	30	40	50	60	70	80	90	100	110	114
True speed:	11	20	28.5	38.5	48	58	69	80	91	101	112	114

DATA

PRICE (basic), with two-seater body, **£843.**
British purchase tax, **£422 17s.**
Total (in Great Britain), **£1,265 17s.**
Extras:

	£	s	d
Screen washer	3	0	0
Heater	18	7	6
Adjustable steering column	3	0	0
Oil cooler	13	10	0
Competition seats	9	18	9
Twin horns	2	1	3

ENGINE: Capacity, 1,588 c.c. (96.91 cu in).
Number of cylinders, 4.
Bore and stroke, 75.4 × 88.9 mm (2.97 × 3.5in).
Valve gear, twin overhead camshafts.
Compression ratio, 9.9 to 1.
B.H.P. 108 (nett) at 6,700 r.p.m. (B.H.P. per ton laden 96.5).
Torque, 104 lb ft at 4,500 r.p.m.
M.P.H. per 1,000 r.p.m. in top gear, 17.3

WEIGHT: (with 5 gals. fuel), 19¼ cwt (2,156 lb).
Distribution (per cent): F, 53.9; R, 46.1.
Laden as tested, 22¼ cwt (2,506 lb).
Lb per c.c. (laden), 1.6.

BRAKES: Type, Dunlop disc.
Method of operation, hydraulic.
Disc diameter: F, 10¾in; R, 10¾in.
Lining swept area: F, 247.4 sq in; R, 247.4 sq in.

TYRES: 5.90—15in.
Pressures (lb sq in); F, 18; R, 20 (normal). F, 22; R, 24 (fast driving).

TANK CAPACITY: 10 Imperial gallons.
Oil sump, 12 pints.
Cooling system, 13⅜ pints (plus 1 pint if heater fitted).

STEERING: Turning circle, 32ft 6in.
Between kerbs, 31ft 4in.
Between walls, 33ft 5in.
Turns of steering wheel from lock to lock, 2¾.

DIMENSIONS: Wheelbase, 7ft 10in.
Track: F, 3ft 11 29/32in; R, 4ft 0⅞in.
Length (overall), 13ft.
Height, 4ft 2in.
Width, 4ft 10in.
Ground clearance, 6in.
Frontal area, 13.8 sq ft (approximately).

ELECTRICAL SYSTEM: 12-volt; 51 ampère-hour battery.
Head lamps, Double dip; 50–40 watt bulbs.

SUSPENSION: Front, independent, coil spring and wishbones. Rear, half-elliptic leaf springs with live axle.

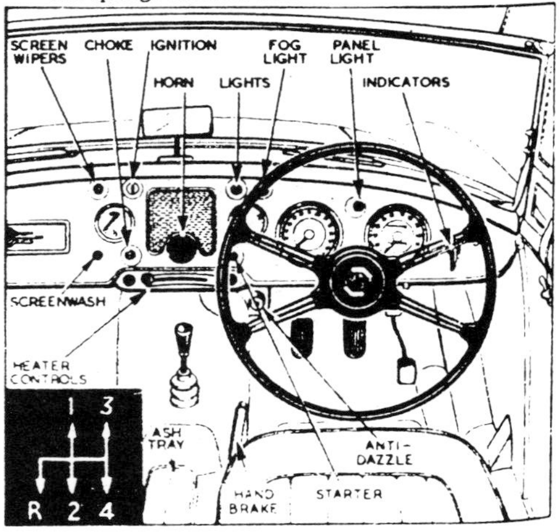

SCREEN WIPERS
CHOKE
IGNITION
FOG LIGHT
PANEL LIGHT
HORN
LIGHTS
INDICATORS
SCREENWASH
HEATER CONTROLS
ASH TRAY
ANTI-DAZZLE
HAND BRAKE
STARTER
1 3
R 2 4

Typically British, this new MGA will almost certainly be as popular in foreign markets as the previous models

IN the tradition of maintaining the breed, the new M.G. MGA 1600 is a direct successor to the MGA which, in its comparatively short existence, has become one of the most popular sports cars not only in England but also abroad. Indeed, as a dollar earner there are few cars which have done better. This new MGA is virtually identical except for an increase in engine capacity, the adoption of disc brakes at the front, and minor restyling attention to the body, including little 1600 motifs secured at either side near the bonnet louvres and on the boot lid.

With an engine capacity of 1,588 c.c. in place of 1,489 c.c., the gross power has been raised from 72 b.h.p. at 5,500 r.p.m. to 79.5 b.h.p. at 5,600 r.p.m. The effect of this increase is apparent as soon as one starts to drive the car, and there is no need of a stop-watch for evidence of the enhanced performance. Acceleration figures have improved over those of the previous model, and this is particularly noticeable in top gear at the higher cruising speeds. The figure for 50-70 m.p.h. in top gear has improved by almost 2sec, and the 60-80 m.p.h. figure by over 3sec. The car is capable of holding a genuine 100 m.p.h., but after several flat-out laps on a high-speed circuit it was noticed that the oil pressure was gradually dropping.

At 80 m.p.h., which appears very quickly on the quite accurate speedometer, the car moves happily at a natural and comfortable gait. There was a tendency for the engine of the test car to become rough and to vibrate at about 5,000 r.p.m., but if the throttle pedal was held down this disappeared as engine speed continued to mount. Members of the staff with experience of the previous MGA feel the more powerful engine to be rather more noisy and harsh. This is unlikely to deter the true sports car enthusiast; nor is the exhaust note. While not obtrusive at lower engine speeds, at 4,000 r.p.m. and above it is, perhaps, a little loud for town use, although the occupants of the car do not suffer from this so much as onlookers.

One of the greatest advantages of the new MGA is that the increased power has improved the flexibility of the engine, and where previously one had to use first and second while crawling in heavy traffic, one can now employ second and third gears quite comfortably. In fact, it was found that the car would pull away from under 10 m.p.h. in top gear, though, of course, it is unlikely that any driver of this type of car would do so.

One has to pay a price for these various benefits in a slightly greater fuel consumption—24 m.p.g. overall for the 1,590 miles of the test. A gentle touring consumption which

involved keeping the speed below 60 m.p.h. and avoiding high engine speeds in the intermediate gears returned a figure better than 31 m.p.g. During the test the car used three pints of engine oil, and the radiator needed considerable topping-up on two occasions.

When the car was delivered, the gear box proved to be extremely stiff; quite often it was necessary to employ both hands to engage reverse gear, and more effort than expected was required to select the other gears. Towards the end of the test, however, the movement had freed itself quite considerably, and it was obvious that in a thousand miles or so this would be a pleasant box to manipulate. Ratios are the same as those on the 1500 MGA, and one gained the impression that this car could have coped adequately with a slightly higher final drive ratio. Smooth to operate, the hydraulically actuated clutch could contend comfortably with violent acceleration from a standstill with a minimum of slip.

While our previous experience of the MGA left us in

Increased in capacity by 82 c.c. and in power by 7.5 b.h.p., the 1600 MGA engine appears identical with its predecessor

slight doubt about the adequacy of the brakes relative to maximum performance, there is no doubt that the brakes of the 1600 are of a very high standard indeed. With Lockheed discs on the front and 10in drums on the rear, the car can be stopped repeatedly from its high cruising speeds very quickly without any trace of fade or loss of directional stability. For a maximum retardation stop a fair amount of pedal pressure is needed, but a mean efficiency of 98 per cent, without any tendency for the wheels to lock, is highly commendable. The comparatively high pedal loads arise because the braking system is not provided with servo assistance. The hand brake, of the fly-off type, is also powerful and held the car without trouble on a 1 in 3 gradient, from which incline the car moved away with plenty of power in hand.

By modern standards the suspension must be considered firm; on smooth roads this is, of course, no disadvantage, and the car could be really hurtled into corners, when it would go round with minimum fuss, sitting squarely on the road and feeling very safe and controllable during the whole performance. This did not apply on rougher surfaces, however, and a feeling that the wheels were hopping and jumping, accompanied by intermittent tyre squeal, indicated that the tyres were not maintaining full contact with the road. With standard tyre pressures there was some oversteer, but an increase in the rear pressures reduced this to a bare trace at the sacrifice of a little ride comfort. The steering—rack and pinion—had little self-centring action, but was commendably direct and precise. A degree of road shock was transmitted to the driver through the steering.

Body alterations centre round the restyling of the side, tail and turn indicator lights in order to bring them into conformity with new regulations in this country. The flasher lights on the front have been coloured amber, while at the rear the wing light units have been changed so that the turn indicators and rear lights are separate.

Side screens are now of the sliding panel type, and the manufacturers claim that these, with the hood up, give as much protection as a saloon car body. During the period that this car was on test the weather remained very fine and sunny, so that it was never possible to ascertain if rain would enter through the largish gap between the body and the leading lower edge of the side screen. A series of pastel shades of paintwork is available for the 1600; the test car was finished in an attractive beige called Alamo.

Since no alterations have been made to the interior, much of what had been said before still applies—the space provided inside is still cramped for a car of its dimensions. Well upholstered, leather-trimmed seats give moderately good support, and only for a very slim person is there any possibility of being insufficiently braced. A grab handle, incorporated in the windscreen mount, is provided for the passenger. An average-sized person found that he needed the driving seat in the fully back position to be comfortable, so that even with an adjustable steering wheel a tall person never seemed really at home in the driving position, his arms being bent considerably at the elbow. A fairly tall driver, however, has the advantage that his view of the nearside wing is unobscured by the centrally mounted driving mirror. Gear change lever and handbrake are conveniently placed, but the facia-mounted horn button—old M.G. practice—is not always found when needed suddenly. Also it is unusual today to find the ignition switch not incorporated with the starter control.

Mounted rather high, the dip switch needed a full stretch of the foot to operate, and the main beam warning light was obscured by the steering wheel. For normal cruising speeds the head lamps are entirely adequate, but if one were in a hurry more powerful beams would be desirable. The commodious door pockets are entirely adequate for all the odds and ends that normally find their way into motor cars, but it is a pity when manufacturers do not provide in an open car which cannot be locked up, a thief-proof facia compartment. On the M.G. this facia space was occupied by a radio; although pleasant at town speeds, the

set became practically inaudible as one accelerated away from speed limits. Wind noise on this car was marked when in open form, but became an irritating roar with the hood up; in the latter trim, visibility was not greatly restricted.

One person can erect the hood, but it is much easier for two; even then it is wise to anticipate rain if one is not to get wet. With hood and sidescreens stowed behind the seats it was rather difficult to reach the boot catch. Much of the small boot capacity is taken up by the spare wheel and tool roll—a flattish suitcase and an air travel bag are about the limit for stowable baggage, and they would have to be taken out to get to the spare wheel.

A quick glance beneath the bonnet would not encourage the private owner to carry out minor adjustments himself, but in fact most of the components which might need servicing or adjustment are fairly accessible.

The M.G., with its powerful, responsive engine, combined with a moderately heavy but low-slung chassis, adequate steering and superlative brakes, and without any little vices or unpredictable traits in behaviour, maintains the traditional high standards of performance and safety of the marque.

M.G. MGA 1600

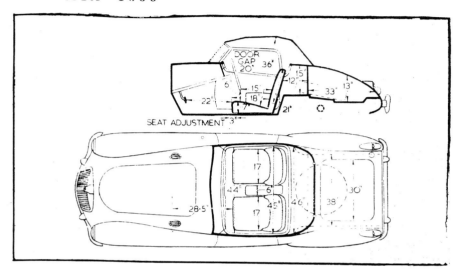

Scale ¼in to 1ft. Driving seat in central position. Cushions uncompressed.

DATA

PRICE (basic), with two seater body and hood, **£663.**
British purchase tax, **£277 7s 6d.**
Total (in Great Britain), **£940 7s 6d.**
Extras: Radio **£24 5s** (**£34 7s 1d** with tax).
  Heater **£12 5s** (**£17 7s 1d** with tax).
  Windscreen washer **£2** (**£2 16s 8d** with tax).

ENGINE: Capacity, 1,588 c.c. (96.9 cu in).
Number of cylinders, 4.
Bore and stroke, 75.39 × 88.9 mm (2.968 × 3.5in).
Valve gear, o.h.v. pushrods.
Compression ratio, 8.3 to 1.
B.h.p. 79.5 (gross) at 5,600 r.p.m. (b.h.p. per ton laden 75.3).
Torque, 87lb ft at 3,800 r.p.m.
M.p.h. per 1,000 r.p.m. in top gear, 17.16.

WEIGHT: (With 5 gals fuel), 18.12 cwt (2,030lb).
Weight distribution (per cent): F, 53, R, 47.
Laden as tested, 21.12 cwt (2,366 lb).
Lb per c.c. (laden), 1.49.

BRAKES: Type, Lockheed. F, Discs. R, Drums.
Method of operation, hydraulic.
Drum dimensions: 10in diameter; 1.75in wide.
Disc diameter, 11in.
Swept area: F, 240 sq in; R, 110 sq in.

TYRES: 5.60—15in.
Pressures (lb sq in): F, 17; R, 20 (normal). F, 21; R, 24 (fast driving).

TANK CAPACITY: 10 Imp. gallons.
Oil sump, 8 pints (including filter).
Cooling system, 10 pints (plus 0.65 pint if heater fitted).

DIMENSIONS: Wheelbase, 7ft 10in.
Track: F, 3ft 11.5in; R, 4ft 0.75in.
Length (overall), 13ft.
Width, 4ft 10in.
Height, 4ft 2in.
Ground clearance, 6in.
Frontal area, 13.77 sq ft (approximately) (hood up).

ELECTRICAL SYSTEM: 12-volt: two 6-volt, 58 ampère-hour batteries.
Head lights: Double dip; 50—40 watt bulbs.

SUSPENSION: Front, coil springs.
Rear, semi-elliptic leaf springs.

PERFORMANCE

ACCELERATION (mean):

Speed range, Gear Ratios and Time in Sec.

m.p.h.	4.3 to 1	5.91 to 1	9.52 to 1	15.65 to 1
10—30	—	8.7	4.7	—
20—40	11.0	7.8	4.6	—
30—50	10.9	6.9	—	—
40—60	10.5	7.5	—	—
50—70	11.9	8.3	—	—
60—80	13.2	—	—	—
70—90	17.0	—	—	—

From rest through gears to:

30 m.p.h.	..	4.6 sec.
40 ,,	..	6.7 ,,
50 ,,	..	10.3 ,,
60 ,,	..	14.2 ,,
70 ,,	..	18.5 ,,
80 ,,	..	26.6 ,,
90 ,,	..	36.4 ,,

Standing quarter mile, 19.3 sec.

MAXIMUM SPEEDS ON GEARS:

Gear			m.p.h.	k.p.h.
Top	..	(mean)	100.9	162.4
		(best)	101.4	163.2
3rd	..	..	77.0	123.9
2nd	..	..	46.0	74.0
1st	..	..	27.0	43.4

TEST CONDITIONS: Weather: dry, overcast. 5-15 m.p.h. wind.
Air temperature: 69 deg. F.

SPEEDOMETER CORRECTION: M.P.H.

Car speedometer:	10	20	30	40	50	60	70	80	90	100
True speed:	11	20	30	39	49	59	68	77	87	97

BRAKES (at 30 m.p.h. in neutral):

Pedal load in lb	Retardation	Equivalent stopping distance in ft
25	0.22g	137
50	0.42g	70
75	0.74g	41
94	0.98g	30.8

FUEL CONSUMPTION:

Steady speeds in top

30 m.p.h.		40.0 m.p.g.
40 ,,		36.3 ,,
50 ,,		33.3 ,,
60 ,,		30.7 ,,
70 ,,		28.5 ,,
80 ,,		26.0 ,,
90 ,,		22.3 ,,

Overall fuel consumption for 1,590 miles, 24.1 m.p.g. (11.72 litres per 100 km).
Approximate normal range 24-31 m.p.g. (11.7-9.2 litres per 100 km).
Fuel: Premium grade.

TRACTIVE EFFORT (by Tapley meter):

				Pull (lb per ton)	Equivalent Gradient
Top	..	..	..	245	1 in 9.1
Third	..		..	345	1 in 6.4
Second	..			550	1 in 3.9

STEERING: Turning circle.
Between kerbs, L, 31ft 2⅜in, R, 31ft 5in.
Between walls, L, 32ft 8in, R, 33ft.
Turns of steering wheel, lock to lock, 2¾.

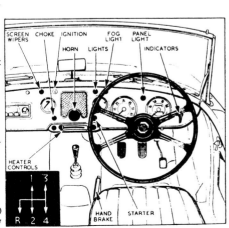

NEW CARS

DESCRIBED

MGA 1600

Mk II

SLIGHTLY LARGER, MORE POWERFUL ENGINE AND STYLING MODIFICATIONS: PRICES UNCHANGED

WHILE development of their new Midget has been under way, Abingdon have also been carrying out a programme of minor changes on the MGA. This model, as a result, now has a 34 c.c. increase in cylinder capacity —from 1,588 to 1,622 c.c.—and detailed styling changes. There has been a considerable re-working of the engine, and maximum power is increased from 83 b.h.p. to 90 b.h.p. without sacrifice of reliability. The object of these changes is to raise the maximum speed comfortably clear of 100 m.p.h., with a proportionate rise in cruising speed.

The larger cylinder capacity has been achieved by increasing the bore diameter from 75·4mm to 76·2mm, retaining the stroke at 88·9mm. To this end, the block casting has been re-cored and the degree of siamezing of the bores increased by reducing the size of the water passages in the cast webs between the individual cylinder barrels. Much work has also been done on the cylinder head. Not only are the inlet valves 0·63in. larger in diameter but the profiles of the inlet and exhaust tracts have been improved as a result of testing on an air-flow rig. As a further aid to improved gas flow the combustion chamber walls have been cut back adjacent to the valve heads and this has increased the chamber volume from 38·2 to 42·5 c.c. No change has been found necessary in either valve or ignition timing, but the quality of the valve steel has been improved. The latest Lucas DM4 distributor with roller weights for the centrifugal advance mechanism will be introduced concurrently with this model.

It is claimed that the changes made to the combustion chamber contours have also improved combustion efficiency, which has enabled the compression ratio to be raised from 8·3 to 1 to 8·9 to 1 and the engine to be free from pinking without demanding Super Premium fuel. The lower compression ratio is optional.

Flat-top Pistons

The higher compression ratio, in conjunction with the larger combustion chamber, has been made possible by replacing the former pistons with slightly concave crowns by new ones having a flat top. They are of the solid skirt type with three compression rings, the upper one chrome-plated, and one oil control ring—all located above the gudgeon pin.

These modifications, as mentioned above, have increased the maximum output from 83 b.h.p. at 5,600 r.p.m. to 90 b.h.p. at 5,500 r.p.m., a very creditable achievement considering the small increase in cubic capacity. This figure, taken under B.M.C. standard conditions, is for the engine without a fan but with air cleaners and gearbox fitted, and a test house exhaust system. Gross rating (S.A.E.) is 95 b.h.p. at 5,000 r.p.m. A maximum b.m.e.p. of 148 at 4,000 r.p.m. is quoted.

To absorb the higher crankshaft loading which this power implies, it has been necessary to increase the crankshaft web section by reducing slightly the width of the main bearings; extensive testing has demonstrated that there was a sufficient reserve of area in the copper-lead bearings to permit this, without affecting reliability. Front and rear main bearings are, therefore, reduced by 0·125in., while the centre one is 0·0625in. narrower. Stiffened connecting rods and larger gudgeon pins —increased in diameter from 0·69in. to 0·75in.—are also specified. The increased torque and power have made possible the use of a higher rear-axle ratio without loss of flexibility, and a ratio of 4·1 to 1 will be offered as standard, compared with 4·3 to 1 on the earlier model. This has raised the road speed in top gear from 17·2 to 17·9 m.p.h. per 1,000 r.p.m.

Power is transmitted through a closely balanced clutch mounted on a new flywheel, 8lb lighter than before. The gearbox casing has also been strengthened, by increasing the depth of the external webs but internally it is the same. Overall ratios with the 4·1 axle are 14·91, 9·08, 5·63 and 4·10 to 1.

Externally, the MGA Mark II is most readily distinguished by the new air intake grille, with inset vertical slats. The rear styling of the car is much improved, and the lighting is brought into step with the latest regulations, by the replacement of the old combined stop-and-tail-lamp fitting with a new cluster housing separate bulbs, mounted horizontally on the rear panel.

Cockpit appearance has been enhanced by covering the top of the scuttle behind the screen with Nuvon, a matt waterproof plastic material. The facia panel is also covered with this product, which gives a workmanlike appearance, free from reflections. Safety-belt attachments, located on the propeller-shaft tunnel but bolted through to the chassis frame, are a standard fitting in the cockpit.

These changes have been made without any increase in cost. The price remains at £663 basic, purchase tax £277 7s 6d, total £940 7s 6d. There is a wide range of optional extras available on the home market; they include a fresh-air heater and demister, an adjustable steering column, and a lower axle ratio of 4·55 to 1. Dunlop disc brakes front and rear, in conjunction with centre-lock wire wheels, are also obtainable, as are Road Speed tyres by the same manufacturer. Other items comprise a competition windscreen, anti-roll bar, competition seats, and sliding side-screens.

The multitude of MGA enthusiasts will welcome these improvements to their old favourite. Reports indicate that the extra performance has given the car a degree of liveliness quite out of proportion to what one could expect from the small increase in engine capacity. It remains to be seen how the car performs in competition, as it now moves into a different international classification, for cars between 1,600 and 2,000 c.c.

Left: Redesigned and repositioned rearlamp clusters on the Mark II are the noticeable differences from behind. Far left: Scuttle top and facia are now covered with matt plastic material

Basic elements of the 948 c.c. Midget are identical with those of the Austin-Healey Sprite, but there are differences in styling, seating and facia layout. The hood can be stowed in the luggage boot and a tonneau cover and detachable hardtop are among a wide range of extra equipment

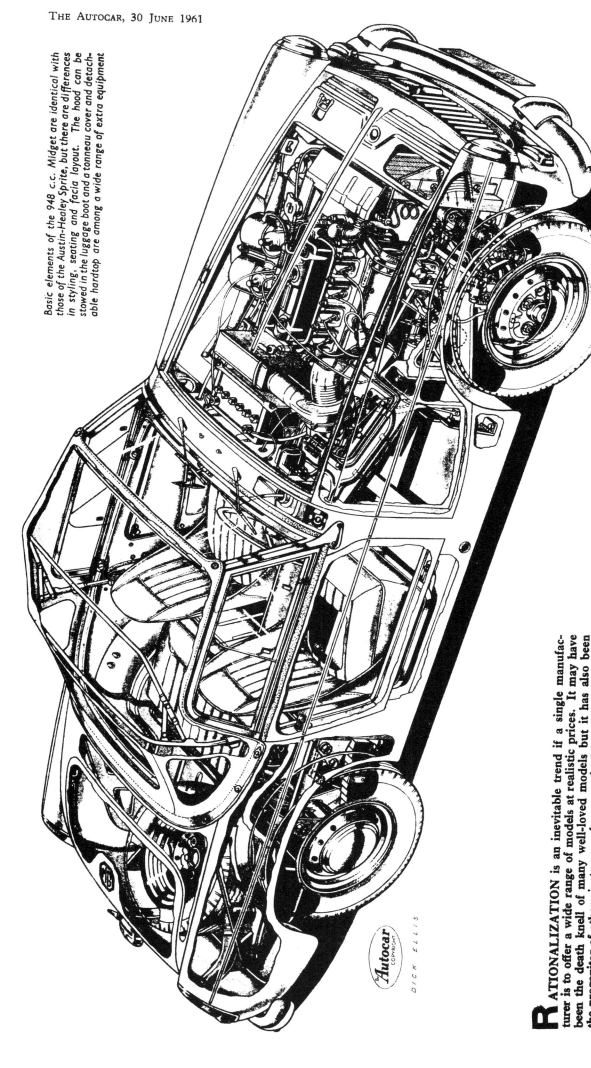

Autocar COPYRIGHT

DICK ELLIS

NEW CARS DESCRIBED

M.G. MIDGET

RATIONALIZATION is an inevitable trend if a single manufacturer is to offer a wide range of models at realistic prices. It may have been the death knell of many well-loved models but it has also been the progenitor of others just as good; as practised by the British Motor Corporation, the results have always been a commercial success, and at the same time have preserved some individuality in an increasingly classless world. Some would regard today's announcement of the M.G. Midget as one more step in a commercial policy: it is much better regarded as the revival of one of the most honoured names in the history of motor sport.

The very first M.G. Midget, the M type, was introduced at the 1928 Olympia Motor Show and was a very rationalized car indeed, being built almost entirely from unmodified production parts taken from the contemporary Morris Minor. From this modest beginning until 1 May

139

Above: a de luxe version fitted with the optional Ace wheel discs which do much to enhance the appearance. The bonnet is rear-hinged and the metal-frame sidescreens with sliding plastic panels are standard equipment: the doors are opened by internal release catches. Below: Leathercloth covering is used for the facia which has a padded safety roll on the top edge

1936, when the last under-1,000 c.c. Midget, a blue PB, was delivered to Hughes of Liverpool, the sporting lists were packed with wins and records by this marque. The words "Magic Midget" indeed came to mean something more than just the name painted on the side of one particular record breaker.

Now the name is reborn and the M.G. Midget takes on a new life with a power unit based on that of the Morris Minor 1000, albeit a much more specialized version than that which powered the original M type. Moreover, the new model will be built in the Pavlova Works at Abingdon-on-Thames, the traditional home of M.G. So enthusiasts for the octagon badge can rest assured that this will be a true M.G.

Examination of the suspension and structure of the car reveals many similarities with the Austin-Healey Sprite Mk. II. In fact, all the monocoque structure and the suspension is common with that model. It will be recalled that the front suspension is by a lower wishbone and upper, combined radius arm and damper, a large diameter coil spring acting as the suspension medium. The live rear axle is suspended on quarter-elliptic springs attached to the chassis centre section by robust U bolts; lateral location is provided by these springs, while driving and braking torque are shared with trailing radius arms located above the spring at each side. To obtain the desired spring rate the designer has chosen 15 thin leaves, five 0·156in. thick and 10 0·125in. thick.

Braking at front and rear is by 7·5in. dia. × 1·25in. Lockheed drum and shoe brakes; pierced road wheels are fitted to promote air flow over the drums.

Motive power for the Midget is provided by the 62·9 × 76·2mm four-cylinder, A series, B.M.C. engine, to sports car specification. Fitted with twin 1·25in. type HS2 S.U. carburettors and a compression ratio of 9 to 1, an output of 46·5 b.h.p. (net) is realized at 5,500 r.p.m. Compared with the Minor 1000 version the camshaft has a longer inlet valve opening period, in conjunction with larger, 1·156in. dia. valves to provide better breathing at high engine revolutions. There is no doubt that B.M.C. have drawn on the data acquired during the course of their work on formula Junior engines in developing this unit, and if the need arose, the know-how exists for much higher outputs.

Clutch housing and gearbox are a one-piece aluminium casting, with a bolted-on tailpiece to carry the mainshaft extension. The gearbox is the standard B.M.C. "A" series unit, with synchromesh on the upper three speeds; however, the ratios are different, a spacing similar to the MGA having been chosen to make possible maximum speeds of 26, 42 and 61 m.p.h. in the intermediates. The 4·22 to 1 rear axle ratio, in conjunction with 5·20 × 13in. tyres, gives a road speed of 15·37 m.p.h. per 1,000 r.p.m. in direct drive and a claimed 85 m.p.h. maximum.

Responsive and quick steering is assured by the rack and pinion layout. Only 2¼ turns are required between locks and the turning circle, kerb to kerb, is little more than 32ft.

Complete equipment and a high standard of finish are the keynotes of the Midget body. By means of a series of clever touches, the body shell has been given a distinctive M.G. look.

Responsible for this impression are the divided air intake with a central strip incorporating the M.G. badge, plated side flashes running the full length of the body at waist level, and a chromium strip on the bonnet centreline which repeats the radiator grille division. The famous octagon motif on the boot lid proclaims the identity of the car from the rear. Bumpers without overriders are a standard fitment.

The cockpit layout and trim have been devised to identify the car with the MGA. For example, the close fitting bucket seats are trimmed with plain side and top panels having a pleated inset; the covering material is synthetic. A leathercloth-

covered instrument panel, carrying the M.G. badge on the passenger side, furthers the resemblance to natural leather.

Moulded rubber mats with a white flecked finish make an attractive and practical covering for the floor of the front compartment and over the gearbox tunnel. This flecked theme is carried through to the pattern of the carpeting, which covers the rear compartment panelwork. This will provide a first-class protection against the rough edges of any articles carried behind the seats. A seat cushion, tailored to fit the luggage shelf, is offered as an extra and will no doubt find ready acceptance among those families with small children. Both front seats are fully adjustable in a fore-and-aft direction, and in keeping with the latest B.M.C. policy, safety belt anchorages as a standard fitting are located on the rear wheel arches and propeller shaft tunnel.

Instrumentation will be found adequate by most owners, for not only are there an engine revolution counter and a trip speedometer, placed in front of the driver, but also a combined oil-pressure and coolant temperature gauge, and a fuel-contents gauge. The steering wheel is finished with a baked golden pearl enamel.

PRICES

Basic £472; purchase tax £197 15s 10d; total £669 15s 10d.

OPTIONAL EXTRAS (home market only)

	Prices with tax		
	£	s.	d.
Wing mirror	1	4	10
Tonneau cover, rail and stowage bag	6	7	6
Ace Mercury wheel discs	15	18	9
White wall tyres	7	5	3
Heavy duty tyres	6	7	6
Twin horns	1	11	2
Rear compartment cushion	4	5	0

(Prices of the hardtop are not yet fixed)

Separate switches for all the electrical equipment, the choke knob and screenwasher plunger occupy the middle of the facia panel. They are well grouped in relation to the steering wheel; the lighting switch is close to hand and the choke control away to the left. A tell-tale for the turn indicators which are not self-cancelling, occupies the space immediately above the steering column, and there are main beam and ignition warning lights within the tachometer and speedometer dials. The horn push is in the centre of the steering wheel boss, unlike all previous M.G. sports cars, on which it was on the facia.

As one would expect from a firm with such a long experience of open bodies, weather protection has been given much thought and is thoroughly effective. The hood is a simple affair, the fabric folding up into a small bundle and the hoodsticks dividing at a centre joint and packing into a neat bag. The sidescreens have robust extruded aluminium frames with channels for the plastic glazing, and both the driver's and passenger's windows have sliding panels.

Colour schemes for the new model are based on combinations of Tartan red, Clipper blue, Farina grey, ivory or black paint schemes in conjunction with red, black or blue trim schemes. Only the Clipper Blue cars will have blue upholstery and a blue hood. Red cars will have red hoods and the others grey.

A wide range of optional extras is to be offered, as the appended list shows; it will be noticed that most of these are concerned with comfort and convenience. No tuning kits have been mentioned so far. It remains to be seen whether this line of country will be left to the specialists, or whether various stages of tune will be recommended by the works, as is done in the case of the MGA.

Undoubtedly this latest M.G. has all the qualities that have carried its predecessors along the road to success. It is well finished, very thoroughly equipped and the price is right. It is interesting to observe that at £472 without tax its cost is rather less than three times that of the original M type, which makes it outstanding value if the decreased value of the pound is taken into account. This is perhaps most important of all, for it will give a lot of young people the chance to own a new M.G. In recent years B.M.C. have shown increasing awareness of the publicity value of motoring sport, particularly in overseas markets, and it is patent that this latest model will become a healthy factor in the sporting field.

SPECIFICATION

ENGINE

No. of cylinders	...	4 in line
Bore and stroke	...	62·9 x 76·2mm (2·48 x 3·0in.)
Displacement...		948 c.c. (57·87 cu. in.)
Valve position	...	Overhead, pushrods and rockers
Compression ratio	...	9 to 1
Max. b.h.p. (gross)	...	49·8 at 5,500 r.p.m.
Max. b.h.p. (net)	...	46·5 at 5,500 r.p.m.
Max. b.m.e.p. (net)	...	138 p.s.i. at 2,750 r.p.m.
Max. torque (net)	...	53 lb ft at 2,750 r.p.m.
Carburettors	...	Two S.U. Type HS2
Fuel pump	...	AC-Delco mechanical
Tank capacity	...	6 Imp. gallons (27 litres)
Sump capacity	...	6·5 pints (3·7 litres)
Oil filter	...	Full flow
Cooling system	...	Pump, fan and thermostat
Battery	...	12 volt, 43 ampère hour

TRANSMISSION

Clutch	...	Single dry plate, hydraulic, 6¼in. dia.
Gearbox	...	Four-speed; synchromesh on 2nd, 3rd and top; central floor change
Overall gear ratios	...	Top 4·22; 3rd 5·73; 2nd 8·08; 1st 13·50; reverse 17·36 to 1
Final drive	...	Hypoid, 4·22 to 1

CHASSIS

Brakes	...	Lockheed hydraulic, drums, front and rear.
Drum diameter, shoe width	...	7in. x 1·25in.
Suspension: front	...	Independent, coil springs and wishbones
rear	...	Live axle, quarter-elliptic leaf springs, and radius arms
Dampers	...	Hydraulic, lever arm
Wheels	...	Ventilated disc, four-stud fixing; 3·5in. rim width
Tyre size	...	5·20—13in.
Steering	...	Rack and pinion
Steering wheel	...	16in. diameter
Turns, lock to lock	...	2.25

DIMENSIONS (Manufacturers' Figures)

Wheelbase	...	6ft. 8in. (203·2 cm)
Track: front	...	3ft. 9·75in. (116·2 cm)
rear	...	3ft. 8·75in. (113·7 cm)
Overall length	...	11ft. 4·25in. (346·1 cm)
Overall width	...	4ft. 5in. (134·6 cm)
Overall height	...	4ft. 1·75in. (126·4 cm)
Ground clearance	...	5in. (12·7 cm)
Turning circle	...	32ft. 1·5in. (9·75 m)
Kerb weight	...	1,566lb, 14 cwt (711kg)

PERFORMANCE DATA

Top gear m.p.h. per 1,000 r.p.m.	...	15·4
Torque lb. ft. per cu. in. engine capacity	...	0·92
Brake surface area swept by linings	...	110 sq. in.
Weight distribution	...	F. 53 per cent; R. 47 per cent.

Left: The optional hardtop is different from that used on the Austin-Healey Sprite, having a much flatter roof line and an inset rear window. Right: A loose cushion can be bought to fit the rear luggage platform for occasional passenger use

The Autocar road tests

M.G. MIDGET

An M.G. badge is incorporated in the radiator grille, and there is a central chromed flash on the bonnet

SINCE the new M.G. Midget was introduced at the end of June, the Chancellor's tax adjustments have increased the U.K. total price by some £20; yet it remains within the £700 bracket. At this price it is still good value as a thoroughly well-planned and soundly constructed little car, and promises to regain the popularity won by its pre-war predecessors. It is no secret that the car is in effect a luxury version of the Austin-Healey Sprite II, and is thus £30 dearer with tax.

Mechanical dissimilarities are few, and the differences in performance between the Midget and the Sprite II (which we tested on 2 June) must be attributed to variations of tune, and mileage run since new by the test cars. Throughout the speed range, the Midget accelerated slightly faster in any given gear, and showed a saving of 3sec, for example, from 60 to 80 m.p.h. in top. In acceleration from rest, some of this advantage was lost by a clutch which was not ideal

for rapid take-offs. It took up the drive rather abruptly over a small part of the long and largely ineffective pedal travel, pulling engine revs below the point of maximum torque. Attempts to slip the clutch during rapid getaways resulted in clutch spin, which also prevented the car from restarting on a 1-in-3 test gradient.

Starting was always immediate, and there was no need for the choke in mild weather. After the car has stood for more than half-an-hour or so, the engine is often a little reluctant to pull straight away; this hesitance disappears rapidly as the engine warms up in the first few hundred yards, and acceleration is then crisp and responsive.

One is immediately impressed by the smoothness of the Midget's power unit. Normally the rev counter needle is held between 2,000 and 4,000 r.p.m. on the open road, but 5,000 r.p.m. may be used without roughness or excess noise from the engine. A noticeable surge of power is felt at 2,500 r.p.m. There was a noticeable engine period between 5,000 and 5,500 r.p.m., it became smooth again up to the valve bounce speed of 6,500 r.p.m. At this speed the unit remained sweet and smooth, so that a watchful eye had to be kept on the rev counter, which is standard equipment. On this an orange warning band starts at 5,500 r.p.m. and changes to red at 6,000 r.p.m.; the calibration extends to 7,000 r.p.m.

An intelligent choice of gear ratios enables full advantage to be taken of the wide span of engine power. When making a fast getaway there is a logical progression through the gears, and after reaching peak revs in bottom and second a useful range of acceleration remains in the subsequent gear. Second is particularly useful up to 45 m.p.h. for spurting past slow-moving traffic, and allows up to 50 m.p.h. Yet the docile behaviour of the engine at low revs enables the car to pull away from a walking pace in second gear.

In third gear the most practical range extends from about 25 m.p.h. to 60 m.p.h., with a 70 m.p.h. maximum in reserve. Complementing these excellent gear ratios are the

Under-bonnet accessibility is fair, although the compartment is unusually crowded on the Midget. The dipstick is below the sparking plug leads

ease and speed with which changes can be made, for the lever can be snatched from one position to the next almost as quickly as the hand can move. For fast upward changes the synchromesh cannot always quite cope, especially if the lever is pulled smartly from bottom to second. Distinctive but unobtrusive gear whine is audible in all the indirects. The gear lever is placed conveniently only a few inches from the driver's left hand on the steering wheel, and its knob is of hard plastic, insulated with rubber.

Bearing in mind the engine's willingness to rev, top gear gives just the right combination of liveliness with high-speed cruising, the road speed being just over 60 m.p.h. at 4,000 r.p.m. The fastest speed reached with the Midget was 86 m.p.h. at 5,600 r.p.m., when the engine is nowhere near the point of "running out of revs." The theoretical maximum, based on the engine's safe rev limit, would be just short of 100 m.p.h.

Factors tending to dissuade one from taking full advantage of the car's abilities were a marked increase in noise above 70 m.p.h., accompanied on this example by vibration, apparently from the transmission. The most comfortable and restful cruising rate is around 60 m.p.h., and the fuel consumption figures at constant speeds show that 60 m.p.h. is relatively economical, for at a steady 70 m.p.h. 10 miles fewer are averaged per gallon. If faster speeds are sustained, as when the car was held at 80 m.p.h. and above for long periods on M1, the oil pressure drops rapidly from its normal 60 p.s.i. maximum to nearer 40 p.s.i. Three pints of oil were consumed in 1,037 test miles, equivalent to nearly 3,000 m.p.g. At the higher speeds also, slight final drive whine was heard.

As for fuel consumption, the best figure obtained was 48.5 m.p.g. on a main road run with restrained use of the performance, but this figure dropped to 34.1 m.p.g. when the same 20-mile stretch of road was covered as fast as the car would go. In city traffic and at sustained high speeds consumption naturally increases, giving the overall figure of 33.4 m.p.g. for the entire test, but any owner in search of economy will have no difficulty in exceeding 40 m.p.g. with the Midget.

The 948 c.c. engine has a compression ratio of 9-to-1, and needs to be run on super premium grades of fuel. The lower compression ratio of 8.3-to-1 is optional to suit normal premium grades of petrol, and any increase in consumption resulting from this would probably be recovered in reduced petrol costs; performance, naturally, would be a little lower. The fuel tank holds only six gallons, so that frequent refuelling is necessary when the car is driven hard.

Directional stability of the Midget at speed is much affected by cross winds, and frequent correction is necessary to maintain a straight course. This characteristic is made less troublesome than it would be otherwise by the excellent precision of the rack-and-pinion steering. The control is completely free from lost movement, and with 2¼ turns of the wheel between the extremes of acceptably wide steering locks, it requires only small or even imperceptible move-

A padded roll runs along the top of the facia. Roomy pockets for maps and oddments are fitted to the inside of both doors. Right: Both seats tilt forward to give access to the rear compartment in which a seat cushion is an optional extra. An ashtray is also available at 7s 9d extra

M.G. Midget

With the hood in place instead of the hardtop the Midget uses the same sidescreens as are fitted to the Austin-Healey Sprite, but the car is still identifiable in this view by the full-length rubbing strip and " MG Midget " motifs on the luggage locker lid

ments of the wheel to control the car on a straight road.

When cornering the basic characteristic of the car is to oversteer, as a result of the rear wheel steering effect of the back axle, which is suspended on quarter-elliptic leaf springs. A newcomer to the car may find at first that the Midget corners unexpectedly sharply, but the handling is never vicious, and in a short time he is able to throw the Midget round corners taking full advantage of the responsive steering to correct any tendency for the tail of the car to move outwards. On winding country lanes and cross-country routes this little M.G. is really at home.

During the test some increase in travel of the brake pedal was noticed, and there was always a rather dead feel to the brakes. However, they do have a good reserve of stopping power, and fade does not occur in normal use. Pedal pressures required are fairly high, but although there is room for improvement in this respect, the driver is soon reassured that if he presses hard on the pedal the car will stop rapidly. The handbrake is controlled by a chromed pull-up lever to the left of the transmission tunnel and held the car without difficulty on the 1-in-3 test hill. The pedals are well-placed and allow easy simultaneous use of the brake and throttle.

Acceptably Soft Suspension

Extremely good bump absorption is provided by the suspension, which is softer than its layout would suggest. On secondary or badly surfaced city roads the car sits down well and does not jolt its occupants. On rough *pavé* the limited vertical wheel travel begins to tell, and the rear suspension bottoms violently on bump stops which seem to be too small.

Severe humps in the road naturally result in some firm upward movement, and when tall drivers were at the wheel they found their heads were near enough to the hardtop for them to hit it as the car bounced.

The stylish and well-made, glass-fibre hardtop with plastic interior linings may be fitted or removed single-handed in a matter of minutes. However, with the hardtop, sidescreens different from those supplied with the standard hood are necessary. As the total cost of the hardtop and sidescreens is some £73, including purchase tax, when they are ordered with the new car, most owners will probably be content with the basic p.v.c. hood as all-the-year-round weather protection. Purchase tax on the hardtop kit is not payable if it is ordered after delivery of the car, and the price is then £50.

The draught-sealing with the hood in place is about as satisfactory as one may ever hope for in a car with detachable sidescreens, and a particularly good seal is made by the rubber surrounds. The sidescreens have light alloy frames with double sliding Perspex windows allowing opening for ventilation at both front and rear. The hood fit is also good, and a metal bar sewn into the leading edge ensures a perfect overlap joint at the top of the windscreen, while the strut springs can be locked, and then released

The toolkit comprises a side-lifting jack, a wheelbrace, and a socket spanner for the sparking plugs. Storage bags are provided for the hood

when the hood is in position. When not in use the struts separate like tent poles at the centre and fold away into a bag for stowage in the luggage locker. At above 70 m.p.h. wind pressure causes the leading edge of the sidescreens to bow out.

A generously large luggage locker is provided with an exterior lockable handle—an important point since the car doors do not lock. Although the spare wheel lies flat in the centre of the boot floor there is ample room around it for carefully packed luggage. At the forward end of the compartment some space is lost when the folded hood is stowed in the bag provided. The boot is held open by a swivelling prop which proved annoyingly clumsy.

Visibility is particularly good, and the driver sits high enough to see over the steering wheel and scuttle without difficulty, and with both front wings and the bonnet in sight. The windscreen pillars are slender and offer little or no obstruction to visibility even when the car is closed. To the rear of the windscreens with the hood in place, vision is better than when the hardtop is fitted, as rear quarter windows are incorporated in the hood.

Self-parking wipers have blades as long as allowed by the depth of the windscreen, but a large portion is left unswept at both ends. The interior mirror is mounted too low and vibrates; for safety's sake we added a suction-fitting interior mirror to the screen of the test car.

Well-upholstered seats are adjustable fore-and-aft, and covered in black p.v.c. with a red-painted car. The cushion is comfortable and the backrest provides good lateral support, but it is too firm at the top, and tends to make the occupants slump forward; more support is needed in the small of the back. The occasional rear seat fitted to the test car costs £4 5s, and is adequate for two children if the adults have their seats well forward to provide rear legroom. The floor and gearbox housing are covered with dark moulded rubber flecked with red. Carpet is used behind the seats and, for protection, on the lower portions of the folding seat backrests. Both front floor mats are readily removable.

A plain but functional instrument layout is provided, with the main rev counter and speedometer on either side of the steering column. A fuel gauge is on the right, and a combined oil pressure gauge and coolant thermometer is fitted on the left, where it is partly masked by the driver's left hand on the steering wheel. Provision of a trip mileometer in the speedometer is particularly welcome. The steering wheel and column surround adjoining the facia are of yellowy

plastic material somewhat out of keeping with the character of the rest of the car.

Tumbler switches are used for the wipers and for the lamps, which are the latest sealed-reflector and filament pattern. They give ample main beam illumination for the speed potential of the Midget, and have a generously long reach on dipped beam without dazzling oncoming drivers. A switch similar to that for the lamps is mounted centrally on the facia to control the winking indicators. They are not self-cancelling, but a bright warning lamp is fitted above the steering wheel boss.

Twin windtone horns fitted to the test car are a specially desirable extra, priced at £1 12s 1d including tax. A fresh-air heater is another practically essential optional fitting, and costs £17 10s with tax. This was also among the £116 worth of accessories on the Midget tested, and gave a good flow of air through inlets with cut-off flaps to either side of the engine bulkhead. An overriding air control is fitted on the facia, and a tap on the engine allows the hot water supply to be turned off for the summer. There is no provision for a reversing lamp to be fitted. Twelve grease points require attention every 1,000 miles.

This new M.G. is an endearing little car with a remarkable capacity for nipping about among heavy traffic. It is easy and safe to drive, and certainly is approaching the ideal for the market which it is intended to serve.

M.G. MIDGET

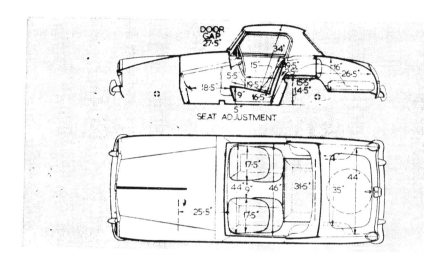

Scale ⅛in. to 1ft. Driving seat in central position. Cushions uncompressed.

DATA

PRICE (basic), with open two-seater body, £472.
British purchase tax, £217 11s 5d.
Total (in Great Britain), £689 11s 5d.
Extras, incl. p.t.:
Hardtop and sidescreens, £70 16s 8d; Tonneau cover, £6 11s 3d; Heater, £17 10s 0d; Fresh air unit, £5 16s 8d; Twin horns, £1 12s 1d; Cigarette lighter, £1 12s 1d; Whitewall tyres, £7 9s 6d; Heavy duty tyres, £6 11s 3d; Radio, £30 5s 2d; Laminated windscreen, £4 0s 2d; Ace Mercury wheel discs, £16 8s 1d; Luggage carrier and wing mirror, £12 15s 2d; Rear compartment cushion, £4 7s 6d.
ENGINE: Capacity, 948 c.c. (57.9 cu. in.).
Number of cylinders, 4.
Bore and stroke, 62.9 × 76.2 mm (2.48 × 3.0 in.).
Valve gear, o.h.v., pushrods and rockers.
Compression ratio, 9.0 to 1 (8.3 to 1 optional).
B.h.p. 41.6 (net) at 5,500 r.p.m. (b.h.p. per ton laden 49.3).
Torque, 53lb. ft. at 3,000 r.p.m.
M.p.h. per 1,000 r.p.m. in top gear, 15.4.
WEIGHT: (With 5 gal fuel), 13.9 cwt (1,554lb).
Weight distribution (per cent); F, 52.7; R, 47.3.
Laden as tested, 16.9 cwt. (1,890 lb).
Lb per c.c. (laden), 2.
BRAKES: Type, Lockheed hydraulic.
Drum dimensions: F and R, 7in. dia.; 1.75in. wide.
Total swept area: 110 sq. in. (131 sq. in. per ton laden).
TYRES: 5.20—13in. Dunlop Gold Seal Nylon tubeless.
Pressures (p.s.i.); F, 18; R, 20 (normal). F, 24; R, 26 (fast driving).
TANK CAPACITY: 6 Imperial gallons.
Oil sump, 6.5 pints.
Cooling system, 10 pints (including heater).
DIMENSIONS: Wheelbase, 6ft 8in.
Track: F, 3ft 8.75in.; R, 3ft 9.75in.
Length (overall), 11ft 4.25in.
Width, 4ft 5in. Height, 4ft 1.75in.
Ground clearance, 5in.
Frontal area, 12.4 sq. ft. (approx.).
Capacity of luggage space, 11.5 sq. ft. (approx.).
ELECTRICAL SYSTEM: 12-volt; 43 ampère-hour battery.
Headlamps, 60-45 watt filaments.
SUSPENSION: Front, coil springs and wishbones, lever-type dampers.
Rear, live axle, trailing quarter-elliptic leaf springs, radius arms, lever-type dampers.

PERFORMANCE

ACCELERATION TIMES (mean):
Speed range, Gear Ratios and Time in Sec.

m.p.h.	4.22 to 1	5.73 to 1	8.09 to 1	13.5 to 1
10—30	—	10.1	6.3	—
20—40	13.3	8.6	6.2	—
30—50	14.1	9.5	7.1	—
40—60	15.7	11.2	—	—
50—70	17.9	16.5	—	—
60—80	28.6	—	—	—

From rest through gears to:

30 m.p.h.	..	6.3 sec.
40 „	..	9.4 „
50 „	..	14.4 „
60 „	..	20.2 „
70 „	..	32.8 „
80 „	..	56.8 „

Standing quarter mile 21.9 sec.

MAXIMUM SPEEDS ON GEARS:

Gear			m.p.h.	k.p.h.
Top		(mean)	84.7	136
		(best)	86	138.4
3rd	..	..	70	112
2nd	..	..	50	81
1st	..	..	30	48

TRACTIVE EFFORT (by Tapley meter):

		Pull (lb per ton)	Equivalent gradient
Top	..	180	1 in 12.4
Third	..	240	1 in 10.8
Second	..	350	1 in 15.8

BRAKES (at 30 m.p.h. in neutral):

Pedal load in lb	Retardation	Equiv. stopping distance in ft
25	0.16g	187
50	0.39g	77
75	0.92g	32.8

FUEL CONSUMPTION (at steady speeds in top gear):

30 m.p.h.	51.6 m.p.g.
40 „	54.8 „
50 „	47.2 „
60 „	43.0 „
70 „	33.8 „

Overall fuel consumption for 1,037 miles, 33.4 m.p.g. (8.4 litres per 100 km.).
Approximate normal range 32-34 m.p.g. (8.8-5.9 litres per 100 km.).
Fuel: Super Premium.

TEST CONDITIONS: Weather: dry; sunny intervals, 10 m.p.h. wind gusting to 25 m.p.h.
Air temperature, 68 deg. F.

STEERING: Turning circle:
Between kerbs, L, 30ft 0in. R, 30ft 3in.
Between walls, L, 31ft 5in. R, 31ft 8in.
Turns of steering wheel from lock to lock, 2.25.

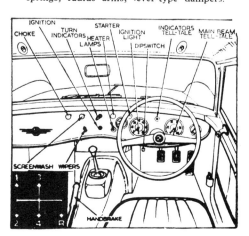

SPEEDOMETER CORRECTION: m.p.h.

Car speedometer	..	..	..	10	20	30	40	50	60	70	80
True speed	..	..	..	10	19	29	40	50	60	70	80

M.G. MGB 1800 1,798 c.c.

WHATEVER the diehard enthusiast may say to the contrary, and however hard the traditionalist may cling to a superseded model, there is no doubt that the new M.G. MGB 1800 is a much superior car to its predecessor, the MGA in all its forms. One cannot think of any aspect of this new sports car which does not show appreciable advantage in comparison with the previous model.

In terms of performance, ever important in this class of car, the gains are particularly marked. The standing quarter-mile time is some half a second quicker, at 18·7sec, and acceleration from rest to 90 m.p.h. takes 32·6sec compared with 36·1sec obtained in our last test of the MGA. Throughout the range, all performance figures are progressively faster with the new car.

Both models weigh almost exactly the same, and the improved performance is largely what one would expect to be achieved as a result of the increase in engine capacity from 1,622 to 1,798 c.c. It is significant that the new engine has lost the harshness but none of the low-speed traction of

its predecessor, while at the upper end of the range the engine has much more freedom to rev. Previously, 6,000 r.p.m. was regarded as a maximum safe limit, but now the engine may be taken up to 6,800 r.p.m. This allows 34, 55 and 91 m.p.h. respectively to be reached in the three indirect ratios, but it also permits an easy 70 m.p.h. in third gear, which is a very useful ratio for fast overtaking and main road cornering. A pink segment marked on the rev. counter from 5,500 r.p.m. changes to red at 6,000, and this should be regarded as a normal safety limit for the owner. Within this range, the engine remains relatively quiet, and runs through no vibration periods. An easy 100 m.p.h. is available with the MGB, and cruising at 5,000 r.p.m. allows 90 m.p.h. to be sustained without evidence of stress. The one-way maximum of 105 m.p.h. is 3 m.p.h. more than with the MGA. For overseas markets an oil cooler is standard, and is an optional extra in the U.K., recommended for those who habitually drive fast. Fitted to the test car, it prevented any reduction in oil pressure from the normal figure of 65 p.s.i. even after sustained high speeds.

Only a moment's use of the choke is necessary for the first start of the day, after which the engine pulls strongly and without hesitation. It seemed that the mixture on the car tested was set fairly rich for highest performance, with the result that the tickover when hot was rather lumpy, with a tendency to stall unless a touch of throttle was used to speed up the idling rate.

The overall fuel consumption of 21·4 m.p.g. is within 1 m.p.g. of the figure (22·3 m.p.g.) obtained with the MGA Mk. II, while all the fuel consumptions measured at constant speeds were more economical with the new car. The overall figure, of course, reflects performance testing, hard driving and considerable high-speed work, but it would be folly to think that anyone will buy the MGB simply to dawdle; and accordingly consumption in the region of 22-24 m.p.g. is to be regarded as normal.

Fuel tank capacity is 10 gallons, and normally less than

PRICES						
2-door sports	..	..	..	..	£690	
Purchase tax	..	..	..	..	£259 15s	3d
			Total (in G.B.)		£949 15s	3d
Extras (including tax)						
Heater	..	..	..	..	..	£16 16s 11d
Wire wheels	..	..	..	..	..	£34 7s 6d
Folding hood	..	..	..	..	..	£5 10s 0d
Full-length tonneau cover	..	..	..	..	£11 0s 0d
Anti-roll bar	..	..	..	..	..	£2 15s 0d
Ashtray	..	..	..	..	..	£1 7s 6d
Luggage grid	..	..	..	..	..	£14 15s 0d
Oil cooler	..	..	..	..	..	£8 18s 9d
Twin horns	..	..	..	..	..	£1 17s 10d

Make · M.G.   Type · MGB 1800

Manufacturer: The M.G. Car Co. Ltd., Abingdon-on-Thames, Berks.

Test Conditions

Weather ... Mist, brightening later,
with 0-5 m.p.h. wind
Temperature ... 13 deg. C. (56 deg. F.). Barometer
29·9in. Hg.
Dry concrete and asphalt surfaces.

Weight

Kerb weight (with oil, water and half-full fuel
tank) 18·5cwt (2,072lb-972kg)
Front-rear distribution, per cent F, 52·4; R, 47·6
Laden as tested .... 21·5cwt (2,408lb-1,092kg)

Turning Circles

Between kerbs .... L, 32ft 0in.; R, 32ft 10in.
Between walls .... L, 33ft 4in.; R, 34ft 2in.
Turns of steering wheel lock to lock .... 2·9

Performance Data

Top gear m.p.h. per 1,000 r.p.m. .... 17·9
Mean piston speed at max. power ... 3,150ft/min.
Engine speed at mean max. speed ...... 5,770 r.p.m.
B.h.p. per ton laden .... 88·3

FUEL AND OIL CONSUMPTION

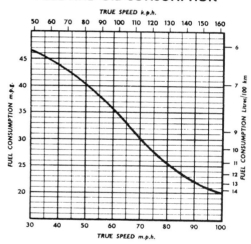

FUEL .... Premium Grade
(97 octane RM)
Test Distance .... 1,144 miles
Overall Consumption .... 21·4 m.p.g.
(13.3 lit/100 km.)
Normal Range .... 20—29 m.p.g.
(14.3—9.8 lit/100 km.)
OIL: S.A.E. 30 ... Consumption: 4,500 m.p.g.

HILL CLIMBING AT STEADY SPEEDS

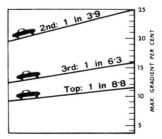

GEAR	Top	3rd	2nd
PULL	255	350	550
(lb per ton)	1 in 8·7	1 in 6·3	1 in 3·9
Speed range			
(m.p.h.)	48-52	42-46	34-38

MAXIMUM SPEEDS AND ACCELERATION (mean) TIMES

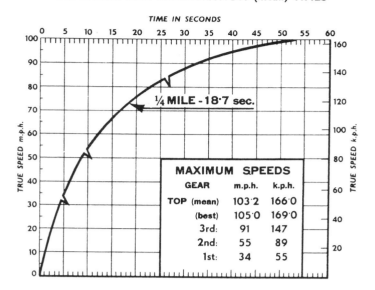

¼ MILE - 18·7 sec.

MAXIMUM SPEEDS		
GEAR	**m.p.h.**	**k.p.h.**
TOP (mean)	103·2	166·0
(best)	105·0	169·0
3rd:	91	147
2nd:	55	89
1st:	34	55

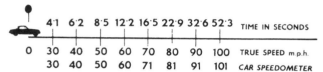

								TIME IN SECONDS
	4·1	6·2	8·5	12·2	16·5	22·9	32·6	52·3
0	30	40	50	60	70	80	90	100	TRUE SPEED m.p.h.
	30	40	50	60	71	81	91	101	CAR SPEEDOMETER

Speed range and time in seconds

m.p.h.	Top	3rd	2nd	1st
10—30	—	8·1	4·3	3·3
20—40	11·4	6·9	4·4	—
30—50	9·7	6·1	4·9	—
40—60	8·7	7·0	—	—
50—70	10·4	8·1	—	—
60—80	12·0	10·2	—	—
70—90	15·7	18·0	—	—
80—100	29·8	—	—	—

BRAKES	Pedal Load	Retardation	Equiv. distance
(from 30 m.p.h.	25lb	0·20g	152ft
in neutral)	50lb	0·42g	72ft
	75lb	0·75g	40ft
	100lb	1·0g	30·2ft
Handbrake		0·40g	75ft

CLUTCH   Pedal load and travel—40lb and 4·5in.

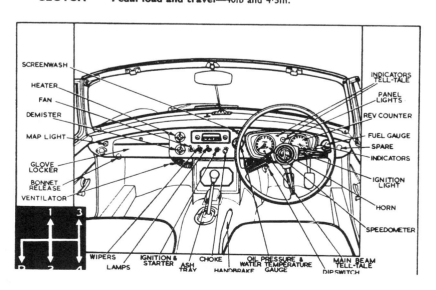

A map light on the left of the facia may be turned on when the exterior lamps are in use. The ashtray on the transmission hump is an optional extra. A padded roll above the facia is extended along the top edge of each door

200 miles are covered between refuelling stops, which may be considered only just adequate. For the standard high compression engine fitted to the MGB (8·75 to 1), fuel of at least 98 octane is recommended; but in fact the engine did not pink and only occasionally ran on with the normal premium grades of fuel (97 octane) which were used throughout the test.

Clutch take-up is delightfully smooth, and the pedal operating load is relatively light; the car had no difficulty in restarting on the 1 in 3 test hill.

A higher ratio final drive compensates for the smaller wheels fitted (14in. instead of 15in. as on the MGA), and top gear speed per 1,000 r.p.m. is almost the same at 17·9 m.p.h. (previously 17·7 m.p.h.). Bottom gear is slightly lower than before, but a higher second gear ratio would be appreciated, though there is the advantage with the present gearing that the car will start from rest smoothly in second without judder. There is thus no need to engage the un-synchronized bottom gear when on the move in traffic, and when bottom gear is reluctant to engage at rest—which does happen occasionally—there is no difficulty in moving away in the next higher gear. The gear change itself is both precise and rigid, and a joy to use. Synchromesh on the three upper ratios was never beaten, even in the snatched gear changes of performance testing. Reverse is easily engaged if the lever is knocked to the left, instead of attempting to lift and push it against the safety spring.

Rack-and-pinion steering is retained, and by incorporating a universal joint in the steering column a "straight-on" wheel angle has been obtained. Some drivers found that the steering wheel was a little too large and mounted rather high, so that the top of the rim interfered with forward vision, but all were agreed that the steering itself is above criticism. It combines the virtues of lightness at low speeds, and a turning circle of only 32ft between kerbs, with a superb degree of accuracy. No lost movement is present, and hairline steering corrections control the course of the car at speed; cross wind effects are scarcely, if ever, noticed. A popular complaint against rack-and-pinion steering—wheel shock and tremor over rough surfaces—does not apply with the MGB.

A fine compromise between the needs for sports car firmness and the superior comfort to be expected from this much improved car has been achieved in the design of the

suspension. Small, firm, vertical movement of the car is felt in most conditions, particularly at speed on an indifferent surface; yet there is remarkably good insulation from the larger irregularities of road surface, and the way in which the car rode over a typical badly neglected secondary road at 70 m.p.h. was outstanding. Again, on very rough going, such as irregular *pavé* taken at 50 m.p.h. (which is decidedly fast for such conditions), the occupants are aware of the work being done by the suspension, but still are not shaken about. Aeon rubber buffers at the rear absorb the shock of severe spring deflection without trans-

Whether with hood raised or with the optional full length tonneau cover fitted, the car looks impressively neat and well-finished. Both doors may be locked with the key; the passenger door has a locking catch

Apart from the distributor, which is obscured by the pipes to the oil cooler, all components are commendably accessible. The oil cooler, which is optional on home market cars, is visible ahead of the radiator

An inconvenient prop has to be fixed in position to hold the boot lid open. Luggage space is severely restricted by the positioning of the spare wheel

M.G. MGB 1800 . . .

mitting any severe bottoming to the back of the car over the roughest tracks. This car would certainly be at home for high-speed cruising on fast but ill-surfaced roads of the Continent.

For owners of the MGA, one of the greatest joys of the model has always been the tidy, surefooted and easily controllable handling characteristics; and the new MGB is even better. There is slight understeer until the limit of adhesion is approached, when the rear wheels begin gently to break away. The response to steering correction is immediate, and at speed on twisting country roads the M.G. is most satisfying to handle.

Allied to the responsive nature of the car is its feeling of tautness. There is no scuttle shake, and the whole car feels immensely sturdy and rigid. The same is true with the hood in place, when there is still freedom from rattles.

Lockheed brakes are fitted, with discs at the front. There

is no servo assistance, yet reassuring response is available without need for excessively heavy pedal effort. It is certainly creditable that like the last B.M.C. sports car road tested—the Austin-Healey 3000 Mk. II Convertible—the MGB's brakes returned a deceleration figure of 1g (the theoretical maximum) at 30 m.p.h. with 100lb pedal pressure. Higher pedal pressures resulted in a tendency to wheel lock, and slight slewing towards the left, but without any marked loss of efficiency. On the road they are superb brakes for fast driving with safety.

Just to the left of the driving seat is the handbrake lever, ideally placed for convenient use. It held the car securely on the 1 in 3 test hill.

It is obvious that a great deal of work has gone into the design of the bad weather equipment for this more refined model. A choice of hoods is available, the standard version being entirely detachable and stowed in the luggage compartment. On the test car, the optional version was fitted, which costs £5 10s extra including tax. When lowered, it lies in the well behind the driving seat, while when raised it makes a thoroughly neat and weatherproof finish to the car. It could not be said that raising and lowering the hood were simply the "work of a moment," as with some true convertibles. On each side there are three press studs, four Lift-the-Dot fasteners, two slides and one over-centre windscreen clip to be operated; and if the driver is alone he is involved in quite a battle, and a succession of trips from one side to the other, to convert the car from the open or closed condition. With practice, times can be reduced.

A Valued Extra

A short tonneau cover is provided as standard equipment and there is also available a full-length tonneau cover with detachable rail, which makes a smart finish to the MGB when open. This is virtually essential for the effort saved by not having to erect the hood, in case of rain, every time the car is parked. It is well tailored, covering the lowered side windows, and including zip-up slots for use with safety belts.

More attention is needed to draught-sealing when the hood is raised, at the point where the side window nestles against the hood flap; but in other respects the car is very cosy when closed. The hood seal along the top of the windscreen is first class, and is tightly secured by the two over-centre clips mentioned earlier. With the hood lowered, the cockpit seems to enclose a pocket of fairly still air, and the occupants are not buffeted or exposed to severe draughts. The side windows wind smoothly and easily.

On the test car the efficiency of the optional extra heater was impaired because its fan was not working, and the usual low-temperature thermostat fitted to B.M.C. cars left the coolant too cold to be of much use in the heater. However, air delivery by ram effect above the scuttle is good, and is governed by rotary controls on the facia; and with better temperature maintenance the heater would be amply effective. A small trap door on each side of the heater console allows the supply of hot air to be cut off absolutely in warm weather, and for use when it is very hot there is a cold air vent with two-position control beneath the facia. This had the rare distinction of admitting air which was really cold.

Ahead of the heater console is a large loudspeaker mounting which serves a second duty by assisting in the commendable scuttle rigidity. On the test car the Smiths all-transistor Radiomobile receiver provided good tone quality and a wide range of undistorted volume. Speech from the radio is clearly audible even at 100 m.p.h. with the hood down. This also emphasizes the low level of wind noise.

A windscreen tie rod securing the upper rail is also used as the mounting for the rear mirror, with the useful feature that the mirror can be adjusted to the correct height for maximum rearward vision, to suit the individual driver. Although the screen is shallow and fairly far forward, visibility is good, and the quarter windows are not unduly obstructive. Comfortable and softly padded seats, upholstered in leather, are appreciated, and give good support in the small of the back and right under the thighs, as well as holding the occupant securely in fast cornering. They have ample range of fore-and-aft adjustment to suit all drivers,

149

and the angle of rake of the squab may also be reset. A sturdy hook at the bottom of each backrest prevents it from tilting forward, but if, as we found, it is preferred to be able to tilt the seats forward to give easy access to the rear "trench" for luggage, these may be unbolted and reversed.

For some drivers the pendant pedals are mounted too high, as also is the foot-operated dipswitch. Heel-and-toe operation of brake and accelerator is not practicable; the side of the foot has to be used, which is possible, but awkward.

Instrumentation is excellent, and it is worthy of special note that the speedometer was accurate within 1 m.p.h. right up to maximum speed. Ignition and headlamp main beam warning lights are incorporated in the rev counter and speedometer, and there is variable brightness control for the instrument illumination. The oil pressure gauge and coolant thermometer are in a combined dial to the left of the speedometer. A singularly vague and inaccurate fuel gauge indicated anything between full and empty according to whether the car was accelerating or braking.

Three identical tumbler switches to the left of the ignition-starter keyhole control the heater blower, wipers and lights. As a result of the layout, it is difficult to find the switch for the lights quickly—a specially bad point as a headlamp flasher which such a car certainly should have is not fitted. The wipers work quite vigorously, at one speed, and clear a good area of the windscreen. A direct-pressure windscreen washer is fitted, and is convenient to use. A finger-tip control beneath the steering wheel operates the winking indicators, which are self-cancelling and have well-placed repeater lights ahead of the driver—valuable advances over the MGA time switch arrangement.

Ample illumination for the top performance to be used at night is provided by the sealed filament headlamps, although these were set too high on the test car. Twin horns, sounded by the steering wheel boss button (with MG octagon), are optional at £1 17s 10d extra.

Considerable improvement has been made in the provision of luggage accommodation, both behind the seats, and in the lockable boot. The spare wheel occupies much of the boot space, but there is still room for a fair amount of well-stowed luggage; a self-fixing stay would be preferable to the prop provided. A different key from that for the ignition and door locks is used for the boot, and for the diminutive facia locker. The passenger door is locked from the inside by turning a catch. Neither door, when locked, can be opened by its interior handle—a wise provision to discourage theft when the car is left with the tonneau cover fitted.

There was much desirable optional equipment on the car tested—to a total value of some £83 which would have increased the tax-paid cost of the car to £1,032. But in standard form, this MGB is still an altogether superior car to its predecessor.

Specification

ENGINE

Cylinders	...	4
Bore	...	80·3mm (3·16in.)
Stroke	...	89·0mm (3·5in.)
Displacement	...	1,798 c.c. (109·6 cu. in.)
Valve gear	...	Overhead, pushrods and rockers
Compression ratio		8·8 to 1
Carburettors	...	Twin S.U. HS4 semi-downdraught
Fuel pump	...	S.U. HP electric
Oil filter	...	Tecalemit full flow
Max. power	...	95 b.h.p. (net) at 5,400 r.p.m.
Max. torque	...	110 lb. ft. at 3,000 r.p.m.

TRANSMISSION

Clutch	...	Borg and Beck, 8in. dia. single dry plate, diaphragm spring type
Gearbox	...	Four-speed synchromesh on 2nd, 3rd and top, central floor change
Overall ratios	...	Top 3·91, 3rd 5·37, 2nd 8·66, 1st 14·21, Reverse 18·59
Final drive	...	Hypoid bevel, 3·91 to 1

CHASSIS

Construction	...	Integral with steel body

SUSPENSION

Front	...	Independent, coil springs and wishbones; Armstrong lever-type dampers forming top link.
Rear	...	Live axle; semi-elliptic leaf springs; Armstrong lever-type dampers
Steering	...	Rack and pinion. Wheel dia., 16·5in.

BRAKES

Type	...	Lockheed, hydraulic, disc front, drum rear; no servo
Dimensions	...	F. 10·75 in. dia. discs; R. 10in. dia. drums, 1·75in. wide shoes.
Swept area	...	F. 203 sq. in; R. 107 sq. in. Total: 310 sq. in (335 sq. in. per ton laden)

WHEELS

Type	...	Pressed steel disc, 4 studs; centre-lock wire wheels extra
Tyres	...	5·60-14in. Dunlop RS5

EQUIPMENT

Battery	...	12-volt 58-amp. hr (2 x 6-volt)
Headlamps	...	Lucas sealed-filament 50-40-watt
Reversing lamp	...	None
Electric fuses	...	2
Screen wipers	...	Single speed, self-parking
Screen washer	...	Standard, manual plunger
Interior heater	...	Extra, Smith's fresh air with electric booster
Safety belts	...	Extra, anchorages provided
Interior trim	...	Leather on wearing surfaces
Floor covering	...	Pvc mats; carpet over transmission tunnel
Starting handle	...	Standard
Jack	...	Side lifting, rotary handle
Jacking points	...	1 below each door
Other bodies	...	None

MAINTENANCE

Fuel tank	...	10 Imp. gallons
Cooling system	...	9·5 pints (plus 0·5 pints in heater)
Engine sump	...	7·5 pints. Change oil every 3,000 miles; change filter element every 6,000 miles
Gearbox	...	4·5 pints SAE30. Change oil ever 6,000 miles
Final drive	...	2·25 pints SAE90. Change oil every 6,000 miles
Grease	...	8 points every 3,000 miles
Tyre pressures	...	F. 17; R. 20 p.s.i. (normal driving). F. 23; R. 26 p.s.i. (fast driving). F. 20; R. 24 p.s.i. (full load)

Scale : 0·3in. to 1ft.

Cushions uncompressed.

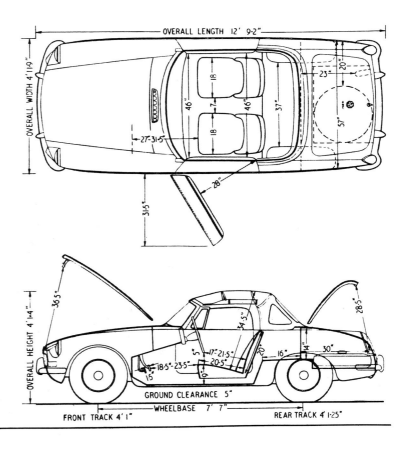

Autocar
ROAD
TEST
NUMBER 2159

M.G. MGC 2,912 c.c.

AT A GLANCE. New derivative of MGB with six-cylinder engine. Lack of low speed torque and engine reluctant to rev. Very noisy fan. New all synchromesh gearbox works well, but has odd choice of ratios with overdrive. Heavy fuel consumption. Light brakes, with some fade. Good ride; strong understeer; steering low geared. Lots of legroom. Heater extra. Good finish.

MANUFACTURER
MG Car Co. Ltd., MG Division, British Motor Corporation, Abingdon-on-Thames, Berkshire.

PRICES
Basic	..	..	£895	0s	0d
Purchase Tax	..		£206	16s	6d
Seat belts (pair)		..	£6	0s	0d
Total (in GB)		..	£1,111	16s	6d

EXTRAS (inc. P.T.)
Overdrive	..	..	£61	9s	2d
Wire wheels	..	..	£30	14s	7d
Heater	..	..	£15	1s	2d
Radio	..	..	£20	0s	0d

PERFORMANCE SUMMARY
Mean maximum speed		120 mph
Standing start ¼-mile..		17.7 sec
0-60 mph		10.0 sec
30-70 mph (through gears)	..	9.8 sec
Fuel consumption	..	19 mpg
Miles per tankful	..	228

THERE has been talk of a new big sports car from BMC now for a couple of years. Rumours of a new big Austin-Healey with this or that kind of new engine, and of various coupés from the Abingdon stable have all been doing the rounds. After all these exciting stories, the new MGC must have come as a disappointment to many, because it looks just like the MGB and only a keen car spotter would notice the bulging bonnet hiding the six-cylinder engine. Inside there have been a few changes; all these also apply to the four-cylinder "B". Squeezing the bigger engine into the MGB shell has called for quite a number of engineering changes, so what in effect is much more than just the engine option it seems, adds £154 to the total price.

For the moment the Austin-Healey 3000 continues as a parallel model priced at £24 more than the MGC. In effect it shares the same engine, although that in the "C" has three extra main bearings and a revised cylinder block. Our issue of the 19 October described the new car in some detail, so we will run over only the essential statistics again here.

Basically the 3-litre engine has not changed its layout; it still uses push-rods and rockers for its valve gear, but the block has been redesigned to make it shorter and a little lighter. Somewhere along the line a few horsepower have been lost (either in extra bearing friction or as windage losses from the reduced crank web clearances) and the MGC engine develops 145 bhp net compared with the Healey's 150. Maximum torque is about the same with 170 lb. ft. at 3,500 rpm.

To match the revised engine the gearbox has been brought up to date by adding synchromesh to first, and without overdrive the ratios are much the same as those of the MGB, with an appropriate raising of the final drive ratio from 3.91 to 3.07 to 1. With overdrive a 3.307 axle is used, and for a reason BMC have not explained to us, a much higher first gear is fitted as well, with only slightly raised other indirects. Our test car had the latter arrangement, and while the long-legged, easy cruising at 27 mph per 1,000 rpm in overdrive top was appreciated on the continent, the gap between second and third spoilt an otherwise excellent set of ratios. Even without overdrive the MGC revs at only 4,200 rpm at 100 mph, so

Autocar road test number 2159

Make: M.G.
Type: MGC 2,912 c.c.

TEST CONDITIONS
Weather: Sunny. Wind: 8 mph
Temperature: 11 deg. C. (53 deg. F.)
Barometer: 29·3in. Hg.
Humidity: 55 per cent
Surfaces: Dry concrete and asphalt

Figures taken at 2,900 miles by our own staff at the Motor Industry Research Association proving ground at Nuneaton.

WEIGHT
Kerb weight 22·1 cwt (2,477lb–1,125kg) (with oil, water and half-full fuel tank)
Distribution, per cent: F, 55·7; R, 44·3
Laden as tested: 25·5 cwt (2,853lb–1,294kg)

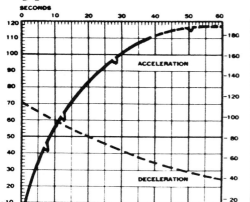

MAXIMUM SPEEDS

Gear	mph	kph	rpm
OD Top (mean)	120	193	4,450
(best)	121	195	4,490
Top	120	193	5,450
OD 3rd	115	185	5,550
3rd	97	156	5,750
2nd	62	101	5,750
1st	44	71	5,750

Standing ¼-Mile 17.7 sec 79 mph
Standing Kilometre 32 sec 103 mph

TIME IN SECONDS	4·0	5·6	7·6	10·0	13·8	18·0	23·1	29·3	40·9	
TRUE SPEED MPH	30	40	50	60	70	80	90	100	110	120
INDICATED SPEED	31	42	51	62	71	82	92	101	111	121

Mileage recorder 0·9 per cent over-reading.   Test distance 1,031 miles.

Speed range, gear ratios and time in seconds

mph	OD Top (2·68)	Top (3·31)	OD 3rd (3·54)	3rd (4·32)	2nd (6·82)	1st (9·86)
10— 30	—	11·1	10·4	7·6	4·5	3·4
20— 40	13·2	9·6	9·0	6·3	4·4	3·3
30— 50	11·4	9·1	8·5	7·0	4·0	—
40— 60	11·5	10·0	9·1	6·8	4·3	—
50— 70	14·2	10·7	9·3	7·3	—	—
60— 80	16·9	11·1	10·1	8·5	—	—
70— 90	13·8	12·8	11·9	9·0	—	—
80—100	25·3	15·4	13·9	—	—	—
90—110	33·6	18·3	19·0	—	—	—

FUEL CONSUMPTION

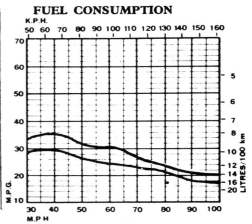

(At constant speeds—mpg)

	OD Top	Top
30 mph	33·1	29·4
40	35·1	29·2
50	32·0	27·0
60	30·8	24·5
70	26·8	22·9
80	24·4	21·4
90	22·2	19·2
100	19·7	17·3

Typical mpg 19 (14·9 litres/100km)
Calculated (DIN) mpg 20·8 (13·6 litres/100km)
Overall mpg 17·5 (16·1 litres/100km)
Grade of fuel, Premium, 4-star (min 97RM)

OIL CONSUMPTION
Miles per pint (SAE 20W/40) .. 1,000

BRAKES (from 30 mph in neutral)

Load	g	Distance
25 lb	0·25	100 ft
50 ,,	0·58	52 ,,
75 ,,	0·98	30·7 ,,
100 ,,	1·03	29·2 ,,
Handbrake	0·36	84 ,,

Max. Gradient, 1 in 3
Clutch Pedal: 35lb and 5in.

PEDAL PRESSURE (lb) FOR 0·5g
STOPS AT ¼ MILE INTERVALS FROM 70 M.P.H

TURNING CIRCLES
Between kerbs L, 35ft 9in.; R, 35ft 9in
Between walls L, 36ft 9in.; R, 36ft 9in
Steering wheel turns, lock to lock .. 3·5

HOW THE CAR COMPARES:

MAXIMUM SPEED (mean) MPH

100	110	120	130
MG MGC			
Austin-Healey 3000 Mk III			
MG MGB			
Reliant Scimitar 3-litre			
Triumph GT6			

0-60 MPH (sec)

30	20	10
MG MGC		
Austin-Healey 3000 Mk III		
MG MGB		
Reliant Scimitar 3-litre		
Triumph GT6		

STANDING START ¼-MILE (sec)

30	20	10
MG MGC		
Austin-Healey 3000 Mk III		
MG MGB		
Reliant Scimitar 3-litre		
Triumph GT6		

MPG OVERALL

10	20	30
MG MGC		
Austin-Healey 3000 Mk III		
MG MGB		
Reliant Scimitar 3-litre		
Triumph GT6		

PRICES

MG MGC	£1,102
Austin-Healey 3000 Mk III	£1,126
MG MGB	£948
Reliant Scimitar 3-litre	£1,516
Triumph GT 6	£985

M.G. MGC . . .

it is hard to see why this option is listed. For the first time there is the alternative of Borg-Warner automatic transmission.

The engine is something of an enigma. It is smooth and flexible, but completely lacking in sporty characteristics. Whilst it pulls evenly from very low revs (below 500 rpm in top), there is very little low speed torque *and* the engine seems reluctant to rev or develop much top end power. This impression is borne out by the top gear acceleration figures, which are less quick than those of MGB for every 20 mph increment up to 70 mph (20–40 mph : 8·6 sec MGB, 9·6 sec MGC; 30–50 mph : 8·7 sec MGB, 9·1 sec MGC; 40–60 mph : 9·1 sec MGB, 10·0 sec MGC). Overall through the gears, however, the new car is appreciably quicker with a 0 to 60 mph time of 10·0 sec (MGB: 12·9), and a fast standing quarter-mile in 17·7 sec (MGB: 18·9).

Usually the engine is sweet and docile, but once or twice we experienced slight plug fouling after fairly long spells in heavy traffic. For the first few minutes after a cold start it was particularly difficult to keep the engine from dying, and when accelerating hard oil surge caused clouds of blue smoke from the exhaust. A new moulded plastic cooling fan in a metal cowl whines and whirrs all the time very loudly, and at high revs the driver hears a loud noise like a supercharged vacuum cleaner. To avoid the fuss and bother of making the engine rev, one never goes much above 3,000 rpm for everyday driving, except for the occasional burn-up away from the lights.

Getting the car away from rest quickly was hampered by clutch slip when we tried over 3,500 rpm for take-offs, and by a definite lack of torque below these revs. Even so, a 0 to 100 mph time of under 30 sec is pretty brisk, and might even be faster on the non-overdrive car with better gearbox ratios. Our in-the-gears maxima of 44, 62 and 97 mph at an indicated 5,500 rpm (5,750 actual) show up the odd spacing mentioned earlier. Overdrive third takes the car on to 115 mph, and in both direct top and overdrive top we recorded mean maxima of 120 mph. The Laycock overdrive is operated by a little cranked toggle switch on the facia under the wheel rim on the right; it engaged and disengaged very smoothly, but with a definite delay on the upward shift.

The gearbox has a firm and robust-feeling remote control with a nice large ball-shaped knob rather spoilt by a sharp-edged nut underneath it. Movements are very positive and the powerful synchromesh stood up perfectly to all the punishment we could

The 6-cyl. engine fills all the available space, but everything needing routine attention is easily reached, especially the oil filter, on the left of the block

give it during acceleration runs. The gate is very narrow and there is spring loading towards the first and second gear plane; this makes it harder to be sure one is in neutral, and initially the change up from second to third feels strange. All the indirect gears are very quiet, except for a slight whine on the over-run.

For maximum speed runs we took the MGC to Belgium and found it cruised very well at 100 mph with arrow-like stability. Wind roar round the hood drowns out all conversation and the radio, and anyone preferring to tour over long distances rather than have the option of fresh air would be better off with the alternative GT version.

Compared with the Austin-Healey 3000, the new MG is slightly slower in both top speed (121 mph for the Healey) and acceleration (0 to 100 mph : 25·7 sec for the Healey). Fuel consumption is also not as good as that of the Healey and much heavier than the MGB's. Overall we man-

aged only 17·5 mpg with the MGC, although at a steady 70 mph, for example, it covers nearly 23 mpg in direct top and 26·8 mpg in overdrive; overall figures for comparison are 22·0 mpg for the MGB (with overdrive) and 20·3 mpg for the Healey (again with overdrive).

Of course, the new car is not as heavy as the Healey, but it weighs a full 350 lb more than the MGB. The six-cylinder engine is 210 lb heavier than the B-series unit, and the new gearbox is larger. Considering all this amounts to 16·4 per cent extra on the weight of the MGB, it must have been very hard for the manufacturers to keep the weight distribution reasonably balanced. The front-end weight is up from 52·6 to only 55·7 per cent of the total, and a corresponding increase in the recommended tyre pressure differential (from equal front and rear to a 4 psi front bias) restores handling. To lighten the steering load a lower geared rack is used and the king-pins have been de-castored.

The boot holds a remarkable amount of soft luggage, but there is no trimming. With the hood down the cover and irons take up a good deal of room. A strut has to be used to hold the lid open

KOV 259F

Left: The facia layout is identical to the MGB's. The standards of fit and finish are very high, with leather on the seats and rubber floor mats. Right: There is a vast amount of adjustment on the seats. The flap type door handles are very neat and easy to use

Even so, the steering is heavy and it is by no means a delicate car to drive. For a start the steering wheel feels huge (it has a 16·5in. dia.) and there are now 3·5 turns needed for a 35ft 9in. turning circle instead of 2·9 turns for a 32ft 4in. one. It was no help that our car pulled strongly to the left and the steering wheel was not straight on its splines. It now has a stitched on leather glove over its rim.

Apart from the low-geared steering there is strong understeer which makes the front end slow to respond. In the low gears there is enough torque to help the back round, but on wet surfaces we found it very hard indeed to catch the tail if it got out of line, so we settled for a slow-in, fast-out (once it was straight) technique. The MGC lacks the "chuckability" of both the MGB and the Austin-Healey 3000; it is better suited to *Routes Nationales* than mountain *cols*.

MGC wheels are an inch bigger in diameter and an inch wider than those of the MGB, and Dunlop SP 41 radial-ply tyres are standard. Grip is good and it is virtually impossible to spin the rear wheels on wet roads. Once or twice, however, we locked a front wheel when braking hard. There is little thump from the tyres on ridges and catseyes, but they are prone to squeal during hard cornering, even in the wet.

To get the new engine in the MGB frame the front cross-member has been discarded, and to transfer the suspension loads back to the stiff scuttle area, longitudinal torsion bars replace the coil springs used on the "B". For a sports car the ride is quite soft and almost in the saloon car class for comfort. Firm damping retains something of the traditional taut feel, and there is no pitch and very little roll at any time. Only on very rough roads does the vertical motion become harsh, but even then there is surprisingly little body shake

and no scuttle flexing.

Braking has been revised to suit the new weight distribution and there is a vacuum servo. Pedal loads are light and progressive up to a maximum of over 1·0g at 80lb. Surprisingly for a sports car we measured a lot of fade during ten stops from 70 mph at ¾-mile intervals, and the front discs got very hot and smoked. The hand-brake is powerful and held the car on a 1-in-3 facing either way; the cranked brake lever, fitted in between the driving seat and the tunnel, is convenient to use and well placed.

Unlike most two-seater sports cars, the MG is built for big people. Even our 6ft testers did not need the seat right back; there is an abundance of legroom and enough foot room in spite of the wider tunnel. On the other hand, our shorter staff found that they sat too low in the car and therefore had difficulty in seeing enough of the bonnet to locate themselves on the road. By the latest

standards, the windscreen seems shallow, especially on a dark, wet night, and the wiper blades park on the screen obscuring some of the driver's view of the left-hand kerb. At last the wipers have two speeds.

Some features of the revised interior have been dictated by the new American safety requirements. The flush interior door handles are neat and practical, but the rubber knobs on the window winders repeatedly came off. The glove locker lid can be held shut only by locking it with its key, which also locks the boot. There is another key for the ignition and doors.

The heater is a £15 extra, and it is controlled by two rotary knobs on the left of the facia. The top one works a simple water valve, which seems to have no intermediate temperature between hot and cold, and the lower one directs the air to screen or footwells. There is no ram effect at all, so the single-speed fan must be used all the time heat or demisting is

Reversing lamps are built into the tail panel. From the rear, only the small MGC sign above the octagon badge shows which model this is

required. A separate cold-air intake is worked by a lever under the left of the facia.

The hood is still one of those detachable pvc and tubular frame affairs which must be taken off and folded up before stowing it in the boot, or in settled climates leaving it at home. Putting it up in a hurry is quite quick, but experience helps a lot in reducing the frequent trips from side to side when doing this alone. Sealing round the doors is not completely stormproof.

We were amazed to find the boot has no self-propping strut for its lid, and this is a real nuisance when loading or unloading an armful of odds and ends. With the optional wire wheels one really needs several soft bags for luggage as the hub of the spare pokes up in the way of a normal suitcase.

Probably our impressions of the MGC would have been more favourable if we had taken it for a holiday to the south of Spain and back. As it is, we were able to use it only around England and for a brief day trip to the Jabekke road in Belgium. The MGC is the latest example from a very famous factory which has regularly produced classic sports cars in the past; somewhere in the large BMC complex it has lost the "Abingdon touch."

SPECIFICATION: M.G. MGC (FRONT ENGINE, REAR-WHEEL DRIVE)

ENGINE
Cylinders	6, in line
Cooling system	Water; pump, fan and thermostat
Bore	83·4mm (3·28in.)
Stroke	88·9mm (3·50in.)
Displacement	2,912 c.c. (177·7 cu. in.)
Valve gear	Overhead; pushrods and rockers
Compression ratio 9-to-1: Min. octane rating: 98 RM
Carburettors	2 SU HS6
Fuel pump	SU electric
Oil filter	Full flow, renewable element
Max. power	145 bhp (net) at 5,250 rpm
Max torque	170 lb. ft. (net) at 3,400 rpm

TRANSMISSION
Clutch	Borg and Beck diaphragm spring, 9in. dia.
Gearbox	Four-speed, all synchromesh; overdrive on Third and Top.
Gear ratios	Top 1·0; OD Top 0·82 OD Third 1·07; Third 1·31; Second 2·06; First 2·98; Reverse 2·67
Final drive	Hypoid bevel, 3·31-to-1

CHASSIS and BODY
Construction	Integral with steel body

SUSPENSION
Front	Independent, torsion bars, wishbones, telescopic dampers, anti-roll bar
Rear	Live axle, half-elliptic leaf springs, lever arm dampers

STEERING .. Rack and pinion
Wheel dia. 16·5in.

BRAKES
Make and type	Girling discs front, drums rear
Servo	Girling vacuum type
Dimensions	F, 11·06in. dia.; R, 9in. dia. 2·5in. wide shoes
Swept area	F, 226·2 sq. in.; R, 127·2 sq. in Total 353·4 sq. in. (277·3 sq. in./ton laden)

WHEELS
Type	Pressed steel disc standard—optional 72-spoke wire wheels on test car, 5in. wide rim
Tyres —make	Dunlop
—type	SP41 radial-ply tubed
—size	165—15 mm.

EQUIPMENT
Battery	12-volt 58-amp. hr. (2 × 6-volt)
Alternator	Lucas 16AC 33-amp
Headlamps	Lucas sealed filament 100-180-watt (total)
Reversing lamp	2 standard
Electric fuses	2
Screen wipers	2-speed, self-parking
Screen washer	Standard, manual plunger
Interior heater	Extra, water valve type
Heated backlight	Not applicable on roadster

Safety belts	Extra, anchorages built in
Interior trim	Leather and pvc seats
Floor covering	Carpet and rubber mats
Starting handle	No provision
Jack	Screw pillar
Jacking points	One each side under sills
Windscreen	Laminated
Underbody protection	Phosphate treatment prior to painting

MAINTENANCE
Fuel tank	12 Imp. gallons (no reserve) (54·8 litres)
Cooling system	18·5 pints (including heater) (10·5 litres)
Engine sump	12·8 pints (7·2 litres) SAE 20W/40. Change oil every 6,000 miles; Change filter element every 6,000 miles
Gearbox and overdrive	14·5 pints SAE 20W/40. Change oil every 6,000 miles
Final drive	1·75 pints SAE 90EP. No oil change needed, check level every 6,000 miles
Grease	4 points every 3,000 miles
Tyre pressures	F, 26; R, 22 p.s.i. (normal driving). F, 28; R, 32 p.s.i. (fast driving)

PERFORMANCE DATA
Top gear mph per 1,000 rpm	22·12
Overdrive top mph per 1,000 rpm	26·95
Mean piston speed at max power	3,060ft/min
Bhp per ton laden	113·7

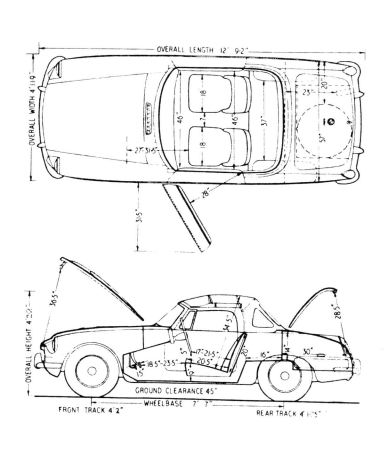

155

AUTOTEST
MG MIDGET MK III
(1,275 c.c.)

AT-A-GLANCE: BLMC's familiar small sports-car in latest paintwork and trim, with some detail improvements. Higher gearing increases top speed slightly but not acceleration. Excellent handling, firm ride, good value and good fun.

MANUFACTURER
British Leyland Motor Corporation Ltd., (MG Division), Abingdon-on-Thames, Berkshire.

PRICES
Basic	£692	0s	0d
Purchase Tax	£213	14s	9d
Seat belts (approx.)	£10	0s	0d
Total (in G.B.)	£915	14s	9d

EXTRAS (inc P.T.)
*Tonneau cover and rail	£11	15s	0d
*Radial ply tyres	£9	2s	9d
Wire wheels	£32	12s	9d
Oil cooler	£13	1s	1d
Anti-roll bar	£3	18s	4d
Hard top	£65	5s	7d
Headrests (pair)	£10	8s	1d

*Fitted to test car

PRICE AS TESTED £936 12s 6d

PERFORMANCE SUMMARY
Mean maximum speed	94 mph
Standing start ¼-mile	19.6 sec
0-60 mph	14.1 sec
30-70 mph through gears	15.8 sec
Typical fuel consumption	30 mpg
Miles per tankful	180

THERE are, surprisingly, still too few contenders for the role of the young man's (or young woman's) first sports-car. With still-steeper insurance one might have thought that the demand for a proper open two-seater of acceptably nippy performance, nimble handling, sports-car appointments and—by today's inflated standards—middling low price, was bigger than ever. At £906 Austin-Healey Sprite-cum-MG Midget in its latest form still remains perhaps the best car of the type available. Performance, though good, is still not as good as a number of saloon cars, but the Midget (which is the "badge" we tested) is undeniably a true sports-car.

The body shape dates back to 1961 when the highly distinctive "frog-eyed" Sprite was restyled to a more conventional—and perhaps less original—shape. Later, a more important change in one way, the unusual quarter-elliptic leaf-sprung back axle was altered to ordinary half-elliptic springing which more or less eliminated the car's marked and—once you'd got to know it—amusing tendency to slight rear-axle steer. The faithful BMC A-series engine fitted has gradually gone up in capacity and power; it stands now at 1,275 c.c. in the inexplicably mild 64 bhp at 5,800 rpm form. (Its saloon stablemate the MG1300 Mk II is allowed 5 bhp more and is at some points slightly faster). Most recent alterations are a 3.9-to-1 final drive (in place of 4.22), black paint on the sills giving the effect of particularly heavy side-flashes, the words "Midget" in heavy chrome also on the sides, nave-plateless wheels (wire-wheels remaining an option), and self-propping boot and bonnet stays (at last).

From the performance point of view, the gearing change is the most important, the overall figure going up from 15.4 to 16.5 mph per 1,000 rpm on the Michelin ZX 145 SR-13in. radial-ply tyres on the test car (cross-ply tyres are standard). (Owners with other tyres fitted should note that in this particular size there are different rev-per-mile figures for the various makes, giving different overall gearing.) Previously the same-size Midget's top speed of 93 mph was seen after peak-power engine speed—6,000 rpm—but the higher-geared test car achieved 94 mph mean at 5,700 rpm, with a best figure on one leg of MIRA's banked circuit in good conditions of 96 (5,800 rpm). One does not notice much difference in cruising refinement subjectively, though there is obviously some improvement. Fuel consumption overall, compared with the lower-geared car which took part in the Midget-Spitfire double test (*Autocar* 10 April 1969), seems hardly affected. We averaged 29.6 mpg over 1,270 miles with best and worst consumptions of 26 and 35 mpg, depending of course on how one responded to the car's obvious willingness to work hard.

Acceleration is very slightly slower, to a degree only noticed by the ink-recording stopwatch. Showing the double-test car in brackets, from a standing start 50 mph comes up in 9.6sec (9.5), 60 in 14.1 (13.8), the ¼-mile in 19.6 (19.3), and 80 in 29.7 (28.3); the new car will however just achieve 90 mph within the length of MIRA's twin horizontal mile—in 51.3sec—which the other would not. Corresponding figures for the MG 1300 MkII are respectively 9.4sec, 14.1, 19.6, and 28.3, with 90 mph seen at 49.2sec.

Good car in traffic

Such cold comparisons are not to the Midget's advantage, and do less than justice to its likeable character. Coupled with good smooth-road handling and brakes (of which more anon), and good visibility whether or not the hood is down, the performance is more than enough to provide the keen driver with a lot of fun. Clearly what advantages the little MG has are at their best in traffic; one has more than enough to stay master of most traffic situations. The engine is always willing, beginning to pull hard from 3,000 rpm, though not baulking if you ask it to work from speeds only a little above its tickover. Recommended brief maximum speed is 6,300 rpm on the revcounter, which under-read by 100 rpm at this speed, but the engine feels happy to go higher without signs of valve-bounce. Exhaust and mechanical noise from the engine are not obtrusive; it is the gearbox which offends most clearly here. First gear would not seem out of voice in one of the lower-priced Vintage-period popular cars. It is very noisy on most examples we have tried. Second and 3rd are only somewhat better.

Gear ratios are well-chosen, giving maximum speeds of 33, 55 and 78 mph at 6,400 rpm. Useful maxima for everyday use at 6,000 rpm are 31, 52 and 73 mph. The gearchange is extremely precise, with nothing rubbery about it, and very much in character for the type of car. The Midget shares with its main competitor the Triumph Spitfire the distinction of lacking synchromesh on 1st gear, which omission stands out more clearly as the years roll by. One learns to judge engine and road speeds correctly for double-declutching changes down, but it isn't easy here. On the other hand the renowned flexibility of the A-series engine will enable the lazy or less-skilled driver to use 2nd instead in many instances. The clutch is equally tolerant, coping adequately with the

considerable revs needed to re-start two-up on the 1-in-3 test slope.

The Midget's steering is everything a sports-car's ought to be—light, very accurate, highly responsive, highly geared and, once the rack is fully run-in, giving good feel without too much kickback. There is no slop worth mentioning, so that on first driving it, having got out of almost any other car, one tends to "over-steer". The car's obviously rigid construction shows through to the driver on a twisty road; it feels very much all one piece. Slippery roads are fun in the Midget, which is unusually well balanced. Handling characteristics are completely safe; slight initial understeer changing progressively to middling tail-breakaway when you try really hard. There is no suggestion of treachery at any stage, though such a light car obviously badly needs all-independent suspension. Ride is distinctly firm, the live-axled back end hopping outwards somewhat on bumpy bends taken quickly. As usual with an open car one is not conscious of suspension noise to any degree.

Brakes are unassisted discs front, drums

Unlike several other sports-cars, the Midget's hood does not need a lot of practice to furl properly

This view shows how comparatively little three-quarter-rear vision is lost by the large-windowed hood. Rubber-faced overriders are a sensible feature

Neat trim lines still, though you can only buy the car now with the black side-strip paint. There are no nave-plates on the wheels. Right: Wide-angle, lens-distorted view of the Midget in its most pleasant form, with hood down

rear. They work well, giving 1g stopping power on a dry track with the rear wheels just locking at a not-too-heavy 80lb pedal pressure. There is adequate fade resistance for all normal purposes, though anyone using the car at all competitively does well to fit hard pads and linings (available, like much other speed equipment at extra cost, from British Leyland Special Tuning at Abingdon). The handbrake holds the car facing up or down the 1-in-3 slope.

The driving position remains somewhat old-fashioned. Taller drivers have to sit closer to the large steering wheel than they may prefer, and have just enough legroom. The quickness of the steering means that the first objection doesn't matter too much; the second could only be improved by a major redesign of the car. Door openings are rather cramping for getting out, and the too-stiff door releases are much too far back for easy reach. There is however a pleasant feeling of snugness once you're in the very comfortable driving seat. No major control is remote from you, the gearchange falls readily to hand, and the pedals are well arranged.

Heel-and-toe changes come easily, and there is room to rest the left foot on the foot dip-switch. The horn is in the most natural place, the large padded centre of the steering wheel, and makes a surprisingly "quality" noise. Visibility is of course superb with the hood down, except perhaps through the somewhat fussy clutter of the front quarter-lights. It is better-than-average with the hood up, with no serious blind spots.

The facia is pleasingly straightforward, with no ostentatious transatlantic lips and jowls. One would however like to see some extra attention paid to more efficient design—combination of wiper and washer switch and plunger for one thing and, on each door, a more substantial-feeling but less stiff-winding window handle. When it broke away from its fixing screws we learnt that the quite generous parcel shelf on the passenger's side is made of something resembling cardboard. Uprating the crude water-valve may increase the heat output, but it does nothing towards proper control of temperature.

Hood erection and furling is easier than on most British sports-cars. The windscreen-frame clamps need a lot of effort, so does buttoning down the hood-cover press-studs. If one fitted a wireless it would, with the hood up, only be any real use at slow speeds, as wind noise becomes too loud above 60 mph. Keen enthusiasts who prefer to carry out their own servicing will find the Midget's engine accessibility pretty good. They will however need a lot more in tools than comes with the car—in the usual scruffy bag lying loose in the boots of so many British cars. Boot space is limited by the spare wheel, but careful stowage with squashy bags will get quite a lot in.

As stated at the beginning, there is not very much competition for the Midget (and the Sprite). It is a model that fills a large need, and one we would like to see developed considerably without losing its worthy character of sports-car primer for the not-so-well-off younger driver (and slightly dashing shopping car for two-car families). As it is, it remains an excellent little car which certainly achieves its primary object—that of being fun to drive. □

MG MIDGET MK III (1,275 c.c.)

ACCELERATION

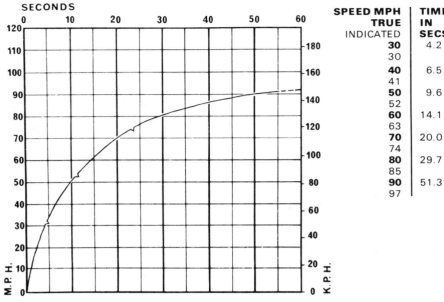

SPEED MPH TRUE INDICATED	TIME IN SECS
30	4.2
30	
40	6.5
41	
50	9.6
52	
60	14.1
63	
70	20.0
74	
80	29.7
85	
90	51.3
97	

SPEED RANGE, GEAR RATIOS AND TIME IN SECONDS

mph	Top (3.9)	3rd (5.29)	2nd (7.47)	1st (12.48)
10-30	—	8.0	5.5	4.0
20-40	10.7	7.4	5.2	—
30-50	10.4	7.2	6.3	—
40-60	10.7	8.3	—	—
50-70	12.3	10.3	—	—
60-80	16.9	—	—	—
70-90	31.8	—	—	—

Standing ¼-mile
19.6sec 69 mph
Standing kilometre
36.6sec 85mph
Test distance
1,270 miles
Mileage recorder
0.7 per cent
over-reading

PERFORMANCE
MAXIMUM SPEEDS

Gear	mph	kph	rpm
Top (mean)	94	151	5,700
(best)	96	155	5,800
3rd	78	126	6,400
2nd	55	89	6,400
1st	33	53	6,400

BRAKES

(from 70 mph in neutral)
Pedal load for 0.5g stops in lb

1	55-50	6	55-50
2	55-50	7	55-50
3	52-48	8	55-52
4	52-47	9	55-50
5	53-48	10	55-50

RESPONSE (from 30 mph in neutral)

Load	g	Distance
20lb	0.16	188ft
40lb	0.34	89ft
60lb	0.57	53ft
80lb	1.0	30.1ft
Handbrake	0.37	81ft
Max. Gradient 1 in 3		

CLUTCH
Pedal 35lb and 4.5 in.
MOTORWAY CRUISING

Indicated speed at 70mph	74mph
Engine (rpm at 70mph)	4,240rpm
(mean piston speed)	2,260ft/min.
Fuel (mpg at 70mph)	35.7
Passing (50-70mph)	10.4sec

COMPARISONS

MAXIMUM SPEED MPH
MG 1300 Mk II 2-door	(£968)	97
Ford Escort 1300GT 2-door . . .	(£966)	95
MG Midget Mk III	**(£906)**	**94**
Triumph Spitfire 4 Mk 3	(£876)	92
Mini 1275GT	(£894)	86

0-60 MPH, SEC
Ford Escort 1300GT 2-door	12.2
Triumph Spitfire 4 Mk 3	14.0
MG Midget Mk III	**14.1**
MG 1300 Mk II 2-door	14.1
Mini 1275 GT	14.7

STANDING ¼-MILE, SEC
Triumph Spitfire 4 Mk 3	19.4
Ford Escort 1300GT 2-door	19.5
MG Midget Mk III	**19.6**
MG 1300 Mk II 2-door	19.6
Mini 1275 GT	19.8

OVERALL MPG
Triumph Spitfire 4 Mk 3	31.3
Mini 1275GT	30.2
MG Midget Mk III	**29.6**
Ford Escort 1300GT 2-door	27.5
MG 1300 Mk II 2-door	26.8

GEARING (with 145-13in. Michelin ZX tyres)
Top	16.5 mph per 1,000 rpm
3rd	12.15 mph per 1,000 rpm
2nd	8.62 mph per 1,000 rpm
1st	5.16 mph per 1,000 rpm

TEST CONDITIONS:
Weather: Fine. Wind: 5-10 mph. Temperature: 16 deg. C. (60 deg. F). Barometer: 29.7in. hg. Humidity: 40 per cent. Surfaces: Dry concrete and asphalt.

WEIGHT:
Kerb weight 13.8 cwt (1,546lb — 702kg) (with oil, water and half full fuel tank). Distribution, per cent F, 52.5; R. 47.5. Laden as tested: 17.3cwt (1,934 — 878kg).

TURNING CIRCLES
Between kerbs L, 32ft 3in.; R, 32ft 0in. Between walls L, 33ft 7in.; R, 33ft 4in., steering wheel turns, locks to lock 2¼.

Figures taken at 3,200 miles by our own staff at the Motor Industry Research Association proving ground at Nuneaton.

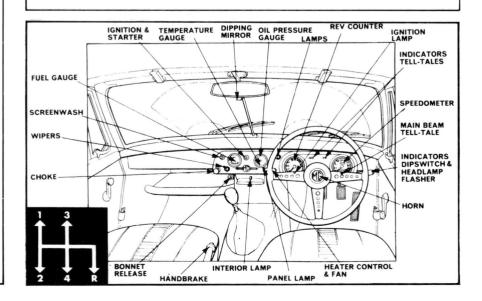

MG MIDGET MK III (1,275 c.c.)

CONSUMPTION

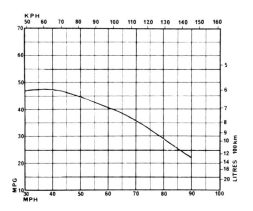

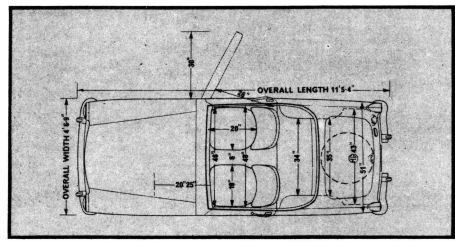

STANDARD GARAGE 16ft x 8ft 6in.

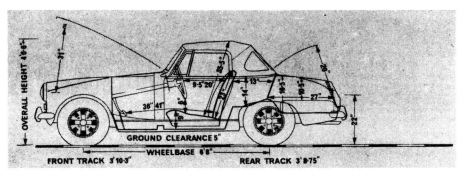

SCALE 0.3in. to 1ft
Cushions uncompressed

FUEL
(At constant speeds—mpg)

30 mph	. . . .	47.0
40 mph	. . . .	47.6
50 mph	. . . .	44.9
60 mph	. . . .	40.4
70 mph	. . . .	35.7
80 mph	. . . .	28.5
90 mph	. . . .	22.8

Typical mpg	. . . 30	(9.4 litres/100km)
Calculated (DIN) mpg	32.5	(8.7 litres/100km)
Overall mpg	. . . . 29.6	(9.5 litres/100km)
Grade of fuel	Premium, 4-star (min. 97 RM)	

OIL
Miles per pint (SAE 10W/40) 1,200

SPECIFICATION FRONT ENGINE, REAR-WHEEL DRIVE

ENGINE
Cylinders . . .	4, in line
Main bearings .	3
Cooling system .	Water; pump, fan and thermostat
Bore	70.6mm (2.78 in.)
Stroke . . .	81.3mm (3.20 in.)
Displacement. .	1,275 c.c. (77.8 cu.in.)
Valve gear . . .	Overhead: pushrods and rockers
Compression ratio	8.8-to-1 Min. octane rating: 97 RM
Carburettors . .	Twin SU HS2
Fuel pump . .	SU electric
Oil filter	Full-flow, renewable element
Max. power . .	64 bhp (net) at 5,800 rpm
Max. torque . .	72 lb.ft (net) at 3,000 rpm

TRANSMISSION
Clutch	Borg and Beck diaphragm spring 6.5in. dia.
Gearbox. . . .	Four speed, synchromesh on 2nd, 3rd and top
Gear ratios. . .	Top 1.0
	Third 1.357
	Second 1.916
	First 3.2
	Reverse 4.14
Final drive . . .	Hypoid bevel 3.90-to-1

CHASSIS and BODY
Construction . .	Integral, with steel body

SUSPENSION
Front	Independent, coil springs, wishbones, lever-arm dampers, optional anti-roll bar (not fitted to test car)
Rear	Live axle, half-elliptic leaf springs, lever arm dampers

STEERING
Type	Rack and pinion
Wheel dia. . . .	16in.

BRAKES
Make and type .	Lockheed discs front, drums rear, no servo
Dimensions . .	F 8.25in. dia R 7in. dia 1.25in. wide shoes.
Swept area . .	F 135 sq. in. R 55 sq. in. Total 190 sq. in. (220 sq. in./ton laden)

WHEELS
Type	Pressed steel perforated disc, four-stud fixing (wire wheels optional) 4.0 in. wide rim.
Tyres—make .	(cross-ply standard) Michelin on test car.
—type	ZX radial ply tubeless.
—size	145-13 in.

EQUIPMENT
Battery	12 Volt 43 Ah
Generator . . .	Lucas C40 28 amp d.c.
Headlamps. . .	Sealed beam, 120/90 watt (total)
Reversing lamp .	Standard
Electric fuses . .	4
Screen wipers .	Single speed, self-parking
Screen washer .	Standard, manual plunger
Interior heater .	Standard, water-valve
Heated backlight	Not applicable
Safety belts . .	Extra, anchorages built in
Interior trim . .	Pvc seats, pvc headlining
Floor covering .	Carpet
Jack	Screw pillar
Jacking points .	One each side in centre of body
Windscreen . .	Toughened
Underbody protection . .	Phosphate treatment under paint

MAINTENANCE
Fuel tank . . .	6 Imp. gallons (no reserve) (27.3 litres)
Cooling system .	6 pints (including heater)
Engine sump . .	6.5 pints (3.7 litres) SAE 10W/40. Change oil every 6,000 miles. Change filter element every 6,000 miles.
Gearbox. . . .	2.5 pints SAE 10W/40. Top up every 12,000 miles.
Final drive . . .	1.5 pints SAE 90EP. Top up every 12,000 miles
Grease	7 points every 3,000 miles
Tyre pressures .	F 22; R 24 psi (normal driving) F26, R 28 psi (fast driving) F 22; R 26 psi (full load)
Max. payload . .	350 lb (159 kg.)

PERFORMANCE DATA
Top gear mph per 1,000 rpm	16.5
Mean piston speed at max. power . .	3,200 ft/min.
Bhp per ton laden	74

159

AUTO TEST

MG Midget 1500

1,493 c.c.

Smallest British Leyland sports car given much more punch by bigger engine. Quick, accurate steering but handling throttle-sensitive and inclined to oversteer. Harsh ride, excessive wind noise with hood up. Undergeared. Limited range

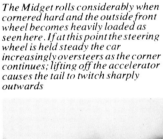

The Midget rolls considerably when cornered hard and the outside front wheel becomes heavily loaded as seen here. If at this point the steering wheel is held steady the car increasingly oversteers as the corner continues; lifting off the accelerator causes the tail to twitch sharply outwards

THERE was an outburst of lamentation from MG enthusiasts when the Midget 1500 was announced, apparently because the A-series engine had been replaced by a Triumph-designed unit. From an engineering point of view the change was almost inevitable. The Midget needed a bigger engine to counteract the effect of safety and antipollution equipment in America, where it sells in its greatest numbers; and at 1,275 c.c., the A-series unit was at the end of its "stretch potential". The answer was to instal the Triumph engine which, while of similar design and vintage, had long ago been given a longer stroke to bring its capacity to 1,493 c.c., its first application being the now-defunct front-drive Triumph 1500.

The purists may decry the move, but Triumph is a name long respected in the sports car business and there is no reason to suppose the Spitfire engine should be unsuitable for the Midget. It might be more in order to complain that a considerable increase in swept volume has resulted in a negligible increase in quoted power, from 64 bhp (net) to 66 bhp (DIN). On the other hand torque, a more important part of a sports car's character, than most people realize, is increased by a greater margin. Against all this has to be balanced the greater weight of the new car, with a kerb weight (our measurement) of 15·3cwt compared with the 13·8cwt of the last 1,275 c.c. Midget we tested.

Performance and economy

The proof of the Midget 1500 is in the stopwatch, and there is no doubt it is substantially quicker than the late-series 1,275 c.c. car. Comparisons are valid because the final drive ratio remains unchanged at 3·9 to 1; the adoption of the single-rail "corporate" gearbox has meant some change in internal ratios, which are wider than before. Tyre size likewise remains the same.

The Midget 1500 is a genuine 100 mph car, and this represents a great advance on the 1275 which managed only 94 mph mean when tested in 1971. Unfortunately maximum speed takes the car over the red line on its rev counter, which over-read by a modest 100 rpm at maximum speed; clearly, therefore the Midget is substantially undergeared to make best use of its peak power, which falls at 5,500 rpm. Higher gearing would not only improve economy, but also permit higher speeds in the intermediate gears.

Although we ran the Midget beyond the 6,000 rpm red line to attain its ultimate maximum speed, we stuck to the limit in the lower gears with the result that first gear would not quite take the car to 30 mph, and third stopped just short of 70 mph. Our figures point up the considerable gap between second (47 mph maximum) and third, which is felt on the road to some extent but is disguised by the spread of useful torque.

Open sports cars always suffer in performance at the top end when they are run with the hood down, and the Midget was no exception. Lowering the hood took the maximum speed down to 94 mph – apart from making life very uncomfortable at that speed. We took no acceleration figures with the hood down, but there is no doubt they would be inferior to those obtained with the hood in place.

TOF 553N

MG Midget 1500

All the Midget 1500 acceleration figures are far superior to those of the 1275, whether from a standing start or in any particular gear. Standing starts are best accomplished without a surfeit of revs and sudden engagement of the clutch, which tends to produce strong and uncomfortable axle tramp. A more gentle procedure, feeding in the clutch fairly fast from a 2,000 rpm starting point, trims half a second off the 1275 time to 30 mph, giving a respectable 3·7sec to this speed. The 1500 proceeds to 60 mph in 12·3sec (a 1·8sec improvement), and to 90 mph in 35·3sec, a better time by no less than 16sec. In like fashion, the standing quarter-mile now takes 18·5sec compared with 19·6 before.

In the gears, every single feature claimed by the 1275 is bettered by a substantial margin. Not only is the torque curve flatter; the 1500 does not run out of breath so quickly at the top end, while flexibility is improved to the extent of being able to pull away from 10 mph in top, which the 1275 would not tolerate.

Comparisons

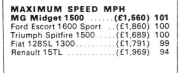

MAXIMUM SPEED MPH
MG Midget 1500	(£1,560)	**101**
Ford Escort 1600 Sport	(£1,860)	100
Triumph Spitfire 1500	(£1,689)	100
Fiat 128SL 1300	(£1,791)	99
Renault 15TL	(£1,969)	94

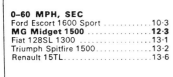

0-60 MPH, SEC
Ford Escort 1600 Sport	10·3
MG Midget 1500	**12·3**
Fiat 128SL 1300	13·1
Triumph Spitfire 1500	13·2
Renault 15TL	13·6

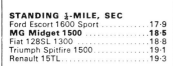

STANDING ¼-MILE, SEC
Ford Escort 1600 Sport	17·9
MG Midget 1500	**18·5**
Fiat 128SL 1300	18·8
Triumph Spitfire 1500	19·1
Renault 15TL	19·3

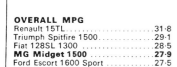

OVERALL MPG
Renault 15TL	31·8
Triumph Spitfire 1500	29·1
Fiat 128SL 1300	28·5
MG Midget 1500	**27·9**
Ford Escort 1600 Sport	27·5

Performance

ACCELERATION SECONDS

True speed mph	Time in Secs	Car Speedo mph
30	3·7	30
40	5·8	40
50	8·5	50
60	12·3	61
70	17·0	71
80	24·0	82
90	35·3	92
100	—	102

Standing ¼-mile
18·5sec 72 mph

Standing kilometre
34·9sec 90 mph

Mileage recorder: accurate

GEAR RATIOS AND TIME IN SEC

mph	Top (3·90)	3rd (5·58)	2nd (8·23)
10–30	9·8	6·2	3·9
20–40	9·2	5·8	4·0
30–50	8·7	5·8	—
40–60	9·6	6·7	—
50–70	10·2	7·9	—
60–80	12·5	—	—
70–90	19·3	—	—

GEARING
(with 145–13in. tyres)
Top	16·44 mph per 1,000 rpm
3rd	11·50 mph per 1,000 rpm
2nd	7·79 mph per 1,000 rpm
1st	4·82 mph per 1,000 rpm

MAXIMUM SPEEDS

Gear	mph	kph	rpm
Top (mean)	101	163	6,140*
(best)	102	164	6,200*
3rd	69	111	6 000
2nd	47	76	6,000
1st	29	47	6,000

*See text

BRAKES
FADE (from 70 mph in neutral)
Pedal load for 0·5g stops in lb
1	35	6	45–65
2	40–45	7	50–65
3	40–60	8	50–65
4	45–65	9	50–65
5	45–55	10	50–60

RESPONSE (from 30 mph in neutral)
Load	g	Distance
20lb	0·22	137ft
40lb	0·46	65ft
60lb	0·70	43ft
80lb	0·96	31ft
Handbrake	0·33	91ft
Max Gradient	1 in 3	

CLUTCH
Pedal 42lb and 4¾in.

Consumption

FUEL
(At constant speed – mpg)
30 mph	48·8
40 mph	44·5
50 mph	39·2
60 mph	34·2
70 mph	29·8
80 mph	26·2
90 mph	22·1
100 mph	17·6

Typical mpg 30 (9·4 litres/100km)
Calculated (DIN) mpg 32·5
(8·7 litres/100km)
Overall mpg 27·9 (10·1 litres/100km)
Grade of fuel Premium, 4-star (min 97RM)

OIL
Consumption (SAE 20W/50) 1,000 mpp

TEST CONDITIONS:
Weather: Fine
Wind: 0·3 mph
Temperature: 15deg C (58deg F)
Barometer: 29·95in. Hg
Humidity: 65 per cent
Surface: Dry concrete and asphalt
Test distance 883 miles

Figures taken by our own staff at the Motor Industry Research Association proving ground at Nuneaton.

All Autocar test results are subject to world copyright and may not be reproduced in whole or part without the Editor's written permission.

Dimensions

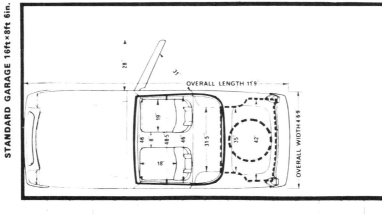

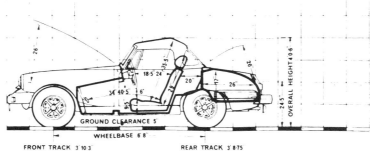

STANDARD GARAGE 16ft × 8ft 6in.

OVERALL LENGTH 11'9"

OVERALL WIDTH 4'6.9"

OVERALL HEIGHT 4'0.6"

GROUND CLEARANCE 5"

WHEELBASE 6'8"

FRONT TRACK 3'10.3"

REAR TRACK 3'8.75"

TURNING CIRCLES:
Between kerbs
L, 30ft 10in.; R, 31ft 11in.
Between walls
L, 32ft 2in.; R, 33ft 3in.
Steering wheel turns,
lock to lock 2¾

WEIGHT:
Kerb Weight 15·4cwt
(1,720lb–780kg)
(with oil, water and half full fuel tank)
Distribution, per cent
F, 53·7; R, 46·3
Laden as tested:
18·0cwt (2,020lb–917kg)

Where economy is concerned, one might expect the 1500 to be less economical because of its larger engine. On the other hand its economy should at least be comparable, because the car remains the same size and there is no reason why any more power should be needed to push it along. Two factors upset this tidy calculation. One is that the Midget in its new form is a good deal heavier; the other is its extra performance, which is used some if not all of the time. As a result, our overall fuel consumption emerged as 27·9 mpg compared with 29·6 mpg for the smaller-engined car. This is not a particularly good figure – worse than the Spitfire 1500 for instance, but then the Spitfire has higher gearing and, for our test, overdrive as well. It was noticeable, though, that the Midget's consumption stayed almost constant whoever the driver and whatever the journey, and at no time did it record a brim-to-brim figure of better than 30 mpg.

This is not to say that 30 mpg is unattainable. Our steady-speed figures show that cruising at a constant 60 mph (with the hood up!) enables the driver to better that figure with ease. If this limit were observed and fierce acceleration avoided, the Midget would prove quite economical; but it is not inherently so, still less the way it is likely to be driven.

Handling and brakes
The Midget sticks to its simple suspension arrangement with double wishbones at the front

Specification MG Midget 1500

FRONT ENGINE, REAR-WHEEL DRIVE

Final drive	Hypoid bevel, ratio 3·90 to 1
Mph at 1,000 rpm in top gear	16·44

CHASSIS AND BODY
Construction	Integral, with steel body

SUSPENSION
Front	Independent: double wishbones, lever arm dampers, anti-roll bar
Rear	Live axle, semi-elliptic leaf springs, lever-arm dampers

STEERING
Type	Rack and pinion
Wheel dia	15½in.

BRAKES
Type	Disc front, drum rear
Dimensions	F 8·25in. dia R, 7·0in. dia, 1·25in. wide shoes
Swept area	F, 135 sq. in., R, 55 sq. in. Total 190 sq. in. (211 sq. in./ton laden)

WHEELS
Type	Pressed steel Rostyle, 4-stud fixing, 4in. wide rim
Tyres – make	Pirelli Cinturato (on test car)
– type	Radial ply tubeless
– size	145–13in.

EQUIPMENT
Battery	12 volt 40 Ah.
Alternator	28 amp a.c.
Headlamps	Sealed beam, 120/90 watt (total)
Reversing lamp	Standard

ENGINE
Cylinders	4, in line
Main bearings	3
Cooling system	Water; pump, fan and thermostat
Bore	73·7mm (2·90in.)
Stroke	87·5mm (3·44in.)
Displacement	1,493 c.c. (91·1 cu. in.)
Valve gear	Overhead: pushrods and rockers
Compression ratio	9·0 to 1. Min octane rating: 97RM
Carburettors	2 SU HS4
Fuel pump	SU mechanical
Oil filter	Full-flow, replaceable cartridge
Max power	66 bhp (DIN) at 5,500 rpm
Max torque	77 lb. ft. (DIN) at 3,000 rpm

TRANSMISSION
Clutch	Diaphragm-spring, 7·25in. diameter
Gearbox	4-speed, all-synchromesh
Gear ratios	Top 1·0
	Third 1·43
	Second 2·11
	First 3·41
	Reverse 3·75

Electric fuses	4
Screen wipers	Single-speed
Screen washer	Standard, manual plunger
Interior heater	Standard, water valve type
Heated backlight	Not available
Safety belts	Static type
Interior trim	Pvc seats
Floor covering	Carpet
Jack	Screw pillar type
Jacking points	One each side
Windscreen	Toughened
Underbody protection	Phosphate treatment under paint

MAINTENANCE
Fuel tank	7 Imp gallons (32 litres)
Cooling system	7½ pints (inc heater)
Engine sump	8 pints (4·5 litres) SAE 20W–50. Change oil every 6,000 miles. Change filter every 6,000 miles
Gearbox	1·5 pints. SAE 90EP. Check every 6,000 miles
Final drive	1·75 pints. SAE 90EP. Check every 6,000 miles
Grease	8 points every 6,000 miles
Valve clearance	Inlet 0·010in. (cold) Exhaust 0·010in. (cold)
Contact breaker	0·015in. gap.
Ignition timing	10deg BTDC (stroboscopic at 650 rpm)
Spark plug	Type: Champion N9Y. Gap 0·025in.
Tyre pressures	F 22; R 24 psi (normal driving) F 26; R 28 psi (high speed) F 22; R 26 psi (full load)
Max payload	420lb (190kg)

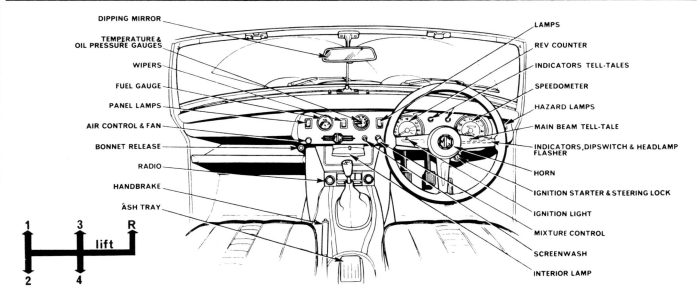

DIPPING MIRROR
TEMPERATURE & OIL PRESSURE GAUGES
WIPERS
FUEL GAUGE
PANEL LAMPS
AIR CONTROL & FAN
BONNET RELEASE
RADIO
HANDBRAKE
ASH TRAY

LAMPS
REV COUNTER
INDICATORS TELL-TALES
SPEEDOMETER
HAZARD LAMPS
MAIN BEAM TELL-TALE
INDICATORS, DIPSWITCH & HEADLAMP FLASHER
HORN
IGNITION STARTER & STEERING LOCK
IGNITION LIGHT
MIXTURE CONTROL
SCREENWASH
INTERIOR LAMP

1 3 R
lift
2 4

Servicing

	6,000 miles
Time Allowed (hours)	3·5
Cost at £4.30 per hour	£15.05
Engine oil	£2.50
Oil Filter	£2.15
Air Filter	£1.08
Contact Breaker Points	£0.52
Sparking Plugs*	£1.48
Total Cost:	**£22.78**

*when required

Routine Replacements:	Time hours	Labour	Spares	TOTAL
Brake Pads – Front (2 wheels)	1·00	£4.30	£3.80	£8.10
Brake Shoes – Rear (2 wheels)	1·35	£5.80	£3.80	£9.60
Exhaust System	0·85	£3.65	£19.50	£23.15
Clutch (centre + driven plate)	8·00	£34.40	£12.83	£47.23
Dampers – Front (pair)	1·55	£6.65	£28.88	£35.53
Dampers – Rear (pair)	1·00	£4.30	£25.52	£29.82
Replace Half Shaft	0·55	£2.35	£13.80	£16.15
Replace Alternator	0·70	£3.00	£27.00	£30.00
Replace Starter	1·60	£6.90	£15.86	£22.76

and a live rear axle located by semi-elliptic leaf springs with no other form of assistance. It worked well enough in the past, given the Midget's very limited wheel travel, but there are signs that the latest car needs something more sophisticated to cope with its greater torque and performance.

Part of the trouble lies in the fact that the Midget, like the MGB, has been given increased ride height at the back to compensate for the greater weight of its "5 mph" bumpers and associated structure. As a result, roll stiffness at the back end has been reduced and there is much more tendency to oversteer. This is despite the heavier engine which means the front wheels bear a greater part of the total weight.

The best feature of the Midget, as always, is its very quick and accurate steering. With less than three turns of the wheel between extremes of an average 32ft turning circle, the driver never has to tie his arms in knots to turn a corner or rescue a situation. Inevitably, there is some kick-back on rough surfaces, but this is by no means the most tiring feature of the car.

Straight-line stability is no better than average, except on ultra-smooth surfaces. Normally, the Midget feels willing enough to keep to a straight course but if the wheel is released for a moment it soon reveals its willingness to wander off-line. The feeling of stability is actually due to the driver

Massive front bumper makes the whole car look bigger than before; inset lights are well protected by lipped extensions. Door mirrors are part of standard equipment. Headlamps are sealed-beam units, not halogen

Standard number plate is mounted beneath the new "5 mph" bumper, rather than below the boot lid as in previous Midgets. Reversing lights are standard and boot lid can be left unlocked if the driver wishes

being barely conscious of the tiny but constant corrections he is applying.

The handling, as we have already said, holds the promise of oversteer. It is not evident at first, for in gentle driving the Midget stays very close to neutral. When driven harder into a corner, if the driver holds the wheel and accelerator steady, the tail will come out steadily until some of the lock has to be paid off before the car gets too sideways. In itself this is no bad thing, for it enables the Midget to be driven in distinctly sporting fashion by someone who knows what he is doing. At the same time it holds the seeds of danger for anyone less clever.

The real snag to the Midget's handling in 1500 form lies in its sensitivity to the throttle. Given the previous situation where the car has been wound hard into a long, tight bend, any sudden re-

lease of the accelerator will bring the tail out very smartly, calling for opposite lock to pin it down. Again, this is a situation beloved of some drivers but it means the Midget is much less predictable, and certainly calls for more skill, than many small saloons of equal performance *and* cornering ability. The drawback is compounded by limited roadholding, which can leave the car well-balanced fore and aft, but skittering sideways onto a wider line than desired. Despite the increased weight and torque, the tyre section remains the same at 145–13in., and it is difficult to avoid the conclusion that the 1500 is somewhat under-tyred.

In the wet, the roadholding is considerably reduced and the Midget tends to skate around on smooth-surfaced corners. In this case, however, it is much more forgiving and the quick

steering really comes into its own.

The brakes need moderate effort and generally work well, giving a well-controlled ultimate stop of 0·95g for a pedal effort of 80lb – well within reasonable limits. The brakes have good "feel", with no sign of sponginess, and no tendency to snatch when cold. Their fade performance is less reassuring with a near-doubling of effort for a 0·5g stop during our ten-stop test, and some smell of linings towards the end; but even then there is no increase in pedal travel.

The handbrake works well, our test car recording a 0·33g stop when the handbrake was used alone on the level. It also held the car well facing either way on the 1-in-3 test hill, on which a restart was easily achieved thanks to the low first gear – but not without a smell of clutch lining.

Comfort and convenience

The Midget could hardly be described as anything but cramped, with difficult entry and exit. It has always been so, and buyers have accepted it. But the statistics tell us that Britons are getting bigger – not to say Americans – and we are surely approaching the point where it may be too small for its own good. Even our largest staff members (the largest of all scaling 16½ stone and 6ft 2in.) found the interior space just sufficient with the driver's seat moved to its back stop, but complained of their inability to shift position to relieve numb spots. More serious were the contortions involved in getting in and out, even with the hood down.

The seats do not look especially inviting, reminding one of the shapeless BMC equipment of a few years ago. This is doing them less than justice. Together with the generally tight confines of the interior they locate driver and passenger well, and they do their best to damp out the effects of the generally mediocre ride. The ride itself will not disappoint Midget enthusiasts and could only be described, euphemistically, as "good for the liver". The limited wheel travel and high spring rates give the Midget no chance of offering a comfortable ride and the result is misery when the car is driven quickly on any uneven surface, let alone a really rough one. On the credit side it is very rare for the suspension actually to bottom, and the 1500 is notably free of the crashes and bangs which afflicted some earlier Midgets, especially when their dampers were past the first flush of youth. Nor is the handling very much affected by suspension movement, so a driver fit enough to withstand the battering can make rapid progress along almost any British road.

Bigger Triumph 1500TC engine does not look unduly large under Midget bonnet, with plenty of length to spare and room for the massive heater trunking. Access to some items is good, but others (such as battery behind heater blower unit) are difficult to reach

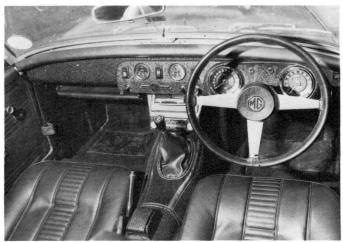

Above: Black crackle-finished facia panel gives slightly vintage air to the interior. Rev counter and speedometer are widely separated but can still be seen inside rim of large steering wheel. Minor dials are less easily read

Left: Midget seats look rather stylized but not very well shaped; in fact they are quite comfortable, damping out the worst effects of the ride, while the small size of the interior ensures good location. Note the awkwardly-placed door handle by the occupant's shoulder

Boot lid is supported by a single self-locking strut. Capacity is strictly limited and there is a low sill over which luggage must be lifted. Spare wheel and fuel tank lie flat on the boot floor and beneath it respectively

The controls are not well laid out, but at least they are easy to understand and are clearly labelled. There are signs of penny-pinching in the single (too slow) speed wipers, the manual-plunger washer, the primitive heater control. Of the major controls, the steering wheel is larger than one might expect and close to the chest by modern standards; the pedals are understandably close together in their narrow tunnel. Clutch effort is high but pedal movement limited, though the clutch takes up sweetly enough. In the test car, however, the accelerator linkage was rather "sudden" and no help to gentle driving. The gearchange is precise but not as quick as some of its rivals.

A major drawback of the Midget is its high interior noise level. For the most part it is made up of wind noise, which drowns the other components to the extent where one is unsure how much contribution the engine is making until one switches off and coasts at high speed. The wind noise itself comes from the hood, and while this may seem inevitable there are other soft-top cars which do not suffer in the same way (or at least, not to the same extent). In the Midget's case it is noticeable that the car is much quieter with the hood down, and the radio easier to hear, at speeds as high as 70 mph. Indeed, with the hood up the radio is almost inaudible above this speed. The

engine actually makes a lot of noise at higher speeds – it simply can't compete with the wind roar. Induction and exhaust noise is high when the car is accelerating hard, at anything over 5,000 rpm; but when the car is driven more gently the 1500 unit is quiet and refined. Noisy or not, it is very smooth right up to the red line and beyond, in a way that may surprise MG diehards.

Even with the hood up, visibility is not bad. At first sight the windscreen is shallow but it seems to provide sufficient view for short and tall drivers; the hinged quarter-lights obstruct the front-quarter view a little, but the "over-the-shoulder" blind spot is cleared by two extra windows let into the hood. Two door mirrors are standard, but on the test car they continually flopped down to a useless position. The wipers clear only a small area of screen and are too slow to cope with heavy rain. Sealed-beam headlights give good illumination at night but the driver's low eyeline prevents him making the most of it. Reversing lights are standard.

The heater is a primitive affair with a single push-pull control for temperature, and a single-speed fan which can only be switched on when full heat is selected. There is no means of selecting airflow to screen or floor, the output being shared arbitrarily. However, the fan is quiet and the heater clears the screen quickly even in humid conditions. There is no direct-flow ventilation other than via the quarter-lights.

Living with the Midget 1500

By comparison with Midget hoods of a few years ago that of the 1500 is easy to contend with. It is not yet a simple one-handed operation either to stow or erect it, though, and in particular it is much easier to fit its leading edge to the windscreen rail if four hands are available. With the hood down one does not get too battered by the airflow, even at high speed, but one driver found that when driving open in light rain the inside of the windscreen soon became covered in droplets and the occupants of the car dampened.

A basic appeal of the Midget is its simplicity, and this is still so with the 1500 which is no more difficult to work on than its predecessors. The most awkward servicing point is the need

to reach the battery at the very rear of the engine compartment under the hinge line of the bonnet; the dipstick is not easy to find, especially in the dark. A link with tradition is the need to attend to eight grease points during the 6,000-mile service – but there are no intermediate service intervals, so an average car requires only twice-a-year attention.

A main drawback of the car is its small (7-gallon) tank, which gives a safe range of less than 200 miles. It is filled via a simple cap in the rear panel, and unlike many modern tanks can be filled quickly to the brim with no danger of blow-back.

There are few accessories to be added to the Midget from the MG option list. A hardtop is expensive but might prove an investment in terms of reduced wind noise and long-journey comfort; wire wheels are available for those who can face the chore of cleaning them; and head restraints may be specified. There is no overdrive option, far less an automatic. Static seat belts are standard – apparently there is no room for inertia-reel units.

In conclusion

There is no doubt that the performance of the Midget has been greatly improved by its change of engine, and there is now a spread of torque which allows the car to be driven sportingly or to be lugged along all the way in top gear by a lazy or tired driver. At the same time the handling has suffered in some respects and the car is no longer as predictable or forgiving as it was.

People are bound to differ on how badly cramped they find the interior (though few will argue with the infuriating difficulty of reaching the interior door handles), but few would quarrel with the conclusion that the ride is harsh and the noise level over-high.

Now that the Midget and the Spitfire share the same engine, the question of their joint survival must arise. For our money – and there is scant price difference between the two – the Spitfire is much more practical and civilized. There will always be those who will scorn it for precisely those reasons, but if further rationalization comes to pass it will be difficult to make out a case for the Midget *vis-à-vis* its stablemate. □

MANUFACTURER:
British Leyland UK Ltd., Austin-Morris Division, Longbridge, Birmingham

PRICES			
Basic	£1,333.00	Insurance	Group 5
Special Car Tax	£111.08		
VAT	£115.53	**EXTRAS (inc VAT)**	
Total (in GB)	**£1,559.61**	Wire wheels	£56.12
Seat Belts, static type	(standard)	Hard top	£112.09
Licence	£40.00	Head restraints *	£18.27
Delivery charge (London)	£15.00	*Fitted to test car*	
Number plates	£6.60		
Total on the Road (exc insurance)	**£1,621.21**	**TOTAL AS TESTED ON THE ROAD**	**£1,639.48**

USED CAR CHOICE

MGB
SPORTS and GT

THE MGB has proved that an impeccable pedigree is a prime essential for a successful sports car, and that technical innovation, though desirable, is not a necessity for success in the field of the sporting car.

The design is depressingly conventional in nearly all respects from the pushrod 4-cylinder engine to the semi-elliptic rear springs and live rear axle, but it shows the successful way in which lessons can be learned from a predecessor, and how modern techniques, when applied to a tried idea, can produce an acceptable contemporary result. The MGB owes a great deal to the previous MGA, sharing the same engine, but in increased capacity form, the same suspension layout and components, and substantially the same interior layout. The most important difference between the two designs is in the method of construction, as the MGB has a unitary construction body unit, as opposed to a separate chassis, as seen on the MGA. The weight penalty of the unitary construction is the main reason for the use of a 1,798 c.c. version of the B-series BMC engine, and although the MGB was one of the first British sports cars to employ this method of construction, the initial sturdy design was good enough to allow well over 300,000 MGBs to be sold since the introduction in September 1962.

During the long and distinguished life of the MGB, the design has remained basically unchanged, and the revisions that have taken place have been of detail only, and the most important of these are detailed in the accompanying table.

When the MGB was first introduced, the B-series engine had three main bearings, and the resultant avoidance of frictional losses meant that these versions were slightly faster than the later five main bearing engines. However, the later engine is considerably smoother, and is capable of higher sustained revs, and is probably the more desirable unit. It is important to remember that both British Leyland and other companies retailing exchange units can only exchange like-for-like, and do not provide five-bearing engines in exchange for three-bearing.

In service, it would be fair to say that the British Leyland B-series engines give remarkable longevity, and the three-bearing engine is good for up to 70,000 miles, only requiring valve and cylinder head attention in the interim. The life of the five-bearing engine is even better, and 100,000 miles can be expected before attention to the bores and crankshaft will be required. All the dealers to whom we spoke were full of praise for the excellent reliability record of the car, and there are clearly few faults of mechanical design.

The most important area for close attention when buying secondhand is the bodywork, as this more than anything affects the price to be paid. The MGB demonstrates better than most cars how important it is to avoid the build-up of mud inside wheel arches, as most of the rust problems with the car stem from the action of mud in the arches. The other bad areas are inside the sills, of which more later.

The guide to approximate "Asking Price" given in the data panel is unavoidably general where examples over four years of age are concerned. By their very nature, sports-cars can be expected to have had a pretty hard life. All-too-often they are bought with very nearly the last penny by people who ought to know how to look after them but in fact, do not. The MGB has a very wide appeal, as it is easy to drive, has very sure-footed handling and in absolute terms, it is not that fast. Therefore, the condition that a used example is in after four or five years depends to a marked extent on the degree of conscientiousness with which it has been serviced and maintained generally. We were interested to hear in our enquiries into the model, that the average length of ownership is less than 18 months, a figure that is more typical of a saloon car than a sports-car. It is likely, therefore, that an older example will have had a number of owners, and that the standard of maintenance will have suffered as a result. It is advisable, in the light of this, to look for an example with as few owners as possible, consistent with the other

Above: Dateless elegance with just a hint of muscle gives tremendous appeal to the open and coupé models (Below)

yardsticks of overall condition such as mileage, complete service record and good visual appearance.

What to look for

All B-series engines sound "tappety", as the tappet clearances are meant to be wide. A noisy top end is therefore not a worry, unless it is very bad. There is little incidence of timing-chain stretch, but care should be taken to be certain to differentiate between excessive "thrash" from the timing chain and the other noisy goings-on at the top of the engine. The usual checks should be applied for big-end and small-end knocking, but in fairness, there is, again, little incidence of these problems.

The engines are generally oil-tight, and one should suspect any car on which there is an excess of oil in the engine bay. The cause may be relatively simple, but it is as well to bear in mind that some eight hours are needed by a garage with all the proper equipment to take the engine out and refit the unit.

This figure of eight hours should be remembered when considering any replacement job involving the engine or the gearbox, as the gearbox cannot be removed without first removing the engine. If the engine unit and gearbox are removed together, the front of the car must be set some 8in. above the normal height on axle stands, as the length of the combined engine and gearbox requires clearance below for the gearbox tailshaft. In order to clear the steering column, it is a good idea to remove the oil filter, as it is this unit that gets in the way.

Before the introduction of the all-synchromesh gearbox in 1967 on the Mk II model, the 2nd gear synchromesh was weak, especially when changing down from 3rd to 2nd gear. If you are taken for a demonstration run by a dealer or a private seller, watch out for a double-declutch when changing down into 2nd. The quoted time to strip and overhaul a gearbox, replacing 2nd gear synchromesh is $5\frac{1}{2}$ hours, so even at today's inflated servicing costs, this would make a considerable saving over an exchange unit at £44.

While back axles do not cause much trouble in service, they are assembled in manufacture with generous tolerances. This may result in a degree of backlash, which will make itself evident as a distinct "clonk" when the drive is taken up, and another one if the car is reversed. It is important to establish whether worn universal joints are contributing, or indeed, causing the backlash. With the car on a lift, there should be no play in the UJs and no signs that the centre spider is moving in the yokes. If there is any wear, the UJs are simply and cheaply changed, and it will then be possible to establish the seriousness of the back-axle play.

Wear in the hubs is unlikely to be worse than average and the normal checks should be made with each wheel individually supported.

Left: The interior of the original MGB shows the leather upholstery, long gearlever and sprung-spoked steering wheel

Right: In contrast, the Series III car has the shorter gearlever, identifying the all-synchromesh gearbox, facia level ventilation and a neat centre console incorporating a glove locker and the ashtray.

Front suspension wear is limited to the bottom trunnion, and the kingpins. Either of these two will show up on the road if the car is put into neutral at less than 10 mph, and the brakes are lightly applied. If there is a "clonk", and then another one when the car **is reversed**, then both the trunnion and the kingpin should be checked.

The steering ball-joints do not wear any faster on the MGB than on other cars with a similar system and the M.o.T. test should therefore ensure that the joints are given at least annual attention. The only other item of steering equipment to look at is the steering column top bush which is prone to wear. This can be checked by trying to move the steering wheel vertically, when there should be no loose movement.

There are no Achilles' heels where the hydraulic brakes are concerned, and the only

aspect of the braking that may cause any trouble is the handbrake. Even on a new car, the handbrake is not very good, and on a used example, the brake may have difficulty in meeting the requirements of the M.o.T. test. It is essential that the cable is freed off fully, and that the handbrake compensators are not jammed. Provided that these items are in order and that the shoes themselves are in good condition and free from grease, the handbrake should be all right, although it is best to consider it as a parking brake only.

That about covers the mechanical and suspension items that should be looked at carefully, so we can move on to the crucial rust problem that is almost certain to be affecting examples over four years old.

There are three areas on the MGB that may be badly affected by rust and each of these result from the design of the car. The most

serious problem is with the sills, and more importantly, the side members contained within the sills. Water and mud are able to get into box formed by the outer sill panel and the side members through the lower join between the two. Once this area is well saturated, rust begins to attack the sill panel from the inside, and the outer and lower faces of the side members. The first signs of the dreaded disease will appear on the outsides of the sill panels which should really be replaced, as any other action will only put off the inevitable day. It is essential to look very carefully at the condition of the side members when the sills are off, as eventually these can be so eaten away that the structural rigidity is affected, and to plate them sucessfully to restore it could well cost a three-figure sum.

The best general advice that one can give is to avoid any car that is showing bad signs

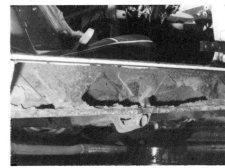

Top left: Early models often have splits in the door tops due to flexing of the quarterlight

Top centre: Rusting from the inside on the rear wings. Water enters between the wing and the wheel arch if the join is not good — it is worth re-sealing this on a used car

Top right: This is what can happen to the side member. If the sills are being replaced, check these

Left: The offending mud-trap at the back of the front wheel arch can be clearly seen. Mud trapped here can lead to the condition seen in the picture below. The cutaway shows the immense rigidity of the monocoque construction

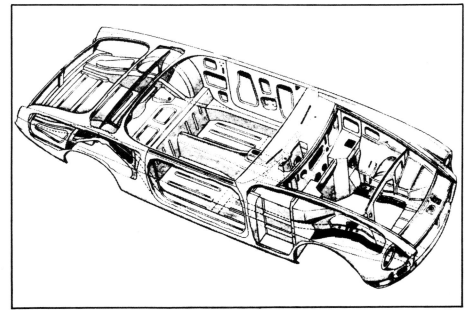

USED CAR CHOICE
MGB . . .

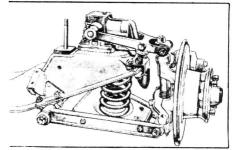

Above: Regular lubrication of the front suspension will help to reduce wear. The lever arm dampers are easily replaced. When checking for front suspension wear, support each side in turn by jacking beneath the coil spring lower support

of rusting in this area, as it is highly likely that the problem is not confined to the sills alone, and could be very serious indeed. If one's budget forces one to look at cars over five years old then do be careful, and remember that if the rust situation is bad here, then any action taken will only prolong the car's life and cannot insure it. The other two areas of rust can be recognized easily, and are not as serious as the sill problem.

Beneath the two front wings, there are bad mud traps at the back of the wheel arches where the wing joins the box member that reinforces the top of the engine bay and the windscreen. Mud collects in the area below the wing top, and its action eventually results in signs of rust showing on the top surface of the wing itself, about 14 in. forward of the windscreen and an inch or so in from the edge of the bonnet. This action is avoided if this area is washed out regularly with a hose, and this is advisable on new or used cars alike.

The last area that should be looked at carefully is on the rear wings. If the join between the inner wheel arch and the rear wing itself is not good, then rust will start inside the space between the two panels. This will show first as paint bubbles about an inch in from the edge of the wheel arch. If the damage appears on the extreme edge of the wheel arch, this is less serious and more easily dealt with, as the action is external rather than within the body itself which is the case in the former example.

Where to buy and how much to pay

As with most sport-cars, there are a number of reputable dealers who specialize to some extent on the MGB. Because they know the bad points both mechanical and structural, they are unlikely to buy-in any examples that are too far gone. It is pretty safe to say, therefore, that the examples that they have for sale are in sound shape. Similarly, the excellent British Leyland Gauntlet Guarantee for 6 months will ensure that the car was up to scratch when it was offered for sale by a BLMH dealer.

On older cars, however, the buyer will be

Above: One of the changes on 1969 cars was the adoption of the recessed grille seen here

left much more on his own to decide on the condition of the car. If there is a warranty on offer on a used example from a dealer, the usual warnings that it should be in writing and preferably to cover parts and labour, apply.

The general rule over how much to pay, is that it is sensible to pay a little over the odds for a particularly low mileage or one- or two-owner car, as the MGB can be kept in good condition if it is maintained properly, and if the owner is aware of the few shortcomings of the design.

Since the model has been in production for over 10 years, there has been time for various specialists to have a good look at the car and to be able to provide a good service as a result. It is possible for instance to buy new hoods from several companies as well as from a British Leyland dealer, and reconditioned engines, gearboxes etc. are available at reasonable prices from a number of sources.

With the reservation over the slight difficulties

over the removal of the engine, it is true to say that the typical "no-nonsense" MG design means that the car is easy to maintain and should give a few problems to the home do-it-yourself man.

As with most British cars, the best value-for-money is a two to three-year-old example with lower than average mileage, which can be kept for a further two years and sold then — before the rot sets in. In this way, someone else suffers the original depreciation and you have the car for the best years of its life.

In the compiling of this guide to the MGB we have been given considerable assistance from both S. H. Richardson of Slough, and also University Motors and to both of these our thanks are due. In the case of Richardsons, as they are about the only dismantlers of MGBs, we were grateful to be able to see beneath the skin of some older examples to be able to appreciate the damage that can be taking place on outwardly reasonable examples. □

Significant data

Mean maximum speed (mph)	3 brg Sports	5 brg Sports	MGB GT	Auto Sports
	103	104	102	104
Acceleration (sec)				
0-30	4.1	4.0	3.8	4.9
0-40	6.2	6.0	6.1	7.1
0-50	8.5	9.0	8.7	10.0
0-60	12.2	12.9	13.0	13.6
0-70	16.5	17.2	17.8	18.5
0-80	22.9	24.1	25.4	26.4
0-90	32.6	35.6	36.9	39.0
Standing ¼-mile (sec)	18.7	18.9	18.5	19.5
Top Gear (sec)				
20-40	11.4	8.6	11.2	—
20-40	11.4	8.6	11.2	—
30-50	9.7	8.7	10.1	6.6 (Inter)
40-60	8.7	9.1	9.6	7.2 (Inter)
50-70	10.4	11.1	10.8	8.8 (Inter)
60-80	12.0	13.2	13.7	14.5 (Top)
70-90	15.7	17.1	19.0	19.4 (Top)
Typical fuel consumption	26	27	24	26

Dimensions		
Length		12ft 9.2 in.
Width		5ft 0 in.
Height		4ft 1.4 in.

	3 brg Sports	5 brg Sports	MGB GT	Auto Sports
Kerb weight (cwt)	18.5	19.0	21.2	19.2
Date of original Road Test	21/9/62	12/2/65	1/7/71	16/4/70

MGB Sports and GT

Model introduced (in open form) in July 1962. 1,798 c.c. 3-main bearing engine. Heater, anti-roll bar, oil cooler and folding hood optional. Price incl. P.T. £950.
1963 changes: strengthened hand brake lever, rear springs modified. Glass fibre optional hardtop available. Laycock overdrive optional.
1964 changes: closed circuit crankcase breather. 5-main bearing crankshaft and oil cooler standard. Electric tachometer.
1965 changes: 12 gal. fuel tank. Sealed propeller shaft (no grease points). MGB GT introduced with opening rear door, at £1,013.
1966 changes: front anti-roll bar standard on Sports and GT.
1967 changes: reversing lamps standard on Sports and GT. Mk II version of Sports and GT introduced with all-synchromesh gearbox, alternator. Door trims and seats revised. Automatic optional extra.
1969 changes: plated radiator grille replaced by matt black vertical grille, with MG emblem in centre. Leather rim steering wheel with perforated spokes. Reclining front seats optional.
1970 changes: ventilation improved, interior courtesy lights, self-locking boot and bonnet stays. Steering lock.
1971 changes: Mk III version of Sports and GT introduced with centre console between seats, rocker switches, facia-level ventilation from grilles in facia centre. Armrest between front seats. Collapsible steering column. Nylon seat inserts on GT.
1972 changes: new grille reverting to original chromed surround, but with latticed centre sections. Padded armrests replace doorpulls. Full nylon seat coverings on GT.

Chassis Identification

Sports (3-bearing):	GHN3 101 onwards
Sports (5-bearing):	GHN3 48766 onwards
GT coupé:	GHD3 71933 onwards
Sports Mk II:	GHN4 138801 onwards
GT coupé MK II:	GHD4 139824 onwards
Sports Mk II: 1969 revisions	GHN5 187170 onwards
GT coupé Mk II: 1969 revisions	GHD5 187841 onwards
Sports Mk III:	GHN5 258001 onwards
GT coupé Mk III:	GHD5 258004 onwards

Approx. selling price range	Normal mileage models available	
	Sports	GT
£150-£250	1962; 1963	
£250-£350	1964	
£350-£450	1965	
£450-£550	1966	1965
£550-£650	1967; 1968	1966; 1967
£650-£750	1969	1968
£750-£850	1970	1968
£850-£950	1970	1969
£950-£1050	1971	1970
£1050-£1150	1972	1971
£1150-£1400		1972

Details of item to be renewed or work to be done	Labour	Spares
Short engine (exchange, £30.00 Deposit pending return of old unit)	£26.40	£71.25
Gearbox (exchange)	£26.40	£44.00
Clutch (Plate, pressure plate and carbon bush)	£28.05	£13.60
Starter ring gear	£36.30	£2.20
Both propshaft UJs	£5.80	£5.50
Exhaust system	£3.30	£14.50
King Pins (both sides)	£14.85	£8.00
Shock absorber (exchange)	£2.45	£10.00
Front wing — Sports	£30.00	£23.00
— GT	£25.00	£23.00
Sills — both sides	£30.00	£10.00
Door		£23.50
Hood		£38.45

Look what's gone

British Leyland have now introduced the long-awaited V8-engined MGB. Unfortunately, the new car will only be available in GT form, and as such, it has stepped into a very competitive sector of the market. The installation is well engineered, and takes account of all immediate European emission regulations. As the all-aluminium V8 weighs only slightly more than the B-series four cylinder engine, the balance is not seriously affected.

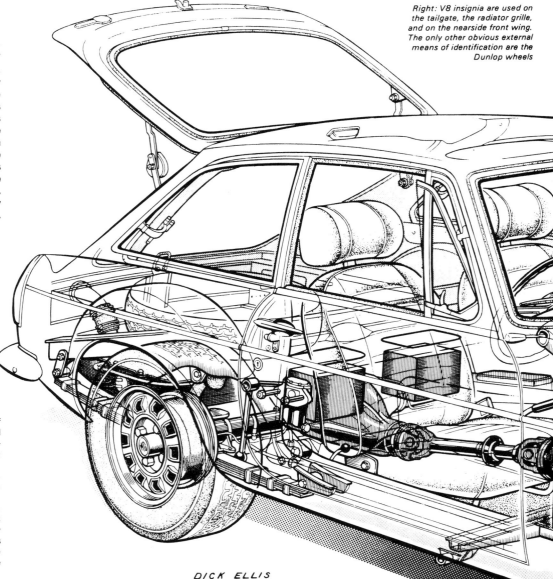

Right: V8 insignia are used on the tailgate, the radiator grille, and on the nearside front wing. The only other obvious external means of identification are the Dunlop wheels

DICK ELLIS M.S.I A

By A. D. Shanks

FOLLOWING the demise of the MGC, British Leyland have re-assessed the available power units and decided that the timeless MGB would combine well with the aluminium Rover V8 engine from the 3500 range. To effect this metamorphosis of the MGB, much work has been involved to shoehorn the wide V8 engine into the narrow engine bay of the B, which up to now, has been plenty wide enough for the in-line fours and sixes that have been used.

To make sufficient room for the Rover engine both the inner wheel arches and the engine bulkhead have been changed in shape, and by setting the engine well back in the bay, it has been possible to retain a near 50/50 weight distribution (50.7/49.3). In order to rationalize, some of the changes that have been made to allow the V8 installation will be introduced on all MGBs, principally because the opportunity has been taken with the MGB V8 to change the datum points of the suspension pickups to gain a better bumper height. It is immediately noticeable that the V8 stands higher off the road than previous MGBs; the height difference being 1 inch.

The variation of the Rover 3528 c.c. V8 used has most in common with that used in the Range Rover, sharing the same dished pistons which give a compression ratio of only 8.25 to 1. The Rover engine is well-known in its application in the Rover 3½-litre as well as in the 3500 and Range Rover, but its suitability in a high performance application has already been well proved in the popular 3500S. Oversquare dimensions and a very sturdy bottom-end permit the engine to retain its smoothness beyond its power peak at 5,000 rpm up to the onset of "pumping up" of the hydraulic tappets. In order to allow the use of the standard

MGB bonnet, it has been necessary to use different inlet manifolding to that employed on either the Rover 3500 or the Range Rover. Instead of mounting the twin carburettors on the top of a penthouse manifold, the MGB application moves the carburettors towards the back of the engine, with forward-facing inlet tracts into a plenum chamber approximately in the centre of the vee. In addition to meeting the requirements for bonnet height, this arrangement gives a slight increase in low-speed torque.

The engine has been developed to meet the ECE 15 European

Emission Regulations and to enable it to do this, neat temperature-sensitive bimetallic valves have been built into the air intakes and are arranged to draw in warm air from sleeves on the exhaust manifolds when occasion demands. The extremely low compression ratio enables the car to run on 97 octane (RON), 4 star petrol. The carburettors are the SU HIF6 (horizontal integral float chamber) type as fitted to the Rover 3500S. A change from the

into the MGB GT

Below: The cutaway diagram reveals the tight fit of the Rover engine. The temperature-sensitive hot/cold air blending valves can be seen forward of the air-cleaner cans. The external oil cooler and oil filter are shown, as are the thermostatically controlled electric cooling fans, with their protective wire mesh cover. Also evident is the very short propeller shaft that contributes much to the smoothness and lack of vibration in the drive line

Above: The all-aluminium Rover 3528 c.c. V8 engine is a snug fit in the engine bay, although routine service items are kept in reach. The new inlet maifold that allows the rearward positioning of the carburettors can be seen

Look what's gone into the MGB GT

specification of the Rover 3500 is the use of an AC Delco alternator as opposed to a Lucas unit.

The maximum power of the engine as installed in the MGB V8 is 137 bhp (DIN) at 5,000 rpm, while maximum torque is 193 lb./ft. at 2,900 rpm, compared with 150 bhp and 204 lb./ft. for the Rover 3500S, and 130 bhp and 185 lb./ft. for the Range Rover.

The gearbox is a modified version of that first seen on the MGC, and now fitted as standard on 4 cylinder MGBs. It has synchromesh on all forward gears and internal ratios of 3.138 (1st) 1.974 (2nd), 1.259 (3rd); top gear is direct. Overdrive is fitted as standard, working on top gear only, and this has a ratio of 0.820. The gearbox casing has had to be changed from that of the 4 cylinder car, as a larger clutch (9½ in. as opposed to 8in.) is required to cope with an increase in torque of 75 per cent over the 4 cylinder engine. The clutch has a ballrace withdrawal race as opposed to the carbon ring of the MGB.

The changes to the suspension are minor, and are to control the increase in torque, rather than to have any effect on handling and ride. The spring rates are 102 lb/in. at the front, and 115 lb/in. at the rear, as opposed to 100 and 105 lb/in. respectively on the MGB 4 cylinder. It was not found

Above: The left-hand fingertip stalk now controls the overdrive, as well as the windscreen wiping and washing. The necessary larger shroud intrudes further into the base of the facia, requiring the use of a smaller-sized speedometer and rev counter

necessary to change either the damper settings or anti-roll bar stiffness, both being as for the MGB.

The most obvious external identification of the V8 car are the Dunlop wheels, which have ventilated cast alloy centres rivetted to chromed steel rims. These wheels are immensely

strong, the life acceptance standards being easily exceeded on rig tests.

To cope with the increased cooling requirements of the V8 engine, the MGB V8 is fitted with a larger radiator than the 4 cylinder car, and twin thermostatically-controlled electric fans are used to reduce noise and power absorption. An oil cooler is fitted as standard, as opposed to being an optional extra as on the MGB.

Inside the car, there are few changes from the normal MGB. The adoption of the American-market column switchgear has meant that a smaller speedometer and revcounter have had to be used, as the shroud of the steering column is larger. The fingertip stalks control the headlights on the right hand side, and overdrive, and windscreen washing and wiping on the left hand.

The price for the MGB V8 includes most of the items that were previously available as optional equipment on the 4 cylinder car, including overdrive, tinted window glass, heated rear window and a door-mounted outside mirror. The only optional extra on offer is inertia reel seat belts which can be specified for factory fitment at £15.85, otherwise the price of £2,293.96 includes all the equipment detailed in this description. □

Below: The body of the MGB GT V8 sits noticeably higher off the road than the normal MGB GT although ground clearance is reduced by ½ in by the larger diameter exhaust system required by the V8 engine. The composite Dunlop wheels have cast aluminium centres rivetted to chromed steel rims

AUTO TEST

MGB GT V8

MG elegance
Rover smoothness

AT-A-GLANCE:
Effective combination of proven MGB GT and superb Rover 3500 V8. Good performance with remarkable economy. Smooth fuss-free engine with good torque but little engine noise. Perennial MGB faults. Too expensive.

FEW cars have been more of an open secret than the MGB GT V8. From the moment that supplies of the Rover V8 engine to Ken Costello were stopped, it was clear that British Leyland themselves were intending to do a similar exercise.

There is a considerable market all over Europe and America for a smart Grand Touring car with comfortable space for two people and their luggage, or for two and their small children or their dogs, and such cars as the Reliant Scimitar GTE and the Lotus Elan +2 have sold well as a result. It must also have worried British Leyland that they were not represented in the "big" sports car range by tne Austin Morris Division, following the termination of the Austin Healey 3000, and the unfortunate public response to the MGC that led to its early demise. As we said when the MGC was first tested, if there were no MGB by which to measure it, the MGC would not have been considered such a bad car, and so it is heartening to see that British Leyland are again prepared to capitalize on the excellent name of "MG" and to try again.

The combination of the timeless lines of the Pininfarina-influenced MGB GT and the smoothness of the lightweight 3,528cc Rover V8 engine ought, on paper, anyway, to make for an excellent high performance sporting coupé. If the end product falls short in any way, it is in the unfortunate perpetuation of the dated features of the MGB. Such shortcomings as excessive wind noise, a harsh ride and heavy steering may be forgiven in an out-and-out sports car, but they have no place in a GT car costing over £2,000. More unfortunate still is the fact that such shortcomings are accentuated by the superb smoothness and relative quietness of the excellent Rover V8 engine, which it must be admitted, goes most of the way to making up for the less likeable facets of the car.

In terms of performance, the Rover engine has moved the MGB GT V8 up into the realms of the fastest European sports cars as it is capable of well over 120mph, and its acceleration both through, and in the gears is excellent. Acceleration from rest to 90mph in under 20 seconds, and a standing ¼mile time of 16.4 seconds are both very good, and the effortless way in which the quiet V8 accelerates from as low as 10mph in top gear is impressive. In direct top gear, each 20mph increment from 10 to 80mph takes less than 8 seconds, while it takes only 10.3 seconds to get from 80 to 100mph.

To provide this sort of performance, while paying attention to European Emission Regulations, British Leyland use a version of the V8 engine that has most in common with the Range Rover, utilizing the same low-compression pistons in both engines. To allow for a sufficiently low carburettor height, the manifold is changed from the penthouse design of the Rover 3500 and Range Rover, and a cast manifold is used, whose inlet tracts point towards the back of the engine, enabling the carburettors to be positioned close to the bulkhead, where there is more available space.

Below: There is little to show that the Rover V8 engine is not the original power unit of the MGB GT, as the installation is neat and well planned. The electrical service items such as fuses and relays are all positioned on the offside of the bay, while the radiator header tank and screen washer reservoir are on the nearside. The reservoirs for clutch and brake hydraulic circuits are positioned high up behind the pedal box, but their proximity to the angle of bonnet and bulkhead makes it difficult to see the fluid level

The gearbox derives from the MGC all-synchromesh unit that was introduced on all MGBs in 1967. As used on the MGB GT V8, only the casing is changed to allow the use of a 9½in dia. clutch, while the internal ratios are higher than those of the 4 cylinder car to suit the increased power and torque of the much larger engine. The ratios are well chosen, allowing up to 40mph in 1st gear, and 100mph in third gear. Although 2nd gear gives up to 60mph, it is spaced a little too close to 1st gear, and would benefit from being a little higher.

Overdrive operates on top gear only and is geared up to give 28.5mph/1000rpm. While this may seem to indicate a strictly "overdrive" gearing, it is surprising how often it can be engaged, even around town, so torquey is the V8 engine. Engagement of overdrive is by the lefthand of two fingertip stalks, and while the unit disengages sweetly enough when the lever is pushed away from the wheel rim, engagement is lazy and unduly speed-conscious, taking longer to engage at low speeds than high, as the inhibitors sort themselves out, and decide whether or not overdrive can be engaged.

One of the nicest features of the car is the complete absence of any snatch, vibration or harshness from the drive-line. From full throttle on to overrun, there is little sign of the considerable torque reversals that are taking place, and this contributes greatly to the pleasure of driving the car. As this feature is present to a lesser degree in the Rover 3500S it is probably due in part to the V8 engine, but the very short propshaft must help considerably in this.

There are absolutely no dramas involved in starting the car, either cold or hot. Under cold-start conditions, the manual mixture enrichment needs to be used sparingly, and can be pushed home within the first mile. In fact, the car runs smoothly without the need for enrichment long before the heater starts to give much appreciated warmth.

Despite a good angle of attack, the clutch effort is inordinately high, and operating it becomes a tiring exercise in town. Perhaps, this is more noticeable as the full movement must be used to avoid any grating on engaging the gears. It is essential to use the full movement of the clutch when engaging reverse, as the gears continue to spin for a long time, and it is often quicker to stop them by engaging 1st gear. The gearchange is also appreciably heavier if the full travel of the clutch is not utilized.

The brakes are excellent, progressive and capable of producing a 1g stop at only 65lb pedal load; the accelerated fade tests revealed only a slight tendency for the pedal load to increase as the brakes became hot, and only on the 10th application from 70mph did they begin to show any loss of performance, and that only slight.

All the MGBs are commendably tractable, and very easy cars to drive. They can all be pottered gently without the need for critical use of gearchange points, and the V8 version distinguishes itself by being even more free of fuss than its smaller-engined brothers. Never before has a sports car in this class been as flexible and forgiving and so easy to drive smoothly, but then never before has such a smooth engine been offered beneath an MG bonnet.

Above: The roomy interior of the MGB GT remains substantially unaltered, only the size of the instruments and calibration of the speedometer to 140 mph indicate the presence of the V8 engine beneath the bonnet. Unfortunately, the opportunity has not been taken to level up the pedals, and therefore it is still not possible to heel-and-toe

Below: A surprising amount of luggage can be fitted into the load area, and the two wells behind the rear wheel arches are particularly useful for stowage. A pram base will not quite fit crossways between the wheel arches, and will not fit longways if the rear seat is in the raised position

AUTOTEST
MGB GT
V8...

Above: Access to the rear of the car is reasonable, and the locking release lever is particularly convenient

Below: The rear seats are really only suitable for children up to about eight, although no doubt older children would put up with the discomfort for the thrill of being driven in the car. The rear seat cushions are retained by "lift-the-dot" fasteners, and when released allow the rear seat back to swing down onto the rear seat

Below: The spare wheel is positioned below the floor of the rear deck, above the petrol tank. The jack and wheelbrace are also stowed here, and there is plenty of additional space for tools or oddments both in and alongside the wheel

What is remarkable is that this marked increase in performance and flexibility is accomplished at little cost in fuel economy. Compared with the last MGB GT that we tested two years ago, the V8 gave 23.4mpg overall, compared with 23.7mpg overall for the smaller-engined car. While it would be possible to get a slightly better "touring" performance from the four cylinder car, this is partially offset by the fact that the Rover V8 engine can run on three star fuel, while the four cylinder engine requires five star, and we would expect that the same driver on the same journeys would get very similar figures in the two cars. When the considerable difference in performance is taken into account, this is a quite outstanding achievement.

Ride and Handling

To cope with the 75 per cent increase in torque that the V8 has brought, the spring rates have been increased at the rear. There is a small balancing increase at the front that goes unnoticed, but the harder rear springs have turned the ride from hard to harsh, compared with the earlier MGB. This excessive rear end roll stiffness contributes to power oversteer that is in conflict with the natural understeering characteristics of the car. This is not a problem on long sweeping fast bends, but at lower speeds, hard acceleration can produce a disconcerting imbalance, as the transition from understeer to oversteer takes place. Further evidence of the imbalanced nature of the car appears when one is forced to lift-off in the middle of a corner that has been entered at too high a speed to allow power oversteer to be induced. If the lift-off is sudden, the car tightens its line quite abruptly, necessitating rapid steering correction. Considering how very predictable the normal MGB is, and how predictable the Costello MGB V8 is, it would seem that the work on the rear suspension has not produced the desired results. It must not be assumed that the foregoing ascribes a serious degree of raggedness to the handling but since the MGB GT V8 must put down half as much power again as the 4 cylinder car and at the higher potential cornering speeds that the excellent Goodyear G800 tyres allow, it would inspire more confidence if the handling was more progressive. Extremely strong castor action contributes considerably to excellent straight-line stability. It also makes for good resistance to side winds but means fairly heavy steering effort.

Interior comfort and fittings

Many young families would consider the MGB GT V8 an ideal car for parents and children up to seven or eight. With the children on the back seat, there is still sufficient room behind for a great deal of luggage, and if the children are to be left at home, the rear seat can be folded forward, further increasing the available load space, and leaving room for such bulky items as school trunks or pram bases. Access to the luggage space is gained through the large rear door that swings well out of the way, and is retained in the open position by two sturdy self-supporting struts. The spare wheel is housed below the floor of the load space, and is properly secured by a large wing-nut. The area around the spare wheel can be used to stow tools and oddments that would otherwise be on display in the luggage area.

In the remainder of the car, stowage space is limited to a small glove locker (which, as we have said many times is infuriating in that it can only be opened and closed by the key, which is inevitably on the key ring — where it belongs) and to a lift-up glove-locker between the seats whose accommodation is aptly described by its title. There is also a useful map-pocket on the passenger's side but this is out of reach, especially when static seat belts are being worn.

All the seats now have nylon facings on their wearing surfaces, and both the front seats can be reclined. Adjustment of the front seats is generous, and drivers of all sizes can be accommodated. The backs of the front seats do, however, lack lumbar support, and leave a space below the small of the back that can lead to some discomfort. The seat backs are high and well shaped, providing good shoulder support, and the gripping nature of the brushed nylon material helps to provide good lateral support. The backs of the seats recline, but only to approximately 45 deg at which angle they come up against the rear seats.

For the driver, the seating position relative to the controls is good, the gear lever falling comfortably to hand, and the relationship of shoulder position to the small leather-covered steering wheel enables a near straight arm posture to be enjoyed. Shorter drivers do, however tend to sit quite low in the car, making visibility of the front corners difficult.

The remainder of the interior appointments are in line with the normal MGB GT, with the exception of the speedometer and rev counter which are the same small size as the American market cars. This is dictated by the larger shroud made necessary by the additional finger tip switch for the overdrive.

Living with the MGB GT V8

Static seat belts at £15.85 including VAT are the only optional extras on offer on the MGB GT V8, and so the price of £2,293.96 has only the normal items of vehicle licence/delivery charge (including VAT) of £18.70 and number plates at £5.00 to give an on-the-road price of £2,352.43 with static seat belts, or £6.08 more if the optional factory-fitted inertia reel belts are specified. The MGB GT V8 package includes all the items that are available as options on the normal MGB GT. Included among these are heated rear window, tinted windows, servo brakes, head restraints, and of course, the overdrive unit.

There should be few problems involved in getting nationwide service for the car, as Leycare now extends to all British Leyland dealers, and this ensures fixed charges for routine servicing anywhere in the country, and also ensures that there are technicians capable of servicing the Rover V8 engine at all MG dealers. The cost of replacement parts is expected to be similar to those for existing MG parts, while prices for the Rover engine should not be excessive.

Routine servicing is recommended every 6,000 miles, while a "safety check" service is recommended every 3,000 miles if the car is used under dusty or arduous conditions. Access to items requiring routine maintenance is good beneath the big aluminium bonnet, and a typically thoughtful feature is the plastic grip on the dipstick, which remains cool. The engine

MGB GT V8 (3,528c.c.)

ACCELERATION

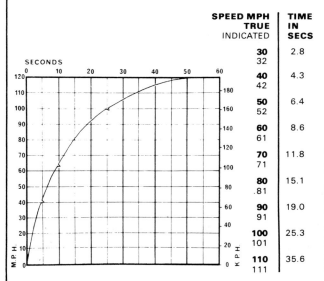

SPEED MPH TRUE INDICATED	TIME IN SECS
30	2.8
32	
40	4.3
42	
50	6.4
52	
60	8.6
61	
70	11.8
71	
80	15.1
.81	
90	19.0
91	
100	25.3
101	
110	35.6
111	

GEAR RATIOS AND TIME IN SEC

mph	o/dTop (2.52)	Top (3.07)	3rd (3.87)	2nd (6.06)
10–30	—	7.5	6.0	3.6
20–40	9.5	6.8	5.3	3.2
30–50	8.8	6.5	4.8	3.2
40–60	8.7	6.6	4.8	3.6
50–70	9.5	6.8	5.7	—
60–80	9.8	7.4	6.2	—
70–90	10.2	8.3	7.1	—
80–100	12.9	10.3	9.7	—
90–110	17.0	14.8	—	—

Standing ¼-mile
16.4 sec 84 mph
Standing Kilometre
30.4 sec 106 mph
Test distance
1,645 miles
Mileage recorder
accurate

PERFORMANCE

MAXIMUM SPEEDS

Gear	mph	kph	rpm
O.D. Top (mean)	123.9	199.4	4,350
(best)	125.4	201.8	4,400
Top	117.0	188.3	5,000
3rd	100.0	160.9	5,500
2nd	64.0	103.0	5,500
1st	40.0	64.4	5,500

BRAKES
FADE
(from 70 mph in neutral)
Pedal load for 0.5g stops in lb

1	35	6	35–40
2	35	7	40
3	35–37	8	42
4	35–37	9	42
5	35–40	10	42–45

RESPONSE (from 30 mph in neutral)

Load	g	Distance
20lb	0.20	150ft
30lb	0.36	84ft
40lb	0.52	58ft
50lb	0.72	42ft
60lb	0.95	31.7ft
70lb	1.05	28.7ft
Handbrake	0.42	72ft
Max. Gradient	1 in 3	

CLUTCH
Pedal 38lb and 4½in.

COMPARISONS

MAXIMUM SPEED MPH

Datsun 240Z	(£2,535)	125
MGB GT V8	**(£2,294)**	**124**
Ford Capri 3000 GXL	(£1,824)	122
Lotus Elan +2 S130	(£2,789)	121
Reliant Scimitar GTE (o/d)	(£2,480)	119

0-60 MPH, SEC

Lotus Elan +2 S130	7.4
Datsun 240Z	8.0
Ford Capri 3000 GXL	8.3
MGB GT V8	**8.6**
Reliant Scimitar GTE (o/d)	9.3

STANDING ¼-MILE, SEC

Datsun 240Z	15.8
Lotus Elan +2 S130	16.0
MGB GT V8	**16.4**
Ford Capri 3000 GXL	16.6
Reliant Scimitar GTE (o/d)	16.9

OVERALL MPG

Lotus Elan +2 S130	26
MGB GT V8	**23**
Datsun 240Z	21
Ford Capri 3000 GXL	21
Reliant Scimitar GTE (o/d)	21

GEARING
(with 175HR 14in. tyres)

O.D. Top 28.5 mph per 1,000 rpm
Top 23.4 mph per 1,000 rpm
3rd 18.6 mph per 1,000 rpm
2nd 11.9 mph per 1,000 rpm
1st 7.4 mph per 1,000 rpm

CONSUMPTION

FUEL
(At constant speed — mpg) o/d top   top

30 mph	40.4	37.0
40 mph	41.7	36.4
50 mph	39.2	33.3
60 mph	34.5	29.9
70 mph	30.8	27.0
80 mph	27.0	23.8
90 mph	24.1	21.2
100 mph	20.9	18.4

Typical mpg 25 (11.3 litres/100km)
Calculated (DIN) mpg 24.6 (11.5 litres/100km)
Overall mpg 23.4 (12.1 litres/100km)
Grade of fuel Economy, 3-star (min. 94RM)

OIL
Consumption (SAE 20/50) 1,700 mpp

TEST CONDITIONS:
Weather: Fine
Wind: 2-10 mph
Temperature: 19 deg. C. (66 deg. F).
Barometer: 29.5 in. hg. Humidity: 70 per cent
Surfaces: Dry concrete and asphalt.

WEIGHT:
Kerb Weight 21.3cwt (2,387lb-1081kg)
(with oil, water and half full fuel tank).
Distribution, per cent F, 50.7; R, 49.3
Laden as tested: 24.4cwt (2737lb-1240kg)

TURNING CIRCLES:
Between kerbs L, 34ft 2in.; R, 32ft 11in.
Between walls L, 35ft 5 in.; R, 34ft 3½in.
Steering wheel turns, lock to lock 2.9.
Figures taken at 1,600 miles by our own staff at the Motor Industry Research Association proving ground at Nuneaton and on the Continent.

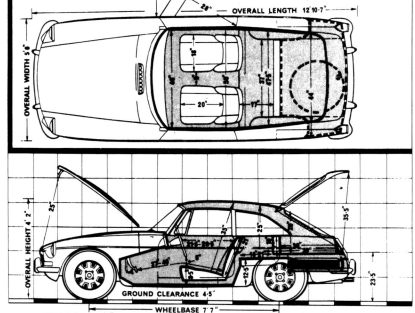

OVERALL LENGTH 12'10.7"
OVERALL WIDTH 5'0"
OVERALL HEIGHT 4'2"
GROUND CLEARANCE 4.5"
WHEELBASE 7'7"
FRONT TRACK 4'1"
REAR TRACK 4'1.25"

STANDARD GARAGE 16ft x 8ft 6in.

SPECIFICATION

FRONT ENGINE, REAR-WHEEL DRIVE

ENGINE

Cylinders	8, in 90 deg vee
Main bearings	5
Cooling system	Water, thermostat and twin electric fans
Bore	88.9mm (3.5in.)
Stroke	71.12mm (2.8in.)
Displacement	3,528 c.c. (215.4 cu. in.)
Valve gear	Pushrod overhead valves, hydraulic tappets
Compression ratio	8.25-to-1. Min. octane rating: 94 RM
Carburettors	Twin S.U. HIF6
Fuel pump	S.U. electric
Oil filter	Full flow, disposable canister
Max. power	137 bhp (DIN) at 5,000 rpm
Max. torque	193 lb. ft. (DIN) at 2,900 rpm

TRANSMISSION

Clutch	Borg and Beck diaphragm spring 9.5in. dia.
Type	
Gearbox	4-speed all-synchromesh, overdrive on top gear
Gear ratios	Top 1.0 OD top 0.820
	Third 1.259
	Second 1.974
	First 3.138
	Reverse 2.819
Final drive	Hypoid bevel, ratio 3.07:1

CHASSIS and BODY

Construction	All steel unitary

SUSPENSION

Front	Independent; upper wishbone incorporating lever-type dampers, lower wishbone, coil springs, anti-roll bar
Rear	Live axle; semi-elliptic leaf springs, lever-type dampers

STEERING

Type	Rack and pinion; collapsible column
Wheel dia	15.5 in.

BRAKES

Make and type	Lockheed; discs front, drums rear
Servo	Lockheed; vacuum
Dimensions	F 10.7 in. dia.
	R 10.0 in. dia. 1.7 in. wide shoes
Swept area	F 231.6 sq. in. R 106.8 sq. in.
	Total 338.4 sq. in. (277 sq. in./ton laden)

WHEELS

Type	Composite — Cast alloy centres, chromed steel rims 5 in. wide rim. (J section)
Tyres—make	Goodyear
—type	radial ply tubeless
—size	175HR 14

EQUIPMENT

Battery	12 Volt 67 Ah. @ 20 hr. rate (2 x 6v in series)
Alternator	AC Delco 43 amp a.c.
Headlamps	Lucas sealed beam 150/100 'watt (total)
Reversing lamp	Standard
Electric fuses	4 in fuse box, 2 in-line
Screen wipers	2-speed, self-parking
Screen washer	Standard, electric
Interior heater	Standard, water-valve
Heated backlight	Standard
Safety belts	Extra
Interior trim	Nylon-faced seats PVC headlining
Floor covering	Carpet and rubber wear mats
Jack	Screw pillar
Jacking points	1 per side beneath sill
Windscreen	Laminated Sundym tinted glass
Underbody protection	Phosphate treatment under paint

MAINTENANCE

Fuel tank	12 Imp. gallons (54 litres)
Cooling system	16 pints (inc. heater)
Engine sump	9 pints (5.1 litres) SAE 20/50 Change oil every 6,000 miles. Change filter every 6,000 miles
Gearbox and overdrive	6.3 pints SAE 90 EP. Change oil and o/d filter every 24,000 miles.
Final drive	1.8 pints SAE 90 EP
Grease	5 points every 6,000 miles
Valve clearance	n/a (hydraulic tappets)
Contact breaker	014-016 in. gap: 28 deg. dwell
Ignition timing	8 deg. BTDC (stroboscopic at 1,000 rpm)
Spark plug	Type: Champion L92Y. Gap 0.035 in.
Compression pressure	155 psi. @ 200 rpm
Tyre pressures	F 21; R 25 psi (normal driving)
	F 26; R 32 psi (high speed)
	F 26; R 32 psi (full load)
Max. Payload	450 lb (202 kg)

DIPPING MIRROR
VENTILATORS
OIL PRESSURE &
TEMPERATURE GAUGE
OVERDRIVE,
2 SPEED
WIPERS &
SCREENWASH
CHOKE
HEATER CONTROL
HEATER FAN
AIR DISTRIBUTION
COURTESY LAMP
FRESH AIR
VENT CONTROL
RADIO
HAZARD
CIGAR LIGHTER
HANDBRAKE
ASH TRAY

LAMPS
SPEEDOMETER
INDICATORS
TELL-TALE
PANEL LAMPS
RHEOSTAT
REV COUNTER
FUEL GAUGE
INDICATORS,
DIPSWITCH &
HEADLAMP
FLASHER
IGNITION LIGHT
HORN
IGNITION,
STARTER &
STEERING
LOCK
MAIN BEAM
TELL-TALE
REAR WINDOW
DEMISTER
REAR WINDOW
DEMISTER
WARNING LIGHT

Service Interval	3,000 miles (optional)	6,000 miles	12,000 miles
Leycare fixed charge	£2.82	£9.55	£9.77
Oil Change	£1.58	£1.58	£1.58
Oil Filter	£1.50	£1.50	£1.50
Air Filter	—	—	£1.50
Contact breaker points	—	—	£2.00 (pair)
Sparking plugs	—	—	£0.77
			£2.60
Total Cost: £5.90		£12.63	£18.22

Routine Replacements:	Time (hours & mins)	Cost (Labour @ £3.30/hr.)	Spares	Total:
Brake Pads — Front (set)	1.00	£3.30	£6.90	£10.20
Brake shoes — Rear (set)	1.21	£4.46	£5.20	£9.66
Exhaust System	0.45	£2.48	£15.50	£17.98
Clutch	9.33	£31.51	£21.47	£52.98
Dampers — Front (pair)	1.27	£4.79	£20.00	£24.79
Dampers — Rear (pair)	1.09	£3.80	£15.06	£18.86
Replace Generator	0.30	£1.65	£29.00	£30.65
Replace Starter	1.39	£5.45	£42.00	£47.45

has a "no-loss" cooling system, and it is essential to check this while the engine is cool.

The electrical circuits are protected by four fuses in a fusebox, while there are two additional in-line fuses to protect the heater fan motor, and the hazard warning flasher unit.

The spare wheel lives below the floor of the rear luggage compartment from which all luggage must be removed in the event of a puncture. However, as the spare is inside the car, it stays clean and dry, although it must be released from its stowed position and turned over for the tyre's pressure to be checked.

The rear compartment of the test car became saturated with water during the course of the test period. At first, poor sealing around the tailgate was suspected, but as the water only gets in when the car is on the move, we would suspect that the grommet around the petrol filler cap was not a good fit. This problem has been noticed with previous MGBs, and attention to this seal at an early stage is advised.

There are no tools supplied with the car apart from a jack and wheelbrace which are stowed in a substantial soft bag in the space occupied by the spare wheel. There is one jacking point on each side of the car, and the jack has a good crank action, raising the car quickly.

Conclusions

To put the MGB GT V8 into perspective in the new market that British Leyland are entering, it must be compared with a number of cars that have already carved a niche for themselves. For instance, there is the Reliant Scimitar GTE at £2,430 or £2,480 with overdrive, the Datsun 240Z at £2,535, the Lotus Elan +2 S130 at £2,789 and of course the Triumph Stag at £2,533, while the Ford Capri 3000 GXL compares favourably at only £1,824. To hope to sell well against this powerful competition, the MGB V8 GT has to rely heavily on its excellent smooth power unit, for in most respects of appointment and comfort, it does not score over the opposition. In terms of handling the MGB GT V8 scores over all but the Datsun and the Lotus Elan +2, while in terms of ride, it must be rated at the back of the field. In view of the fact that the development costs cannot have been high, it is difficult to understand how a £500 differential can be justified between the MGB GT V8 and an MGB GT with the 4 cylinder engine, and the same optional equipment.

Undoubtedly the car will sell well on the MG name alone, but it is a fiercely competitive arena that the MGB GT V8 has stepped into, and if it succeeds, it will be mainly due to the excellent Rover V8 engine for which praise cannot be too high. □

MANUFACTURER:

British Leyland Motor Corporation Limited
Austin Morris Group
Longbridge, P.O. Box 41,
Birmingham B31 2TB

PRICES

Basic	£1,925.00
Car Tax	£160.42
V.A.T.	£208.54
Total (in GB)	**£2,293.96**
Static Seat Belts incl. V.A.T.	£9.77
Licence	£25.00
Delivery charge (London) incl. V.A.T.	£18.70
Number plates	£5.00
Total on the Road (exc. insurance)	**£2,352.43**
Insurance	Group 7

EXTRAS (inc. PT)

* Inertia reel seat belts	£15.85

* Fitted to test car

TOTAL AS TESTED ON THE ROAD £2,358.51

1877 1977

Cheerful facelift for Leyland's veteran sports car.
Suspension modifications restore its enjoyable handling.
New seats and facia cannot disguise the MG's age.
Outperformed in almost every respect by newer designs,
it is fading quietly away in a shrinking corner of the market

MGB GT

NOF 480R

TO DESCRIBE the MGB as an "evergreen" is surely one of motoring's great understatements. Introduced in 1962, it has been an old favourite, or an evergreen, for going on 10 years.

In many ways it symbolises all that is best and worst about British cars. This classic sports car design is one which has sold tremendously well world wide; a credit to its designers. But, on the other hand, it has remained largely unchanged save for cosmetic or safety modifications during its life. Critics have written themselves to distraction pointing out its inadequacies, a monument to that dubious philosophy "If it sells, why bother to improve it"

At least, that seemed to be the case until last year, when much to everyone's surprise a revised MGB appeared with almost all the detailed points of criticism improved. As we said in our news headline at the time: "Facelift for MGB — at last". The 14-years-on improvements were a restyled facia, new heater controls, fabric seats, modified pedal layout, and a variety of minor mechanical changes.

These latter were mainly aimed at improving the handling and roadholding which had suffered when the B's ride height was raised to accommodate the American specification bumpers a year previously. Though the ride height remained unaltered, the open car was given a front anti-roll bar, having previously not had one, while the GT's was increased to the same thickness. Both models also gained a rear anti-roll bar for the first time. At the same time the steering wheel size was reduced to 15in. and the rack ratio increased from three to three-and-a-half turns from lock to lock.

Despite its rarely changing specification and performance that is bettered by more family saloons each year, the MGB goes on, selling in numbers that surprise even some Leyland executives. The detail changes give us reason to re-examine the MGB GT, a model that we last "re-examined" in 1971.

Like Wimbledon, the MGB seems to have becomes part of the British summertime sporting tradition and it too has compromised only a little to meet changing demands. The massive, rubber faced Federal safety bumpers are viturally the only exterior styling change to the GT

Performance

The weight increase caused by the massive American bumpers has not helped performance, but, more significantly, during the MGB's lifetime the whole concept of what is acceptable performance has changed. The GT's acceleration must now rate as slow, even by family car standards; yet when it first appeared, back in 1965, this sort of performance was quite acceptable.

Maximum speed in direct top corresponds closely with the 5,500 rpm power peak at 99 mph, the best leg of the MIRA banking giving 101 mph. Overdrive is available on both top and third gears, gearing up top by some 20 per cent. But the car is not keen to pull the higher gearing and the overdrive maximum is very wind-dependent. With the wind slightly in its favour, the GT's one-leg best was 104 mph, but the mean was still just 99 mph.

Straight line acceleration is really very modest. The B manages 60 mph in 14 seconds, which is a second slower than the GT we tested six years ago. Power output has not changed significantly over the years, so the main reason for the lower acceleration must be that kerb weight is up from 21.2 to 21.6 cwt.

Power output is currently 84 bhp at 5,500 rpm, and maximum torque 105 lb. ft. at 2,500 rpm. The quoted figures have varied slightly during the past few years as the B-series engine has been modified for emission control regulations, and these regulations have also been responsible for the loss of some of the unit's former character.

Never noted for its free-revving liveliness, the B-series engine was always a solid, durable unit with a broad spread of power and a complete absence of fussiness. Unfortunately, the emission-inspired changes have seen the delightful low speed torque replaced by a succession of flat spots. Our test engine was also seriously guilty of running on, a not uncommon B-series problem, and pinked under load — fairly familiar problems with some emission modified engines.

The B's gearchange is one of its most characteristic features, and one which has not been spoiled by the advancing years. It is the true sports car shift; a short, gaitered lever, ready to hand and offering notchy, firm, yet very precise movements through its accurate gate. Overdrive is, of course, standard, and one of the improvements on the latest car has been to re-locate the operating switch away from the facia and onto the gear-lever knob. For the first time, an MGB driver can now change gear and operate the overdrive without taking both hands off the wheel!

Gear ratios are unchanged and so the rather low second gear remains

More dramatic changes inside where the scattered dashboard has been re-fashioned and the seats given a new deckchair striped cloth facing

The rear bench is really a nominal plus-two, being flat and hard with very limited head and legroom for all but the smallest children

MGB GT

— even holding on to 6,000 rpm only gives a maximum of 50 mph. On the other hand, overdrive third, allowing up to 95 mph, is a superb ratio and the car can be driven over give-and-take routes for miles, flicking between third and overdrive third.

Economy

The B-series engine is inherently an economical unit, and even in MGB tune it returns impressive consumption figures. Of course, overdrive is a great asset in the pursuit of good fuel consumption. Our steady-speed fuel consumption figures show what sort of difference it makes — around 14 per cent at 70 and 80 mph, the sort of speeds at which it is most likely to be used. Indeed, overdrive makes 30 mpg motorway cruising a ready possibility, as the figures show, and our own journeys confirmed this. While our overall consumption dropped to 25.7 mpg, journeys with a large element of motorway all hovered near the 30 mpg mark.

Handling

The 1½ in. increase in ride height needed to meet American bumper regulations had quite disastrous effects on the handling and roadholding of the B which was formerly a well-balanced, eminently driveable sports car. Instead, the open version which we tested shortly after the change was found to have heavy roll oversteer and a very twitchy response.

Thankfully, the anti-roll bar modifications have now largely cleared up the problem — though it must remain a mystery why Leyland did not provide them from the start. With the changes, the car has now reverted a good way back to its original levels of handling and roadholding.

The B has never been the sort of sports car to set standards in roadholding; its crude lever arm dampers and basic, leaf-spring rear axle see to that. Rather the pleasure of driving it has come from its taut and predictable reactions. An initial modest understeer gives way, as cornering speeds build up, to readily controllable oversteer. Ultimate levels of roadholding are not high, but the car's controllability makes it fun to drive.

The lower-geared rack has made the steering significantly lighter, its heaviness being a noticeable feature of past MGs. Though the steering wheel is a little smaller, it is still too large for some tastes, and certainly its rim is too thin.

Brakes are first class, with servo assistance allowing near 1g stops with only 60lb pedal effort. The 10-stop fade test showed up no problems.

Ride and noise

Once again, the B has been overtaken by later designs in the handling/ride compromise. Newer cars have managed to combine good handling with a higher all-round level

of ride comfort than the MG's. Its ride is quite firm — hard if compared with saloons of similar performance — and would once have been thought typically sports car-ish if more recent cars had not proved otherwise. The harshness is especially noticeable on rougher roads, when the lever arm dampers and leaf springs get caught out from time to time over successions of bumps.

However, worst aspect of overall driving comfort is the noise level inside the GT. The door window sealing is very poor and at any speed above 60 mph the roar of wind completely drowns conversation or radio. It is a long-standing problem, yet it appears to have received no attention. The engine is also surprisingly noisy; despite now having an electric fan it still suffers from just the sort of noise one would expect from a big, belt-driven fan.

Behind the wheel

The MG has the sort of cockpit that marks it out as a sports car of the traditional school; seats are set close to the floor and legs stretch out horizontally along the sides of the large central tunnel. The facia and steering wheel dominate the small cabin.

The new facia is certainly a pleasant change, even if it has been a long time coming. The dashboard shape is unchanged, as is the material, but its black crackle finish has been toned down to a more restrained grey. It is the instrumen-

The new facia is a considerable improvement, though the new shape steering wheel masks the smaller dials and the piano key switches can be confusing. Speedometer and rev counter face the driver with a fuel gauge between and oil pressure, water temperature to the left and right. The left stalk operates wipers / washers and the right lights and indicators, while a small flip switch by this is the lights master control. The ignition key is hidden awkwardly forward and below these. Below the central piano key switches for heated rear screen, map light, fan and hazard flashers are the manual choke, map light and rotary heater controls

ENGINE	
	Front; rear drive
Cylinders	4-in-line
Main bearings	5
Cooling	water
Fan	Electric
Bore, mm (in.)	80.26 (3.16)
Stroke, mm (in.)	88.90 (3.50)
Capacity, c.c. (in³)	1,798 c.c. (109.7)
Valve gear	Ohv
Camshaft drive	Chain
Compression ratio	9.0-to-1
Octane rating	97 RM
Carburettors	Twin SU HIF4
Max power	84 bhp (DIN) at 5,500 rpm
Max torque	105 lb.ft. at 2,500 rpm

TRANSMISSION		
Type four-speed, all synchromesh, o/drive on 3rd and 4th		
Gear	Ratio	mph/1000rpm
O/d Top	0.820	21.83
Top	1.000	17.90
O/d 3rd	1.133	15.81
3rd	1.382	12.96
2nd	2.167	8.26
1st	3.036	5.20
Final drive gear	Hypoid bevel	
Ratio	3.909-to-1	

SUSPENSION	
Front—location	Double wishbones
—springs	Coil
—dampers	Lever
—anti-roll bar	Yes
Rear—location	Live axle
—springs	Leaf
—dampers	Lever
—anti-roll bar	Yes

STEERING	
Type	Rack and pinion
Power assistance	No
Wheel diameter	15.0 in.

BRAKES	
Front	10.75 in. dia disc
Rear	10.00 in. dia drum
Servo	Yes

WHEELS	
Type	Steel
Rim width	5J
Tyres—make	Pirelli Cinturato
—type	Radial ply
—size	165SR14

EQUIPMENT	
Battery	12 volt 66 Ah
Alternator	45 amp 18 ACR
Headlamps	55-55 watt halogen
Reversing lamp	Standard
Hazard warning	Standard
Screen wipers	Two-speed and flick wipe
Screen washer	Electric
Interior heater	Water valve
Interior trim	Fabric seats, pvc headlining
Floor covering	Carpet
Jack	Pillar
Jacking points	4
Windscreen	Laminated
Underbody protection	Bitumastic

MAINTENANCE	
Fuel tank	11 Imp gal (50 litres)
Cooling system	12 pints (inc heater)
Engine sump	6 pints SAE 20w/50
Gearbox	6 pints SAE 20w/50
Final drive	1½ pints SAE 90
Grease	7 points
Valve clearance	Inlet 0.013 in. (hot) Exhaust 0.013 in. (hot)
Contact breaker	0.014-0.016 in. gap
Ignition timing	10 deg BTDC (stroboscopic at 1,000 rpm)
Spark plug —type	Champion N9Y
—gap	0.025 in.
Tyre pressures	F21; R24 psi (normal driving)
Max payload	394 lb (179 kg)

Maximum Speeds

Gear	mph	kph	rpm
O/d Top			
(mean)	99	159	4,520
(best)	104	167	4,750
Top	99	159	5,500
O/d 3rd	95	153	6,000
3rd	78	125	6,000
2nd	.50	80	6,000
1st	31	50	6,000

Acceleration

True mph	Time (sec)	Speedo mph
30	4.8	31
40	7.0	40
50	9.3	50
60	14.0	60
70	19.1	70
80	28.5	80
90	35.7	90

Standing ¼-mile:
19.1 sec, 70 mph
Kilometre:
36.4 sec, 91 mph

mph	O/d Top	Top	O/d 3rd	3rd	2nd
10-30	—	12.5	—	7.6	4.4
20-40	17.1	11.5	9.1	6.8	4.3
30-50	16.3	9.9	8.3	6.8	5.0
40-60	16.8	10.9	10.2	7.7	—
50-70	16.7	16.9	14.1	9.3	—
60-80	21.8	22.2	16.4	11.7	—
70-90	—	32.0	22.0	—	—

Consumption

Fuel
Overall mpg: 25.7
(10.99 litres/100km)
Calculated (DIN) mpg: 27.1
(10.42 litres/100km)

Constant speed:

mph	mpg	O/d Top
30	48.0	55.6
40	41.3	50.5
50	37.2	44.2
60	34.2	36.7
70	29.8	33.7
80	25.6	29.2
90	22.9	25.1

Autocar formula
Hard driving, difficult conditions
23.1 mpg
Average driving, average conditions
28.3 mpg
Gentle driving, easy conditions
33.4 mpg
Grade of fuel: Premium, four star
(97 RM)
Mileage recorder: 1.8 per cent
over-reading

Oil
Consumption negligible

Brakes

Fade (from 70 mph in neutral)
Pedal load for 0.5g stops (lb)

	start/end		start/end
1	30/30	6	30/30
2	35/35	7	30/35
3	30/35	8	30/35
4	30/35	9	30/35
5	30/35	10	30/35

Response (from 30 mph in neutral)

Load (lb)	g	Distance (ft)
20	0.25	120
40	0.65	46
60	0.95	31.7
Handbrake	0.35	86

Max gradient: 1 in 3

Clutch
Pedal 25lb and 5½ in

Test Conditions

Wind: 5-20 mph
Temperature: 12 deg C (54 deg F)
Barometer: 29.6 in. Hg
Humidity: 100 per cent
Surface: wet Ashphalt and concrete
Test distance 1,224 miles

Figures taken at 9,500 miles by our own staff at the Motor Industry Research Association proving ground at Nuneaton.

All Autocar test results are subject to world copyright and may not be reproduced in whole or part without the Editor's written permission

Regular Service

Interval (miles)

Change	3,000	6,000	12,000
Engine oil	Check	Yes	Yes
Oil filter	—	Yes	Yes
Gearbox oil	Check	Check	Check
Spark plugs	—	Clean	Yes
Air cleaner	—	—	Yes
C/breaker	—	—	Yes
Total cost	**£7.15**	**£23.24**	**£31.85**

(Assuming labour at £5.50/hour)

Parts Cost

(including VAT)

Brake pads (2 wheels)—front	£14.04
Brake shoes (2 wheels)—rear	£8.86
Silencer(s)	£38.34
Tyre—each (typical advertised)	£29.50
Windscreen	£22.95
Headlamp unit	£4.86
Front wing	£52.38
Rear bumper	£27.81

Warranty Period
12 months/unlimited mileage

Weight

Kerb, 21.8 cwt/2,442lb/
1,108 kg
(Distribution F/R, 52/48)
As tested, 25.0 cwt/2,800lb/
1,271 kg

Boot capacity: 9.6 cu.ft.

Turning circles:
Between kerbs L, 33ft. 11in. R,
35ft. 1 in.
Between walls L, 34ft. 2in. R,
35ft. 4 in.
Turns, lock-to-lock: 3.5

Test Scorecard

(Average of scoring by
Autocar Road Test team)

Ratings: 6 Excellent
5 Good
4 Above average
3 Below average
2 Poor
1 Bad

PERFORMANCE	3.16
STEERING AND HANDLING	3.83
BRAKES	4.20
COMFORT IN FRONT	3.00
DRIVERS AIDS	3.37
(instruments, lights, wipers, visibility, etc)	
CONTROLS	3.50
NOISE	2.83
STOWAGE	3.33
ROUTINE SERVICE	3.90
(under-bonnet access dipstick, etc)	
EASE OF DRIVING	4.00
OVERALL RATING	**3.52**

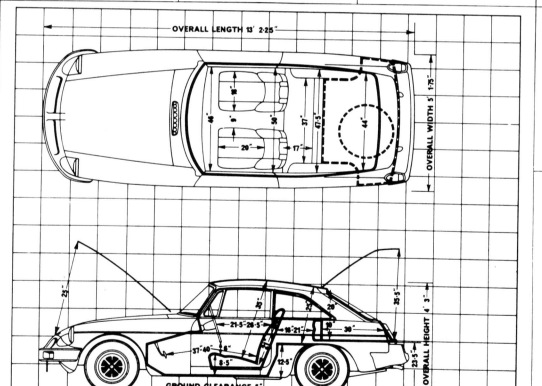

OVERALL LENGTH 13' 2·25"
OVERALL WIDTH 5' 1·75"
OVERALL HEIGHT 4' 3"
GROUND CLEARANCE 5"
WHEELBASE 7' 7"
FRONT TRACK 4' 1"
REAR TRACK 4' 1·25"

Comparisons

Car	Price (£)	Max mph	0-60 (sec)	Overall mpg	Capacity (c.c.)	Power (bhp)	Wheelbase (in.)	Length (in.)	Width (in.)	Kerb wt lb	Fuel (gal)	Tyre size
MGB GT	**3,576**	**99**	**14.0**	**25.7**	**1,798**	**84**	**91.0**	**158.3**	**61.8**	**2,442**	**11.0**	**165x14**
Colt Celeste 2000GT	3,349	104	11.2	24.9	1,995	98	92.1	162.0	63.0	2,190	9.9	165x13
Toyota Celica Liftback ST	3,413	102	12.7	27.6	1,968	96	98.2	166.9	63.8	2,356	12.8	165x14
Triumph TR7	3,371	109	9.1	26.4	1,998	105	85.0	160.0	66.3	2,206	12.0	175/70x13
Fiat X1/9	3,298	99	12.7	30.7	1,290	73	86.8	150.8	61.8	2,016	10.5	165/70x13
Ford Capri 2000S	3,522	106	10.4	24.0	1,993	99	101.0	171.0	67.0	2,273	12.7	165x13

tation and switchgear that has been most thoroughly revised and improved.

Speedometer and rev counter still sit in front of the driver, viewed through the steering wheel, with its new four-spoke design, but the oil pressure and water temperature gauges are now separated and lie to the outside of the main dials. The fuel gauge sits in the centre, between the two main instruments. Though the dials are crisply numbered and easily read, unfortunately the oil and water gauges are hidden by the driver's hands.

The formerly chaotic muddle of switches has also been rationalized into a tidy row under the central pair of fresh-air vents, operating heated rear screen, map light, heater fan, and hazard flashers. The piano-key switches are all clearly labelled but pose the problem common to this sort of layout, in that it is easy to flip the wrong one until touch-familiar with their location. Stalk controls operate wipers and indicators together with light dipping and flashing. The lights master switch sits to the right of the steering wheel at the base of the column. Near it is the ignition switch, which is fiddly and awkward to use, buried deep in the column and having a tiny tab to release the key from the lock.

The map light is now a small, rotateable affair, mounted on top of the centre console between the cigarette lighter and choke lever. Below is space for the optional radio and ranged below that again are the heater controls, with a clock set between them. The heater is the same old water-valve unit, which means that the temperature is awkward to regulate accurately. But the controls have been usefully improved and now comprise two clearly-marked circular knobs, for attempted temperature regulation and distribution. The two fresh-air vents give a good airflow, but extraction is improved by opening a rear-quarter window.

A very visible improvement to the MGB is the new seating material, a vivid deckchair-striped nylon cloth that faces the wearing surfaces. Our test car was trimmed in discreet shades of grey, but there are other, much more lurid trim colours available. The material looks very *chic*, just the sort of thing for the market the car is aimed at, and is certainly a lot more comfortable than the old vinyl.

The seats are unchanged in design and are as comfortable as ever, with plenty of lateral support around the thigh and back. They can be partially reclined, but by awkward-to-use levers mounted on the backrests. Adjustable headrests are also fitted. The straight-legged seating position allows drivers of most heights to find a comfortable position behind the wheel. Revised pedal positions allow heeling-and-toeing -- 14 years after we complained in our road test of the then new car that this was impossible.

Behind the front seats is a candy-stripe bench which is really

Familiar B-series engine has lost some of its sparkle through emission tuning, which has also cluttered the engine bay with pipework

The modest boot extends usefully in size when the rear seat back is folded and loading is easy through the deep tailgate. Below: Spare wheel and jack stow under the floor

only suitable for small children, leg and headroom being much too restricted to carry anyone larger except perhaps a single adult sitting crosswise. The bench is crude and flat, held in place just by "lift-the-dot" style fasteners, so that it can be easily removed for access to the battery. The seat back can be unclipped and folded down on it to extend the luggage area.

The MG is, of course, much more of a pure sports car than most of its newer two-plus-two rivals, and, in consequence, its boot space is fairly modest. It does extend usefully, however, if the rear seat is folded flat. The wheel arches, which have the large inertia reels of the seat belts mounted awkwardly on top of them, do intrude to some extent, and the spare wheel is stowed along with the jack under the boot floor.

Access to the boot is easy through the full-depth tailgate, but the latter's remarkably strong springs send it slamming down hard at the slightest provocation. Aside from the boot, stowage space is very restricted; just the glovebox, a map bin in front of the passenger's door, and a small box under the central armrest. But, at last, the glovebox can be opened without a key (though it is still lockable) so saving the owner the irritation of having to stop and remove the ignition keys to read a map.

In service

The MGB is a straightforward, uncomplicated car, as easy to service and maintain as it is to drive. Starting is straightforward, using the manual choke, but the car does not run happily from cold, being rather jerky and fluffy.

Under the bonnet, the once-so-simple B-series engine is how heavily disguised by emission plumbing. But it is still essentially a straightforward engine to service. The distributor and spark plugs are accessible, the rocker box easily removed for tappet adjustment, and items like the coil and fluid reservoirs are all to hand.

The fuel tank holds 11 gallons and fills through an unobstructed neck that has a twist-off cap. Reversing lamps, two exterior mirrors, a laminated screen, and

halogen headlamps are all now fitted as standard. Service interval is 6,000 miles, with an optional 3,000 mile check, and the Supercover warranty can be extended to two years for a modest charge.

Where it fits in

Now that the V8 GT has been discontinued, there are two versions of the MGB -- the open sports and the GT. The latter is considerably more expensive, at £3,576, compared with the open car which costs £2,854.

There are now a number of other sporting two-plus-twos, some more obviously sporting than others. The Ford Capri is perhaps the most attractive, at £3,522, the 2000S at £3,522 being a close price rival for the MGB GT.

The Japanese also have recent rivals to offer; from Colt, the 2-litre Celeste at £3,349, and from Toyota the 2000ST liftback at £3,413. The VW Scirocco at £4,161 is perhaps a little expensive for comparison, but there are a number of other coupés that do not have hatchbacks which come into the price range — the Opel Manta 1.9SR, Lancia Beta 1600, and even the Ford Escort RS2000.

Conclusion

The MGB is now so aged and out-paced as to be strictly a minority taste; it is easily outsold by Leyland's newer sports car, the TR7. Certainly the modifications improve it, but it is incredible to think that one has had to wait 14 years for little things like the glovebox lock alteration.

The facia is tidier and the seating material very smart, but they are reminiscent of the facelift on an ageing film star — they cannot hide all the cracks. Presumably the MGB is now in that sort of ageing car's limbo where its sales generate enough profit to keep it in production but not sufficient to encourage the sort of substantial re-design it needs.

As it is, it remains a pleasant to drive, easy to service and maintain GT car, with classically sporting lines and predictable handling, yet very modest performance.

MANUFACTURER:	
Leyland Cars	
Grosvenor House	
Redditch, Worcestershire	

PRICES	
Basic	£3,056.00
Special Car Tax	£254.67
VAT	£264.85
Total (in GB)	**£3,575.52**
Seat belts	Standard
Licence	£50.00
Delivery charge (London)	£47.50
Number plates	£7.50
Total on the Road	**£3,680.82**
(exc insurance)	
Insurance	Group 6
EXTRAS (inc VAT)	
Wire wheels	£80.84
TOTAL AS TESTED	
ON THE ROAD	**£3,680.82**

Premature Obituaries

AUTOCAR, w/e 12 July 1980

MG: the end of the line?

BL says losses can't go on as rescue deadline passes

JUST A faint hope of success was held out by Alan Curtis, architect of the bid to save MG when he responded to BL's ultimatum on the Abingdon closure last week. Confidence in British industry, and particularly in the British motor industry, had run out, he said. As a result, the promise of financial backing in Britain – from several sources – had been withdrawn and the collapse here had then prompted the withdrawal of American support which had accounted for about 25 per cent of the total. The

flicker of hope that remained was the interest shown in the project in Japan.

"With hindsight," said Curtis, "I would have done better to have concentrated my efforts to raise all the funding in Japan instead of in America and here." He did not want to raise any false hopes at this late stage but last Wednesday was waiting with his colleagues for a call which could send him "leaping on to the next plane for Tokyo". That could result in re-opening the negotiation with BL. The

outcome of this remote possibility would be known after we closed for press.

BL announced that they were to go ahead with the MG plant closure on 1 July, three months after they had made an "agreement in principle" with the Curtis consortium. Because MGB sales are currently slow, the Abingdon factory has been working a three day week since May and stocks of unsold cars are high. BL say that their losses on MG will be over £20 million this year if production continues.

The rescue bid was formulated in January and at first seemed unlikely to be given much consideration by BL, who had already indicated their intentions for the Abingdon site and made plans for the use of the MG name on other models. By April, Curtis, of Aston Martin, with the backing of British Car Auctions, Norwest Holst, Peter Cadbury, Lord George-Brown and others, had BL's approval for their ideas to keep the MGB going. They had undertaken a re-design of the MGB which they hoped to launch in 1981. On paper, the proposition was a doubtful one. BL claim to be losing £900 on each MGB sold in America. Curtis' researches produced different figures: "I don't believe it is an unprofitable car," he said.

Things started to go wrong with the consortium six weeks ago and then escalated with the evaporation of business confidence. Curtis didn't blame the government for the situation. There had been a meeting with Industry Secretary Sir Keith Joseph but Curtis appreciated his reasons for declining any solid help to go with abundant sympathy offered. Identity of the Japanese interest on which final hopes rested was not to be revealed, other than confirming that it was "not Honda" and that it was a company with motor industry connections.

Curtis also confirmed that the consortium's intention was that John Symonds, former head of BL's Pressed Steel Fisher and now chief executive of Aston Martin Lagonda, would head the management team of the new MG production company.

BL have yet to reveal their plans for the MG name if and when MGB production ends. ☐

AUTOCAR, w/e 1 November 1980

End of an era

it's finally come for Abingdon

Last of the line

THE FINAL MGB was produced last week at Abingdon, the marque's home since 1929. The plant is up for sale – with a price tag of around £5 million – and the workforce is looking for new employment.

More than half a million MGBs were built since the model's introduction in 1962 and, without an immediate replacement, it will become increasingly a collector's

car. However, it may take as long as six months to sell the "several thousand" new MGBs still in the pipeline between factory and dealers at home and abroad. And it will take until Christmas to fully run-down the Abingdon plant.

Last year, when BL announced the plan to cease MG production, there was an outcry –

from dealers in the USA, MG clubs and other enthusiasts. BL's original intention was to use the site for packing CKD – completely-knocked-down – kits for despatch to plants abroad. This would have freed space at the crowded Cowley plant for the *un*-packing of components from Honda for the Bounty which goes

into production at Cowley next year.

In the meantime a consortium led by Aston Martin boss Alan Curtis made a protracted but failed attempt to put together a rescue deal. And changing circumstances have meant that BL has been able to accommodate both CKD packing and unpacking at Cowley.

The future location of BL Motorsport, now housed in a purpose-built facility on the Abingdon site, is uncertain. It doesn't affect operation of the plant, so it could stay there indefinitely as a sitting tenant. But a buyer might want the site free of such encumbrances and, if so, a new home will have to be found for Motorsport. ☐

MG's new vintage

The new MG RV8 is launched today and goes on show at Birmingham next week. In the first of our motor show previews, Steve Cropley finds the reborn roadster quick, plush and full of MG spirit

Reach for the stringbacks and death to MG Montego. For the first time in more than a decade, Britain has an MG sports car which is worthy of the octagonal badge on its nose. This week the wraps come off the MG RV8, Rover's 3.9-litre B-based two-seater roadster, and a new era of MG sports car motoring begins.

A carefully orchestrated flow of Rover teasers and tip-offs alerted us, months ago, to the fact that the car was coming. Also that it would be based on the *new* MGB body which, four years ago, was put back into production for the benefit of classic car restorers. But none of that fully prepares British sports car enthusiasts for the MG RV8 as it stands today: it is fast, luxurious, roomy and well proportioned and, well, pretty convincing. Some had feared the RV8 would be an overdressed version of a rickety old car: it's far from that.

The idea of a 'new MG' has lingered since before the old one went out of production in 1980. Plans became better focused when Peter Mitchell and his team at British Motor Heritage, Oxfordshire, began to build MGB shells again in 1988. But Heritage hadn't the resources to build complete cars and, anyway, it was doubtful that anyone would want an ordinary B, a car which passed its sell-by date in about 1975.

The MG RV8 was finally brought to fruition by Rover Special Projects, a team of 30 planners, engineers and designers based at Gaydon, Rover's test track in Warwickshire. RSP director Steve Schlemmer says that, starting at the beginning of 1990, his people formed the nucleus of a dedicated team drawn from all corners of Rover. Calling the project 'Adder', (in recognition of the Anglo-American Cobra of the '60s), their objective was to re-create the MGB as it would have been had it never left production.

The truth is that they've probably done better than that. The car has a wide-tracked chunkiness and a level of luxury to which the tired old black-bumpered two-seater of 1980 could never have aspired. MG owners' groups have already given it the unconditional thumbs-up.

Yet, curiously, Rover's high-hats seem anything but overcome by the emotion of their latest launch. They are quite dispassionate about the great occasion, firmly denying that the car is any confirmation that modern MGs are on the way. They concede only that the RV8 will be a jolly profitable way of celebrating the 30th anniversary of the MGB's debut, and admit only grudgingly that the RV8's launch is a fine way of keeping the MG name warm.

In fact, as we've made clear in past issues, Rover's management knows it would be plain crazy not to launch some new MGs, so great is the interest and demand. The company has two front-running projects: PR3, a mid-engined two-seater due in 1995, and a Stag-style four-seater, due a couple of years later.

The MG RV8, to cost £26,500, will start going out to customers in April or May next year. Rover has started taking deposits of just under £3000 from customers, and quoting firm delivery dates in return. A couple of weeks before the Birmingham motor show there had been 1000 enquiries, 200 of which were serious enquiries that had turned into 100 firm orders. The motor show debut should produce many more. Rover says it plans a two to three-year life for the car (which is tantamount to admitting that there will be something else with an MG badge for the later '90s) and 20-odd artisans at Cowley, Oxford, will build about 15 cars a week. If demand is heavy, that can rise to 20 cars.

The MG RV8 is a UK-only programme "at this stage", says Schlemmer. Building for other markets would have slowed the project and added to the cost which he describes as "miniscule" on a normal motor industry scale. Since news of the project has broken, it has become clear that the Japanese, who also drive on the right, would love

Refined cruising rather than race-track handling is the RV8's forte. It's much more than a dressed-up MGB

RV8 has wider tracks than MGB, hence flared wings. Foglights set in body-coloured plastic bumper

some RV8s, but Schlemmer will only say the company "will look at it" when the size of the demand crystallises.

If you read between the lines, it is probable that RSP will only turn its attentions to export markets if demand in the UK isn't as strong as exports. MG-loving nations other than Britain will have to exist on a trickle of UK-spec personal imports or possess their souls with patience until the new-generation MGs arrive, sometime around 1994

In the flesh, the MG RV8 has an obvious relationship with the old MGB, but is satisfactorily different. The basic structure is the Heritage body, built (Rover says with surprising candour) to slightly higher standards than when formerly made. The all-steel unitary chassis is deemed plenty strong enough to carry the 3.9-litre alloy V8, even though, in the car's heyday, there was never a factory-produced V8 roadster. (There was an MGC roadster powered by a huge iron six, which probably weighed 50 per cent more than a fully equipped V8).

In the MG RV8 every panel has at least a single-side zinc coating, and the car carries a six-year guarantee against corrosion, just like all other Rovers.

On to the Heritage shell go new flared front and rear wings to cover the wider track. The bumpers are formed in body-colour plastic, the lights front and rear are all-new and there's a new bonnet with a power bulge. The grille is derivative in style, but different. Even the distinctive windscreen frame is all-new, though it

Thick-rimmed wheel

looks the same. "The old frame was a particularly nasty mixture of castings and extrusions," says Schlemmer. "Ours is made from steel in a single piece." The doors are original MGB, though they have their quarter-lights

Hood revised from MGB

removed and have a new set of body-colour exterior mirrors. The hood, based on the old shape and frame, has been revised by Tickford but functions largely in the same way as MGB hoods.

The engine is the same pushrod 3950cc alloy V8 which Land Rover supplies to its other sports car customers, such as Morgan and TVR, and is very closely related to the 3.5-litre which was used in the 2500-odd MGB V8 GTs made between 1973 and 1976.

But whereas in the '70s it

was fed by carburettor and produced 137bhp, today's engine has 187bhp at 4750rpm and 231lb ft of torque at 3200rpm, is fed by electronic fuel injection and puts exhaust gases through a pair of closed-loop catalysts.

Power goes through a Land Rover-built 77mm gearbox, basically a much-improved version of the old Rover SD1 gearbox. Top gear (in which the car will happily pull from 30mph) is a 0.79:1 overdrive, giving a top gearing of just under 29 mph/1000 rpm.

From there, drive goes to a live rear axle which has a Quaife torque sensing differential. Schlemmer says Rover's tests have shown this kind of diff is the only one which can cope with a long life of V8-sized helpings of torque.

The biggest suspension news is that the MGB's infernal lever arm dampers have been dropped in favour of tubular units. The front suspension now has a proper double wishbone system with coil springs and concentric tubular dampers (the damper arm used to ▶

The MG RV8 is the product of Rover's group of niche market specialists

THE MG RV8 IS ROVER SPECIAL PROJECTS' SIXTH COMPLETED project, even though this Gaydon-based group of 30 planners, engineers and designers was only formed at the beginning of 1990. Boss Steve Schlemmer says the group's job is to spot opportunities to produce low-volume niche products, to sell the ideas to management, and to bring them to fruition.

So far, RSP's products have included the limited edition Mini Cooper (the 1000-off version which preceeded the car's return as a fully fledged production model), the two-door 'handling pack' Range Rover CSK, a specially equipped, old-shape Rover 800 to speed that model's run-out, and a US-only limited edition version of the newly launched Land Rover Defender, to raise the model's profile.

First return of Cooper...

"We draw the people and resources we need from all over the company, for the relatively short terms that one of our projects lasts," says Schlemmer. "That allows us to stay small and flexible. We have another four projects on the go at present, and at least one of them is a high-profile job like the MG RV8."

...CSK Range Rover...

Schlemmer will say nothing about it, but one of RSP's key jobs must surely be readying the Mini Cooper S, slated for full production launch quite soon. But there's always a bottom line to consider: RSP is always deadly serious about making its image cars into profit-earners, Schlemmer says. "It's easy to have exciting ideas," he comments, "but you have to ask yourself if there is a person out there who will buy it."

For the MG RV8 project, detailed research was carried out to prove that demand for such a car actually existed. The Special Projects team found a 'significant' number of well-off people who were very interested in the idea of an MG in the classic style, but weren't really classic car or DIY types.

"We found people who thoroughly understood the proposition of the MG," says Schlemmer. "They admired the competence of modern cars but wanted something with a little more character, though not for day-to-day use.

"They were looking for great performance, but not a car that would have to justify itself against a Porsche or a TVR Griffith. The first performance priority, they told us, was that the car should just roll along beautifully. That's the car we've given them."

...RV8: all work of Rover Special Projects team

◄ be the top link), though geometry is not much changed. The RV8's steering, like the MGB's, remains unassisted rack and pinion.

Not much sophistication about the rear suspension either: it continues to use MGB-style semi-elliptics, but Rover chooses to describe them as 'twin-taper leaf' springs. Unlike a conventional semi-elliptic set-up, their two leaves are spaced apart to reduce friction and wear. Telescopic shock absorbers provide the damping, and twin lower torque control arms limit axle tramp. As at the front, there is an anti-roll bar.

The front brakes are large ventilated discs with twin-pot calipers; the rears are 230mm drums rather similar to the original MGB ones. They are power assisted, of course, but anti-lock brakes are "not a priority".

The combination of revised suspension and much chunkier wheels and tyres (205/65 VR15s on specially designed alloy wheels with 6J rims) means front and rear tracks are several inches wider. That helps both looks and handling.

Inside, the accent is predictably enough on wood and leather. RSP's planners reckoned a luxurious MG interior would do a lot to sell it, so they have given the car a burr-elm laminate across the facia and on the centre console. The bucket seats are leather covered, as are the steering wheel, gearstick and armrests, while the tunnel sides and door panels are in leather-look vinyl.

The switch and control layout is modern, but very much in the spirit of a classic British roadster. The steering wheel is sporty in style, but thick-rimmed, there's a full set of VDO black-on-white instruments, and the steering column stalks are latest-spec Rover 800 items. In short, there's nothing revolutionary about the MG cockpit, but the effect is very pleasing, especially since the MGB cabin was always well planned and roomy.

Though everyone — both Rover and their potential MG customers — seems to agree that this won't be a high-mileage, day-to-day car, lots of trouble has been taken to make the car durable.

Factfile

MG RV8

How fast
0-60mph	5.9secs
Top speed	135mph
MPG: urban	n/a
56mph	n/a
75mph	n/a

All manufacturer's claimed figures

How much?
£26,500 **On sale in UK** spring 1993

How big?
Length	4010mm (158ins)
Width	1694mm (67ins)
Height	1320mm (52ins)
Wheelbase	2330mm (92ins)
Weight (claimed)	1280kg (2822lb)
Fuel tank	51 litres (11 galls)

Engine
Max power 187bhp/4750rpm
Max torque 231lbft/3200rpm
Specific output 47bhp/litre
Power to weight 155bhp/tonne
Installation longitudinal, front, rear-wheel drive
Capacity 3946cc, 8 cyls in vee
Made of aluminium alloy
Bore/stroke 94mm/71mm
Compression ratio 9.35:1
Valves 2 per cyl, single cam
Ignition and fuel breakerless electronic ignition, Lucas multi-point fuel injection

Gearbox
Type 5-speed manual
Ratios/mph per 1000rpm
1st 3.32/6.9 2nd 2.09/11.0
3rd 1.40/16.4 4th 1.00/22.9
5th 0.79/29.0
Final drive ratio 3.31

Suspension
Front independent, double wishbone, coils springs, dampers, anti-roll bar
Rear live axle, twin taper-leaf half-elliptic springs, dampers, control arms, anti-roll bar

Steering
Type rack and pinion
Lock to lock n/a

Brakes
Front 270mm ventilated discs
Rear 230mm drums Anti-lock n/a

Wheels and tyres
Size 6x 15ins Made of cast alloy
Tyres 205/65VR

Made and sold by
Rover Cars, Canley Road, Canley, Coventry CV4 9DB Tel: 0203 670111

Besides the rustproofing and the hood revisions, the MG RV8 has a completely new wiring harness using 1993-spec cable, fusing, connectors and relays. The system which includes a similar alarm system to that recently introduced in the Rover 200 cabriolet, now runs inside the car, not underneath it as the MGB's did.

To finish the package Rover has made a special effort with paint choices. There are six standard Rover colours — two solids, two metallic, two pearlescent

Cabin is well planned, roomy and luxuriously appointed with elm and leather everywhere. Steering is unassisted

But the highest demand, Rover predicts, will be for four new colours specifically designed for the MG RV8 and offered for £750 extra: Le Mans Green metallic, Willow Woodcote Green, Oxford Blue pearlescent and Old English White.

Production MG RV8s will be distinctly thin on the ground until delivery begins in four to five months' time. Most current testing has been conducted on two prototypes, 'Red Adder' and 'Black Adder', though Schlemmer says the proto-type count will total about 12 by the time RV8s are in the hands of customers.

The car was never expected or planned to have the highest levels of race-bred handling, says Schlemmer. "It handles very predictably," he says, "and tracks as straight as an arrow at motorway cruising speeds. Besides, if you corner it hard, it will still hang on much longer than most drivers expect. It's a forgiving car, and we think that's the main thing."

The steering has very good

Modern control layout

centre-feel, points out Schlemmer, which is one benefit of its lack of power assistance. It isn't the lightest of cars to manoeuvre into parking spaces, he says, but effort levels are acceptable.

If Rover didn't see race-track handling as a priority, they certainly put effortless performance high on the list. And the RV8 has got it. Though it weighs about 2800lb at the kerb, which is plenty for a two-seater, its copious low-end power gets it swiftly off the mark with 0-60mph claimed to take just

5.9secs, and, according to early estimates, the 100mph in about 14secs. Top speed is conservatively estimated at 135mph, at which stage it's only pulling 4600rpm.

The MG's other side is as an effortless cruiser. Owners who like autobahn touring (work for which the car seems ideal) will soon discover that a genuine 100mph requires only 3500rpm in top. The touring range might be a problem, though; at 22-24mpg, the car will only do about 180-200 miles comfortably. Knowing it isn't a truly modern car, buyers may excuse the foible.

Throughout the project, Rover has insisted that the MGR V8 is "not the new MG", merely a convenient way to celebrate 30 years of the MGB, keep the MG name warm, and turn in a profit — all at a same time.

In the flesh, it doesn't look or feel new. But the RV8 is a fast, good-looking and engaging car, which is well built and should be long lasting. If not the new MG, it is certainly a real MG. That, many buyers will think, is a more important accolade. ■

Land Rover's 3.9 V8 gives 187bhp, 231 lb ft torque

MG RV8

A British legend is back. But has 13 years on ice left Rover's favourite roadster out in the cold?

WHAT DO A SWIMMING pool, a speedboat and an oil painting all have in common? Together they are considered by Rover to constitute the principal opposition for its £25,440 MG RV8 roadster. And if this sounds like a strange collection of rivals for a motor car, Rover would like you to see it instead as 'a recreational pursuit which just happens to take the form of a motor car.'

Rover claims that it is promoting its heavily revised MGB like this not out of fear of how it might compare to other, similarly priced, two-seater roadsters but because, it asserts, 90 per cent of the 2000 customers it is aiming for over the next two years will be weighing it up against the likes of the speedboat and oil painting, not another car.

So what is it about the RV8 that leads its makers to suggest it should be seen as a hobby on wheels rather than a modern motor car?

Simply put, and no-one argues this point, it is not a modern car but a modern interpretation of a car which was born 31 years ago. The essential bones of the original structure remain, from the bodyshell (now made by British Motor Heritage) to the live rear axle, basic suspension design and most of the bodywork, from the bonnet and doors to the bootlid.

To look at, though, the changes Rover has made to exhume the most popular MG after 13 years in the grave are obvious and, by and large, successful. New wings front and rear give a more modern, integrated look while new bumpers and headlamps are a vast improvement on the ugly rubber mouldings that ruined the front and rear of all post-1974 MGBs.

The car looks lower too, thanks to flared wheel arches, an increased track and fat, low profile tyres. Office opinion varied on the overall effect of the update but most agreed it fell somewhere between the elegance of the original design and the polluted, Federalised version of the mid to late '70s.

The best news from a mechanical point of view is the installation of the 3.9-litre version of the all-alloy, pushrod V8 that has now been Rover's fast car mainstay for 26 years. Though this is not the first time this engine has seen service in an MGB — the coupe version was available with ▶

STAN PAPIOR

Price as tested £26,030 **Top speed** 136mph
0-60mph 6.9secs **MPG** 20.2

....

For Strong engine, beautifully built, feels pleasantly quaint
Against Poor handling, unrefined and rather lumpen ride

◄ a 137bhp, 3.5-litre variant from 1973 to 1976 — this is the first time it has been factory-installed in the convertible. Power has risen to 190bhp at 4750rpm while 234lb ft of torque is at your disposal at 3200rpm.

Even if you accept Rover's contention that the RV8 is a car without four-wheeled rivals, there's no escaping the fact that there are a number of similar-sized roadsters available for a similar price. The most obvious of these is the £26,250, four-litre TVR Chimaera which, given its design brief to be both a sports car and a sophisticated tourer, is so clearly in competition with the RV8 that we have pitted the two together, starting on page 74.

It is also hard to ignore such similarly powered and ancient designs as the £24,081 Marcos Mantara 4.0 and the Morgan Plus Eight at £24,898.

If, however, it is a more civilised, modern convertible you're after, Audi will part with an 80 2.3 Cabriolet in exchange for £22,199 while Mazda's sweet looking and handling MX-5 can be specified in ritzy SE trim for just £18,686. At the other end of the spectrum you will find Porsche's 968 Cabriolet at £37,175 and by August BMW will have its ultra-sophisticated 325i Cabriolet to tempt you at about £28,000.

Performance

The RV8 fulfils the first requirement of a sports tourer with ease: it feels fast. That this impression is not entirely backed up by the performance figures is not something that will worry you on the open road. With a light alloy V8 making exactly the right noises, from its low rev woofle to its flat-out roar and supplying ample doses of torque at any engine speed you like, it simply never occurs to you that you're not actually travelling that quickly. Not by TVR Chimaera standards anyway.

Rover's own performance claims say the RV8 will scrape under 6secs for the 0-60mph sprint, a time which, had we been able to replicate it, would have seen the RV8 banging on the door of the supercar club. However, it was all we could do to coax it under 7secs, suggesting that the RV8 is merely very swift. After that, despite the aerodynamic limitations of a design older even than that of the Porsche 911, it still accelerates hard, hitting 100mph in 18.5secs and eventually reaching 136mph.

To put it another way, the RV8 posts a near-identical set of figures to the Volkswagen Golf VR6, which is

0.2secs slower to 60mph and 100mph, has a top speed just 2mph higher, and records an identical 30-70mph time of 6.4secs.

Yet such statistics fail to show the RV8 in its best light. Its engine is far stronger in the midrange than screaming at the 5900rpm rev limit so the technique is to change up early and let the torque do the work. Drive like this and the engine's flexibility becomes a joy, dispatching every 20mph increment between 20 and 80mph in fourth in less than 5.6secs. Added bonuses are the clean shifting gearchange and well-cushioned, progressive clutch.

Economy

There are few cars in our road-test history whose thirst for petrol has varied as greatly as that of the RV8. Drive it fast enough to keep pace with a TVR Chimaera over the Brecon Beacons and, as we found, it will gulp down fuel at 13-15mpg all day. Conversely, gently cruise the motorways and 35mpg is not an uncommon sight, thanks, in the main, to a top gear ratio which adds 29mph to the speed of the rear wheels for each additional 1000rpm.

Overall it managed 20.2mpg in our hands, a good result considering the car's power and the manner in which it was driven. It was a disappointment, then, to note that our touring route, a blend of towns, country roads and motorway, tackled at a suitably relaxed pace, could yield only 26.9mpg.

Handling

Rover has worked hard to keep the RV8's chassis out of the dark ages, widening its track, replacing the lever arm dampers of old with telescopic Konis and fitting ultra-modern fat 205/65 ZR 15 section Michelin MXV3 tyres.

Yet the live rear axle with its leaf springs remains and as a result, though grip has been markedly improved, the RV8's handling is still firmly rooted in a previous generation.

The first thing you learn about driving the RV8 fast is not to do anything at all which might upset it. No sudden movements of the arms, no over-zealous applications of the throttle.

Do so and, as one tester put it, you'll read the whole book of handling vices from cover to cover in one corner. Try to bully the RV8 along and the entire gamut of horrors from terminal understeer to roll oversteer will unfold before you. And if the road is wet or the least bit bumpy, you'd be better off not trying to hustle it along at all.

The roads the RV8 likes are smooth and dry with no hidden camber changes or bumps. Angle its nose gently into a sweeping bend and it will follow your command faithfully, provide more than enough grip and, thanks to steering that is impressively communicative, give you the feeling of being in touch with the car and the road surface that is essential to any sports car. Under such conditions the RV8 is a delight. The problem is, it takes so little to upset it as it lacks both the damping control to tackle ►

More modern than meets the eye

OVER AND ABOVE ITS NEW, GLASS-FIBRE WINGS, ROVER HAS GONE TO CONSIDERABLE lengths to update the shape of the RV8. Integrated bumpers visually top and tail the car while a widened track serves to give it a more modern and aggressive stance — look at the 1962 MGB roadster next to an RV8 (right).

The headlamps, uncannily like those fitted to the Porsche 911, slope backwards in place of the convex bulge of old. The rear lights, meanwhile, have a new, smoother profile.

There is a new badge in the grille, while fog lamps have now found their way into front bumpers. The bonnet has been reprofiled to accommodate the V8 engine. The windscreen surround is now a single-piece design. As well as improving aerodynamics, it should also ease maintenance.

Heaven is a smooth, dry road; bumps unsettle the RV8

MG RV8

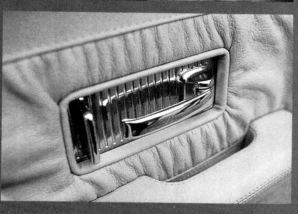

Walnut door cappings and dash **plus leather trim and** seats **give an air of class lacking in the rather tacky vinyl-and-cheap-carpet MGB ancestor. The** cabin, **however, is hardly roomy**

Instruments **are standard British sports car issue, familiar from much other homegrown machinery. They are clear and legible, though**

Venerable all-alloy ex-Buick Rover V8 engine, **in 3.9-litre incarnation, fills the bay**

Hefty, heavily chromed interior door handles are Jaguar-like, and aid the car's overall feel of solidity and quality

The bespoke steering wheel **boss is neat and distinctive**

Boot **is mostly full of spare wheel. Space is just about adequate for a weekend away but leave the full set of Louis Vuitton luggage at home**

Both front **and rear aspects are massive improvements over the rubber bumpered '70s versions of the MGB. Headlamps now slope backwards**

The Autocar Road Test

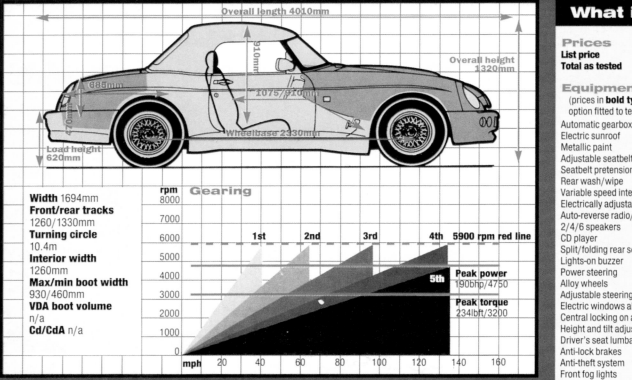

Overall length 4010mm
910mm
685mm
470mm
Overall height 1320mm
Load height 620mm
1075/910mm
Wheelbase 2330mm

Width 1694mm	
Front/rear tracks 1260/1330mm	
Turning circle 10.4m	
Interior width 1260mm	
Max/min boot width 930/460mm	
VDA boot volume n/a	
Cd/CdA n/a	

Gearing

rpm: 8000, 7000, 6000, 5000, 4000, 3000, 2000, 1000, 0

1st, 2nd, 3rd, 4th, 5900 rpm red line, 5th

Peak power 190bhp/4750
Peak torque 234lbft/3200

mph 20 40 60 80 100 120 140 160

What it costs

Prices
List price £25,440
Total as tested £26,030

Equipment
(prices in **bold type** denote option fitted to test car)

Automatic gearbox	–
Electric sunroof	–
Metallic paint	★
Adjustable seatbelt height	–
Seatbelt pretensioners	–
Rear wash/wipe	–
Variable speed intermittent wipe	★
Electrically adjustable mirrors	–
Auto-reverse radio/cassette player	★
2/4/6 speakers	4
CD player	£590
Split/folding rear seat	–
Lights-on buzzer	–
Power steering	–
Alloy wheels	★
Adjustable steering column	–
Electric windows all round	★
Central locking on any door	–
Height and tilt adjustable driver's seat	–
Driver's seat lumbar adjustment	–
Anti-lock brakes	–
Anti-theft system	★
Front fog lights	★

★ standard – not available

Insurance group 17

Depreciation n/a

Warranty
12 months unlimited mileage, 6 years anti-corrosion, 12 month recovery

Servicing
Major 12,000 miles, service time n/a
Interim 6000miles n/a

Parts costs

Set spark plugs	£18.40
Brake pads front	n/a
Brake pads rear	n/a
Exhaust (exc cat)	£220
Door mirror glass	n/a
Tyre (each, typical)	£160
Windscreen	£100
Headlamp unit	£60
Front wing	£180
Rear bumper	£250

Specification

Engine
Layout	8cyls in a vee, 3946cc
Max power	190bhp/4750rpm
Max torque	234lb ft/3200rpm
Specific output	48.7bhp/litre
Power to weight	172bhp/tonne
Installation	longitudinal, front, rear-wheel drive
Made of	aluminium block, head
Bore/stroke	94.0/71.12mm
Comp ratio	9.35:1
Valves	2 per cyl, ohv
Ignition and fuel	fully mapped breakerless ignition, Lucas multi-point fuel injection, catalyst

Gearbox
Type five-speed manual
Ratios/mph per 1000rpm
1st 3.32/6.91 **2nd** 2.09/10.98
3rd 1.40/16.4 **4th** 1.00/22.9
5th 0.79/28.97 **Final drive** 3.31:1

Suspension
Front double wishbones, telescopic dampers, anti-roll bar
Rear Live axle, elliptic leaf springs, telescopic dampers, anti-roll bar

Steering
Type rack and pinion
Lock to lock 3.1 turns

Brakes
Front 270mm ventilated discs
Rear 228mm drums
Anti-lock not available

Wheels and tyres
Size 15x6ins
Made of aluminium alloy
Tyres 205/65 VR15
Spare full size

Made and sold by
Rover Cars, Canley Road, Coventry CV5 6QX. Tel: 0203 670111

Performance

Maximum speeds
Top gear 136mph/4694rpm
4th 135/5900 **3rd** 97/5900
2nd 65/5900 **1st** 41/5900

Acceleration from rest
True mph	Secs	Speedo mph
30	2.4	35
40	3.7	45
50	5.0	56
60	6.9	66
70	8.8	76
80	11.2	87
90	14.5	98
100	18.5	109
110	23.6	120

Standing qtr mile 15.2secs/92mph
Standing km 27.9secs/116mph
30-70mph through gears 6.4secs

Acceleration in each gear
mph	top	4th	3rd	2nd
10-30	–	6.1	4.1	2.6
20-40	7.8	5.6	3.9	2.4
30-50	7.7	5.5	3.7	2.6
40-50	7.6	5.4	3.6	3.4
50-70	7.7	5.2	3.8	–
60-80	7.9	5.4	4.4	–
70-90	8.5	6.0	5.6	–
80-100	9.6	7.0	–	–
90-110	11.0	8.4	–	–

Fuel consumption
Overall mpg on test 20.2
Best/worst on test 37.1/10.4
Touring* 26.9
Range 301 miles
Govt tests (mpg):
urban 17.2 56mph 40.9 75mph 32.5
Tank capacity 51 litres (11.2 galls)

** Achieved over a pre-set test route designed to replicate an average range of driving conditions. **The figures** were taken at the Lotus proving ground, Millbrook, with the odometer reading 2100 miles. Autocar & Motor test results are protected by world copyright and may not be reproduced without the editor's written permission.*

Brakes
Distance travelled under max braking
Track surface dry
Anti-lock no

30mph	11.3m
50mph	33m
70mph	68m
st qtr mile (92mph)	114m

Fade tests
Consecutive brake applications at 0.5g retardation from st qtr terminal speed
(figures on the right represent pedal pressures)

50lb, 40, 30, 20, 10, 0

Weight
Kerb (incl half tank) 1101kg
Distribution f/r 51/49%
Max payload 220kg
Max towing weight 1310kg

1 Voltmeter 2 Ventilation controls 3 Analogue clock 4 Hazard warning switch 5 Water temperature gauge 6 Stereo radio/cassette 7 Indicator stalk 8 Rev-counter 9 Fuel gauge 10 Speedometer 11 Windscreen wiper stalk 12 Front fog lamps 13 Rear fog lamps 14 Interior adjustable mirrors

Handling goes to pieces under pressure, despite modernisation of chassis. Grip is good — while the going is good

◀ undulations with confidence and the suspension travel to soak up the kind of mid-corner bumps that an independently sprung car would scarcely notice.

Ride

The RV8 falls prey to its live rear axle again. At medium effort on unchallenging roads or motorways its suspension is well controlled and comfortable, fuelling the notion that here is a car more concerned with light cruising than more serious driving. Its composure, however, is seriously challenged both by urban potholes and twisting country roads, where you find yourself patrolling the horizon for bumps to avoid.

Brakes

At just 1100kg, the RV8 hardly needs a headline-grabbing brake specification. Big ventilated discs at the front and much smaller rear drums may not seem adequate to slow a car with such a performance potential but, on the road,

there are no such worries.

Pedal feel is excellent and retardation, so long as you don't encounter a bump which can cause premature lock-up, is strong and in all normal use fade-free. Anti-lock brakes are unavailable which, were this any other kind of car costing this much, would be seen as a disgrace.

For some reason though, open British sports cars seem to have excused themselves from fitting such basic and essential safety equipment. The truth is that the RV8, like any car with a top speed close to 140mph, should have anti-lock as standard.

At the wheel

The RV8's driving position is hugely undermined by the fact that the unadjustable steering wheel is severely off-set towards the centre of the car. Were this not the case, you would sit exactly as you'd wish in a low slung British sports

car: reclined, legs reaching to well spaced pedals with your hands gripping a chunky steering wheel right in front of you. In reality though, it is hard to escape from the feeling that your arms are operating a wheel that's in a different part of the car to the rest of you.

The instruments are standard fare for our indigenous sportsters, populating cars from the cheapest Caterham to the mighty Lotus Esprit S4. Though small, they work well and add to the flavour of Britishness. Column stalks,

minor switches and the steering wheel, if not its newly designed MG boss, come courtesy of Rover's parts bin and blend in well with rest of the interior.

Accommodation and comfort

The RV8 is a strict two-seater. Though hood-up headroom is just sufficient, tall drivers will have to drive the RV8 barefoot to make enough space to work the pedals comfortably. The hood itself is ▶

Rear view is neat but hood cover is difficult to attach properly

Wind noise is obtrusive at speed by modern cabrio standards; new wings subtly update evocative lines of original

◀ essentially the MGB hood of old. To raise it, you simply pull it forward. clamp it to the trailing edge of the windscreen and attach four pop studs to keep the loose ends from flapping at speed.

Lowering the hood is nearly as straightforward — just reverse the process. The hood bag, however, essential if a tidy appearance is to be maintained, is fiddly to attach and needs to be fitted over a small metal skeleton to provide the correct tautness.

The boot is large enough to swallow enough squashy bags for a fortnight's casual holiday, but thoughts of packaging large, formal suitcases should be dismissed immediately .

Noise

Noise suppression has come a long way since the days of the MGB and, in the RV8, it shows. At speed, excessive wind noise is a constant companion (though the situation is much improved with the hood in place) and this is exacerbated if the manual

aerial is raised — it creates such a loud whistle that you can't hear the radio that you lifted the aerial for in the first place.

Off the motorway, the RV8's noises make much more pleasant companions as they emanate almost entirely from the sweet-sounding V8.

Build quality and safety

You quite simply cannot quibble with the way the RV8 is pieced together. The quality of the interior materials, especially the leather, is top drawer, while you'd have to look a long way indeed to find a paint finish better than that which adorned the test RV8.

Lovely touches like the heavy, chromed door handles inside and out give the RV8 a pleasant period feel of solidity, too.

Unfortunately this is not backed up by the addition of modern safety features like side

impact bars, pre-tensioned seat belts, anti-lock brakes or an airbag. If you have an accident in the RV8 it will be the car's inherent strength, rather than any clever safety features, that saves you from injury.

Equipment and value

The RV8 comes with its beautiful leather upholstery, lavish walnut trim, neat alloy wheels, superb paintwork and an immobilis-

er as standard. Look for electric windows, mirrors or power steering though and you'll be dis-appointed. The only option listed is a £590 CD player fitted in the boot.

Whether the RV8 is good value or not depends on how you perceive it. If you judge it simply on its capabilities, it is hard to justify the expense.

Look at it as a piece of nostalgia which provides both a trip down memory lane plus decent performance and the £25,440 purchase price is easier to swallow.

Verdict

Every time you drive the RV8 you are reminded that it owes its existence to a design that is now more than 30 years old.

For those who buy British sports cars for their dynamic ability, the RV8 rules itself out of the running almost immediately. Rover realises this, which is why it is so eager to distance itself from cars like the TVR Chimaera. It knows there are people, MGB owners of old for instance, who care less about point-to-point speed and pin-sharp responses than they do about being in, and being seen in, a pleasantly styled, familiar old friend which now goes and sounds like never before. For them, the RV8 may well prove irresistible.The bottom line is, and Rover admits it, that the RV8 exists as much to be a status symbol as a car in which to enjoy driving. To us the RV8 is an anachronism, albeit a strangely likeable one. It is nowhere near as good a new car as a TVR or an old one as a Morgan but on the right day, in the right conditions, it is easy to enjoy and even fun to drive in an agricultural, vintage manner. If, however, you asked us whether we would part with £25,440 for the pleasure of its company, we would regrettably have to decline.

MG RV8

★★ **£25,440**

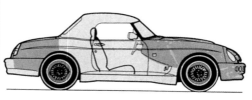
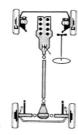

Length 4010mm **Width** 1694mm **Front track** 1260mm **Wheelbase** 2330mm
Height 1320mm **Rear track** 1330mm **Weight distribution front/rear** 51/49

The MGB is back, albeit in revised form with a V8 in the convertible body for the first time. This means straight-line performance is strong enough for most tastes even if, with its live rear axle, its handling leaves rather a lot to be desired. A likeable, if seriously flawed car that will certainly appeal to marque enthusiasts. Others may wonder its purpose.

Capacity	3946cc
Power	190bhp/4750rpm
Torque	234lb ft/3200rpm
Max speed	136mph
0-60mph	6.9secs
30-70mph through gears	6.4secs
Standing quarter mile	15.2secs
30-50mph in fourth	5.5secs
50-70mph in top	7.7secs
Mpg overall/touring	20.2/26.9
Mph/1000rpm in top	29.0
Kerb weight	1101kg
Date tested	16.6.93

Audi 80 Cabriolet

★★★ **£22,199**

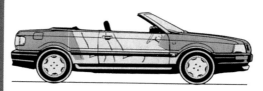

Length 4366mm **Width** 1716mm **Front track** 1453mm **Wheelbase** 2545mm
Height 1379mm **Rear track** 1447mm **Weight distribution front/rear** n/a

Chopping the top off the 80 has turned a good-looking car into a great one. Unfortunately it's still the same underneath, which means performance is barely adequate for a car costing this much and handling, while pleasant, is hardly the stuff of dreams. Best driven slowly, when you have more time to appreciate its superb build, rigid structure and all the looks it draws.

Capacity	2309cc
Power	133bhp/5500rpm
Torque	137lb ft/4000rpm
Max speed	123mph*
0-60mph	10.8secs*
30-70mph through gears	n/a
Standing quarter mile	n/a
30-50mph in fourth	n/a
50-70mph in top	n/a
Mpg overall/touring	n/a
Mph/1000rpm in top	21.9
Kerb weight	1350kg
Date tested	n/a

*manufacturer's claim

Marcos Mantara 4.0

★★★ **£24,081**

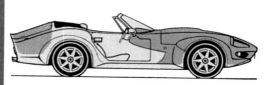
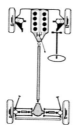

Length 4267mm **Width** 1588mm **Front track** 1448mm **Wheelbase** 2273mm
Height 1080mm **Rear track** 1397mm **Weight distribution front/rear** n/a

Thirty years on, Jem Marsh's design looks set for many more years yet. A restyle and a change of name from Mantula to Mantara have cost some visual panache but has earned limited volume Type Approval. With power coming, naturally, from the ubiquitous 3.9-litre Rover V8, the Mantara proves able to provide a blast from the past as well as fine top-down touring.

Capacity	3946cc
Power	190bhp/4750rpm
Torque	234lb ft/3200rpm
Max speed	140mph*
0-60mph	5.4secs*
30-70mph through gears	n/a
Standing quarter mile	n/a
30-50mph in fourth	n/a
50-70mph in top	n/a
Mpg overall/touring	n/a
Mph/1000rpm in top	29.0
Kerb weight	1020kg
Date tested	n/a

*manufacturer's claim

Mazda MX-5 SE

★★★★ **£18,686**

OUR CHOICE

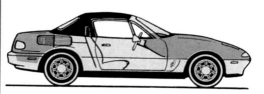
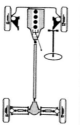

Length 3975mm **Width** 1675mm **Front track** 1410mm **Wheelbase** 2265mm
Height 1219mm **Rear track** 1430mm **Weight distribution front/rear** 52/48

The SE version of Mazda's seminal sportscar boasts anti-lock brakes, new alloy wheels and a leather interior with a wooden steering wheel. Paintwork is any colour you like so long as it's black. Your money also buys one of the best looking cars of the '90s as well as one of the finest handling. It only seems like a lot of money until you drive it.

Capacity	1597cc
Power	115bhp/6500rpm
Torque	100lb ft/5500rpm
Max speed	114mph
0-60mph	9.1secs
30-70mph through gears	9.5secs
Standing quarter mile	17.4secs
30-50mph in fourth	7.5secs
50-70mph in top	13.9secs
Mpg overall/touring	24.0/34.1
Mph/1000rpm in top	18.8
Kerb weight	950kg
Date tested	14.3.90

Morgan Plus 8

★★★ **£24,898**

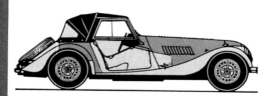

Length 3962mm **Width** 1600mm **Front track** 1371mm **Wheelbase** 2489mm
Height 1219mm **Rear track** 1371mm **Weight distribution front/rear** 49/51

Those who buy these Morgans couldn't care less about the dreadful ride, terrible weather equipment and appalling lack of refinement. What attracts them is the joy of old car motoring with the security of modern, mass-produced mechanicals. That this also buys them one of the most evocative and just plain beautiful cars around is merely icing on their cake. We don't blame them.

Capacity	3946cc
Power	190bhp/4750rpm
Torque	235lb ft/2600rpm
Max speed	121mph
0-60mph	6.1secs
30-70mph through gears	6.1secs
Standing quarter mile	15.1secs
30-50mph in fourth	4.1secs
50-70mph in top	6.3secs
Mpg overall/touring	20.1/23.5
Mph/1000rpm in top	27.6
Kerb weight	935kg
Date tested	15.5.91

Porsche 968 Cabrio

★★★★ **£37,175**

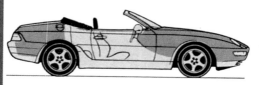
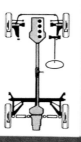

Length 4320mm **Width** 1735mm **Front track** 1472mm **Wheelbase** 2400mm
Height 1275mm **Rear track** 1450mm **Weight distribution front/rear** 45/55

There are few convertibles money can buy that are as capable as this Porsche. Whether you wish to relish one of the best chassis around, cruise the open autobahn at an effortless 130mph or just admire the car as a piece of engineering, the 968 will not disappoint. A pity, then, that it looks strange and that, with the optional Tiptronic gearbox, its acceleration is unexciting.

Capacity	2990cc
Power	240bhp/6200rpm
Torque	225lb ft/4100rpm
Max speed	145mph
0-60mph	8.3secs
30-70mph through gears	7.1secs
Standing quarter mile	15.9secs
30-50mph in kickdown	2.9secs
50-70mph in kickdown	4.2secs
Mpg overall/touring	23.0/24.1
Mph/1000rpm in top	24.4
Kerb weight	1472kg
Date tested	24.6.92

*car tested with Tiptronic semi-automatic gearbox

MGF

Enthusiasts have been holding their breath to see what the new MG would be made of. Now we know — and in the next 10 pages we chart the genesis of Britain's most important sports car since the E-type

Words by Steve Cropley

is go!

Photography by Stan Papior

Feast your eyes, car enthusiasts, on the sleek lines and rich specification of the new MGF roadster, revealed at the Geneva motor show today, and be glad that these are not the 'good old days'.

Why?

Because the arthritic group of companies from which today's Rover Group has so remarkably sprung would never have built a car like the MGF. Because in the UK's new would-be sporting flagship Rover has given us practically everything on our MG wish list, whereas in the old days life wasn't quite like that.

On paper, the MGF is exactly the mid-engined, affordably priced, all-independent, all-disc roadster we have hoped for and speculated upon for years. Not only that, but it is also better packaged and more sophisticated mechanically than its near-rivals, the Mazda MX-5, Fiat Barchetta and Toyota MR2. Its styling studiously avoids anything of a 'retro' look, which might have pleased a few near-sighted purists but which made the MG RV8 such a disappointment.

The F-type introduces two new 1.8-litre versions of Rover's much-acclaimed K-series family of modular engines. The higher-powered version has an all-new variable valve timing system that gives it a horsepower per litre figure that would do justice to a modern turbo four.

And — amazingly — it brings Alex Moulton's time-tested Hydragas suspension system into the new generation of ▶

Mid-engined MGF will start at £16,000 when it goes on sale in June. It promises much dynamically

Design

To Canley via Frankfurt

Rover's EX-E sowed the seeds of the MGF, says Iain Robertson

It's 10 years since Rover stormed a European motor show with an all-new MG sports car, but the success of the exotic EX-E concept unveiled at 1985's Frankfurt motor show was a turning point for the marque.

The EX-E was never intended for production – although some say it inspired Honda's NSX – but the essential MGF design cues were already there. There are mechanical similarities, too: the engine was mounted behind a two-seat cockpit and even the running gear, like much of the MGF, was borrowed from the Metro (the EX-E's 250bhp V6 started life in the raucous Metro 6R4 rally car).

By 1989 the MG programme had been dubbed "Phoenix Revival" and PR codenames assigned to a series of prototypes.

Spurred on by the success of Toyota's MR2 and the imminent arrival of Mazda's MX-5, Rover's special products department opted for the mid engine/rear drive layout of PR3, as the car was initially known. Dynamically superior to front-drive prototypes, it was also to be cheaper to build than traditional MGs with their front engine/rear drive layout.

Aware that its new mid-engined roadster would take at least four years to develop, Rover also sanctioned PR4 – better known as the low-volume MGB-based RV8 – to pave the way by re-establishing the MG marque.

In January 1991, with its own designers working flat out on models like the 600, Rover commissioned styling proposals from IAD (now part of the Mayflower Group that produces MGF bodies for Rover), MGA Developments and the Luton-based consultancy ADC.

Of the three, Coventry's MGA gave the MGF its basic shape. Former MGA designer Steve Harper recalls the brief. "It was very open, really. We were given a simple mechanical package and a list of cars that

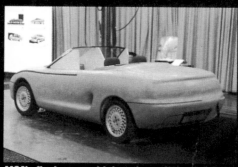

1985's EX-E provided inspiration for MG rebirth

MGA's final proposal takes shape. Note air intake

'Twin cockpit' cabin enhances driver appeal and safety; power comes from 118 or 143bhp K-series 1.8

captured some of the spirit they were after –
including the EX-E, the XJR-15, the original
MR2, the Elan and BMW's Z1. Plus it had to
be obviously British and unmistakably MG."

A delegation from Rover's in-house studio
visited twice to follow MGA's progress – once
early on to view initial sketches and again to
see the full-size clay model.

Harper remembers their reaction. "The
feedback we got was very positive. The high
rear deck went down well, as did the bodyside
surfacing and the car's squat stance, but the
front end treatment drew some criticism –
too anonymous, not MG."

Harper and his team were dispatched to

nearby Styling International, where designers
and modellers were putting the finishing
touches to the RV8's familiar nose.

"We tried a similar look, with the round
indicators and sidelights and the distinctive
MG grille shape above the bumper line, but it
wasn't fully resolved."

By the end of May – after just four and a
half months – MGA had signed off its MGF
proposal and the clay model was shipped to
Rover's Canley design studio, where in-house
designer Gerry McGovern started work on the
production version. He insists that the final
version is very different from MGA's 1991

proposal and he's right. The windscreen is
new, the waistline has been lowered, every
body surface has been altered and it's shorter
and prettier. But the basic profile and many of
the details are still there.

The most significant advances occurred at
the front. By reducing the front overhang and
raising the height of both front wings and
bonnet, Rover's team has not only made
space for a vertically mounted full-size spare
wheel but created the classic MG 'face' that
was missing from the MGA version. The rear
is sharper, too – more like the EX-E – and
every surface has been honed, reducing visual
bulk and increasing the feeling of tension.

Effort to mimic RV8 nose was ditched by MGA

whose final design reverted to recessed lights

Early McGovern rendering sparked Rover changes

Rovers, and becomes the first sports roadster in living memory with a gas-fluid suspension that connects the front and rear wheels.

Given the obvious care with which the MGF's shape and specification have been compiled, it's a surprise to learn that the MGF has only been on Rover's official model plan since 1992. For years, the idea of an all-new MG was sidelined by a management more interested in getting its mainstream models properly up to class standards.

Yet by 1992 engineers and designers had done a great deal of preparatory work. Several design consultants had finished full-size MGF concept models (see p18). Rover's styling staff had already gathered a number of traditional MG cars and reference material for what they called "The MG Event" to identify the qualities and hardware that they believed made a true MG. In the end, Rover Design decided to handle the project in-house, believing that the concepts lacked the elusive quality of 'Britishness'. They wanted, in particular, to give the body some of the 'tension' which distinguished the MG EX-E prototype shown at the Frankfurt motor show in 1985.

To strike the right balance of sporting character and practicality, MG engineers started by scanning dozens of magazine and newspaper road tests, believing that cars in the MGF class were widely bought as a result of what was written about them. They studied tests of the MR2 and MX-5, of course, but went back as far as the old MGB and even analysed comments about the most sporting of hot hatches, the Peugeot 205 GTi 1.9. Engine sound and response were highly valued, they found, along with crisp, faithful handling. Many tests emphasised a sports car's need to have a good touring range. And Rover's researchers were pleased to discover (in the interests of keeping insurance costs down) that top speeds and 0-60mph times were of relatively little importance.

But first they had to determine the MGF's true character, charting a way between the expectations of the flat-capped owners of old MGs and lovers of stripped-to-the-bone high-performance cars. The MGF, Rover says, is a sporting car in every way, but comfortable enough to cruise long distances (in a way an MX-5, for instance, is not) and be used as an owner's sole means of transport. It was also built to undercut both key Japanese rivals on service costs to 60,000 miles, through the use of components like long-life spark plugs and air filters.

Starting in 1989, three years before an MGF programme had been officially recognised, Rover's engineers built three prototypes — transverse mid-engined, front engine/front-wheel drive and front engine/rear drive. By 1992 they had already decided that the mid engine layout offered conclusive advantages in weight distribution and handling 'tuneability'. They built prototypes with all-steel suspensions, too, but concluded that a modified Metro ▸

K-series too big for its boots? Try new boots

Rover used some ingenious engineering solutions to increase the size of its award-winning engine. Julian Rendell reports

The big-capacity K-series is an engine that should never have been built. Conceived as a family of small engines, the design squeezed so much into its compact dimensions that Rover persistently denied any chance of more capacity.

Yet six years after its first appearance, Rover has successfully stretched the all-alloy engine to 1.6 and even 1.8 litres. The MGF is the first to use the engine in both regular and variable valve timing forms.

"I'm delighted that what I said five years ago was wrong," says Sivert Hiljemark, engineering director of Rover Group Powertrain.

Driven by a need to replace its expensive, bought-in Honda 1.6, Rover spent "less than £200 million" and six years working on the big-block K, solving its problems with ingenious and innovative engineering.

The key features of the big block are new cylinder liners, called 'damp liners', which allow an increase in the cylinder size by squeezing bigger bores into the same overall block length. For both 1.6 and 1.8-litre engines that means 80mm bores (they're 75mm in the 1.4).

Rover's engineers have perfected the damp liners to such an extent that they rest on a lip only 1.4mm wide. The bore walls are only 3mm wide and the water cooling jacket around the liners is just 0.65mm. Despite the close tolerances, Rover is convinced that reliability, put to the test in more than two million miles and 50,000 test bed hours, is peerless.

The new bores are enough to boost capacity to 1.6 litres, but to get to 1.8 there's a new long-stroke crank with an 89.3mm throw.

Despite the internal alterations, the K's unique bolt-through sandwich construction, by which a single bolt holds cylinder head, block and sump, stays on unchanged.

Rover has pioneered 'damp liner' technology to squeeze extra capacity from K-series engine

Taking an opportunity to use the latest design techniques, the 1.8 crank has a larger diameter but shorter pins to which the big end caps/conrods are bolted, with 40 per cent more stiffness and 25 per cent more web stiffness. Courtesy of an alloy sump, block stiffness is increased threefold. Both engines have new, ultra-lightweight pistons that tip the scales at an extraordinary 194g each, nearly half the weight of the 1.4's pistons.

All this helps smoothness and refinement. "Normally bigger-capacity engines are less refined — typically second order forces go up five per cent — but we've managed to cut them by 12 per cent," says Derek Crabb, Rover's chief engineer for petrol engines.

Q&A

Alex Stephenson
Managing director,
Rover Group
Powertrain

Why go for variable valve timing?
We looked at everything, including turbos and superchargers, but VVC offered the best package of performance, fuel economy and exhaust emissions.

Why not use a turbocharger instead of increasing capacity?
We ditched the turbo because it would have given a peaky power delivery for such a tiny engine as a 1.4. Also, the turbo adds a lot of cost. On its own it's 25 per cent of the total engine cost, but with an intercooler it's one third. We also wanted to avoid any insurance and theft problems of a car plastered with turbo badges.

And a supercharger?
We watched sales of the Volkswagen G-Lader with great interest — and it never took off. It also adds a lot of expense.

What about reliability of the VVC?
The stresses involved are lower than those experienced every day in diesel engine parts like injector pumps, so it's not a problem.

Can you apply VVC to other engines — say, the forthcoming KV6?
That's in the 'yet to be dealt with' basket. One of the problems we must solve is setting up the drive on the vee engine. With three cylinders per bank, we need two hydraulic drive units and that's not cheap — or easy.

Rover's Variable Valve Control

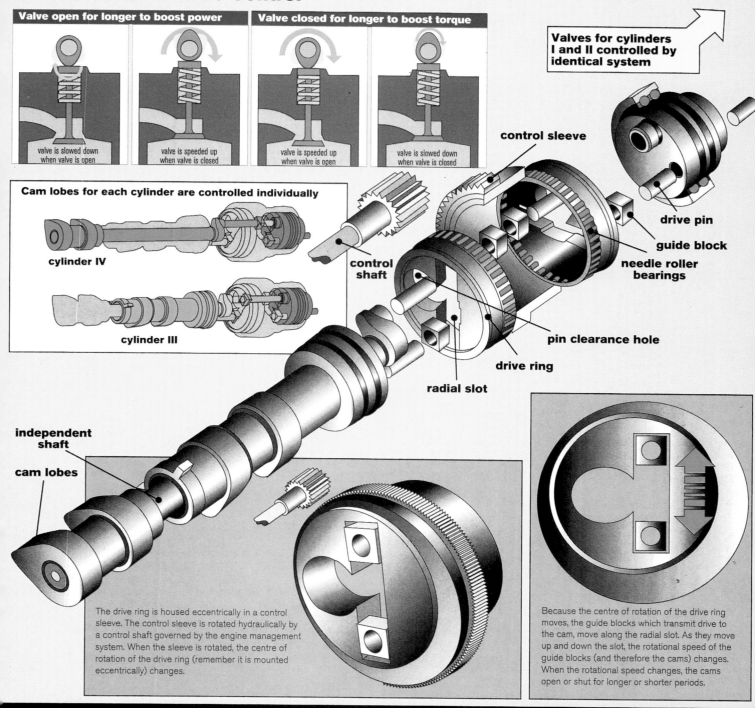

Valve open for longer to boost power

- valve is slowed down when valve is open
- valve is speeded up when valve is closed

Valve closed for longer to boost torque

- valve is speeded up when valve is open
- valve is slowed down when valve is closed

Valves for cylinders I and II controlled by identical system

Cam lobes for each cylinder are controlled individually

- cylinder IV
- cylinder III

control sleeve

drive pin

guide block

needle roller bearings

control shaft

pin clearance hole

drive ring

radial slot

independent shaft

cam lobes

The drive ring is housed eccentrically in a control sleeve. The control sleeve is rotated hydraulically by a control shaft governed by the engine management system. When the sleeve is rotated, the centre of rotation of the drive ring (remember it is mounted eccentrically) changes.

Because the centre of rotation of the drive ring moves, the guide blocks which transmit drive to the cam, move along the radial slot. As they move up and down the slot, the rotational speed of the guide blocks (and therefore the cams) changes. When the rotational speed changes, the cams open or shut for longer or shorter periods.

K-series VVC links cams and drive mechanically, keeping inlet valves open for longer at engine speeds above 4000rpm. The result: 143bhp at 7000rpm

How variable valve timing works

Under the codename Hawk, Rover first researched variable valve control (VVC) for the K-series engine in 1989, but it wasn't until Easter 1993 that the first development engine ran. Tests quickly showed that Rover's design increased power and torque over a wide engine speed band, yet emissions and fuel economy were not adversely affected.

Given the go-ahead, Rover's engineers started to fine-tune their design, which was based on a lapsed patent held in the '70s by piston-maker AE. The result was a 1.8 engine with peak power of 143bhp at 7000rpm and maximum torque of 128lb ft at 4500rpm.

Described as 'third generation', Rover's VVC is technically ahead of BMW's cam phasing system and Honda's VTEC-E. Unlike cam phasing, which just alters valve overlap, and the Honda system, which

switches between two different inlet cams, Rover's VVC can continuously vary the inlet cam period. It allows better combustion over a wider range of engine speeds, boosting power and torque.

The secret to VVC is the clever mechanical link between the inlet camshaft and its drive. An eccentric rotating disc, controlled by the engine management system, alters the relationship between the camshaft and the crankshaft. The effect is to keep the inlet valves open longer at more than 4000rpm, which, with bigger 9.5mm inlet valves, flows more air into the engine.

Low-profile pram-style hood, engineered by Pininfarina, folds away under tonneau. There's no power version, but there will be an optional hard-top

◀ Hydragas system suited a sporting car, perhaps even better than it did a cooking saloon.

Once the primary decisions had been made, the body structure was engineered by Rover and Mayflower's Coventry-based Motor Panels business. It has now begun making bodies to match the anticipated first-year production rate of 15,000 at Rover's Longbridge works in Birmingham, rising to 30,000 in subsequent years.

All along, the F-type was intended to make best possible use of existing Rover components, but engineers now insist that this was not a constraint in the key areas of suspension type and geometry, engine layout and cabin design. The F-type could have been front-engined and rear-wheel drive if that had been appropriate, they insist, even though Rover's saloons all have transverse powerplants. The car is built to last a long time in production, Rover insists, and all decisions on shape and specification have been taken in the light of that.

The MGF's dimensions, in every direction, are within a few of millimetres of those of its closest roadster rivals, the new Fiat Barchetta and five-year-old Mazda MX-5 — even though neither

of those cars shares its transverse mid engine layout. And the MG weighs 1060kg at the kerb — almost exactly the same as the others.

The MG's body is a unitary, all-steel structure with a high degree of rigidity. Rover engineers estimate that its torsional strength equals that of a modern three-door hatchback, making it far more rigid than other convertibles and most specialist two-seaters on the market. The mid engine layout helps here, concentrating the mechanical mass in the strongest part of the car's structure.

Hydragas units are the springing medium for an all-independent suspension system which uses double wishbones at either end of the car. Unlike other Hydragas applications, the MGF system has both separate tubular dampers and an anti-roll bar, which Rover's handling experts claim provide the high degree of body control needed for a sports car.

It is the Hydragas system's interconnection, front to rear, that gives it conclusive advantages over rival set-ups, Rover says. The percentage difference in an MGF's weight, laden to unladen, is low compared with a small saloon's, and the

system has allowed designers to make better use of the car's total wheel travel and improve ride.

There are two MGF models — a £16,000 car with a 118bhp version of the new 1.8-litre engine and a £18,500 model with variable valve timing and 143bhp (see p20). The torque outputs of the two engines are similar, giving rise to the thought that the lower-powered engine will suit drivers who depend most on an engine's mid-range power. The base 1.8 has 122lb ft at 3000rpm; the VVC unit produces only 6lb ft more at 4500rpm.

Both MGFs run on 6Jx15in alloy wheels with 185/55 VR15 tyres at the front and 205/50 VR15 at the rear. The VVC model has a new speed-sensitive power steering system which uses a micro-controlled electric motor to provide its servo effect (which reduces with speed) instead of the more complicated, more common Toyota MR2-style device of an electric motor powering a nose-mounted hydraulic system. The VVC also has anti-lock brakes as standard, which remain an option on the cheaper car.

Inside, designers have created a 'twin cockpit' theme, dividing the cabin ▶

Why the gas man is still laughing

The inventor of Hydragas suspension tells Steve Cropley why it's ideal for the MGF

[D]r Alex Moulton says he's "rather pleased" [th]at Rover has decided to use his Hydragas [su]spension system, now more than [40] years old, for its new MG sports car. [B]ut he isn't all that surprised.

Although critics of the system have [fo]recast its demise for decades, Moulton [b]elieves it has conclusive advantages for [a] small roadster in compactness and [lo]w cost of manufacture. "The tooling [w]as paid for many years ago," he says.

The best Hydragas property, Moulton [s]ays, is that it interconnects the car's [fr]ont and rear suspension systems. [It] de-fidgets the car," he says.

"In a little roadster there is a higher [th]an usual potential for the car to become [u]nsettled on rough surfaces, and the MG [p]erforms much better than the competition [i]n that area, while continuing to handle and [s]teer the way a sports car should."

Given that he has argued (successfully) [i]n the past against separate dampers and [a]nti-roll bars in Hydragas installations, [M]oulton is relaxed about the use of them [th]is time. He still believes the system could [b]e adapted so that it doesn't need them [b]ut admits that tuning the car's handling [i]s easier if you have them.

He'll be driving his first final-spec MGF [a]bout the time you read this but has [a]lready heard from trusted sources within [R]over that the car handles extremely well, [w]hile providing ride comfort beyond that [o]f its competitors.

Moulton, an engineering consultant [w]ho was also responsible for a city bicycle [w]hich had its own rubber suspension, is [b]ullish about the future. While some are [a]lready forecasting the MG application as [th]e last for Hydragas, Moulton demurs. He [b]elieves his unique system has history on [i]ts side: nearly 10 million cars have been [b]uilt with Hydragas suspension.

He has already managed to get BMW [c]hairman Bernd Pischetsrieder to drive an ["o]ptimised" Hydrolastic Mini he built years [a]go, and stands ready to assist with the [n]ew Mini programme in any way he can. "The future," he says, "is tantalising."

CHARLES BEST

with a prominent centre console and using substantial screen pillars and relatively high sides. They believe the move makes the car feel considerably more secure than rivals, while physically making the MGF safer. In fact, crashworthiness has been one of Rover's preoccupations; it claims the car exceeds all current and anticipated crash regulations easily, aided by the mid engine layout, which allows plenty of 'crush space' to cope with head-on impacts.

In common with the MGF's exterior, the cabin has few gimmicks, although the cream-faced instruments do hark back to the MGs of yore. But Rover has considerably fine-tuned the MG octagon badge, which appears on the car's nose and wheels, in a bid to give it modern impact while preserving a traditional look.

Both models have electric windows and what Rover describes as a "good quality" stereo. Two-level locking — incorporating a remote 'superlocking' system — goes into both models. They also feature a manually operated, pram-style soft-top, designed by Rover and engineered at Pininfarina. Although designers saw no need for an electric option, there is an optional hard-top.

Equipment unique to the VVC includes leather trim for the new MGF steering wheel, which incorporates a driver's airbag, and half-leather covering for the sports bucket seats.

The F-type will be launched in the summer — the first cars are expected to hit the road in June — but early buyers will only get the 118bhp 1.8i version. The higher output VVC model, whose engine is still being worked on, won't appear until later in the year, probably in October.

The MGF will be handled by 125 so-called 'specialist' dealers, who will be expected to take one car for stock and one demonstrator at launch. Rover is coy about its initial British volume but anticipates a lively demand for the car across Europe and in Japan as well as from its home market.

No details of a US debut have been announced, although it's worth bearing in mind that US demand made a success of all previous post-war MG models, and Rover could hardly ignore the country that has clamoured for a new MG roadster for so long.

All in all, it seems Britain has a new sporting flagship, and on first acquaintance, it seems to contain the right ingredients to meet the tough competition head-on and — more importantly — to please those legions of car lovers who have waited so long for a new MG. It's not quite so good as getting the Empire back, but nearly. ●

MGF LAUNCH
COMING SOON
IN THE NEXT FOUR WEEKS
GORDON SKED ON DESIGN.
HOW MAYFLOWER WORKS
AND OUT ON TEST
WITH ROVER

Sculpted, modern design maintains MG character

Boot bigger than you'd expect but soft bags only

Cream dials echo old MGs, but retro look shunned

Smart new alloys have modified MG octagon

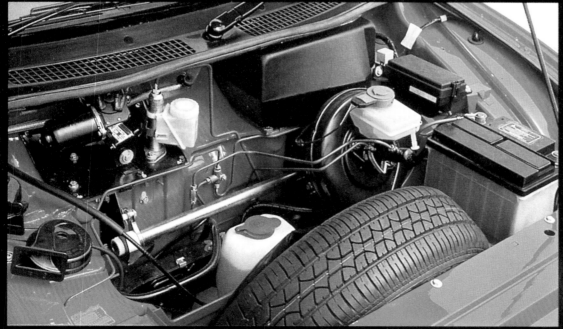

Clever packaging has enabled Rover to fit full-size spare. VVC-powered car has anti-lock brakes as standard

FACTFILE

ROVER MGF
1.8i/1.8i VVC

HOW FAST?
0-60mph	8.5/7.0sec
Top speed	120/130mph
MPG: urban	30.0/tbc
56mph	54.0/tbc
75mph	42.0/tbc

All manufacturer's claimed figures

HOW MUCH?
£16,000/£18,500
On sale in UK June/October

HOW BIG?
Length	3913mm (154.1in)
Width	1628mm (64.1in)
Height	1264mm (49.8in)
Wheelbase	2375mm (93.5in)
Weight (claimed)	1060/1070kg (2337/2359lb)

ENGINE
Max power
118bhp at 5500rpm/143bhp at 7000rpm
Max torque
122lb ft at 3000rpm/128lb ft at 4500rpm
Specific output 65bhp/79bhp per litre
Power to weight 111bhp/134bhp per tonne
Installation mid, transverse, rear-wheel drive
Capacity 1796cc, four cylinders in line
Made of alloy head and block
Bore/stroke 80/89mm
Compression ratio 10.5:1
Valves 4 per cylinder, dohc with hydraulic tappets
Ignition and fuel Rover's own Mems direct injection electronic ignition, multi-point sequential fuel injection, adaptive fuelling control
Gearbox type PG1-u, 5-speed manual

SUSPENSION
Front independent, double wishbones, Hydragas springs, anti-roll bar
Rear independent, double wishbones, Hydragas springs, anti-roll bar

STEERING
Type speed-sensitive electric power-assisted rack and pinion

BRAKES
Front discs **Rear** discs **Anti-lock** standard on VVC, optional on 1.8i

WHEELS AND TYRES
Size 6Jx15in **Made of** alloy
Tyres 185/55 VR15 (f), 205/50 VR15 (r)

SOLD BY
Rover Cars
PO Box 395
Longbridge
Birmingham B31 2TB
Tel: 0800 620820

ON THE ROAD
WITH THE

MGF

Why is the new MG mid-engined and what's it like to drive? After an exclusive day with Rover's project team, Steve Cropley can tell you

MGF TESTING

'Even in its raw form, Pocket Rocket had the edge over the other proposals'

There was a time, not long ago, when the car to relaunch MG to the world wasn't going to be mid-engined or powered by a four-cylinder engine. Back at the beginning of the '90s, there was an even chance that it would be Longbridge's answer to the TVR Griffith.

Serious people within Rover were proposing that the fruit of Project Phoenix be a rear-drive, part-spaceframe car with a meaty pushrod V8 under its long and bulbous bonnet. Indeed, they foresaw two V8 versions, one with plastic body panels and one with steel, and put them up against two entirely different MG proposals.

The V8 cars were PR2 (plastic panels) and PR4 (steel), standing for Phoenix Route Two and Four. The other 'routes' were PR1, a transverse, front-engined, front-wheel-drive alternative, using the 16-valve M16 engine and a collection of Maestro components in a unitary pressed steel chassis, and PR3, a Midget-sized car using Metro components in a steel chassis, clad with plastic panels and with a 1.4-litre K-series powerplant mounted transversely behind the occupants.

The designers and engineers called this last one Pocket Rocket, and even in its raw form it had the edge over the others in terms of sportiness and character. There was instant preference for Pocket Rocket when Rover's management saw the cars in mid 1990, but they decided that the next phase — still well short of adopting the car for future production — should to be to 'grow' it to MGB size.

The other alternatives were swiftly eliminated. There was something crude about the PR2 and PR4 V8s and the company

Above: late 'QP2' prototype undergoes structural tests. Below left: model indicates final cabin shape. Right: rig shows ingenious hood/engine access

MGF MID-ENGINED METRO SIMULATOR

One of mid-engined Metro vans used to develop Rover's K-series engine for PR3's transverse mid engine layout. This one dates back to mid 1992

E268 ODF

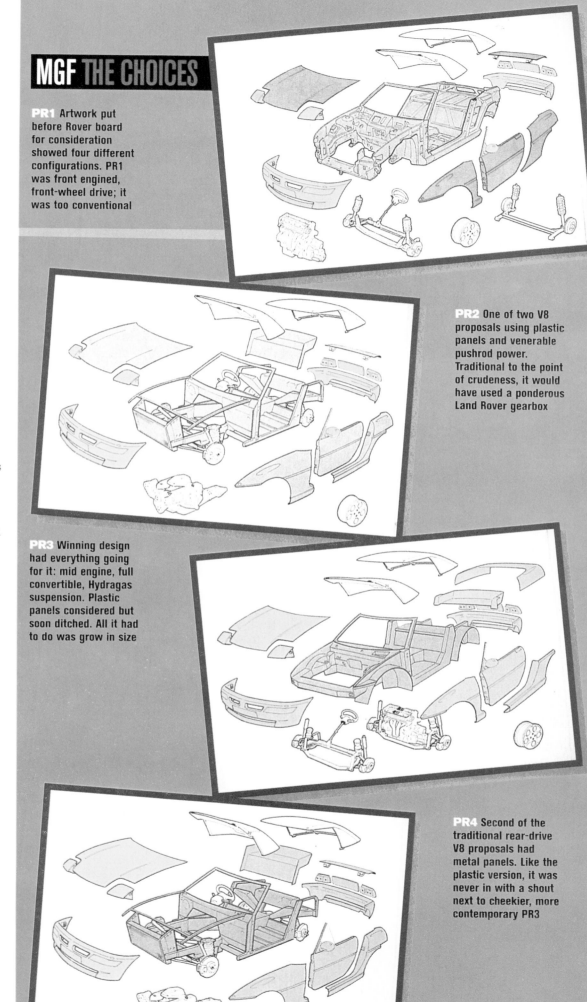

MGF THE CHOICES

PR1 Artwork put before Rover board for consideration showed four different configurations. PR1 was front engined, front-wheel drive; it was too conventional

PR2 One of two V8 proposals using plastic panels and venerable pushrod power. Traditional to the point of crudeness, it would have used a ponderous Land Rover gearbox

PR3 Winning design had everything going for it: mid engine, full convertible, Hydragas suspension. Plastic panels considered but soon ditched. All it had to do was grow in size

PR4 Second of the traditional rear-drive V8 proposals had metal panels. Like the plastic version, it was never in with a shout next to cheekier, more contemporary PR3

no longer had a tradition of fat-engined, rear-drive cars. What was more, the V8s would need to use a bulky, slow-changing Land Rover gearbox. And they would cost.

The front-wheel-drive PR1 risked comparison with the current crop of supermini cabriolets and would lack technical innovation.

The PR3 concept held no worries on either of those scores; on the contrary, a full convertible with a mid-mounted engine would make it unique in Europe. And though the Metro's image remained linked to the likes of the Allegro and Princess in the eyes of some, the revised car was showing that Hydragas suspension (which uses gas-filled springs interlinked front to rear) promised something special in the ride/handling department.

But the PR3 pretty soon lost its plastic panels: Rover's expertise lay in steel fabrication, and plastic (in the news at the time because of the recent Lotus Elan launch) would have required too much hand finishing.

There were plenty of reasons why Pocket Rocket needed to get bigger. The components didn't fit too well (the fuel tank needed to grow from 27 to 45 litres, the rear-mounted radiator needed to be relocated in the nose) and bigger size would allow the car to justify a more viable price. Most important of all, the cars that sold best in the '60s and '70s were the MGB-sized models, not the smaller Spitfires and Spridgets.

While Pocket Rocket was getting bigger (by about 200mm), it lost the drop-down panels that shrouded its headlights in daytime. Both these and pop-up headlights were proposed, but both were dropped when the designers agreed that the car needed a face, and there had been no precedent for retracting ◗

'The Metro front suspension worked well but at the rear it was all wrong'

Car we photographed on the move displayed all the poise and finesse that Rover engineers have led us to expect. Little needs fine tuning, they say

◀ lenses in previous MGs.

At the same time a power steering system, originally considered superfluous, was fitted. But instead of the Toyota MR2 solution of a nose-mounted, electrically driven hydraulic pump to provide the servo assistance, Rover adopted a lighter, more elegant electrical system, again unique in Europe.

The system was originally designed only to assist parking, and only for the Japanese market, but it worked so well in testing that it was adopted to provide speed-sensitive assistance across the board.

Once the Metro-based PR3 layout was adopted, it was always clear that the car would have to use Hydragas suspension, mounted — as in the Metro — on steel fabricated subframes.

But there were problems. The Metro front suspension, without engine, worked well

enough under the nose of the MGF, but that same suspension, governing the rear wheels, was all wrong. Its built-in anti-dive became a mechanism for allowing the tail to rise under braking and squat under the power; its tendency to toe out under braking destabilised the car in cornering. Rover had no budget to design a new rear suspension geometry and no will to produce it for such a small production run.

So the MG chassis men came up with a neat and amazingly cost-effective solution. It employed the existing subframe, but dispensed with the bottom suspension A-arm in favour of three new lower suspension components — bottom link, track control arm and brake reaction rod — anchored in different places on the subframe to provided optimal rear suspension geometry.

The proof will be in the driving, of course, but Rover

MGF D02/19 HANDLING PROTOTYPE

Similar to car that appeared in early scoop shots, D02/19 was used for cold climate and handling tests. Body gives some clues to finished article

MGF THE COMEBACK DIARY

September '85 MG EX-E launched at Frankfurt motor show.
August '89 Rover's initial sports car investigation begins.
June '90 Rover board reviews four MG options (PR1 to PR4). Requests more detailed evaluation of Midget-sized PR3 (Pocket Rocket), increased to MGB size.
January '91 Consultants IAD and MGA commissioned to prepare mid-engined PR3 proposals.
March '91 Rover management backs mid-engined concept. Engineers begin work on spec, proposing 1.4 K-series engine.
May '91 Clinic of three PR3 styling proposals focuses on need for more performance. Gerry McGovern starts work on Rover 'look'.
July '91 Rover board approves direction of in-house design which is bigger than original Pocket Rocket. Proposed power units now 1.6-litre and 1.6 supercharged K-series engines.
Jan '92 Definitive PR3 shape approved. Definitive interior two months away. 'Simulators' built to evaluate steering, chassis, engine installation, suspension, aerodynamics.
April '92 MG Day at British Motor Heritage, Gaydon. Collaborative deal proposed with body panels manufacturer Mayflower.
November '92 Rover board approves programme. Engineers decide 1.8 K-series (standard and VVC) needed for performance and economy. Key spec issues all decided.
July '94 D1 pre-production cars built, mainly using final tooling.
April '95 'M' pre-production cars built, including press test cars.
July '95 First production cars scheduled to roll off line.

chassis man Guy Sutton swears that the geometry is as pure in practice as that of a uniquely designed system, a fact that has brought accolades from his co-workers. The rear wheels toe in under braking or on the overrun (to promote stability) and toe out under power (to resist oversteer).

The front suspension is largely Metro, though the steering arm is shortened to speed up the steering ratio and improve the 'Ackermann effect' (by which each front wheel describes a different curve through a corner in order to sharpen the steering and reduce wheel scrub).

Where the Hydragas units anchor into the top suspension arm, front and rear, the MG uses a new kind of low-friction joint that allows the Hydragas unit to begin moving at lower loads than it does in earlier applications. The result, Rover says, is even less ride

fidget than the system would otherwise have.

Sutton confides that the Hydragas system's designer, Alex Moulton, would like the same joint used on the Rover 100 — and on any future Hydragas applications, too. But in a very cheap car, it's a fairly expensive component.

No model set for worldwide export could get by without thorough durability testing and Rover has taken the MGF to the heat, dust and chassis-wracking washboard roads of Arizona and to the frozen wastes of the Arctic Circle. The car has also lapped the Nardo test track in southern Italy, at top speed in mid-summer. Results have been substantiated by continual rig testing.

Mostly, the design has survived well, but small modifications have been inevitable. The heating — a difficult issue in a mid-engined car — was much modified ▶

MGF K-SERIES MR2

Toyota MR2 was key target for MGF, as was Mazda MX-5. Like Metro simulator, this MR2 was fitted with K-series engine to develop layout

F828 RRT

'Count the test cars up and you have 239 experimental MGs or mules'

for extra output after the first cold trip. A 'bib' was added under the front bumper to create negative pressure and draw air through the radiator.

The location of the engine bay fan was found to be critical in the US desert. And the plenum panel, the plastic shroud below the wipers, was built with slots instead of holes because early versions expanded and cracked in the sun. Grilles in the rear deck, dropped after Pocket Rocket, were reinstated to let engine heat out. In short, the car's development was thorough.

To date, Rover has built more than 100 experimental cars for the project, some of which look like MGFs, many of which don't. The programme started with so-called simulators, cars that test some aspect of the proposed design but possibly look nothing like it. Rover has a selection of 15 mid-engined Metro vans, K-series-engined

Toyota MR2s and other assorted 'mules' that fit this category. About half of these, project director Nick Fell says, look "a bit like a PR3".

After the first hand-built engineering prototypes came the DO2 cars, which all looked like the proposed production car and were good enough for initial on-road, crash, aerodynamic and maybe emissions tests. A further 26 of those were built. Next came the D1 cars, plainly MGFs with a higher proportion of parts produced by the production tooling process. Thirty-four of those were built between July and August last year, and they're still being used for validation tests.

Sixty-four 'QP' (quality proving) cars are now being built to prove the actual production process, and just before production of saleable cars begins on 10 July the line will make 100 so-called M-cars, from which early production

Design and engineering team late last year; it was a relatively small group that facilitated rapid exchange of information. Full production starts in July

line test cars will be drawn. Those cars test that the process is repeatable at the line rate contemplated.

Count them up and you have 239 experimental MGs or mules. In bygone days the early ones would be crushed. This time, the most interesting

of them will be preserved.

Ironically, while the production cars they spawned will go right around the world, the prototypes themselves will travel barely half a mile: from Rover's Gaydon test facility to the British Motor Heritage Museum right next door. ●

MGF PR1 PROTOTYPE

Front-drive PR1 used M16 power from Maestro. Pop-up headlights were proposed for production car but designers opted instead for MG 'face'

MGF WHAT IT'S LIKE TO DRIVE, BY ROVER

Pitch the new MGF into a corner and you'll find it grips like a limpet, displays a whiff of initial understeer on turn-in, then stays neutral until the cornering speeds reach the suicidal. Try hard enough and you'll make it oversteer, but only as a result of full-noise power applications in slippery, fairly low-speed corners.

Naturally, Britain's new two-seater throttle steers very neatly, tightening its line when you throttle off. The independent rear suspension's geometry has been tuned to make that happen. The rack and pinion steering itself is light at parking speeds, but when you're pressing on the assistance practically disappears and you're left with all the feedback of a well-bred, unassisted sports car system.

The MG's two rivals in our market are the Mazda MX-5 and Toyota MR2. Throw the three protagonists around any skid pan and you'll soon discover that the Mazda's cornering attitude is highly adjustable, but that it slides off line relatively early. The Toyota goes to the other extreme, gripping beautifully but showing reluctance to change its attitude when you throttle steer or make small wheel inputs. The MGF takes the best from both sides, gripping well wet or dry, but offering adjustability at the same time.

It should probably not surprise us that the MGF's ride is far better than those of its two main rivals, Toyota and Mazda. The most recent application of its interconnected Hydragas suspension — in the Rover 100 — shows suppleness and refinement. But the MG's ride rates are still quite a lot firmer than the Rover's: the main difference between the MGF and the others is the comfort it continues to offers on rough, broken surfaces. The comfort, testers say, is exceptional for a sporting two-seater.

How do we know all this? Because Rover's engineers told us — and in our experience engineers never lie. If they have a general tendency, it is to understate the scale of their achievement. The MG team has been carrying out exhaustive tests on their F for several years and is still doing them now, with the car no more than a couple of months from volume production.

Hydragas suspension means that individual wheel rates are high but body remains flat in corners and over bumps. Blundell was impressed

Rare photograph of MGF in testing was taken covertly during hot weather runs in Arizona; Rover had decreed that no 'holiday' snaps were allowed

"The MG's ride is not quite as compliant as Alex Moulton might have liked," says project director Nick Fell, "but the car really is the best riding of sports cars.

"The brilliance of Hydragas is that it offers the low pitch rate of an interconnected system with the relatively high individual rates a sports car needs. We think this is the most successful Hydragas application yet."

Rover's people are particularly content with the long-distance ability of their car, which they believe definitely shades the short-haul Mazda, while offering more driver entertainment than the Toyota. The car was not conceived to have a benign nature, Rover admits. It seems to have been bred into the car by its sophisticated mechanical layout and idealised suspension geometry.

Not content with their own findings, last year Rover's suspension men asked McLaren grand prix driver Mark Blundell to drive the car very quickly indeed.

"The speeds at which he pitched the car into bends were incredible," says Nick Fell, who sat in with Blundell. "Once it was actually cornering, though, it felt very secure." Blundell rated the car very highly on chassis rigidity and liked the 'maturity' of its ride and handling, but asked for a little more steering sharpness on turn-in.

The fact that they were already working on it gives Rover confidence that the finished product will meet the needs not only of Mark Blundell, but of more average drivers, too.

MGF 1.8i

This is the first proper MG for a generation with both the specification and looks to take Britain's most popular sportscar marque back to its glory days

If it is surprising that we have waited over thirty years for this, the next new MG, it is altogether more amazing that it is here at all. Since the MGB appeared in 1962, the marque has had to survive on a diet of increasingly old and unappetising product, suffer the indignity of having its name poached and plastered across a range of largely undeserving cars and, in between, long periods on the shelf. Most marques would have given up the struggle.

Yet still the name retains its magic. Were this not the case, the MGB would never have been disturbed let alone exhumed, reworked and sold as recently as last year as the dynamically challenged RV8.

The thinking is simple. If the RV8, obsolete twenty years before it was built, can sell then a proper, state of the art MG sportster should have them queuing around the corner.

But the MGF is more than that. It is also the first all-Rover car since the launch of the Montego in 1984. As such it stands or falls on its own merits.

At first glance, those merits seem compelling. Beautiful in photographs, it's close to stunning in the flesh, making the Fiat Barchetta look contrived and the Mazda MX-5 seem old. And unlike these principle rivals, its design is genuinely innovative. Where the Fiat uses a hatchback-derived front drive layout and the Mazda a traditional front engine, rear drive arrangement, the MG places its 1.8-litre twin cam 16-valve engine directly behind its driver making it the world's first affordable mid-engined convertible.

With that name, those looks and a basic list price of £15,995, its potential is clear. Question is, does it live up to it?

Performance

★★
★★

There are two versions of Rover's 1796cc K-series engine for the MGF. The standard version is seen ▸

LIST PRICE £15,995 **TOP SPEED** 123mph
0-60MPH 8.7sec **30-70MPH** 8.7sec **MPG** 26.4

FOR Beautiful and clever styling, engineering integrity, huge grip, superb brakes, exceptional build quality
AGAINST Considerably less fun to drive than an MX-5, dowdy looking cabin, compromised driving position

here with 118bhp at 5500rpm and 122lb ft of torque at 3000rpm. An extra £2000 buys the VVC version (variable valve control) pushing the outputs up to 143bhp at 7000rpm and 128lb ft of torque at 4500rpm.

In standard tune, the MGF feels reasonably swift. The engine is as smooth as we now expect from the K-series but, thanks to its longer stroke, it has an even spread of torque meaning easier progress and fewer gearchanges. There is, if anything, not quite enough drama in its progress meaning the MG feels slower than it is. An MX-5, slower on paper, feels faster on the road.

Even so, few will find fault with the MG's 0-60mph time of 8.7sec even if that figure is aided somewhat by the natural traction advantage of having the engine's weight on the rear wheels. All out it tops the 120mph claimed by Rover by 3mph, auguring well for the 130mph claimed for the swifter VVC variant.

In-gear performance is solid but hardly exhilarating. It requires 12.1sec to cover the 50-70mph increment in top, enough to earn your attention but still hardly spellbinding stuff by the standards of many cheaper hot hatches.

Here lies the first clue to its overall purpose. It is an overwhelmingly calm performer, feeling no need to dress its acceleration in gaudy engine noise, or hurl its driver through gear ratios stacked like sardines in its five-speed box. Though the change quality is quite exceptional by all standards bar those of the MX-5, its ratios are widely spaced and relaxed, promoting refinement and economy but reducing in-car entertainment.

Economy

It should be no surprise that with its light-weight, aerodynamic shape, long gears and efficient engine, that the MGF is a reasonably frugal sports car.

During testing it returned 26.4mpg, rising to 33.8mpg on a leisurely motorway run. Most disappointing is the fuel tank which, at a miserly 50 litres, means each tankful rarely lasts more than 280miles.

Handling

A mid-mounted engine with double wishbones at each corner is a layout more usually associated with Ferraris than affordably cute convertibles. Add in tyre sizes that vary from 205/50 VR15 at the back to 185/55 VR15 up front and Alex Moulton's brilliant Hydragas springing, and the potential of the MGF's chassis is obvious. But by no means will everyone feel that it has been realised to the full.

Rover has clearly decided to dedicate the MGF's chassis talent to covering the ground as swiftly and with as little fuss as possible. That this means true driver involvement has been seriously compromised will be seen as a crying shame for those hoping for a car with the same sense of fun as the MX-5.

The MGF is nothing like as amusing to drive as the MX-5. But there's no denying the MG, in its chosen role, is supremely effective. It will corner easily at speeds which would have the Mazda skittering nervously. Its body control is top drawer and even at its limit it remains absolutely faithful in its responses. No other car with ♦

MARK BLUNDELL ON THE NEW MGF

'An approach was made because Rover wanted someone in the car to give feedback from a different angle. I haven't done any road car work before, my experience has been in the quickest things there are.

'I did one day's driving at the Gaydon test circuit, trying different configurations.

'I came back and spoke to the engineering staff. We had a small meeting and I also spoke to a couple of other guys who had been testing the vehicle.

'I came across as a race driver, but also took the view that the car is not just for the guy who thinks he can race the pants off somebody. It is also for the driver who needs to think about parking and shopping.

'And I said "It is a bit too much like this, it is a bit too like that…". In some areas, I was already on the right track as the Rover guys were thinking on these lines. I think I just put a bit of top spin on those thoughts…

'I gave them some pointers to which they were very receptive. It gave them something to think about and I think it allowed them to make a step forward with the car.

'For me, the MGF is a good, solid, sportscar. We did comparison tests with other manufacturer's vehicles – they were not in the same league.

'It can be pushed to the limit and not give the driver a fright. Predominantly, you have under rather than oversteer.

'I feel, for the average driver, that this is much safer because you can back off the throttle and bring in the front end, as opposed to trying to use a lot of ability to catch it.

'The variable valve timing engine was the hot ticket. The standard engine is very good, nippy and responsive, but for anybody who is looking for outright performance, the VVC engine is best. That was the one that gave me the biggest buzz.'

Hood does little to spoil smart lines. Optional hard top costs a cool £995

Badge is back where it belongs

Remote central locking is standar

Racy looking filler is a nice touch

Hood mechanism is a doddle to

Cabin is spacious but disappointingly drab. Rover missed an opportunity to carry the style of its exterior into the cockpit. Instrument dials help, though

Boot space excellent, engine access poor. Very little extra room in nose

Gorgeous alloys are standard and well protected with lockable nuts

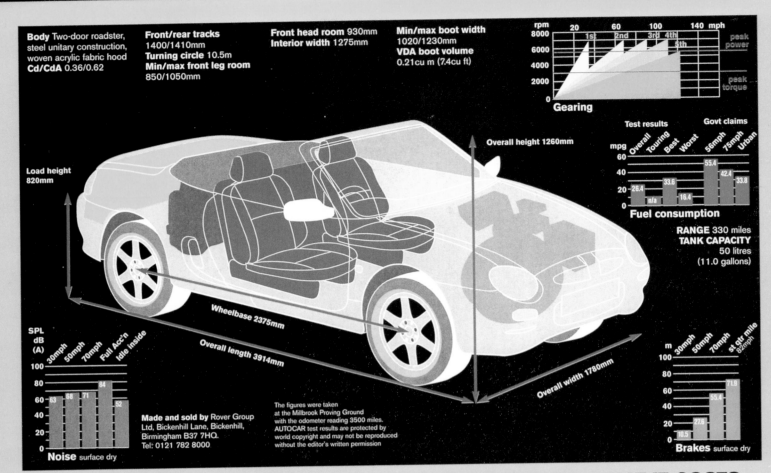

Body Two-door roadster, steel unitary construction, woven acrylic fabric hood
Cd/CdA 0.36/0.62

Front/rear tracks 1400/1410mm
Turning circle 10.5m
Min/max front leg room 850/1050mm

Front head room 930mm
Interior width 1275mm

Min/max boot width 1020/1230mm
VDA boot volume 0.21cu m (7.4cu ft)

Overall height 1260mm
Overall length 3914mm
Overall width 1780mm
Wheelbase 2375mm
Load height 820mm

Gearing

Fuel consumption

mpg	Test results				Govt claims		
---	Overall	Touring	Best	Worst	56mph	75mph	Urban
	26.4	33.6	n/a	16.4	55.4	42.4	33.8

RANGE 330 miles
TANK CAPACITY 50 litres (11.0 gallons)

Noise surface dry

SPL dB (A)	30mph	50mph	70mph	Full Acc'n	Idle inside
	53	68	71	84	52

Brakes surface dry

m	30mph	50mph	70mph	st qtr mile 82mph
	10.5	27.6	55.4	71.9

Made and sold by Rover Group Ltd, Bickenhill Lane, Bickenhill, Birmingham B37 7HQ. Tel: 0121 782 8000

The figures were taken at the Millbrook Proving Ground with the odometer reading 3500 miles. AUTOCAR test results are protected by world copyright and may not be reproduced without the editor's written permission

SPECIFICATION

ENGINE
Layout	4 cylinders in line, 1796cc
Max power	118bhp at 5500rpm
Max torque	122lb ft at 3000rpm
Specific output	66bhp per litre
Power to weight	110bhp per tonne
Torque to weight	114lb ft per tonne
Installation	transverse, mid, rear-wheel drive
Construction	aluminium alloy head and block
Bore/stroke	80/89mm
Valve gear	4 valves per cylinder, dohc
Compression ratio	10.5:1
Ignition and fuel	MEMS electronic ignition, multi-point fuel injection

GEARBOX
Type 5-speed manual
Ratios/mph per 1000rpm
1st 3.17/5.3 2nd 1.84/9.2 3rd 1.31/12.9
4th 1.03/16.4 5th 0.77/22.1 Final drive ratio 3.94

SUSPENSION
Front double wishbones, Hydragas springs, anti-roll bar **Rear** double wishbones, Hydragas springs, anti-roll bar

STEERING
Type rack and pinion, optional speed-sensitive electric power assistance (fitted on test car)
Turns lock to lock 3.1 (3.4 without EPAS)

BRAKES
Front 240mm (9.0in) ventilated discs
Rear 240mm (9.0in) discs **Anti-lock** optional

WHEELS AND TYRES
Wheel size 6Jx15in **Made of** cast alloy
Tyres 185/55 VR15 (f), 205/50 VR15 (r)
Goodyear Eagle Touring **Spare** space saver

PERFORMANCE

MAXIMUM SPEEDS
5th gear 123mph/5560rpm 4th 115/7000
3rd 90/7000 2nd 64/7000 1st 37/7000

ACCELERATION FROM REST
True mph	sec	speedo mph
30	2.8	34
40	4.3	45
50	6.2	55
60	8.7	66
70	11.5	77
80	15.4	87
90	20.3	98
100	27.0	108
110	39.2	119

Standing quarter mile 16.6sec/82mph
Standing kilometre 30.2sec/103mph
30-70mph through the gears 8.7sec

ACCELERATION IN GEARS
mph	5th	4th	3rd	2nd
10-30	–	–	5.8	3.8
20-40	11.9	7.8	5.7	3.7
30-50	11.6	7.4	5.6	3.9
40-60	11.5	7.3	5.7	4.5
50-70	12.1	7.9	6.0	–
60-80	13.4	8.5	6.9	–
70-90	18.4	9.3	9.0	–
80-100	23.5	11.8	–	–

WEIGHT
Kerb (including half tank of fuel)	1073kg
Distribution front/rear	45/55 per cent
Gross vehicle weight	1320kg
Max payload	260kg
Max towing weight braked	n/a
Max towing weight unbraked	n/a

WHAT IT COSTS
List price	£15,995
Total as tested	£17,540

EQUIPMENT
(**bold type** denotes options fitted to test car)
Automatic gearbox	–
Metallic paint	£230
Driver's airbag	●
Passenger's airbag	£345
Seatbelt pre-tensioners	●
Electrically adjustable mirrors	●
Auto reverse radio/cassette player	●
Electric aerial	●
Power steering (electric)	£550
Alloy wheels	●
Adjustable steering column	●
Electric windows	●
Remote central locking	●
Tilt adjustable driver's seat	●
Anti-lock brakes	£650
Front foglights	£188 (DO)
Anti-theft system	●

● standard – not available DO dealer option

INSURANCE GROUP   12

WARRANTY
12 months/unlimited mileage, 6 years anti-corrosion, 3 years cosmetic paintwork, 12 months recovery

SERVICING
Initial 3000 miles, 0.5 hours, free
Interim/major 12,000 miles, 1.5 hours, n/a parts

PARTS PRICES
Oil filter	£7.32
Air filter	£12.22
Brake pads front/rear	£58.00/96.35
Exhaust (excluding cat)	£498.20
Door mirror glass	£18.80
Tyre (each, typical)	£129 (f), £160 (r)
Windscreen	£117.50
Headlamp glass	£38.78
Front wing	£82.25
Rear bumper	£141.00

Dial for oil temperature is standard and suits the MG well

Gear lever would be better if it were short and stubby

Electric windows difficult to reach unless you look

Cream dials help offset the largely plain cabin ambience

Driver has an airbag as standard but passenger bag optional

Stalks are from Honda; only parts that spoil detailing

◀ an engine behind the seats has ever felt this safe to drive fast.

But while we applaud this attention to safety, we lament the monopoly it holds over the MGF's handling characteristics. It provides no opportunity for altering your line with the throttle, no alternative to the steady understeer that arrives when you press hard through a corner. You feel you have no more than a front row seat at a show which, while beautifully produced, is to be appreciated more for the way it has been directed than the excitement it contains. By comparison the MX-5 gives you the lead role in an all-action blockbuster. The MGF's optional electric power steering is pleasingly weighted but lacks feel and has too many turns across a poor lock.

Ride

 Another deeply significant clue to the MGF's character: it rides superbly. Scuttle shake is minimal while it boasts a prodigious appetite for mid-corner bumps. Tackle any country road in an MX-5 followed by the MG and you'd swear someone had resurfaced it as you swapped seats. Half of this is the legacy of its mid mounted engine, a naturally ride-enhancing configuration thanks to the much softer front springs it allows. The other half is the Hydragas springing which, in the MG, has provided all the compliance we have come to expect from the system yet with none of the bounce. It is almost impossible to severely upset its suspension as even deep urban pot-holes are sponged away with little more than a small shudder. Only transverse ridges on country roads are felt particularly, a characteristic that's more apparent under braking. Even so, you'd be hard pressed to call it a serious fault.

Handling characteristics are dominated by fine grip and poise. It's so safe but insufficiently involving for some

Brakes

 There's precious little to fault here. We spent an entire day lapping the Croft racetrack for next week's Best Driver's Car feature and not once did the four discs fail to slow the MG with anything other than masterful authority.

We would, however, prefer to have seen anti-lock brakes as standard on this car.

At the wheel

 The driving position is too high and restricted by its unadjustable steering wheel. Though the coloured instruments work well, the Honda-derived column stalks are nasty and fiddly to operate. Such a range of faults are a shame in such an otherwise complete car. The excellent visibility and competent ventilation system do little to make amends.

Accomodation and Comfort

 Unlike the MX-5, the MGF is a practical daily driver for someone without a family. The boot is big enough for holiday luggage as well as the weekly shop while the cabin boasts significantly more leg room, elbow room and hood-up head room than the MX-5.

The roof mechanism owes more than a little to the Mazda system, allowing you to snap undone the two retaining clips

on the windscreen and throw the roof over your head. If you're quick and don't bother to unzip the rear screen (Rover says it's not strictly necessary), you can lower the hood in rather less than 5secs.

Noise

 Hood down, the MGF is extremely refined, proving resistant to wind buffeting at all speeds you're likely to reach in the UK. With the roof in place, it could almost be a coupe, so resistant is it to the intrusions of wind and road noise.

Build quality and safety

 The MGF feels hugely strong and beautifully built. Paint quality and panel fit exceed the impressive standards of the

MX-5 and the sense of body integrity is perhaps unique among small open sportscars.

Safety features include a standard driver's airbag, seat belt pretensioners and side intrusion beams though a passenger airbag and, a little disappointingly, anti-lock brakes remain an optional extra.

Equipment and value

 As you'd expect, the MG comes with alloy wheels, an alarm, central locking and electric windows. If you want power steering, anti-lock brakes or a passenger air-bag, they'll add £1545 to the list price.

On paper, the MG's price is at least competitive with its rivals while many might consider its engineering, construction and the magic of its badge to be well worth a few pounds more.

LOVES
Fantastic feel through the brake pedal; oil temperature gauge; nicely detailed filler cap; properly designed and shaped boot; the looks it gets everywhere it goes

HATES
Terrible, fiddly hood bag; lack of on-board stowage space; plastic rimmed steering wheel feels cheap to the touch; gear lever should be two inches shorter

THE AUTOCAR VERDICT

 The MGF is going to sell like lottery tickets on a roll-over week. What's more, it will deserve to. It would have been so easy for Rover to have put an MG badge on the nose of a mediocre car and once more rely on the marque's image to do the selling. This has not happened. Rover has instead created what is, in all probability, the world's most complete and affordable open two-seater. From traditional MG fans to those wanting something more stylish than the chopped-about hatchbacks that pass for convertibles these days, the MGF should prove a blessing. It is an all-British car of which we can be unusually proud.

The only people who will feel left out are those who had hoped for a genuinely thrilling driving experience. For all its talents, it is the one service the MGF manifestly fails to provide. Many see this as the first priority of an open two-seater sportscar and some will rule the MG out on those grounds alone. And while they would be missing out on a truly great new car, we, enthusiasts all, understand how they feel.

MAKING OF THE MARQUE

In just 12 years Cecil Kimber built his MG sports car company up from a specialised body manufacturer to an internationally respected marque. Demand for his cars grew rapidly as MG won race after race. Then Kimber incurred the wrath of Lord Nuffield. By Wilson McComb

MG's PRACTICE CAR FOR THE 1932 Ulster TT was a stark, blown 750 just back from its second appearance in the German Grand Prix at the Nurburgring. With that howling Powerplus, minimal weather protection, rock-hard suspension and a wheelbase of 81ins, the C-type Midget was scarcely ideal for a 175-mile road journey. Yet one August afternoon the managing director of the MG Car Company climbed into the 100mph projectile and drove from Abingdon to Liverpool. Crossing on the night ferry to Belfast, he headed next day for the nearby Craigantlet hillclimb. There Cecil Kimber (pictured top left) made second fastest time of the day to a 1½-litre works Lea-Francis, taking three class firsts and four seconds.

The trip was a fair performance for a middle-aged businessman – Kimber was approaching his 45th birthday – and one that few in his position would even attempt let alone achieve today. It tells us much about Kimber that he did not mind a spot of discomfort in a well-prepared sports car, that he had guts and knew how to drive and that he was enough of an enthusiast to throw caution to the wind.

Born on 12 April, 1888 in a London suburb, Kimber moved to Manchester as a child where his father opened a branch of the family printing-ink business, which Kimber joined after leaving school. The family had been wealthy but the new offshoot failed to prosper and, it seems, young Kimber was bored by it. He found more pleasure riding motorbikes until, in his early 20s, he was hit by a car. This left him with a permanent limp but he won about £700 in compensation, part of which he spent on a new 1913 Singer 10.

Kimber left home when his father asked him to invest the remainder of his money in the declining family business and there

was a row about his refusal. He went to the Yorkshire firm of Sheffield-Simplex for a time, then worked for AC Cars, followed by a spell with motor industry supplier E G Wrigley in Birmingham.

In 1921 he joined W R Morris's retail garage business as sales manager and was promoted to general manager the following year. Besides managing Morris Garages, he started designing specialised bodies for the contemporary Bullnose Morris models, an enterprise that succeeded remarkably well. By 1924 his 'MG' sports cars were becoming so popular that he had to keep moving to bigger premises. In late 1929 he made his final move, to Abingdon-on-Thames, where MG was registered as a limited company the following year.

All through the early '30s, Kimber made every effort to turn his brainchild into a well-known and respected marque. He succeeded brilliantly – mainly by daring attacks one very branch of motor sport – and the MG marque cashes in on his hard work to this day.

But his boss Lord Nuffield – as W R Morris had now become – disapproved of motor racing as a publicity medium for roadgoing cars. He called a halt when MG announced a new single-seater racing Midget in 1935. The R-type not only had a Zoller-blown engine giving almost 200bhp/litre in sprint form, but also torsion-bar independent suspension front and rear. Kimber pleaded that the R-type, like his previous racers, was essentially a prototype for future road-going cars and a pointer towards a new range of technically-advanced production MGs that other sports car builders would find hard to match. Nothing doing, said Nuffield: the racing department was closed down in mid-

season, the development of advanced ohc models ceased and future MGs were designed around the Nuffield Group parts bin.

So Kimber's dream of producing new super MGs in the later '30s – and a monoposto Magnette for a 1½-litre GP formula – was rudely shattered, and he never quite recovered the power and influence he lost at that time. There is some evidence that Nuffield resented Kimber's fame. Kimber was frequently seen at Brooklands race meetings or the many social functions staged by the MG Car Club and was on friendly terms with the likes of Howe, Campbell, Eyston and Nuvolari. Even Kimber's remarriage soon after the death of his first wife in 1938 earned the disapproval of the straitlaced Nuffield.

At the onset of the Second World War Kimber secured a valuable contract to build the main section of the Albemarle bomber at the Abingdon factory. But this independent move angered the ambitious Nuffield Group vice-chairman Miles Thomas, who forced Kimber to resign from his own company towards the end of 1941.

Coachbuilder Charlesworth took him on to reorganise its factory for wartime production, after which he moved to Specialloid Pistons to do similar work there. As the war drew to a close he was approached by John Black, of the Triumph Company, to advise on postwar sports car designs, but he never had time to take up this offer.

In February 1945 he boarded a King's Cross train to Peterborough. The engine developed wheelspin 10 minutes after setting off and when the train started to run backwards a panicky signalman threw the points, derailing the last coach. Cecil Kimber, not yet 57, was one of two passengers killed.